WORDSWORTH

THE PRELUDE

OR

GROWTH OF A POET'S MIND

1805

WILLIAM WORDSWORTH

Born at Cockermouth, Cumberland, 7 April 1770
Died at Rydal Mount, Westmorland, 23 April 1850

WORDSWORTH

THE PRELUDE

OR

GROWTH OF A POET'S MIND

(TEXT OF 1805)

─────

Edited from the manuscripts
with an Introduction and Notes by
ERNEST DE SELINCOURT

Corrected by
STEPHEN GILL

Oxford New York
OXFORD UNIVERSITY PRESS

Oxford University Press, Walton Street, Oxford OX2 6DP

Oxford New York Toronto
Delhi Bombay Calcutta Madras Karachi
Kuala Lumpur Singapore Hong Kong Tokyo
Nairobi Dar es Salaam Cape Town
Melbourne Auckland

and associated companies in
Beirut Berlin Ibadan Mexico City Nicosia

Oxford is a trade mark of Oxford University Press

ISBN 0-19-281074-X

The 1805 text of The Prelude first published 1933 by
Oxford University Press
This second edition first published 1970 as an
Oxford University Press paperback
Reprinted 1975, 1978, 1979, 1983, 1984, 1985

Printed in Great Britain by
Richard Clay (The Chaucer Press) Ltd.
Bungay, Suffolk

CONTENTS

PREFACE TO THE SECOND EDITION

In 1926 Ernest de Selincourt published his great edition of *The Prelude*, which presented parallel texts of the well-known version of 1850 and the as then unknown version completed in 1805. His belief in the 1805 text was justified by the interest it aroused, and in 1933 that text alone was issued in a handy volume, which has become the standard text for most students. Some corrections and additions, bringing text and notes into line with the revised parallel-text edition of 1959, were made by Helen Darbishire in a revised impression of 1960. The present edition continues the work of correction necessitated by the research of scholars currently studying the text and interpretation of the Wordsworth canon. The word 'continues' is used advisedly, for corrections and additions will be needed for many years to come. Difficulties in understanding the complicated relations of the various manuscripts and in interpreting the relevance of recent new manuscript discoveries suggest that the ideal, once-for-all authoritative text (that dream of scholarship!) will not appear for some time. This edition thus rests on the de Selincourt edition, attempting only to correct it and to alter emphases wherever modern scholarship directs.

The Text: The text has been checked against MS. A and a number of changes made. It now follows that manuscript more exactly than in earlier editions, in that not only have errors of transcription been corrected, but W. W.'s spelling, punctuation, and capitalization habits have been respected. Breaks between sections of the narrative, the Book titles and running heads, which are largely de Selincourt's, have been retained because they do help us to read a long poem. (Wordsworth called the books 'Parts' and in the MS. left them without titles.) Numbers in square brackets in the right-hand margin refer to the 1850 text in the 1959 edition of the parallel-text *Prelude*.

Introduction: Although scholars would now perhaps want to challenge de Selincourt's emphases, the sections in which he compares the early and late versions of the poem in discussion of Wordsworth's development must stand as he wrote them. The sections on the origin and growth of the poem, however, valuable as they are, do need most careful examination, especially on three points. The first is that de Selincourt fused the chronology of Wordsworth's preparations for writing *The Recluse* with that of his developing conception of a poem on his own life. Thus the date in the sentence 'It was in the early months of 1798' (p. ix) may be pushed at least one year later, and the interpretation of Coleridge's comments (p. x), and the dating of the 'Prospectus' to *The Recluse* (p. ix) may be reconsidered. The second point is that scholars have overemphasized the drama of the break in composition after Books I–II were completed. De Selincourt remarks that after October 1800 'the poem was almost entirely laid aside till January 1804', but new evidence reveals that Wordsworth was at work on the poem into 1801 and had taken it up once more by early 1803. The recent discovery of another very important *Prelude* manuscript casts doubt, moreover, on the sequence of composition suggested by the earlier hypothesis of the big break. De Selincourt constructed three poems: the two-book *Prelude*; the five- or six-book *Prelude* of 1804, the thirteen-book *Prelude* of 1805. The first of these seems fairly secure from scholarly attack, and the last is presented in this edition. The 'shorter *Prelude*' (p. xi), however, now seems to sustain only a precarious existence in the light of recent work on the poem. The third point, bound up with the second, is that scholars have mistaken the relationship between 'Home at Grasmere', *Recluse* Book I, and *The Prelude*. The usual account of the chronology of composition is as follows: In 1798 Wordsworth conceived the great philosophic poem *The Recluse* and out of this stemmed the poem on his own life, Books I–II, which were complete by 1800. In this year also Wordsworth attempted to get on with *The Recluse* but managed only to complete Book I before giving up. The years 1800–4 were spent in self-examination and the composition of short lyrics. In 1804–5 *The Prelude* was completed in a sudden burst of energy and then the philosophic poem was continued, the completed part of which eventually appeared as

The Excursion. It now seems, however, that *Recluse* Book I, 'Home at Grasmere', was written in 1806 at the earliest and that many current ideas concerning Wordsworth's intentions, achievements, and state of mind during this period need to be re-examined.

Footnotes in square brackets, followed by my initials, will be found at a few points in the Introduction that require direct qualification. For detailed information concerning the growth of *The Prelude* and related poems the reader should consult Mark Reed, *Wordsworth: The Chronology of the Early Years 1770–1799* (Harvard, 1967); the second volume, covering the *Prelude* years, is forthcoming. Essays by John Finch on the dating of the 'glad preamble' and 'Home at Grasmere' are to be published in 1970 in *Wordsworth: Bi-Centenary Studies*, ed. Jonathan Wordsworth (Cornell).

Notes: Those of de Selincourt's notes which referred only to the 1850 text have been removed. Some errors of fact or reference have been silently corrected. Helen Darbishire's notes to the text have been inserted in sequence, in square brackets and with initials, as have my own.

STEPHEN GILL

October 1969

INTRODUCTION

§ 1. *Origin, Growth, and Structure of 'The Prelude'*

THE Prelude is the essential living document for the interpretation of Wordsworth's life and poetry; any details, therefore, that can be gathered of the manner and circumstances of its composition must be of interest alike to biographer and critic. But of more vital importance than these is a knowledge of its original text. It has long been known that Wordsworth revised *The Prelude* in his later years, and conjectures have been inevitable on the character and extent of that revision. How far does the authorized text, as it was given to the world by the poet's executors, actually represent what he had written nearly half a century before, when he was in the fullness of his powers? Did he confine himself to purely stylistic correction and embellishment, or did he go further, and in any real sense rehandle his theme, in the spirit of his later thought? A study of this volume will supply the answer. The original version[1] may now be compared with the edition published in 1850; and if the comparison does not show a change as fundamental as some critics have anticipated, it reveals much that is highly significant in the history of the poet's mind and art.

It was in the early months of 1798 that Wordsworth conceived the idea of writing a history of the growth of his own mind. Partly on the suggestion of Coleridge,[2] and spurred on by his enthusiastic encouragement, he had determined to compose a great philosophic poem to be entitled *The Recluse, or Views on Man, Nature, and Society*. It seems probable that a rough draft of those lines afterwards printed as the *Prospectus to the Recluse* was struck off in the first heat of this resolve. He had already written *The Ruined Cottage* and other verse which would naturally find its place in his comprehensive scheme; 'indeed,' he wrote, 'I know not anything which will not come within the scope of my

---

[1] Referred to in this Introduction and the notes as the A text. Other abbreviations used throughout are listed at p. 243.

[2] Coleridge, *Table Talk*, 21 July 1832.

plan'. In the eager confidence with which he embarked on the enterprise he anticipated its completion in less than two years; but the 'paramount impulse not to be withstood' soon gave way to doubt. Has he the strength to assume so awful a burthen? Would it not be wiser to await those 'mellower years' that 'bring a riper mind'? Are his misgivings justly founded, or are they mere timidity and laziness, a subtle form of selfishness cloaked in 'humility and modest awe'? The answer can only be found by taking stock of himself and examining how far Nature and Education have qualified him for his task. And so he wrote *The Prelude*. In the summer of 1798 he had little time to give to it, but during the following winter, when he was in Germany, he wrote many of those passages which describe the experiences of his boyhood, and it is probable that Books I and II were finished by October 1800. Then the poem was almost entirely laid aside till January 1804, when he began again in good earnest: it was completed in May 1805.

It is clear that in its initial stages Wordsworth regarded his spiritual autobiography as an integral part of *The Recluse*, and not as a separate poem preparatory to it. More than a year later, in October 1799, Coleridge refers to it as *The Recluse*, and it seems likely that until the early months of 1800, when *Home at Grasmere* was written to form the introductory book of his great poem, the history of his early life was not viewed as an independent work.[1] Even then it was given no definite title. Wordsworth refers to it as 'a poem on my own earlier life'. Dorothy calls it 'the poem to C.' or 'the poem on his own earlier life'. Coleridge, as late as February 1804, still speaks of it as *The Recluse*,[2] and in *The Friend* (1808-9) refers to it as 'an unpublished Poem on the Growth and Revolutions of an Individual Mind'. Only on publication after the poet's death did it receive, from Mrs. Wordsworth, the name by which it is known to-day.

[1] [The letter of 12 Oct. 1799 in fact makes it clear that whereas Wordsworth was already regarding the poem addressed to Coleridge as apart from *The Recluse*, Coleridge wanted it to be a tailpiece to the greater philosophic poem. S. G.]

[2] [Coleridge's comment in his letter to the Wordsworths of 8 Feb. 1804 most probably does not support the interpretation given here. S. G.]

Its independence of the larger poem followed naturally from its growth under his hand to a length he had not foreseen. It is possible that even in the five books which, as late as March 1804, were to complete the poem, he had already exceeded his original conception of it. This shorter *Prelude* would have taken his history no further than his first Long Vacation, and its culminating episode was to be the consecration of his life to poetry upon the heights above Hawkshead (IV. 320–45). But though this was, perhaps, the great moment of his life, he realized that to stop there would not fulfil his purpose. The experiences of the next six years—his hopes and his despair for the Revolution in France, his life in London and in the country, homeless, and without means of livelihood, his sudden glad release from the bondage of circumstance, his settling at Racedown with Dorothy, and his friendship with Coleridge—had all 'borne a part, and that a needful one', in making him the poet that he was. And eight more books were added.

But in writing thus fully of himself he encroached inevitably upon his first design. *The Recluse*, 'as having for its principal subject the sensations and opinions of a poet living in retirement', was itself essentially autobiographical—even in *The Excursion*, which was intended to be dramatic, not only the hero but also the Solitary and the Vicar were thinly veiled portraits of their author—and much of the poetry he wished to write would, in fact, be equally well suited to either work. There can be no doubt that the wealth of *The Prelude* impoverished *The Recluse*. But this cannot be regretted. The ambitious design of *The Recluse* demanded a philosophic unity which Coleridge, indeed, might confidently anticipate, but which it was not in Wordsworth to supply; from the first it was doomed to failure. In *The Prelude*, which had a unity springing directly from the poet's own mind and personality, Wordsworth produced a masterpiece.

As it stands *The Prelude* has not merely a unity of design; it has something of epic structure. It opens with an outburst of joy that after years of anxiety the poet is at last free to devote his life to its true vocation: its 'last word of personal concern' records his gratitude for the gift which brought him that freedom. Within this frame he places the history of his life from the seedtime of infancy to those days when, chaunting alternate songs with Coleridge as they roamed the Quantock hills together, he was first fully conscious that his genius was bearing fruit. Books I–IV lead up, through an account of his early life, to the first great climax, his poetic consecration; after which there is a pause in the narrative, whilst he reviews, in Book V, his early debt to literature. Books VI and VII resume his life's history, and carry it down to the moment before the second great climax—the awakening of his passionate interest in man (Book IX). But before this, the narrative pauses once more, whilst in Book VIII he gives a philosophic retrospect of his whole period of preparation. Book X leads up to and records the catastrophe—the destruction of his hopes for man in so far as they were identified with the French Revolution, and his consequent despair of mind: Books XI–XIII give the reconciliation, his recovery from despair, the rebuilding of his hopes for man upon a sounder basis and, as a consequence, his entrance into his poetic heritage.

Wordsworth was in evident agreement with Milton on the true nature of the epic subject. Both of them repudiated military exploits, 'hitherto the only argument heroic deemed', in the desire to bring within its confines a more spiritual conflict. Only the pedant will dissent from their conception; and those who regard the mind of Wordsworth as both great in itself and essentially representative of the highest, the imaginative type of mind, will recognize its adventures as a fit theme for epic treatment. But Wordsworth himself, though he claimed this dignity for *The Recluse*, where his theme was the 'mind of man', was humbler in his comments on *The Prelude*. He admitted, indeed, that 'it was a thing unprecedented in literary history that a man should talk so much about himself'. 'It is not self-conceit', he wrote truly, 'that has induced me to do this, but real humility. I began the work because I was unprepared to treat any more arduous subject, and diffident of my own powers. Here, at least, I hoped that to a certain degree I should be sure of succeeding, as I had nothing to do but describe what I had felt and thought; therefore could not easily be bewildered. This might certainly have been done in narrower compass by a man of more address; but I have done my best.'[1] Yet, in truth, Wordsworth was never more eloquent than when he spoke of himself, and his best in *The Prelude* has never been rivalled in its own kind.

§ 2. *Preparation for writing 'The Prelude'*

For the task before him Wordsworth was well equipped by his wide knowledge of the literature of the past. The servant-maid at Rydal Mount, who told a visitor that her master's study was in the fields, touched unquestionably upon the main source of his inspiration, but her pretty epigram did not comprise the whole truth of the matter; and the poet who spoke of books as 'Powers only less than Nature's self, which is the breath of God', was not likely to neglect them. Yet the superficial critic has always tended to underrate their influence upon him. *The Prelude* foresaw this error, but gave some countenance to it; for the section entitled 'Books' takes us no further than his school-days, and is rather a general discourse on the value of imaginative literature than a detailed account of his actual reading. Yet it tells us, at least, that as a boy he read voraciously; and no habit acquired in childhood is easily discarded. As a matter of fact he retained the habit till his middle age, and only gave it up when his eyes declined their office. At Cambridge 'many books were skimmed, devoured, or studiously perused'—in Greek and Latin, Italian, French and Spanish, as well as in his mother tongue—and not poetry alone, but history also. There is evidence that when he settled at Racedown he not only read widely, but was convinced that success in his art could not be acquired otherwise. In his search for a metaphysical basis to his theory of life he studied the philosophers of the eighteenth century: De Quincey bore witness later to his extensive knowledge of ancient history. He had at all times a passion for the literature of travel, and insisted on its value in widening his outlook and enriching his experience. 'If', he wrote to a friend in March 1798, 'you could collect for me any books of travels, you would render me an essential service, as without much of such reading my present labours cannot be

[1] To Sir George Beaumont, 1 May 1805 (*E.Y.* 587).

brought to a conclusion'; and the pages of *The Prelude* are studded
with simile, metaphor, and allusion drawn from the narratives
of famous navigators, and explorers of unknown continents. But
naturally his chief reading was in English poetry. Few poets could
equal Wordsworth in a knowledge of their forerunners. Of his
intimacy with the minor poets of the eighteenth century *The
Evening Walk* and *Descriptive Sketches* bore painful witness: in *The
Prelude* he was to show his true ancestry. 'When I began', he says,
'to give myself up to the profession of a poet for life, I was im-
pressed with a conviction that there were four poets whom I must
have continually before me as examples—Chaucer, Shakespeare,
Spenser and Milton. These I must study, and equal *if I could*:
I need not think of the rest.'[1] He was true to his conviction. The
quintessence of Spenser's charm he could distil into two perfect
lines:

> Sweet Spenser, moving through his clouded heaven
> With the moon's beauty and the moon's soft pace,

and the fragrance of Spenser is recalled on several pages of
The Prelude. The poem abounds in reminiscence of Shakespearian
scene and phrasing. Of Milton there is still more. It was his
avowed ambition to be the Milton of his age; nor, as Keats
recognized, was that ambition ill-founded. He had the same lofty
conception of his art, the same passionate devotion to it, and like
Milton, though in his own way, he strove 'to justify the ways of
God to man'. Throughout *The Prelude* there are signs of devout
Miltonic study. Not only does the style of the poem in its more
eloquent passages take on a distinctly Miltonic manner, but
constantly, in places where they would least be expected, Miltonic
echoes can be heard. That Wordsworth himself was probably
unconscious of them is only a proof of the completeness with which
he had absorbed his master, so that Milton's phrase and cadence
had become a natural and inseparable element in his own speech.

[1] *Memoirs*, ii. 470. Cf. also letter to Alaric Watts, 16 Nov. 1824: 'I am
disposed strenuously to recommend to your habitual perusal the great poets
of our own country, who have stood the test of ages. Shakespeare I need
not name, nor Milton, but Chaucer and Spenser are apt to be overlooked. It
is almost painful to think how far these surpass all others.' (*L.Y.* 159.)

This study of the supreme artists was supported by prolonged meditation on both the principles and the technical minutiae of his art.[1] He chose the metre for his poem with a full consciousness of its pitfalls. It is significant to find copied into the notebook that contains the earliest fragments of *The Prelude* the warnings which Dr. Johnson had uttered on the peculiar dangers incident to the writing of blank verse.[2] From the contorted and unnatural phrasing of the *Descriptive Sketches* he was already in revolt. *The Prelude* was not written, like some of *The Lyrical Ballads*, to illustrate a theory of poetic diction; yet it demonstrates clearly enough that 'a selection from the real language of men in a state of vivid sensation is adapted to the purposes of poetic pleasure'—at least when the man Wordsworth is addressing his closest friend. For its language is selected from the whole of his experience, and the style to which he moulds it rises with the character and the intensity of the emotion it has to express.[3] And with Coleridge he had not only discussed the cardinal points of poetry,[4] but had

[1] In 1831 J. S. Mill noted that 'when you get Wordsworth on the subjects which are peculiarly his, such as the theory of his own art, no one can converse with him without feeling that he has advanced that great subject beyond any other man, being probably the first person who ever combined, with such eminent success in the practice of the art, such high powers of generalization and habits of meditation on its principles'. The foundations of this achievement were laid in 1797-8.

[2] 'Dr. Johnson observed, that in blank verse, the language suffered more distortion to keep it out of prose than any inconvenience to be apprehended from the shackles and circumspection of rhyme. This kind of distortion is the worst fault that poetry can have; for if once the natural order and connection of the words is broken, and the idiom of the language violated, the lines appear manufactured, and lose all that character of enthusiasm and inspiration, without which they become cold and insipid, how sublime soever the ideas and the images may be which they express.' *Alfoxden MS. Notebook*, 1798.

[3] 'In these little poems . . . he wrote, at times, too much with a sectarian spirit, in a sort of bravado. But now he is at the helm of a noble bark; now he sails right onward; it is all open ocean and a steady breeze, and he drives before it, unfretted by short tacks, reefing and unreefing his sails, hauling and disentangling the ropes. His only disease is the having been out of his element; his return to it is food to famine; it is both the specific remedy and the condition of health.' Coleridge on *The Prelude, Anima Poetae*, p. 30.

[4] *Biographia Literaria*, chap. xiv. In July 1802 Coleridge told Southey that 'the Preface' (i.e. of *The Lyrical Ballads*) 'is half a child of my own brain'.

argued upon matters of form and style. His main conclusions, despite occasional overstatement, the natural reaction from the false ideals of his youth, kept him, as Coleridge himself admitted, in the great tradition. The epithets ' simple ' and ' natural ', commonly applied to Wordsworth's poetry, alike for praise and blame, suggest a general ignorance of the intense study and careful artistry that lay behind it. But the popular view is in itself a tribute to the powerful originality of his mind and manner. His style is Wordsworthian as truly as Milton's is Miltonic.

§ 3. 'The Prelude' a posthumous work, but much revised throughout the poet's life

Some time before *The Prelude* was finished Wordsworth had given up all ideas of immediate publication. His high hopes in the poetic future that lay before him, and the spiritual history on which those hopes were founded, might indeed be confided to the friend who was his second self, but could not, without arrogance, be proclaimed to the world before he had given some solid earnest of their fulfilment. 'This poem', he wrote to De Quincey (6 March 1804), 'will not be published these many years, and never during my lifetime, till I have finished a larger and more important work to which it is tributary.'[1] Moreover, he was himself dissatisfied with it. 'When I looked back upon it,' he wrote only a fortnight after its completion, 'it seemed to have a dead weight about it— the reality so far short of the expectation. It was the first long labour that I had finished, and the doubt whether I should ever live to write *The Recluse* and the sense which I had of this poem being so far below what I had seemed capable of executing depressed me much.'[2] Nearly ten years later, as a first instalment of *The Recluse*, he published *The Excursion*; and there can be no doubt that his depression sank deeper, even as it was more fully justified. *The Prelude* had at least won the enthusiastic praise of Coleridge, but Coleridge made it quite clear that he was disappointed with *The Excursion*; and as Wordsworth read his friend's cool and measured commendation of this

[1] *E.Y.* 454.   [2] *E.Y.* 594.

later work, and recalled the glowing tribute accorded to the earlier:

> an Orphic song indeed,
> To its own music chaunted!

he had little heart to continue his great task. How soon the scheme of *The Recluse* was definitely abandoned we do not know;[1] but its abandonment would only strengthen his resolve that *The Prelude* should remain in manuscript till after his death.

But *The Prelude* was not laid aside and forgotten. Though he thought it inferior to what it might have been, he was fully conscious of its worth. The vital intimacy of its theme, which, doubtless, had made him peculiarly sensitive to its shortcomings, made him all the more anxious to perfect it. His resolve that the poem was to appear posthumously did not lessen his interest, for he knew that the destiny of all his writings lay with posterity, not with his immediate public; it only gave him a larger leisure in which to review it. For thirty-five years he continually went back to *The Prelude*, retouching and revising. The poem which appeared in 1850 differed in many respects from that which he read to Coleridge in 1806. From the MSS., now for the first time examined in detail, we are able to note the nature and the extent of the alterations introduced into the text; and a fresh light is thrown, not only upon the changes which came over the poet's mind, but also upon his principles and methods as an artist.

---

[1] In March 1821 D. W. was evidently urging him to it, for she writes: 'W. is very busy, though he has not looked at *The Recluse* or the poem on his own life; and this disturbs us. After fifty years of age there is no time to spare, and unfinished works should not, if it be possible, be left behind. This he feels, but the will never governs *his* labours. How different from Southey, who can go as regularly as clockwork, from history to poetry, from poetry to criticism, and so on to biography, or anything else. If their minds could each spare a little to the other, how much better for both!' (*M.Y.* 28.) And again in December 1824 she writes, 'My brother has not yet looked at *The Recluse*; he seems to feel the task so weighty that he shrinks from beginning with it, yet knows that he has now no time to loiter if another great work is to be accomplished by him' (*C.R.* 132). Wordsworth probably knew by this time that he would never go on with *The Recluse*, though his family still talked of its completion.

Even if Wordsworth had published *The Prelude* on its completion in 1805, it would not have appeared exactly as it is found in the A text; for no poet ever revised his work for press more meticulously than he. Writing in 1816 of some minor pieces which he had just composed he calls them 'effusions rather than compositions, though in justice to myself I must say that upon the correction of the style I have bestowed, as I always do, great labour'.[1] 'The composition of verse',[2] he wrote later, 'is infinitely more an art than men are prepared to believe, and absolute success in it depends on innumerable *minutiae*. . . . Milton speaks of pouring "easy his unpremeditated verse". It would be harsh, untrue, and odious to say there is anything like cant in this, but it is not *true* to the letter, and tends to mislead.' He might have added that his own description of poetry as 'the spontaneous overflow of powerful feelings' was liable to the same misconstruction. For experience had taught him that this 'spontaneous overflow' was no more than the raw material of art. It was easy enough to give those feelings a loose impressionistic language adequate to record them for himself. But such language was not poetry: it had not really expressed them, and could not transmit them to others. The poet, Wordsworth knew well, was a craftsman, who must toil with unremitting patience at every detail of his work, till it has gained a clearer outline, a fuller substance: not otherwise could it acquire that organic power which is the sure touchstone of art:

The vital spirit of a perfect form.[3]

---

[1] *M.Y.* 713.   [2] *L.Y.* 586.

[3] Cf. the following fragment of verse, found in an (unpunctuated) autograph manuscript belonging to 1798–1800, which shows how fully Wordsworth understood a principle underlying all great art:

> nor had my voice
> Been silent oftentimes had I burst forth
> In verse which, with a strong and random light
> Touching an object in its prominent parts,
> Created a memorial which to me
> Was all sufficient, and, to my own mind
> Recalling the whole picture, seemed to speak
> An universal language. Scattering thus
> In passion many a desultory sound,

The labour that Wordsworth bestowed on revision was at least equal to that of first composition, and was pursued when less scrupulous artists would have been well content to leave their work untouched. To Coleridge in 1798 *The Ruined Cottage* was 'superior to anything in our language which in any way resembles it', yet three years later Wordsworth is found wearing himself out in trying to make it better. The slightness of the difference between many passages found in the rough notebooks, where they were jotted down in the hurry of immediate inspiration, and the form they have assumed in the A text, affords ample proof that Wordsworth was postponing correction rather than that he was satisfied with his work as it stood. It is reasonable, therefore, to suppose that had he prepared it for press in 1805 he would have introduced into the text many of those changes which made their first appearance at a much later date.

§ 4. *Comparison of the texts in point of style— later improvements*

No one would doubt that the 1850 version is a better composition than the A text. Weak phrases are strengthened, and its whole texture is more closely knit. The A text leaves often the impression

> I deemed that I had adequately cloathed
> Meanings at which I hardly hinted, thought
> And forms of which I scarcely had produced
> A monument and arbitrary sign.

There is a lacuna in the MS. here: the argument clearly requires some such words as When I reviewed this random and desultory verse I saw its worthlessness, and came to realize that an artist reveals his true power only

> In that considerate and laborious work
> That patience which, admitting no neglect,
> By slow creation doth impart to speach
> Outline and substance even, till it has given
> A function kindred to organic power,
> The vital spirit of a perfect form.

So, in a letter to Beaumont (20 July 1804; *E.Y.* 491), he praises Reynolds for his 'deep conviction of the necessity of unwearied labour and diligence, and the reverence for the great men of his art'. Wordsworth's own reverence for the great masters, and his strenuous efforts to gain perfection of form, are seldom sufficiently realized. Cf. also VI. 600–5.

of a man writing rapidly, thinking aloud or talking to his friend without waiting to shape his thought into the most concise and telling form, satisfied for the moment if he can put it into metre by inverting the prose order of the words. It is not difficult to point in A to halting lines, and to tame or diffuse expressions, which called for drastic treatment. Thus tricks of speech, such as 'I mean', 'we might say', 'for instance', 'with regret sincere I mention this', and the like, tend later to disappear. The awkward circumlocution

> Yet do not deem, my Friend, though thus I speak
> Of Man as having taken in my mind
> A place thus early which might almost seem
> Pre-eminent, that this was really so,   (VIII. 472–5.)

is shortened to

> Yet deem not, Friend! that human kind with me
> Thus early took a place pre-eminent;

And in the same way the verbose

>   Officers
> That to a regiment appertain'd which then
> Was station'd in the City   (IX. 127–9.)

is later, with no loss to the sense, cut down to

> Officers, Then stationed in the city.

The 1850 version, while bracing the limp style of the earlier text, often gives form and outline to a thought before but vaguely suggested. The feeble statement

> Where good and evil never have that name,
> That which they ought to have, but wrong prevails,
> And vice at home   (IX. 360–2.)

is strengthened to

> Where good and evil interchange their names,
> And thirst for bloody spoils abroad is paired
> With vice at home.

Here he has carried to a further stage the idea which was at the back of his mind in 1805, but which never reached expression. Such changes as these exemplify no difference in theory of style, but simply the difference between good and bad writing. The desire for an exacter and more vivid picture leads him more than twenty times in the poem to substitute, for the auxiliary 'to be', a verb with more definite meaning. No better example of this could be given than the description of the morning of his poetic dedication. In the first version it runs:

> Magnificent
> The morning was, a memorable pomp,
> More glorious than I ever had beheld.
> The Sea was laughing at a distance; all
> The solid Mountains were as bright as clouds.　　(IV. 330–4.)

Many a poet would have rested satisfied with those lines as they stood, but no one can miss the gain in strength and vividness effected by the simple changes:

> Magnificent
> The morning rose, in memorable pomp,
> Glorious as e'er I had beheld—in front
> The sea lay laughing at a distance; near,
> The solid mountains shone, bright as the clouds.[1]

In the same way he gets rid of other auxiliaries which tend to weaken his sentence: of this the change from 'did soon become a patriot' to 'erelong became a patriot' is a typical example. Moreover, on re-reading his work, he detected many a jingle or inharmonious phrase, and for the sake of euphony altered 'betwixt' to 'between', 'itself' to 'herself', and 'which' to 'that', wherever it could be done without confusion to the sense. He noticed, too, an unfortunate predilection for the words 'sweet' and 'beauteous',

---

[1] A well-known example of the same change is found in the sonnet 'It is a beauteous evening' etc. (1802), where the line 'The gentleness of heaven broods o'er the sea' originally read 'is on' for 'broods o'er.' Wordsworth seems at this time to have an almost mystical feeling for the verb 'to be'. Cf. a remark he makes on an early reading in *Resolution and Independence*'. 'What is brought forward? A lonely place, "a pond by which the old man was, far from all house or home;" not *stood*, nor *sat*, but *was*—the figure presented in the most naked simplicity possible.' But here as elsewhere 'naked simplicity' is resigned for the sake of vividness.

and banished them from many lines in favour of a more exact appropriate epithet.[1] The cumulative effect of such changes, each one perhaps trifling in itself, cannot easily be over-estimated.

Wordsworth retained his critical acumen far longer than his creative energy; and some of his best corrections, in *The Prelude* as in other poems, are among the last. And to the end he was capable of writing a superb line. Those who accept with too much literalness the obvious truth that what is great in Wordsworth belongs to a single decade (1798–1807), will do well to note that two lines on the statue of Newton,

> The marble index of a mind for ever
> Voyaging through strange seas of Thought, alone,   [III. 62–3.]

were written when he was over sixty years of age, and that only about the same time a fine description of autumn in the Lake Country reached its climax in the lovely phrase

> Clothed in the sunshine of the withering fern.   [VI. 11.]

To study the development of this and other passages[2] from their first conception is a lesson in the craftsmanship of letters.

The Prelude, as Wordsworth left it, had reached a high level of workmanship—so high indeed, that the few remaining banalities, such as 'My drift, I fear, is scarcely obvious', or 'Alas, I fear that I am trifling', stand out conspicuous, making us wonder how they escaped his vigilance. Little survived that was slovenly or careless. Flats, of course, there are, such flats as are inevitable to so comprehensive a design as his; for some of the elements that went to make up the poet's mind were refractory to poetic handling. His lines drag their slow length along whilst he labours to express in exact intellectual terms a philosophic position which, when all is said, is more truly a faith than a philosophy. And there was a matter-of-fact side to his nature which no truthful autobiography

---

[1] Hutchinson notes that in 1827 the word 'sweet' was removed from ten places in the poems, in 1836 from ten, in 1840 from one, in 1845 from three; — 24 in all.

[2] Note, e.g. the development through succeeding texts of VI. 63–4:
> And yet the morning gladness is not gone
> Which then was in my mind.

could gloss over, and which would only be falsified by the coloured draperies of fancy. But alike from what is too abstract for poetry and from what is too common-place, he can rise without effort to his noblest flights of song; and not seldom his most pregnant reflections spring from what seemed barren soil. Viewed as a whole the style is adequate to its theme. It has often been falsely judged. Wordsworth has been ridiculed for failing to attain to the great manner when he was not attempting it, but was playing upon his youthful foibles that gentle mockery which naturally takes a mock-heroic form:[1] more often he has been attacked as prosaic when his simple matter called for the plainest speech. His first aim, as it was his great achievement, was sincerity; and the sole stylistic error of his later revision lies in a too generous concession to the vulgar taste for poetical ornament.

§ 5. *Comparison of the texts in point of style— later deterioration*

Not all the changes of manner introduced into the final text are for the better. In the years when his inspiration was flagging, Wordsworth tended to fall back on that same abstract and artificial language from which his own theories, and his own best practice, had been a reaction. His true disciple, who has learnt from him to recognize the unmistakable ring of sincerity in style, will be the first to detect the false note in his master's work, the last to be cajoled into the delusion that prose can be turned into poetry by the use of unnatural diction or elaborate periphrasis. Nothing is gained poetically by changing the word 'friend' into 'the partner of those varied walks', nor 'human creature, be he who he may', to 'human creature howsoe'er endowed'. 'Thought and quietness' is a more truly Wordsworthian phrase than 'meditative peace'.[2] I find it hard to understand or to forgive the transformation of 'the Woman, and her garments vex'd and toss'd' (XI. 315) into a 'female'. The account of how, when he was

---

[1] Cf. Book III. 15–54, and notes.
[2] And also more suited to the context, a description of his state of feeling as a youth of eighteen.

'dead to deeper hope', he could yet rejoice in the life that is in nature:

> Plants, insects, beasts in field, and birds in bower,   (XI. 28.)

makes less impression upon us when the birds are pompously described as

> boldly seeking pleasures nearer heaven
> On wings that navigate cerulean skies.

Such lines would have adorned *The Seasons* : *The Prelude* can spare them. In the last version of the poem there is a fine but somewhat mannered description of how, with his sister, he lay upon the battlements of Brougham Castle,

> Catching from tufts of grass and hare-bell flowers
> Their faintest whisper from the passing breeze,
> Given out while mid-day heat oppressed the plains;

but the voice of the authentic Wordsworth is more distinctly heard in the delicate simplicity of the rejected lines:

> Lay listening to the wild flowers and the grass,
> As they gave out their whispers to the wind.   (VI. 231–2.)

In the A text his encounter with the discharged soldier has this preface:

> A favourite pleasure hath it been with me,
> From time of earliest youth, to walk alone
> Along the public Way, when, for the night
> Deserted, in its silence it assumes
> A character of deeper quietness
> Than pathless solitudes.   (IV. 363–8.)

The sentence opens lamely enough, though by the third line it has recovered; but as it stands, it is more in key with the bare impressive narrative that is to follow than is the grandiloquent exordium of the later version:

> When from our better selves we have too long
> Been parted by the hurrying world, and droop,
> Sick of its business, of its pleasure tired,
> How gracious, how benign is Solitude!

and so on, succeeded by far-sought similes of the watchman and the hermit—sixteen lines in all, of good but inappropriate writing, in the place of five and a half which needed but slight emendation to make them wholly adequate.[1] This anxiety to write up his poem, and give it a more definitely literary flavour, creates in places the impression of pompous phrase-making, which is farther removed than overbald simplicity from the true Wordsworthian spirit.

§ 6. *Changes in the text due to change of audience*

Other changes in the text, though in part matters of style, are more properly regarded as due to a change in the audience for whom the poem was destined. The A text was not merely dedicated to Coleridge, it was *addressed* to him, as to one

> Who in my thoughts art ever at my side;

its whole atmosphere is suggested by the parenthesis inserted in the tale of his sufferings during the Reign of Terror:

> (I speak bare truth
> As if to thee alone in private talk;)

it has the tone of intimate conversation, or of a personal letter written without reserve, in the confidence that no detail will be accounted too trivial among friends 'who love as we do', that no confession about himself will be misconstrued as vain or empty egoism.[2] *The Prelude* never lost this intimate character; but it was inevitable that when the poet reviewed it with an eye to publication, he should desire to tone down or to omit matter which, to a wider and less sympathetic audience, might seem irrelevant or superfluous. Thus the pronoun 'I', common in the A text, often gives way to a passive construction. In the A text we find a reference to his slender means in London, so that theatre-going, though a 'dear delight', was but a rare luxury with him; we have an

---

[1] This change in the text is all the more regrettable as it led to the omission of ll. 375–95, a passage of great beauty and penetrating psychology.

[2] Cf. also VI. 269–71:

> Throughout this narrative
> *Else sooner ended,* I have known full well
> For whom I thus record *etc.* (The italics are mine.)

explicit statement of his reasons both for going to France and for returning to England; we are told the name of the companion that he lost on the Penrith moor; and we learn that the lake on which he had his momentous adventure in the stolen boat was not Esthwaite, as has so often been surmised, but Ullswater, for he was staying at the time at Patterdale, on his way home for the holidays. Throughout the later versions he tends to eliminate place-names. An early reviewer of *The Prelude* remarked, with some naïveté, that finding the place-names of his district unsuited for verse the poet was obliged 'to make up for this by descriptive circumlocution'; but if Wordsworth could begin a sonnet with the name of Jones, he would hardly boggle at Cockermouth, or Patterdale, or Hawkshead, names endeared to him by rich associations. Of a still deeper interest are those early readings which shed light upon his character. To Coleridge he can write lines protesting his innocence of the passions of envy and dissolute pleasure (III. 532–6), and allude more than once to that strain of constitutional melancholy (VI. 192, X. 868–9) which often destroyed his peace of mind; but while we appreciate the motives that led him to suppress these confidences, we may yet be glad to recover them. Poetically, indeed, much of this detail is nugatory, and some of it, as Wordsworth himself was inclined to think, 'beneath the dignity of verse'. But we value it in no spirit of mere vulgar curiosity. *The Prelude* is a great poem, but it is also the frank autobiography of a great man. It cannot be judged solely by poetic canons, any more than a letter can be judged by the same criteria as an essay: like a letter, it owes its peculiar charm to intimate revelation of the writer. Over many of his readers Wordsworth exerts a truly personal spell. To them he is not a poet only, but a friend; and among our friends the most trivial admissions are often welcomed because, in their very triviality, they seem to bring us nearer to the object of our love.

§ 7. *Changes of idea:* (a) *Life at Cambridge*

To the student of the poet's mind the first version of *The Prelude* is chiefly valuable because it presents us with the history of his spiritual growth as he saw it when his powers were still at their

height, and when he was writing those poems on which his great-
ness rests most securely. No man is the same at seventy years of
age as he was at thirty-five, and Wordsworth, perhaps, changed
more than most of us; for though, like others, he descended into
the vale of years, he descended from far more glorious heights.
The Wordsworth who, when the conversation turned upon
Orleans, could say to his wife 'I wonder how I came to stay there
so long, and at a period so exciting', was either a very different
man from his younger self, or he had a keener sense of humour
than is usually allowed him. When he wrote *The Prelude* he was
gifted with a penetrative imagination that none of our poets, save
Shakespeare, can surpass; but even then the gift came to him
fitfully:

> I see by glimpses now, as age comes on
> May scarcely see at all.

The pathetic prophecy was fulfilled; as age came on, his sight was
dimmed; and not only did he see less, but he tended to lose com-
plete confidence in his earlier vision. He still towered above his
fellows. As late as 1841 he could impress John Stuart Mill with
the 'extensive range of his thoughts and the expansiveness of his
feelings'. But compared with what he had once been he was nar-
row, and he was timid; and many of the later changes in the text
of *The Prelude* are criticisms directed by a man of seventy winters
against his own past.

It is not to be expected that he would find much to alter in
his reminiscences of childhood; nor had he written anything of
Cambridge that would seriously disquiet his more prudent age.
He knew the darker side to the picture, for he told De Quincey
that 'the manners of the young men were very frantic and disso-
lute at that time'; but to this he barely alludes in *The Prelude*.
For there 'his tale was of himself', and the 'baser pleasures of the
place' were 'by him unshared, and only now and then observed'.
There could hardly be stronger testimony to the soundness of his
early education and the strength of his character than that he
could pass unscathed through the Cambridge of his day:

> For me, I grieve not; happy is the man,
> Who only misses what I miss'd, who falls
> No lower than I fell.

The University had, in fact, little of academic worth to offer him; but the very apathy of those in authority, and the barren curriculum which they prescribed, had justified him in indulging his incorrigible passion for liberty. He had re-echoed in his heart the comment passed on Cambridge by his latest poetic predecessor—'If these are the profits of the place, give me the amusements of it'; but looking back from a maturer manhood, he saw little in this to regret. If his reading had been desultory, it had been far wider than is generally supposed. At Cambridge, too, he had learnt one of the supporting truths of his life, 'the spiritual presences of absent things'. Moreover he never ceased to recognize that he 'was not for that hour, Nor for that place'. But when he revised the book he made some slight concessions to the susceptibilities of his Alma Mater. He retained his attack on compulsory College chapel, but compensated for it by inserting here and there a few phrases which give the book a more religious flavour. He now defends his own idleness with less defiance, and exonerates his University from some of her responsibility for it. The later omission of lines, such as—

> Why should I grieve? I was a chosen son . . .
> I was a Freeman, in the purest sense
> Was free, and to majestic ends was strong,

and the inclusion of others—

> Yet why take refuge in that plea? the fault
> This, I repeat, was mine, mine be the blame,

sufficiently indicate a change of tone, befitting one who had sons of undergraduate age, and whose brother was Master of Trinity.

§ 8. *Changes of idea:* (b) *Attitude to the French Revolution*

From the first he was uncertain how he should deal with those fateful years that followed his departure from Cambridge. His original intention was to leave them out of *The Prelude* altogether, and reserve all reflections upon the French Revolution for more dispassionate and impersonal treatment in *The Recluse*;

and when he saw that to follow this course would leave the history of his mind's growth incomplete, he seems to have hesitated as to the amount of detail he should introduce. After recounting his return to England, the narrative, up to this point clear and consecutive, becomes involved and wavering; he goes backwards and forwards, so that the progress of events is not easy to trace. The order in which Books VII and IX were written suggests, at least, that at one time the book devoted to London was to follow and not precede the account of his residence in France; had it done so it must have included not merely the first impressions of an eager, bewildered stranger 'in the vast metropolis', but some details of those exciting months when, with his revolutionary ardour at its height, he was associating with the English radical leaders; and also of that later time when, in the bitter mood of disenchantment, he clung to such straws of hope as he could clutch from the abstract principles of Godwin. There is no part of his life of which we know so little as that which intervened between his departure from France and his settlement at Racedown; there is none of which we would fain know more. His references to it in later years were often vague and misleading; but even when he wrote *The Prelude* he felt no inclination to say more of it than was barely necessary to explain his recovery and release from it.

Critics who approach Wordsworth with a strong revolutionary bias have sometimes expected that the first version of *The Prelude* would reveal a poet far more after their own heart than they have found in the version of 1850. They forget that in the year 1804 he was already heart and soul with his own country in her struggle with Napoleon, convinced that the cause of true liberty depended on her ultimate triumph. Then, as later, in speaking of his Revolutionary ardour, 'juvenile errors' were his theme. The words with which in 1821 he met the charge of apostasy express a conviction that he held as firmly when he wrote *The Prelude*: 'You have been deluded by places and persons, while I have stuck to principles. I abandoned France and her rulers when they abandoned Liberty, gave themselves up to tyranny, and endeavoured to enslave the world.' In point of fact his renunciation of France preceded the full blossoming of his poetic genius.

All later political changes came gradually, insensibly to himself. He never regretted his enthusiasm for the Revolution in its early days of promise, and retained to the last that democratic idealism, inherent in his nature, which had first attracted him to it. Nor was he ever in theory the solid Tory that he became in practice. There was always, he said, something of the Chartist in him. But with the passage of years, as he himself admitted, he lost courage; and his revision of *The Prelude* shows clear signs of his growing conservatism.

Book IX, which relates his conversion, under the inspired guidance of Beaupuy, to the cause of France, he could leave almost untouched:[1] he revised more drastically those books which recorded a sympathy with the Revolution that seemed less justifiable. As time passed, he grew more severe upon France, more indulgent to English foreign policy, more apologetic for himself. *The Prelude* records how the September massacres, though they appalled him, did not damp his ardour; for he was buoyed up by the faith that one great man might still save France from the Jacobins and restore her to her ideals. 'Enflamed with hope', the phrase with which he describes this faith in 1804, gives probably a truer impression of his emotion at the time than the more sober 'Cheered with this hope' which later he substituted for it. Moreover, in 1804 he could still endorse it in the pregnant words

Creed which ten shameful years have not annulled.

The removal of this line from his text not only points to a loss of faith, it removes the implication that his own country bore her part in the shame which those years brought forth. The originally bare account of his reluctant return homewards was elaborated into a passionately patriotic tribute to Albion's sacred shores, which was hardly his sentiment at the time of which it was written. To the motives which he had given for the French declaration of a republic (September 1792) he now added others that were less worthy, and were quite foreign to his thoughts

[1] His omission of *Vaudracour and Julia* from Book IX is discussed in the notes at the end of the volume (*v.* p. 295).

either then or in 1804; and though he admitted later[1] that he had 'disapproved of the war against France at its commencement, thinking, which was, perhaps, an error, that it might have been avoided' (note the 'perhaps', he is not sure of it even in 1821), he could not leave unmitigated the terms in which, in the A text, he had denounced it. In 1804 he had attributed it to 'the unhappy counsel of a few weak men', and laid greater stress on the extent of English sympathy with the Revolutionary cause, whilst his condemnation of the government for their persecution of the English radicals, severe, indeed, in the final text, was before at once more passionate and more contemptuous:

> Our Shepherds (this say merely) at that time
> Thirsted to make the guardian Crook of Law
> A tool of Murder; they who ruled the State,
> Though with such awful proof before their eyes
> That he who would sow death, reaps death, or worse
> And can reap nothing better, child-like long'd
> To imitate, not wise enough to avoid,
> Giants in their impiety alone,
> But, in their weapons and their warfare base
> As vermin working out of reach, they leagued
> Their strength perfidiously, to undermine
> Justice, and make an end of Liberty.   (X. 645–56.)

This is strong language to use against an English cabinet, and we cannot be surprised that it was modified upon revision.

But more significant, perhaps, is the introduction into Book VII, some time after 1820, of an enthusiastic tribute to Burke. There is no trace of this eulogy in the original text. Burke's oratory would, doubtless, have stirred the poet on his visits to London in either 1791 or 1793, but it would have stirred him to very different emotions from those which inspired the added lines. It is possible that even in 1804 he might have written them, but their insertion in the account of his early impressions of London, when he had lately returned from a holiday across a Europe which

> was thrilled with joy,
> France standing on the top of golden hours,
> And human nature seeming born again,

[1] Letter to James Losh, 4 Dec. 1821.

creates a misleading impression as to the state of his mind in that period of which the book professes to be the record.

§ 9. *Changes of idea:* (c) *Philosophy of life and religion*

But most to be regretted are those alterations in the text which have obscured the statement of that religious faith which is reflected in all the poet's greatest work. When Wordsworth wrote *The Prelude* he had in nothing swerved from the faith that inspired the *Lines composed a few miles above Tintern Abbey*. This faith need only be referred to here in the barest outline. Starting from a fervid belief in the inherent goodness of human nature, Wordsworth attributes the growth of the whole moral and intellectual being—from infancy through the stages of childhood and adolescence to maturity—to impressions made upon the senses, bound together, reacting on one another, and ever growing in fullness and intensity by means of the law of association. The philosophical parentage of this conception is unmistakable; it is the direct offspring of the sensationalism of the eighteenth century, and in particular of David Hartley,

> he of mortal kind
> Wisest, he first who marked the ideal tribes
> Up the fine fibres of the sentient brain,[1]

but it is Hartley transcendentalized by Coleridge, and at once modified and exalted by Wordsworth's own mystical experience. For to him there was always this great paradox, that though it is simply by the proper exercise of eye and ear that man reaches his full moral and intellectual stature, so that he can recognize

> In Nature and the language of the sense
> The anchor of my purest thoughts, the nurse,

[1] Coleridge, *Religious Musings*. [A number of studies of Wordsworth's debts to eighteenth-century philosophy are of value. Among the most rewarding are Arthur Beatty, *William Wordsworth: His Doctrine and Art*, 2nd ed. (Madison, 1927); N. P. Stallknecht, *Strange Seas of Thought*, 2nd ed. (Bloomington, 1958); Melvin M. Rader, *Wordsworth: A Philosophical Approach* (Oxford, 1967); Jonathan Wordsworth, *The Music of Humanity* (London, 1969). S. G.]

> The guide, the guardian of my heart, and soul
> Of all my moral being,

yet revelation flashes upon him when 'the light of sense goes out'; and 'laid asleep in body', he becomes deeply conscious of the presence of God within him. In the highest mood of ecstasy this consciousness of complete oneness with God is so overwhelming, that his other attributes as man seem to fall from him, and he knows only that

> one interior life
> In which all beings live with God, themselves
> Are God, existing in the mighty whole,
> As indistinguishable as the cloudless east
> Is from the cloudless west, when all
> The hemisphere is one cerulean blue.[1]

How far this intense mystical experience is compatible with Christianity let theologians determine. Coleridge, whether, like a bee that draws its food from many different flowers, he took his nourishment from the Neo-Platonists, or Hartley, or Spinoza, or, as later, from the German metaphysicians, always contrived to give his honey some Christian flavour; and Wordsworth himself strayed no further from orthodoxy than Coleridge had done in *Religious Musings* and *The Eolian Harp*. When Coleridge described his friend as a semi-atheist he was not objecting to his positive faith, but rather reflecting on what he regarded as its incompleteness. Certainly at this time Wordsworth's faith was in no way tinged with dogmatic Christianity. It is doubtful whether ever, except in those dark years of scepticism when he had wholly lost his bearings, he would have regarded himself as an opponent to Christianity: but Christianity had in youth no special message for him. With Coleridge's attempt to fuse philosophy and religion he was wholly unconcerned. His philosophy, as far as he was a philosopher, *was* his religion; he never examined its logical implications, and any analysis that seemed to disturb its integrity he would have set down to 'that false secondary power by which we multiply distinctions', appealing against it to the tribunal of his

---

[1] From a fragment found in a MS. notebook containing *Peter Bell*.

own deepest experience. His faith was a passionate intuition of
God present in the Universe and in the mind of man; his philo-
sophy no more than the struggle of his reason to account for it.
And to the end of his life this intuition remained the living centre
of his creed; something

> Which neither listlessness nor mad endeavour,
> Nor all that is at enmity with joy,
> Can utterly abolish or destroy.

He always resented that cruder orthodoxy 'which considers
the Supreme Being as bearing the same relation to the Universe
as a watchmaker bears to a watch'. The Temple in which he
worshipped most devoutly was still one not made with hands,
the Bible in which he read the deepest lessons was still 'the
Bible of the Universe, as it speaks to the ear of the intelligent,
and as it lies open to the eyes of the humble-minded'. But later
the vision grew dim, and though at times it was 'by miracle
restored', it was no longer sufficient to meet his needs. Gradually,
therefore, he turned more consciously to the Christian faith. This
change was the almost inevitable outcome of his experience of
life. The Wordsworth of 1798–1804 was the exultant champion
of 'man's unconquerable mind': 'dignity', 'majesty', 'sovereignty'
are words again and again applied to the human mind in the
early *Prelude*, and again and again qualified in the later texts.
Inspired by a passionate sense of the spiritual greatness of man, he
forgot man's natural weakness. But the inevitable yoke brought
by the years taught him the need of humility. We may resent
the intrusion into a passage which in magnificent verse eulogizes
man as 'of all visible natures crown' (VIII. 631–40) of what seems
the unnecessary reminder that he is 'born of dust and kindred to
the worm'.[1] But the inserted phrase tells something that was

---

[1] Cf. also the lines:

> Dust, as we are, the immortal spirit grows
> Like harmony in music,   [I. 340–1.]

which were first written (with no reference to our dusty origin)

> The mind of man is fram'd even like the breath
> And harmony of music.   (I. 351–2.)

Here, unquestionably, the passage has gained by the fine contrast introduced
between the body and the spirit of man.

essential to Wordsworth's later thought. Christian meekness had come to have a real meaning for him, and the more so because, of all the Christian virtues, it was for him the hardest to achieve.

Moreover, he felt a deep sense of responsibility as a teacher, and he had good reason to know that he was misunderstood. Both *Lines composed . . . above Tintern Abbey* and the *Ode: Intimations of Immortality* had proved a stumbling-block to many. He was accused, even by readers of *The Excursion*, of not distinguishing 'Nature as the work of God and God himself', and he felt it incumbent on him to remove from *The Prelude* all that might be interpreted as giving support to the heresy, and to bring that poem into accord with the later modifications of his faith. He took pains to relate, as far as possible, his naturalistic religion to a definitely Christian dogma. He toned down passages that savoured too much of independence. He inserted lines here and there which might lull asleep the watchful eye of the heresy hunter. Sometimes these are merely what might be called pietistic embroidery, in no way affecting the argument, but creating, by the use of conventional phraseology, a familiar atmosphere of edification. In this spirit he adds a reference to matins and vespers [I. 45], includes among possible themes for poetic treatment 'Christian meekness hallowing youthful loves' [I. 185], changes the simple phrase 'as were a joy to hear of' into the more elaborate

> To which the silver wands of saints in Heaven
> Might point with rapturous joy,   [X. 485–6.]

qualifies a statement that seems to him overbold with the line

> So, with devout humility be it said,   [X. 447.]

and adds, as a reason for the respect due for man as man, that he is

> Here placed to be the inheritor of Heaven.   [VIII. 336.]

These are small matters in themselves, but they give a new colour to his work, and are foreign to its original spirit.

He is, throughout, careful, by a small change in word or

phrase, or the addition of a sentence, to cover up the traces of his
early pantheism. Thus

> A soul divine which we participate,
> A deathless spirit   (V. 16–17.)

becomes

> As might appear to the eye of fleeting time,
> A deathless spirit,

and

> God and Nature's single sovereignty   (IX. 238.)

becomes

> Presences of God's mysterious power
> Made manifest in Nature's sovereignty.

Most noticeable is his relapse from that religion of joy which
springs from feeling, the reward of 'glad hearts without reproach
or blot', to a less spontaneous, a disciplined emotion. The spirit
of the early *Prelude* is that of one who, with God and nature
communing,

> saw one life and felt that it was joy.   (II. 430.)

But even to this simple utterance he adds the gloss

> Communing in this sort through earth and heaven
> With every form of creature, as it looked
> Towards the Uncreated with a countenance
> Of adoration, with an eye of love.

Nothing could be more significant than the change of

> I worshipp'd then among the depths of things
> As my soul bade me . . .
> I felt, and nothing else   (XI. 234–8.)

to

> Worshipping then among the depths of things
> As piety ordained . . .
> I felt, observed, and pondered.

(Of 'natural piety', indeed, the original *Prelude* is full: of what is
ordinarily called piety there is nothing.)

In the same way

> The feeling of life endless, the great thought
> By which we live, Infinity and God   (XIII. 176-7.)

becomes later

> Faith in life endless, the sustaining thought
> Of human Being, Eternity and God.

The highest achievement of that Power which he has learnt to reverence in Nature was, in the A text, that it 'lifts the being into magnanimity', i.e. to that greatness of soul which raises us above our petty selves to realize the 'Godhead that is ours, as natural beings in the strength of nature'. In the later version this same power

> Trains to meekness and exalts by humble faith.

And so, that imaginative rapture, that is 'balanced by a Reason which indeed Is reason' (XIII. 257-8), is later presented as

> balanced by pathetic truth, by trust
> In hopeful reason, leaning on the stay
> Of Providence,

and its lasting inspiration, 'sanctified By reason and by truth' (ib. 436-7), is later

> sanctified by reason, blest by faith.

By changes such as these, the last Book in particular, which is the philosophical conclusion of the whole matter, leaves a totally different impression from that created by the earlier text. The ideas he has introduced are from the brain that wrote the *Ecclesiastical Sonnets*; they were entirely alien to his thought and feeling, not only in that youth and early manhood of which *The Prelude* recounts the history, but in that maturer period when it was written; and they have no rightful place in the poem. Whether he ought to have felt them, or wished, when he was reviewing his work, that he had felt them, is another matter. The essential point for us to realize is that their intrusion has falsified our estimate of the authentic Wordsworth, the poet of the years 1798-1805.

The first signs of the change which dictated this revision are seen in the very months during which he was completing the poem—in the *Ode to Duty*, where he renounces his reliance on the genial sense of youth

> When love is an unerring light
> And joy its own security,—

and in the second half of the 'immortal *Ode*'. But though he undoubtedly passed through a period of spiritual change, accentuated by grief at the loss of his brother John, which led to suspension of his work on *The Prelude*, he completed it in the spirit in which it had been begun, with no sign of wavering from his early faith. In the first version of *The Prelude* he wrote nothing that he might not have felt on that eventful day when he revisited Tintern Abbey; and of 'that serene and blessed mood' to which the lines then written give utterance, Wordsworth is the inspired interpreter.

The revised *Prelude* represents another, less independent creed. The position into which he had now withdrawn was not for him a false position. He was sincere, now as ever. But if he was conscious of a change, as it is abundantly clear that he was, he would surely have done better to leave as it stood what he had first written for Coleridge, and, instead of disguising his former faith, to have expounded in a book of *The Recluse*, or elsewhere, the reasons that led him to move from it, and the manner in which it could be reconciled with the tenets of an historic Church. In truth that compromise, which provided so secure a haven for his later years, was worthy of a finer exposition than he was ever able to give it. It may have brought him peace, but it never stirred him to that rapture of which great art is born. When his poetry was commended for the purity of its morals he insisted that he, on the other hand, valued it according to the power of the mind which it presupposed in the writer and excited in the hearer. That work of his which most triumphantly stands this test belongs to the years 1798–1807; and of the vital source and hiding-places of its power the original *Prelude* is the frankest and most direct confession.

1932   E. DE S.

BOOK FIRST

INTRODUCTION—CHILDHOOD AND SCHOOL-TIME

OH there is blessing in this gentle breeze
That blows from the green fields and from the clouds
And from the sky: it beats against my cheek,
And seems half-conscious of the joy it gives.
5 O welcome Messenger! O welcome Friend!
A captive greets thee, coming from a house
Of bondage, from yon City's walls set free,
A prison where he hath been long immured.
Now I am free, enfranchis'd and at large,
10 May fix my habitation where I will.
What dwelling shall receive me? In what Vale　　　[10]
Shall be my harbour? Underneath what grove
Shall I take up my home, and what sweet stream
Shall with its murmurs lull me to my rest?
15 The earth is all before me: with a heart
Joyous, nor scar'd at its own liberty,　　　[15]
I look about, and should the guide I chuse
Be nothing better than a wandering cloud,
I cannot miss my way. I breathe again;
20 Trances of thought and mountings of the mind
Come fast upon me: it is shaken off,　　　[20]
As by miraculous gift 'tis shaken off,
That burthen of my own unnatural self,
The heavy weight of many a weary day
25 Not mine, and such as were not made for me.
Long months of peace (if such bold word accord
With any promises of human life),　　　.　[25]
Long months of ease and undisturb'd delight
Are mine in prospect; whither shall I turn
30 By road or pathway or through open field,
Or shall a twig or any floating thing
Upon the river, point me out my course?　　　[30]

I

Enough that I am free; for months to come
May dedicate myself to chosen tasks;
35 May quit the tiresome sea and dwell on shore,
If not a Settler on the soil, at least
To drink wild water, and to pluck green herbs,
And gather fruits fresh from their native tree.
Nay more, if I may trust myself, this hour
40 Hath brought a gift that consecrates my joy;
For I, methought, while the sweet breath of Heaven
Was blowing on my body, felt within
A corresponding mild creative breeze,   [35]
A vital breeze which travell'd gently on
45 O'er things which it had made, and is become
A tempest, a redundant energy
Vexing its own creation. 'Tis a power
That does not come unrecogniz'd, a storm,
Which, breaking up a long-continued frost   [40]
50 Brings with it vernal promises, the hope
Of active days, of dignity and thought,
Of prowess in an honorable field,
Pure passions, virtue, knowledge, and delight,
The holy life of music and of verse.   [45]

55   Thus far, O Friend! did I, not used to make
A present joy the matter of my Song,
Pour out, that day, my soul in measur'd strains,
Even in the very words which I have here
Recorded: to the open fields I told   [50]
60 A prophecy: poetic numbers came
Spontaneously, and cloth'd in priestly robe
My spirit, thus singled out, as it might seem,
For holy services: great hopes were mine;
My own voice chear'd me, and, far more, the mind's   [55]
65 Internal echo of the imperfect sound;
To both I listen'd, drawing from them both
A chearful confidence in things to come.

2

Whereat, being not unwilling now to give
A respite to this passion, I paced on   [60]
70 Gently, with careless steps; and came, erelong,
To a green shady place where down I sate
Beneath a tree, slackening my thoughts by choice,
And settling into gentler happiness.
'Twas Autumn, and a calm and placid day,   [65]
75 With warmth as much as needed from a sun
Two hours declin'd towards the west, a day
With silver clouds, and sunshine on the grass,
And, in the shelter'd grove where I was couch'd
A perfect stillness. On the ground I lay   [70]
80 Passing through many thoughts, yet mainly such
As to myself pertain'd. I made a choice
Of one sweet Vale whither my steps should turn
And saw, methought, the very house and fields
Present before my eyes: nor did I fail
85 To add, meanwhile, assurance of some work
Of glory, there forthwith to be begun,
Perhaps, too, there perform'd. Thus long I lay   [80]
Chear'd by the genial pillow of the earth
Beneath my head, sooth'd by a sense of touch
90 From the warm ground, that balanced me, else lost
Entirely, seeing nought, nought hearing, save
When here and there, about the grove of Oaks
Where was my bed, an acorn from the trees
Fell audibly, and with a startling sound.   [85]

95   Thus occupied in mind, I linger'd here
Contented, nor rose up until the sun
Had almost touch'd the horizon, bidding then
A farewell to the City left behind,
Even with the chance equipment of that hour
100 I journey'd towards the Vale that I had chosen.
It was a splendid evening; and my soul
Did once again make trial of the strength   [95]
Restored to her afresh; nor did she want

3

Eolian visitations; but the harp
105 Was soon defrauded, and the banded host
Of harmony dispers'd in straggling sounds
And, lastly, utter silence. 'Be it so,
It is an injury,' said I, 'to this day
To think of any thing but present joy.'   [100]
110 So like a Peasant I pursued my road
Beneath the evening sun, nor had one wish
Again to bend the sabbath of that time
To a servile yoke. What need of many words?   [105]
A pleasant loitering journey, through two days
115 Continued, brought me to my hermitage.

I spare to speak, my Friend, of what ensued,
The admiration and the love, the life
In common things; the endless store of things
Rare, or at least so seeming, every day   [110]
120 Found all about me in one neighbourhood,
The self-congratulation, the complete
Composure, and the happiness entire.
But speedily a longing in me rose
To brace myself to some determin'd aim,   [115]
125 Reading or thinking, either to lay up
New stores, or rescue from decay the old
By timely interference, I had hopes
Still higher, that with a frame of outward life,
I might endue, might fix in a visible home
130 Some portion of those phantoms of conceit   [120]
That had been floating loose about so long,
And to such Beings temperately deal forth
The many feelings that oppress'd my heart.
But I have been discouraged; gleams of light
135 Flash often from the East, then disappear   [125]
And mock me with a sky that ripens not
Into a steady morning: if my mind,
Remembering the sweet promise of the past,
Would gladly grapple with some noble theme,

4

140 Vain is her wish; where'er she turns she finds   [130]
    Impediments from day to day renew'd.

    And now it would content me to yield up
    Those lofty hopes awhile for present gifts
    Of humbler industry. But, O dear Friend!
145 The Poet, gentle creature as he is,   [135]
    Hath, like the Lover, his unruly times;
    His fits when he is neither sick nor well,
    Though no distress be near him but his own
    Unmanageable thoughts. The mind itself
150 The meditative mind, best pleased, perhaps,   [140]
    While she, as duteous as the Mother Dove,
    Sits brooding, lives not always to that end,
    But hath less quiet instincts, goadings on
    That drive her as in trouble through the groves.
155 With me is now such passion, which I blame
    No otherwise than as it lasts too long.   [145]

    When, as becomes a man who would prepare
    For such a glorious work, I through myself
    Make rigorous inquisition, the report
160 Is often chearing; for I neither seem
    To lack, that first great gift! the vital soul,   [150]
    Nor general truths which are themselves a sort
    Of Elements and Agents, Under-Powers,
    Subordinate helpers of the living mind.
165 Nor am I naked in external things,
    Forms, images; nor numerous other aids   [155]
    Of less regard, though won perhaps with toil,
    And needful to build up a Poet's praise.
    Time, place, and manners; these I seek, and these
170 I find in plenteous store; but nowhere such
    As may be singled out with steady choice;   [160]
    No little Band of yet remember'd names
    Whom I, in perfect confidence, might hope
    To summon back from lonesome banishment

5

175 And make them inmates in the hearts of men
Now living, or to live in times to come.   [165]
Sometimes, mistaking vainly, as I fear,
Proud spring-tide swellings for a regular sea,
I settle on some British theme, some old
180 Romantic tale, by Milton left unsung;
More often resting at some gentle place   [170]
Within the groves of Chivalry, I pipe
Among the Shepherds, with reposing Knights
Sit by a Fountain-side, and hear their tales.
185 Sometimes, more sternly mov'd, I would relate
How vanquish'd Mithridates northward pass'd,
And, hidden in the cloud of years, became
That Odin, Father of a Race, by whom
Perish'd the Roman Empire: how the Friends   [190]
190 And Followers of Sertorius, out of Spain
Flying, found shelter in the Fortunate Isles;
And left their usages, their arts, and laws,
To disappear by a slow gradual death;
To dwindle and to perish one by one   [195]
195 Starved in those narrow bounds: but not the Soul
Of Liberty, which fifteen hundred years
Surviv'd, and, when the European came
With skill and power that could not be withstood,
Did, like a pestilence, maintain its hold,   [200]
200 And wasted down by glorious death that Race
Of natural Heroes: or I would record
How in tyrannic times some unknown man,
Unheard of in the Chronicles of Kings,
Suffer'd in silence for the love of truth;   [205]
205 How that one Frenchman, through continued force
Of meditation on the inhuman deeds
Of the first Conquerors of the Indian Isles,
Went single in his ministry across
The Ocean, not to comfort the Oppress'd,   [210]
210 But, like a thirsty wind, to roam about,
Withering the Oppressor: how Gustavus found

6

Help at his need in Dalecarlia's Mines:
How Wallace fought for Scotland, left the name
Of Wallace to be found like a wild flower, [215]
215 All over his dear Country, left the deeds
Of Wallace, like a family of Ghosts,
To people the steep rocks and river banks,
Her natural sanctuaries, with a local soul
Of independence and stern liberty. [220]
220 Sometimes it suits me better to shape out
Some Tale from my own heart, more near akin
To my own passions and habitual thoughts,
Some variegated story, in the main
Lofty, with interchange of gentler things. [225]
225 But deadening admonitions will succeed
And the whole beauteous Fabric seems to lack
Foundation, and, withal, appears throughout
Shadowy and unsubstantial. Then, last wish,
My last and favourite aspiration! then
230 I yearn towards some philosophic Song
Of Truth that cherishes our daily life; [230]
With meditations passionate from deep
Recesses in man's heart, immortal verse
Thoughtfully fitted to the Orphean lyre;
235 But from this awful burthen I full soon
Take refuge, and beguile myself with trust [235]
That mellower years will bring a riper mind
And clearer insight. Thus from day to day
I live, a mockery of the brotherhood
240 Of vice and virtue, with no skill to part
Vague longing that is bred by want of power
From paramount impulse not to be withstood, [240]
A timorous capacity from prudence;
From circumspection, infinite delay.
245 Humility and modest awe themselves
Betray me, serving often for a cloak
To a more subtle selfishness, that now. [245]
Doth lock my functions up in blank reserve,

7

Now dupes me by an over-anxious eye
250 That with a false activity beats off
Simplicity and self-presented truth.
—Ah! better far than this, to stray about   [250]
Voluptuously through fields and rural walks,
And ask no record of the hours, given up
255 To vacant musing, unreprov'd neglect
Of all things, and deliberate holiday;
Far better never to have heard the name   [255]
Of zeal and just ambition, than to live
Thus baffled by a mind that every hour
260 Turns recreant to her task, takes heart again,
Then feels immediately some hollow thought
Hang like an interdict upon her hopes.   [260]
This is my lot; for either still I find
Some imperfection in the chosen theme,
265 Or see of absolute accomplishment
Much wanting, so much wanting, in myself,
That I recoil and droop, and seek repose   [265]
In listlessness from vain perplexity,
Unprofitably travelling towards the grave,
270 Like a false steward who hath much received
And renders nothing back.—Was it for this
That one, the fairest of all Rivers, lov'd   [270]
To blend his murmurs with my Nurse's song,
And from his alder shades and rocky falls,
275 And from his fords and shallows, sent a voice
That flow'd along my dreams? For this, didst Thou,
O Derwent! travelling over the green Plains   [275]
Near my 'sweet Birthplace', didst thou, beauteous Stream,
Make ceaseless music through the night and day
280 Which with its steady cadence, tempering
Our human waywardness, compos'd my thoughts
To more than infant softness, giving me,
Among the fretful dwellings of mankind,
A knowledge, a dim earnest, of the calm
285 Which Nature breathes among the hills and groves. [281]

When, having left his Mountains, to the Towers
Of Cockermouth that beauteous River came,
Behind my Father's House he pass'd, close by,
Along the margin of our Terrace Walk.   [286]
290 He was a Playmate whom we dearly lov'd.
Oh! many a time have I, a five years' Child,
A naked Boy, in one delightful Rill,
A little Mill-race sever'd from his stream,
Made one long bathing of a summer's day,   [290]
295 Bask'd in the sun, and plunged, and bask'd again
Alternate all a summer's day, or cours'd
Over the sandy fields, leaping through groves
Of yellow grunsel, or when crag and hill,
The woods, and distant Skiddaw's lofty height,   [295]
300 Were bronz'd with a deep radiance, stood alone
Beneath the sky, as if I had been born
On Indian Plains, and from my Mother's hut
Had run abroad in wantonness, to sport,
A naked Savage, in the thunder shower.   [300]

305   Fair seed-time had my soul, and I grew up
Foster'd alike by beauty and by fear;
Much favor'd in my birthplace, and no less
In that beloved Vale to which, erelong,
I was transplanted. Well I call to mind   [305]
310 ('Twas at an early age, ere I had seen
Nine summers) when upon the mountain slope
The frost and breath of frosty wind had snapp'd
The last autumnal crocus, 'twas my joy
To wander half the night among the Cliffs
315 And the smooth Hollows, where the woodcocks ran
Along the open turf. In thought and wish
That time, my shoulder all with springes hung,   [310]
I was a fell destroyer. On the heights
Scudding away from snare to snare, I plied
320 My anxious visitation, hurrying on,
Still hurrying, hurrying onward; moon and stars

9

Were shining o'er my head; I was alone,
And seem'd to be a trouble to the peace
That was among them. Sometimes it befel
325 In these night-wanderings, that a strong desire
O'erpower'd my better reason, and the bird
Which was the captive of another's toils   [320]
Became my prey; and, when the deed was done
I heard among the solitary hills
330 Low breathings coming after me, and sounds
Of undistinguishable motion, steps
Almost as silent as the turf they trod.   [325]
Nor less in springtime when on southern banks
The shining sun had from his knot of leaves
335 Decoy'd the primrose flower, and when the Vales
And woods were warm, was I a plunderer then
In the high places, on the lonesome peaks
Where'er, among the mountains and the winds,
The Mother Bird had built her lodge. Though mean
340 My object, and inglorious, yet the end
Was not ignoble. Oh! when I have hung   [330]
Above the raven's nest, by knots of grass
And half-inch fissures in the slippery rock
But ill sustain'd, and almost, as it seem'd,
345 Suspended by the blast which blew amain,
Shouldering the naked crag; Oh! at that time;   [335]
While on the perilous ridge I hung alone,
With what strange utterance did the loud dry wind
Blow through my ears! the sky seem'd not a sky
350 Of earth, and with what motion mov'd the clouds!

The mind of Man is fram'd even like the breath
And harmony of music. There is a dark   [341]
Invisible workmanship that reconciles
Discordant elements, and makes them move
355 In one society. Ah me! that all
The terrors, all the early miseries   [345]
Regrets, vexations, lassitudes, that all

10

The thoughts and feelings which have been infus'd
Into my mind, should ever have made up
360 The calm existence that is mine when I
Am worthy of myself! Praise to the end!   [350]
Thanks likewise for the means! But I believe
That Nature, oftentimes, when she would frame
A favor'd Being, from his earliest dawn
365 Of infancy doth open out the clouds,
As at the touch of lightning, seeking him
With gentlest visitation; not the less,
Though haply aiming at the self-same end,
Does it delight her sometimes to employ
370 Severer interventions, ministry   [355]
More palpable, and so she dealt with me.

    One evening (surely I was led by her)
I went alone into a Shepherd's Boat,
A Skiff that to a Willow tree was tied
375 Within a rocky Cave, its usual home.
'Twas by the shores of Patterdale, a Vale
Wherein I was a Stranger, thither come
A School-boy Traveller, at the Holidays.
Forth rambled from the Village Inn alone
380 No sooner had I sight of this small Skiff,
Discover'd thus by unexpected chance,
Than I unloos'd her tether and embark'd.   [360]
The moon was up, the Lake was shining clear
Among the hoary mountains; from the Shore
385 I push'd, and struck the oars and struck again
In cadence, and my little Boat mov'd on
Even like a Man who walks with stately step
Though bent on speed. It was an act of stealth   [361]
And troubled pleasure; not without the voice
390 Of mountain-echoes did my Boat move on,
Leaving behind her still on either side
Small circles glittering idly in the moon,   [365]
Until they melted all into one track

Of sparkling light. A rocky Steep uprose
395 Above the Cavern of the Willow tree
And now, as suited one who proudly row'd
With his best skill, I fix'd a steady view
Upon the top of that same craggy ridge,   [370]
The bound of the horizon, for behind
400 Was nothing but the stars and the grey sky.
She was an elfin Pinnace; lustily
I dipp'd my oars into the silent Lake,
And, as I rose upon the stroke, my Boat
Went heaving through the water, like a Swan;   [375]
405 When from behind that craggy Steep, till then
The bound of the horizon, a huge Cliff,
As if with voluntary power instinct,
Uprear'd its head. I struck, and struck again,   [380]
And, growing still in stature, the huge Cliff
410 Rose up between me and the stars, and still,
With measur'd motion, like a living thing,
Strode after me. With trembling hands I turn'd,   [385]
And through the silent water stole my way
Back to the Cavern of the Willow tree.
415 There, in her mooring-place, I left my Bark,
And, through the meadows homeward went, with grave
And serious thoughts; and after I had seen   [390]
That spectacle, for many days, my brain
Work'd with a dim and undetermin'd sense
420 Of unknown modes of being; in my thoughts
There was a darkness, call it solitude,
Or blank desertion, no familiar shapes   [395]
Of hourly objects, images of trees,
Of sea or sky, no colours of green fields;
425 But huge and mighty Forms that do not live
Like living men mov'd slowly through my mind
By day and were the trouble of my dreams.   [400]

Wisdom and Spirit of the universe!
Thou Soul that art the Eternity of Thought!

12

430 That giv'st to forms and images a breath
And everlasting motion! not in vain,
By day or star-light thus from my first dawn [405]
Of Childhood didst Thou intertwine for me
The passions that build up our human Soul,
435 Not with the mean and vulgar works of Man,
But with high objects, with enduring things,
With life and nature, purifying thus [410]
The elements of feeling and of thought,
And sanctifying, by such discipline,
440 Both pain and fear, until we recognize
A grandeur in the beatings of the heart.

Nor was this fellowship vouchsaf'd to me [415]
With stinted kindness. In November days,
When vapours, rolling down the valleys, made
445 A lonely scene more lonesome; among woods
At noon, and 'mid the calm of summer nights,
When, by the margin of the trembling Lake, [420]
Beneath the gloomy hills I homeward went
In solitude, such intercourse was mine;
450 'Twas mine among the fields both day and night,
And by the waters all the summer long.

And in the frosty season, when the sun [425]
Was set, and visible for many a mile
The cottage windows through the twilight blaz'd,
455 I heeded not the summons:—happy time
It was, indeed, for all of us; to me
It was a time of rapture: clear and loud [430]
The village clock toll'd six; I wheel'd about,
Proud and exulting, like an untired horse,
460 That cares not for its home. —All shod with steel,
We hiss'd along the polish'd ice, in games
Confederate, imitative of the chace [435]
And woodland pleasures, the resounding horn,
The Pack loud bellowing, and the hunted hare.

13

465 So through the darkness and the cold we flew,
And not a voice was idle; with the din,
Meanwhile, the precipices rang aloud, [440]
The leafless trees, and every icy crag
Tinkled like iron, while the distant hills
470 Into the tumult sent an alien sound
Of melancholy, not unnoticed, while the stars,
Eastward, were sparkling clear, and in the west [445]
The orange sky of evening died away.

Not seldom from the uproar I retired
475 Into a silent bay, or sportively
Glanced sideway, leaving the tumultuous throng,
To cut across the image of a star [450]
That gleam'd upon the ice: and oftentimes
When we had given our bodies to the wind,
480 And all the shadowy banks, on either side,
Came sweeping through the darkness, spinning still [455]
The rapid line of motion; then at once
Have I, reclining back upon my heels,
Stopp'd short, yet still the solitary Cliffs
485 Wheeled by me, even as if the earth had roll'd
With visible motion her diurnal round; [460]
Behind me did they stretch in solemn train
Feebler and feebler, and I stood and watch'd
Till all was tranquil as a dreamless sleep.

490 Ye Presences of Nature, in the sky
Or on the earth! Ye Visions of the hills! [465]
And Souls of lonely places! can I think
A vulgar hope was yours when Ye employ'd
Such ministry, when Ye through many a year
495 Haunting me thus among my boyish sports,
On caves and trees, upon the woods and hills, [470]
Impress'd upon all forms the characters
Of danger or desire, and thus did make
The surface of the universal earth

14

500 With triumph, and delight, and hope, and fear,
　　Work like a sea? [475]
　　　　　　　　Not uselessly employ'd,
　　I might pursue this theme through every change
　　Of exercise and play, to which the year
　　Did summon us in its delightful round.

505　We were a noisy crew, the sun in heaven [480]
　　Beheld not vales more beautiful than ours,
　　Nor saw a race in happiness and joy
　　More worthy of the fields where they were sown.
　　I would record with no reluctant voice
510 The woods of autumn and their hazel bowers
　　With milk-white clusters hung; the rod and line, [485]
　　True symbol of the foolishness of hope,
　　Which with its strong enchantment led us on
　　By rocks and pools, shut out from every star
515 All the green summer, to forlorn cascades
　　Among the windings of the mountain brooks. [490]
　　—Unfading recollections! at this hour
　　The heart is almost mine with which I felt
　　From some hill-top, on sunny afternoons
520 The Kite high up among the fleecy clouds
　　Pull at its rein, like an impatient Courser, [495]
　　Or, from the meadows sent on gusty days,
　　Beheld her breast the wind, then suddenly
　　Dash'd headlong; and rejected by the storm.

525　Ye lowly Cottages in which we dwelt,
　　A ministration of your own was yours, [500]
　　A sanctity, a safeguard, and a love!
　　Can I forget you, being as ye were
　　So beautiful among the pleasant fields
530 In which ye stood? Or can I here forget
　　The plain and seemly countenance with which
　　Ye dealt out your plain comforts? Yet had ye [505]
　　Delights and exultations of your own.

15

Eager and never weary we pursued
535 Our home amusements by the warm peat-fire
At evening; when with pencil and with slate,
In square divisions parcell'd out, and all [510]
With crosses and with cyphers scribbled o'er,
We schemed and puzzled, head opposed to head
540 In strife too humble to be named in Verse.
Or round the naked table, snow-white deal,
Cherry or maple, sate in close array, [515]
And to the combat, Lu or Whist, led on
A thick-ribbed Army; not as in the world
545 Neglected and ungratefully thrown by
Even for the very service they had wrought,
But husbanded through many a long campaign. [520]
Uncouth assemblage was it, where no few
Had changed their functions, some, plebeian cards,
550 Which Fate beyond the promise of their birth
Had glorified, and call'd to represent
The persons of departed Potentates. [525]
Oh! with what echoes on the Board they fell!
Ironic Diamonds, Clubs, Hearts, Diamonds, Spades,
555 A congregation piteously akin.
Cheap matter did they give to boyish wit,
Those sooty knaves, precipitated down [530]
With scoffs and taunts, like Vulcan out of Heaven,
The paramount Ace, a moon in her eclipse,
560 Queens, gleaming through their splendour's last decay,
And Monarchs, surly at the wrongs sustain'd
By royal visages. Meanwhile, abroad [535]
The heavy rain was falling, or the frost
Raged bitterly, with keen and silent tooth,
565 And, interrupting oft the impassion'd game,
From Esthwaite's neighbouring Lake the splitting ice,
While it sank down towards the water, sent,
Among the meadows and the hills, its long [541]
And dismal yellings, like the noise of wolves
570 When they are howling round the Bothnic Main.

16

Nor, sedulous as I have been to trace
How Nature by extrinsic passion first   [545]
Peopled my mind with beauteous forms or grand,
And made me love them, may I well forget
575 How other pleasures have been mine, and joys
Of subtler origin; how I have felt,
Not seldom, even in that tempestuous time,   [550]
Those hallow'd and pure motions of the sense
Which seem, in their simplicity, to own
580 An intellectual charm, that calm delight
Which, if I err not, surely must belong
To those first-born affinities that fit   [555]
Our new existence to existing things,
And, in our dawn of being, constitute
585 The bond of union betwixt life and joy.

Yes, I remember, when the changeful earth,
And twice five seasons on my mind had stamp'd   [560]
The faces of the moving year, even then,
A Child, I held unconscious intercourse
590 With the eternal Beauty, drinking in
A pure organic pleasure from the lines
Of curling mist, or from the level plain   [565]
Of waters colour'd by the steady clouds.

The Sands of Westmoreland, the Creeks and Bays
595 Of Cumbria's rocky limits, they can tell
How when the Sea threw off his evening shade
And to the Shepherd's huts beneath the crags   [570]
Did send sweet notice of the rising moon,
How I have stood, to fancies such as these,
600 Engrafted in the tenderness of thought,
A stranger, linking with the spectacle   [575]
No conscious memory of a kindred sight,
And bringing with me no peculiar sense
Of quietness or peace, yet I have stood,
605 Even while mine eye has mov'd o'er three long leagues

Of shining water, gathering, as it seem'd,
Through every hair-breadth of that field of light,
New pleasure, like a bee among the flowers. [580]

Thus, often in those fits of vulgar joy
610 Which, through all seasons, on a child's pursuits
Are prompt attendants, 'mid that giddy bliss
Which, like a tempest, works along the blood
And is forgotten; even then I felt [585]
Gleams like the flashing of a shield; the earth
615 And common face of Nature spake to me
Rememberable things; sometimes, 'tis true,
By chance collisions and quaint accidents
Like those ill-sorted unions, work suppos'd [590]
Of evil-minded fairies, yet not vain
620 Nor profitless, if haply they impress'd
Collateral objects and appearances,
Albeit lifeless then, and doom'd to sleep [595]
Until maturer seasons call'd them forth
To impregnate and to elevate the mind.
625 —And if the vulgar joy by its own weight
Wearied itself out of the memory,
The scenes which were a witness of that joy [600]
Remained, in their substantial lineaments
Depicted on the brain, and to the eye
630 Were visible, a daily sight; and thus
By the impressive discipline of fear,
By pleasure and repeated happiness,
So frequently repeated, and by force [605]
Of obscure feelings representative
635 Of joys that were forgotten, these same scenes,
So beauteous and majestic in themselves,
Though yet the day was distant, did at length
Become habitually dear, and all [610]
Their hues and forms were by invisible links
640 Allied to the affections.
       I began

18

My story early, feeling as I fear,
The weakness of a human love, for days
Disown'd by memory, ere the birth of spring   [615]
Planting my snowdrops among winter snows.
645   Nor will it seem to thee, my Friend! so prompt
In sympathy, that I have lengthen'd out,
With fond and feeble tongue, a tedious tale.
Meanwhile, my hope has been that I might fetch   [620]
Invigorating thoughts from former years,
650   Might fix the wavering balance of my mind,
And haply meet reproaches, too, whose power
May spur me on, in manhood now mature,
To honorable toil. Yet should these hopes   [625]
Be vain, and thus should neither I be taught
655   To understand myself, nor thou to know
With better knowledge how the heart was fram'd
Of him thou lovest, need I dread from thee
Harsh judgments, if I am so loth to quit   [630]
Those recollected hours that have the charm
660   Of visionary things, and lovely forms
And sweet sensations that throw back our life
And almost make our Infancy itself
A visible scene, on which the sun is shining?   [635]

     One end hereby at least hath been attain'd,
665   My mind hath been revived, and if this mood
Desert me not, I will forthwith bring down,
Through later years, the story of my life.
The road lies plain before me; 'tis a theme   [640]
Single and of determined bounds; and hence
670   I chuse it rather at this time, than work
Of ampler or more varied argument.

BOOK SECOND

SCHOOL-TIME—(CONTINUED)

Thus far, O Friend! have we, though leaving much
Unvisited, endeavour'd to retrace
My life through its first years, and measured back
The way I travell'd when I first began
5 To love the woods and fields; the passion yet   [5]
Was in its birth, sustain'd, as might befal,
By nourishment that came unsought; for still,
From week to week, from month to month, we liv'd
A round of tumult: duly were our games
10 Prolong'd in summer till the day-light fail'd;   [10]
No chair remain'd before the doors, the bench
And threshold steps were empty; fast asleep
The Labourer, and the Old Man who had sate,
A later lingerer, yet the revelry
15 Continued, and the loud uproar: at last,   [15]
When all the ground was dark, and the huge clouds
Were edged with twinkling stars, to bed we went,
With weary joints, and with a beating mind.
Ah! is there one who ever has been young,
20 And needs a monitory voice to tame   [20]
The pride of virtue, and of intellect?
And is there one, the wisest and the best
Of all mankind, who does not sometimes wish
For things which cannot be, who would not give,
25 If so he might, to duty and to truth   [25]
The eagerness of infantine desire?
A tranquillizing spirit presses now
On my corporeal frame: so wide appears
The vacancy between me and those days,
30 Which yet have such self-presence in my mind   [30]
That, sometimes, when I think of it, I seem
Two consciousnesses, conscious of myself

And of some other Being. A grey Stone
Of native rock, left midway in the Square
35 Of our small market Village, was the home
And centre of these joys, and when, return'd   [36]
After long absence, thither I repair'd,
I found that it was split, and gone to build
A smart Assembly-room that perk'd and flar'd
40 With wash and rough-cast elbowing the ground
Which had been ours. But let the fiddle scream,   [40]
And be ye happy! yet, my Friends! I know
That more than one of you will think with me
Of those soft starry nights, and that old Dame
45 From whom the stone was nam'd who there had sate
And watch'd her Table with its huxter's wares   [45]
Assiduous, thro' the length of sixty years.

We ran a boisterous race; the year span round
With giddy motion. But the time approach'd
50 That brought with it a regular desire
For calmer pleasures, when the beauteous forms   [50]
Of Nature were collaterally attach'd
To every scheme of holiday delight,
And every boyish sport, less grateful else,
53 And languidly pursued.
                              When summer came
It was the pastime of our afternoons   [55]
To beat along the plain of Windermere
With rival oars, and the selected bourne
Was now an Island musical with birds
60 That sang for ever; now a Sister Isle
Beneath the oaks' umbrageous covert, sown   [60]
With lillies of the valley, like a field;
And now a third small Island where remain'd
An old stone Table, and a moulder'd Cave,
65 A Hermit's history. In such a race,   [65]
So ended, disappointment could be none,
Uneasiness, or pain, or jealousy:

We rested in the shade, all pleas'd alike,
Conquer'd and Conqueror. Thus the pride of strength,
70 And the vain-glory of superior skill   [70]
Were interfus'd with objects which subdu'd
And temper'd them, and gradually produc'd
A quiet independence of the heart.
And to my Friend, who knows me, I may add,
75 Unapprehensive of reproof, that hence
Ensu'd a diffidence and modesty,   [75]
And I was taught to feel, perhaps too much,
The self-sufficing power of solitude.

No delicate viands sapp'd our bodily strength;
80 More than we wish'd we knew the blessing then
Of vigorous hunger, for our daily meals   [80]
Were frugal, Sabine fare! and then, exclude
A little weekly stipend, and we lived
Through three divisions of the quarter'd year
85 In pennyless poverty. But now, to School
Return'd, from the half-yearly holidays,   [85]
We came with purses more profusely fill'd,
Allowance which abundantly suffic'd
To gratify the palate with repasts
90 More costly than the Dame of whom I spake,
That ancient Woman, and her board supplied.
Hence inroads into distant Vales, and long
Excursions far away among the hills,
Hence rustic dinners on the cool green ground,
95 Or in the woods, or near a river side,   [90]
Or by some shady fountain, while soft airs
Among the leaves were stirring, and the sun
Unfelt, shone sweetly round us in our joy.

Nor is my aim neglected, if I tell
100 How twice in the long length of those half-years   [95]
We from our funds, perhaps, with bolder hand
Drew largely, anxious for one day, at least,

To feel the motion of the galloping Steed;
And with the good old Inn-keeper, in truth,
105 On such occasion sometimes we employ'd
Sly subterfuge; for the intended bound   [100]
Of the day's journey was too distant far
For any cautious man, a Structure famed
Beyond its neighbourhood, the antique Walls
110 Of that large Abbey which within the Vale
Of Nightshade, to St. Mary's honour built,
Stands yet, a mouldering Pile, with fractured Arch, [105]
Belfry, and Images, and living Trees,
A holy Scene! along the smooth green turf
115 Our Horses grazed: to more than inland peace
Left by the sea wind passing overhead
(Though wind of roughest temper) trees and towers [110]
May in that Valley oftentimes be seen,
Both silent and both motionless alike;
120 Such is the shelter that is there, and such
The safeguard for repose and quietness.

Our steeds remounted, and the summons given,   [115]
With whip and spur we by the Chauntry flew
In uncouth race, and left the cross-legg'd Knight,
125 And the stone-Abbot, and that single Wren
Which one day sang so sweetly in the Nave
Of the old Church, that, though from recent showers [120]
The earth was comfortless, and, touch'd by faint
Internal breezes, sobbings of the place,
130 And respirations, from the roofless walls
The shuddering ivy dripp'd large drops, yet still,
So sweetly 'mid the gloom the invisible Bird   [125]
Sang to itself, that there I could have made
My dwelling-place, and liv'd for ever there
135 To hear such music. Through the Walls we flew
And down the valley, and a circuit made
In wantonness of heart, through rough and smooth [130]
We scamper'd homeward. Oh! ye Rocks and Streams,

And that still Spirit of the evening air!
140 Even in this joyous time I sometimes felt
Your presence, when with slacken'd step we breath'd   [135]
Along the sides of the steep hills, or when,
Lighted by gleams of moonlight from the sea,
We beat with thundering hoofs the level sand.

145   Upon the Eastern Shore of Windermere,
Above the crescent of a pleasant Bay,
There stood an Inn, no homely-featured Shed,
Brother of the surrounding Cottages,   [140]
But 'twas a splendid place, the door beset
150 With Chaises, Grooms, and Liveries, and within
Decanters, Glasses, and the blood-red Wine.
In ancient times, or ere the Hall was built   [145]
On the large Island, had this Dwelling been
More worthy of a Poet's love, a Hut,
155 Proud of its one bright fire, and sycamore shade.
But though the rhymes were gone which once inscribed
The threshold, and large golden characters   [150]
On the blue-frosted Signboard had usurp'd
The place of the old Lion, in contempt
160 And mockery of the rustic painter's hand,
Yet to this hour the spot to me is dear
With all its foolish pomp. The garden lay   [155]
Upon a slope surmounted by the plain
Of a small Bowling-green; beneath us stood
165 A grove; with gleams of water through the trees
And over the tree-tops; nor did we want
Refreshment, strawberries and mellow cream.   [160]
And there, through half an afternoon, we play'd
On the smooth platform, and the shouts we sent
170 Made all the mountains ring. But ere the fall
Of night, when in our pinnace we return'd   [165]
Over the dusky Lake, and to the beach
Of some small Island steer'd our course with one,
The Minstrel of our troop, and left him there,

24

175 And row'd off gently, while he blew his flute
Alone upon the rock; Oh! then the calm [170]
And dead still water lay upon my mind
Even with a weight of pleasure, and the sky
Never before so beautiful, sank down
180 Into my heart, and held me like a dream.

Thus daily were my sympathies enlarged, [175]
And thus the common range of visible things
Grew dear to me: already I began
To love the sun, a Boy I lov'd the sun,
185 Not as I since have lov'd him, as a pledge
And surety of our earthly life, a light [180]
Which while we view we feel we are alive;
But, for this cause, that I had seen him lay
His beauty on the morning hills, had seen
190 The western mountain touch his setting orb, [185]
In many a thoughtless hour, when, from excess
Of happiness, my blood appear'd to flow
With its own pleasure, and I breath'd with joy.
And from like feelings, humble though intense,
195 To patriotic and domestic love [190]
Analogous, the moon to me was dear;
For I would dream away my purposes,
Standing to look upon her while she hung
Midway between the hills, as if she knew
200 No other region; but belong'd to thee, [195]
Yea, appertain'd by a peculiar right
To thee and thy grey huts, my darling Vale!

Those incidental charms which first attach'd
My heart to rural objects, day by day
205 Grew weaker, and I hasten on to tell [200]
How Nature, intervenient till this time,
And secondary, now at length was sought
For her own sake. But who shall parcel out
His intellect, by geometric rules,

25

210 Split, like a province, into round and square? [205]
Who knows the individual hour in which
His habits were first sown, even as a seed,
Who that shall point, as with a wand, and say,
'This portion of the river of my mind [209]
215 Came from yon fountain?' Thou, my Friend! art one
More deeply read in thy own thoughts; to thee
Science appears but, what in truth she is,
Not as our glory and our absolute boast,
But as a succedaneum, and a prop
220 To our infirmity. Thou art no slave [215]
Of that false secondary power, by which,
In weakness, we create distinctions, then
Deem that our puny boundaries are things
Which we perceive, and not which we have made.
225 To thee, unblinded by these outward shows, [220]
The unity of all has been reveal'd
And thou wilt doubt with me, less aptly skill'd
Than many are to class the cabinet
Of their sensations, and, in voluble phrase, [225]
230 Run through the history and birth of each,
As of a single independent thing.
Hard task to analyse a soul, in which,
Not only general habits and desires,
But each most obvious and particular thought,
235 Not in a mystical and idle sense, [230]
But in the words of reason deeply weigh'd,
Hath no beginning.
               Bless'd the infant Babe,
(For with my best conjectures I would trace
The progress of our being) blest the Babe,
240 Nurs'd in his Mother's arms, the Babe who sleeps [235]
Upon his Mother's breast, who, when his soul
Claims manifest kindred with an earthly soul,
Doth gather passion from his Mother's eye!
Such feelings pass into his torpid life
245 Like an awakening breeze, and hence his mind

Even [in the first trial of its powers]
Is prompt and watchful, eager to combine
In one appearance, all the elements
And parts of the same object, else detach'd
250 And loth to coalesce. Thus, day by day,
Subjected to the discipline of love,
His organs and recipient faculties
Are quicken'd, are more vigorous, his mind spreads,
Tenacious of the forms which it receives.
255 In one beloved presence, nay and more,
In that most apprehensive habitude
And those sensations which have been deriv'd
From this beloved Presence, there exists
A virtue which irradiates and exalts
260 All objects through all intercourse of sense.   [240]
No outcast he, bewilder'd and depress'd;
Along his infant veins are interfus'd
The gravitation and the filial bond
Of nature, that connect him with the world.   [244]
265 Emphatically such a Being lives,
An inmate of this *active* universe;
From nature largely he receives; nor so
Is satisfied, but largely gives again,
For feeling has to him imparted strength,   [255]
270 And powerful in all sentiments of grief,
Of exultation, fear, and joy, his mind,
Even as an agent of the one great mind,
Creates, creator and receiver both,
Working but in alliance with the works
275 Which it beholds.—Such, verily, is the first   [260]
Poetic spirit of our human life;
By uniform control of after years
In most abated or suppress'd, in some,
Through every change of growth or of decay,
280 Pre-eminent till death.   [265]
                        From early days,
Beginning not long after that first time

27

In which, a Babe, by intercourse of touch,
I held mute dialogues with my Mother's heart
I have endeavour'd to display the means
285 Whereby the infant sensibility,   [270]
Great birthright of our Being, was in me
Augmented and sustain'd. Yet is a path
More difficult before me, and I fear
That in its broken windings we shall need
290 The chamois' sinews, and the eagle's wing: [275]
For now a trouble came into my mind
From unknown causes. I was left alone,
Seeking the visible world, nor knowing why.
The props of my affections were remov'd,
295 And yet the building stood, as if sustain'd   [280]
By its own spirit! All that I beheld
Was dear to me, and from this cause it came,
That now to Nature's finer influxes
My mind lay open, to that more exact
300 And intimate communion which our hearts
Maintain with the minuter properties
Of objects which already are belov'd,
And of those only. Many are the joys
Of youth; but oh! what happiness to live   [285]
305 When every hour brings palpable access
Of knowledge, when all knowledge is delight,
And sorrow is not there. The seasons came,
And every season to my notice brought
A store of transitory qualities   [290]
310 Which, but for this most watchful power of love
Had been neglected, left a register
Of permanent relations, else unknown,
Hence life, and change, and beauty, solitude
More active, even, than 'best society',   [295]
315 Society made sweet as solitude
By silent inobtrusive sympathies,
And gentle agitations of the mind
From manifold distinctions, difference

Perceived in things, where to the common eye, [300]
320 No difference is; and hence, from the same source
Sublimer joy; for I would walk alone,
In storm and tempest, or in starlight nights
Beneath the quiet Heavens; and, at that time,
Have felt whate'er there is of power in sound
325 To breathe an elevated mood, by form [305]
Or image unprofaned; and I would stand,
Beneath some rock, listening to sounds that are
The ghostly language of the ancient earth,
Or make their dim abode in distant winds. [310]
330 Thence did I drink the visionary power.
I deem not profitless those fleeting moods
Of shadowy exultation: not for this,
That they are kindred to our purer mind
And intellectual life; but that the soul, [315]
335 Remembering how she felt, but what she felt
Remembering not, retains an obscure sense
Of possible sublimity, to which,
With growing faculties she doth aspire,
With faculties still growing, feeling still [320]
340 That whatsoever point they gain, they still
Have something to pursue.
                              And not alone,
In grandeur and in tumult, but no less
In tranquil scenes, that universal power
And fitness in the latent qualities [325]
345 And essences of things, by which the mind
Is mov'd by feelings of delight, to me
Came strengthen'd with a superadded soul,
A virtue not its own. My morning walks
Were early; oft, before the hours of School [330]
350 I travell'd round our little Lake, five miles
Of pleasant wandering, happy time! more dear
For this, that one was by my side, a Friend
Then passionately lov'd; with heart how full
Will he peruse these lines, this page, perhaps

355 A blank to other men! for many years   [335]
     Have since flow'd in between us; and our minds,
     Both silent to each other, at this time
     We live as if those hours had never been.
     Nor seldom did I lift our cottage latch
360 Far earlier, and before the vernal thrush
     Was audible, among the hills I sate
     Alone, upon some jutting eminence
     At the first hour of morning, when the Vale
     Lay quiet in an utter solitude.   [345]
365 How shall I trace the history, where seek
     The origin of what I then have felt?
     Oft in those moments such a holy calm
     Did overspread my soul, that I forgot
     That I had bodily eyes, and what I saw   [350]
370 Appear'd like something in myself, a dream,
     A prospect in my mind.
                 'Twere long to tell
     What spring and autumn, what the winter snows,
     And what the summer shade, what day and night,
     The evening and the morning, what my dreams   [355]
375 And what my waking thoughts supplied, to nurse
     That spirit of religious love in which
     I walked with Nature. But let this, at least
     Be not forgotten, that I still retain'd
     My first creative sensibility,   [360]
380 That by the regular action of the world
     My soul was unsubdu'd. A plastic power
     Abode with me, a forming hand, at times
     Rebellious, acting in a devious mood,
     A local spirit of its own, at war   [365]
385 With general tendency, but for the most
     Subservient strictly to the external things
     With which it commun'd. An auxiliar light
     Came from my mind which on the setting sun
     Bestow'd new splendor, the melodious birds,   [370]
390 The gentle breezes, fountains that ran on,

Murmuring so sweetly in themselves, obey'd
A like dominion; and the midnight storm
Grew darker in the presence of my eye.
Hence my obeisance, my devotion hence,   [375]
395 And hence my transport.
                              Nor should this, perchance,
Pass unrecorded, that I still had lov'd
The exercise and produce of a toil
Than analytic industry to me
More pleasing, and whose character I deem   [380]
400 Is more poetic as resembling more
Creative agency. I mean to speak
Of that interminable building rear'd
By observation of affinities
In objects where no brotherhood exists   [385]
405 To common minds. My seventeenth year was come
And, whether from this habit, rooted now
So deeply in my mind, or from excess
Of the great social principle of life,
Coercing all things into sympathy,   [390]
410 To unorganic natures I transferr'd
My own enjoyments, or, the power of truth
Coming in revelation, I convers'd
With things that really are, I, at this time
Saw blessings spread around me like a sea.   [395]
415 Thus did my days pass on, and now at length
From Nature and her overflowing soul
I had receiv'd so much that all my thoughts
Were steep'd in feeling; I was only then
Contented when with bliss ineffable   [400]
420 I felt the sentiment of Being spread
O'er all that moves, and all that seemeth still,
O'er all, that, lost beyond the reach of thought
And human knowledge, to the human eye
Invisible, yet liveth to the heart,   [405]
425 O'er all that leaps, and runs, and shouts, and sings,
Or beats the gladsome air, o'er all that glides

31

Beneath the wave, yea, in the wave itself
And mighty depth of waters. Wonder not
If such my transports were; for in all things   [410]
430   I saw one life, and felt that it was joy.
One song they sang, and it was audible,   [415]
Most audible then when the fleshly ear,
O'ercome by grosser prelude of that strain,
Forgot its functions, and slept undisturb'd.

435   If this be error, and another faith
Find easier access to the pious mind,
Yet were I grossly destitute of all   [420]
Those human sentiments which make this earth
So dear, if I should fail, with grateful voice
440   To speak of you, Ye Mountains and Ye Lakes,
And sounding Cataracts! Ye Mists and Winds   [425]
That dwell among the hills where I was born.
If, in my youth, I have been pure in heart,
If, mingling with the world, I am content
445   With my own modest pleasures, and have liv'd,
With God and Nature communing, remov'd   [430]
From little enmities and low desires,
The gift is yours; if in these times of fear,
This melancholy waste of hopes o'erthrown,
450   If, 'mid indifference and apathy
And wicked exultation, when good men,   [435]
On every side fall off we know not how,
To selfishness, disguis'd in gentle names
Of peace, and quiet, and domestic love,
455   Yet mingled, not unwillingly, with sneers
On visionary minds; if in this time   [440]
Of dereliction and dismay, I yet
Despair not of our nature; but retain
A more than Roman confidence, a faith
460   That fails not, in all sorrow my support,
The blessing of my life, the gift is yours,   [445]
Ye mountains! thine, O Nature! Thou hast fed

My lofty speculations; and in thee,
For this uneasy heart of ours I find
465 A never-failing principle of joy,   [450]
And purest passion.
     Thou, my Friend! wert rear'd
In the great City, 'mid far other scenes;
But we, by different roads at length have gain'd
The self-same bourne. And for this cause to Thee
470 I speak, unapprehensive of contempt,   [455]
The insinuated scoff of coward tongues,
And all that silent language which so oft
In conversation betwixt man and man
Blots from the human countenance all trace
475 Of beauty and of love. For Thou hast sought   [460]
The truth in solitude, and Thou art one,
The most intense of Nature's worshippers
In many things my Brother, chiefly here   [465]
In this my deep devotion.
      Fare Thee well!
480 Health, and the quiet of a healthful mind
Attend thee! seeking oft the haunts of men,
And yet more often living with Thyself,
And for Thyself, so haply shall thy days   [470]
Be many, and a blessing to mankind.

BOOK THIRD

RESIDENCE AT CAMBRIDGE

IT was a dreary morning when the Chaise
Roll'd over the flat Plains of Huntingdon
And, through the open windows, first I saw
The long-back'd Chapel of King's College rear
His pinnacles above the dusky groves.   [5]

Soon afterwards, we espied upon the road,
A student cloth'd in Gown and tassell'd Cap;
He pass'd; nor was I master of my eyes
Till he was left a hundred yards behind.
The Place, as we approach'd, seem'd more and more
To have an eddy's force, and suck'd us in
More eagerly at every step we took.
Onward we drove beneath the Castle, down   [15]
By Magdalene Bridge we went and cross'd the Cam,
And at the *Hoop* we landed, famous Inn.

My spirit was up, my thoughts were full of hope;
Some Friends I had, acquaintances who there
Seem'd Friends, poor simple Schoolboys, now hung round
With honour and importance; in a world
Of welcome faces up and down I rov'd;
Questions, directions, counsel and advice
Flow'd in upon me from all sides, fresh day
Of pride and pleasure! to myself I seem'd   [25]
A man of business and expence, and went
From shop to shop about my own affairs,
To Tutors or to Tailors, as befel,
From street to street with loose and careless heart.

I was the Dreamer, they the Dream; I roam'd   [30]
Delighted, through the motley spectacle;

34

30 Gowns grave or gaudy, Doctors, Students, Streets,
Lamps, Gateways, Flocks of Churches, Courts and Towers:
Strange transformation for a mountain Youth,
A northern Villager. As if by word   [35]
Of magic or some Fairy's power, at once
35 Behold me rich in monies, and attir'd
In splendid clothes, with hose of silk, and hair
Glittering like rimy trees when frost is keen.
My lordly Dressing-gown I pass it by,   [40]
With other signs of manhood which supplied
40 The lack of beard.—The weeks went roundly on,
With invitations, suppers, wine, and fruit,.
Smooth housekeeping within, and all without
Liberal and suiting Gentleman's array!   [45]

The Evangelist St. John my Patron was,
45 Three gloomy Courts are his; and in the first
Was my abiding-place, a nook obscure!
Right underneath, the College kitchens made
A humming sound, less tuneable than bees,   [50]
But hardly less industrious; with shrill notes
50 Of sharp command and scolding intermix'd.
Near me was Trinity's loquacious Clock,
Who never let the Quarters, night or day,
Slip by him unproclaim'd, and told the hours   [55]
Twice over with a male and female voice.
55 Her pealing organ was my neighbour too;
And, from my Bedroom, I in moonlight nights
Could see, right opposite, a few yards off,
The Antechapel, where the Statue stood   [60]
Of Newton, with his Prism and silent Face.

60   Of College labours, of the Lecturer's Room,
All studded round, as thick as chairs could stand,   [65]
With loyal Students, faithful to their books,
Half-and-half Idlers, hardy Recusants,
And honest Dunces;—of important Days,

35

65   Examinations, when the Man was weigh'd
     As in the balance,—of excessive hopes,   [70]
     Tremblings withal, and commendable fears,
     Small jealousies, and triumphs good or bad
     I make short mention; things they were which then
70   I did not love, nor do I love them now.
     Such glory was but little sought by me,
     And little won. But it is right to say
     That even so early, from the first crude days   [75]
     Of settling-time in this my new abode,
75   Not seldom I had melancholy thoughts,
     From personal and family regards,
     Wishing to hope without a hope; some fears
     About my future worldly maintenance,
     And, more than all, a strangeness in my mind,   [80]
80   A feeling that I was not for that hour,
     Nor for that place. But wherefore be cast down?
     Why should I grieve? I was a chosen Son.
     For hither I had come with holy powers
     And faculties, whether to work or feel: [89]
85   To apprehend all passions and all moods
     Which time, and place, and season do impress
     Upon the visible universe, and work
     Like changes there by force of my own mind.
     I was a Freeman; in the purest sense
90   Was free, and to majestic ends was strong.
     I do not speak of learning, moral truth,
     Or understanding; 'twas enough for me
     To know that I was otherwise endow'd.
     When the first glitter of the show was pass'd,
95   And the first dazzle of the taper light,
     As if with a rebound my mind return'd
     Into its former self. Oft did I leave
     My Comrades, and the Crowd, Buildings and Groves, [92]
     And walked along the fields, the level fields,
100   With Heaven's blue concave rear'd above my head;
     And now it was, that, thro' such change entire

And this first absence from those shapes sublime
Wherewith I had been conversant, my mind   [95]
Seem'd busier in itself than heretofore;
105 At least, I more directly recognised
My powers and habits: let me dare to speak
A higher language, say that now I felt   [100]
The strength and consolation which were mine.
As if awaken'd, summon'd, rous'd, constrain'd,
110 I look'd for universal things; perused
The common countenance of earth and heaven;   [110]
And, turning the mind in upon itself,
Pored, watch'd, expected, listen'd; spread my thoughts
And spread them with a wider creeping; felt
115 Incumbences more awful, visitings
Of the Upholder of the tranquil Soul,   [120]
Which underneath all passion lives secure
A steadfast life. But peace! it is enough
To notice that I was ascending now   [125]
120 To such community with highest truth.

A track pursuing not untrod before,
From deep analogies by thought supplied,
Or consciousnesses not to be subdued,
To every natural form, rock, fruit or flower,   [130]
125 Even the loose stones that cover the high-way,
I gave a moral life, I saw them feel,
Or link'd them to some feeling: the great mass
Lay bedded in a quickening soul, and all
That I beheld respired with inward meaning.   [135]
130 Thus much for the one Presence, and the Life
Of the great whole; suffice it here to add
That whatsoe'er of Terror or of Love,
Or Beauty, Nature's daily face put on
From transitory passion, unto this
135 I was as wakeful, even, as waters are
To the sky's motion; in a kindred sense   [140]
Of passion was obedient as a lute

37

That waits upon the touches of the wind.
So was it with me in my solitude;
140 So often among multitudes of men.
Unknown, unthought of, yet I was most rīch,
I had a world about me; 'twas my own,
I made it; for it only liv'd to me, [145]
And to the God who look'd into my mind.
145 Such sympathies would sometimes shew themselves
By outward gestures and by visible looks.
Some call'd it madness: such, indeed, it was,
If child-like fruitfulness in passing joy, [150]
If steady moods of thoughtfulness, matur'd
150 To inspiration, sort with such a name;
If prophesy be madness; if things view'd
By Poets in old time, and higher up
By the first men, earth's first inhabitants, [155]
May in these tutor'd days no more be seen
155 With undisorder'd sight: but leaving this
It was no madness: for I had an eye
Which in my strongest workings, evermore
Was looking for the shades of difference [160]
As they lie hid in all exterior forms,
160 Near or remote, minute or vast, an eye
Which from a stone, a tree, a wither'd leaf,
To the broad ocean and the azure heavens,
Spangled with kindred multitudes of stars, [165]
Could find no surface where its power might sleep,
165 Which spake perpetual logic to my soul,
And by an unrelenting agency
Did bind my feelings, even as in a chain.

And here, O Friend! have I retrac'd my life [170]
Up to an eminence, and told a tale
170 Of matters which, not falsely, I may call
The glory of my youth. Of Genius, Power,
Creation and Divinity itself
I have been speaking, for my theme has been

38

What pass'd within me. Not of outward things
175 Done visibly for other minds, words, signs,
Symbols or actions; but of my own heart
Have I been speaking, and my youthful mind.
O Heavens! how awful is the might of Souls, [180]
And what they do within themselves, while yet
180 The yoke of earth is new to them, the world
Nothing but a wild field where they were sown.
This is, in truth, heroic argument,
And genuine prowess; which I wish'd to touch [185]
With hand however weak; but in the main
185 It lies far hidden from the reach of words.
Points have we all of us within our souls,
Where all stand single; this I feel, and make
Breathings for incommunicable powers. [190]
Yet each man is a memory to himself,
190 And, therefore, now that I must quit this theme,
I am not heartless; for there's not a man
That lives who hath not had his godlike hours,
And knows not what majestic sway we have, [195]
As natural beings in the strength of nature.

195   Enough: for now into a populous Plain
We must descend.—A Traveller I am,
And all my Tale is of myself; even so,
So be it, if the pure in heart delight [200]
To follow me; and Thou, O honor'd Friend!
200 Who in my thoughts art ever at my side,
Uphold, as heretofore, my fainting steps.

    It hath been told already, how my sight
Was dazzled by the novel show, and how, [205]
Erelong, I did into myself return.
205 So did it seem, and so, in truth, it was.
Yet this was but short liv'd: thereafter came
Observance less devout. I had made a change
In climate; and my nature's outward coat

Changed also, slowly and insensibly.

210   To the deep quiet and majestic thoughts   [210]
Of loneliness succeeded empty noise
And superficial pastimes; now and then
Forced labour; and, more frequently, forced hopes;
And, worse than all, a treasonable growth

215   Of indecisive judgments that impair'd   [215]
And shook the mind's simplicity. And yet
This was a gladsome time. Could I behold,
Who less insensible than sodden clay
On a sea River's bed at ebb of tide,

220   Could have beheld with undelighted heart,   [220]
So many happy Youths, so wide and fair
A congregation, in its budding-time
Of health, and hope, and beauty; all at once
So many divers samples of the growth

225   Of life's sweet season, could have seen unmov'd   [225]
That miscellaneous garland of wild flowers
Upon the matron temples of a Place
So famous through the world? To me, at least,
It was a goodly prospect: for, through youth,

230   Though I had been train'd up to stand unpropp'd,   [230]
And independent musings pleased me so
That spells seem'd on me when I was alone,
Yet could I only cleave to solitude
In lonesome places; if a throng was near

235   That way I lean'd by nature; for my heart   [235]
Was social, and lov'd idleness and joy.

     Not seeking those who might participate
My deeper pleasures (nay I had not once,
Though not unused to mutter lonesome songs,

240   Even with myself divided such delight,   [240]
Or looked that way for aught that might be cloath'd
In human language), easily I pass'd
From the remembrances of better things,
And slipp'd into the weekday works of youth,

245　Unburthen'd, unalarm'd, and unprofan'd.　　　　[245]
　　Caverns there were within my mind, which sun
　　Could never penetrate, yet did there not
　　Want store of leafy arbours where the light
　　Might enter in at will.　Companionships,
250　Friendships, acquaintances, were welcome all;　　[250]
　　We saunter'd, play'd, we rioted, we talk'd
　　Unprofitable talk at morning hours,
　　Drifted about along the streets and walks,
　　Read lazily in lazy books, went forth
255　To gallop through the country in blind zeal　　　[255]
　　Of senseless horsemanship, or on the breast
　　Of Cam sail'd boisterously; and let the stars
　　Come out, perhaps without one quiet thought.

　　　Such was the tenor of the opening act
260　In this new life.　Imagination slept,　　　　　[260]
　　And yet not utterly.　I could not print
　　Ground where the grass had yielded to the steps
　　Of generations of illustrious Men,
　　Unmov'd; I could not always lightly pass
265　Through the same Gateways; sleep where they had slept,
　　Wake where they wak'd, range that enclosure old
　　That garden of great intellects undisturb'd.
　　Place also by the side of this dark sense
　　Of nobler feeling, that those spiritual Men,
270　Even the great Newton's own etherial Self,　　　[270]
　　Seem'd humbled in these precincts; thence to be
　　The more belov'd; invested here with tasks
　　Of life's plain business, as a daily garb;
　　Dictators at the plough, a change that left
275　All genuine admiration unimpair'd.　　　　　　[277]

　　　Beside the pleasant Mills of Trompington
　　I laugh'd with Chaucer; in the hawthorn shade
　　Heard him (while birds were warbling) tell his tales　[280]
　　Of amorous passion.　And that gentle Bard,

41

280   Chosen by the Muses for their Page of State,
       Sweet Spenser, moving through his clouded heaven
       With the moon's beauty and the moon's soft pace,
       I call'd him Brother, Englishman, and Friend.   [285]
       Yea, our blind Poet, who, in his later day,
285   Stood almost single, uttering odious truth,
       Darkness before, and danger's voice behind;
       Soul awful! if the earth has ever lodg'd
       An awful Soul, I seem'd to see him here   [290]
       Familiarly, and in his Scholar's dress
290   Bounding before me, yet a stripling Youth,
       A Boy, no better, with his rosy cheeks
       Angelical, keen eye, courageous look,
       And conscious step of purity and pride.   [295]

           Among the Band of my Compeers was one
295   My class-fellow at School, whose chance it was
       To lodge in the Apartments which had been,
       Time out of mind, honor'd by Milton's name;
       The very shell reputed of the abode
       Which he had tenanted. O temperate Bard!
300   One afternoon, the first time I set foot
       In this thy innocent Nest and Oratory,   [300]
       Seated with others in a festive ring
       Of common-place convention, I to thee
       Pour'd out libations, to thy memory drank,
305   Within my private thoughts, till my brain reel'd
       Never so clouded by the fumes of wine
       Before that hour, or since. Thence forth I ran   [305]
       From that assembly, through a length of streets,
       Ran, Ostrich-like, to reach our Chapel Door
310   In not a desperate or opprobrious time,
       Albeit long after the importunate Bell
       Had stopp'd, with wearisome Cassandra voice   [310]
       No longer haunting the dark winter night.
       Call back, O Friend! a moment to thy mind,
315   The place itself and fashion of the rites.

Upshouldering in a dislocated lump,
With shallow ostentatious carelessness,
My Surplice, gloried in, and yet despised,
I clove in pride through the inferior throng [315]
320 Of the plain Burghers, who in audience stood
On the last skirts of their permitted ground,
Beneath the pealing Organ. Empty thoughts!
I am ashamed of them; and that great Bard,
And thou, O Friend! who in thy ample mind [320]
325 Hast station'd me for reverence and love,
Ye will forgive the weakness of that hour
In some of its unworthy vanities,
Brother of many more.
                          In this mix'd sort
The months pass'd on, remissly, not given up [325]
330 To wilful alienation from the right,
Or walks of open scandal; but in vague
And loose indifference, easy likings, aims
Of a low pitch; duty and zeal dismiss'd,
Yet nature, or a happy course of things [330]
335 Not doing in their stead the needful work.
The memory languidly revolv'd, the heart
Repos'd in noontide rest; the inner pulse
Of contemplation almost fail'd to beat. [334]
Rotted as by a charm, my life became
340 A floating island, an amphibious thing,
Unsound, of spungy texture, yet withal,
Not wanting a fair face of water-weeds
And pleasant flowers.—The thirst of living praise,
A reverence for the glorious Dead, the sight [340]
345 Of those long Vistos, Catacombs in which
Perennial minds lie visibly entomb'd,
Have often stirr'd the heart of youth, and bred
A fervent love of rigorous discipline.
Alas! such high commotion touched not me; [345]
350 No look was in these walls to put to shame
My easy spirits, and discountenance

Their light composure, far less to instil
A calm resolve of mind, firmly address'd
To puissant efforts. Nor was this the blame [350]
355 Of others but my own; I should, in truth,
As far as doth concern my single self
Misdeem most widely, lodging it elsewhere.
For I, bred up in Nature's lap, was even
As a spoil'd Child; and rambling like the wind [355]
360 As I had done in daily intercourse
With those delicious rivers, solemn heights,
And mountains; ranging like a fowl of the air,
I was ill tutor'd for captivity,
To quit my pleasure, and from month to month, [360]
365 Take up a station calmly on the perch
Of sedentary peace. Those lovely forms
Had also left less space within my mind,
Which, wrought upon instinctively, had found
A freshness in those objects of its love, [365]
370 A winning power, beyond all other power.
Not that I slighted Books; that were to lack
All sense; but other passions had been mine,
More fervent, making me less prompt, perhaps,
To in-door study than was wise or well [370]
375 Or suited to my years. Yet I could shape
The image of a Place which, sooth'd and lull'd
As I had been, train'd up in paradise
Among sweet garlands and delightful sounds,
Accustom'd in my loneliness to walk
380 With Nature magisterially, yet I,
Methinks, could shape the image of a Place
Which with its aspect should have bent me down [376]
To instantaneous service, should at once
Have made me pay to science and to arts
385 And written lore, acknowledg'd my liege Lord,
A homage, frankly offer'd up, like that [380]
Which I had paid to Nature. Toil and pains
In this recess which I have bodied forth

44

Should spread from heart to heart; and stately groves,
390 Majestic edifices, should not want
A corresponding dignity within.   [385]
The congregating temper, which pervades
Our unripe years, not wasted, should be made
To minister to works of high attempt,
395 Which the enthusiast would perform with love;
Youth should be aw'd, possess'd, as with a sense   [390]
Religious, of what holy joy there is
In knowledge, if it be sincerely sought
For its own sake, in glory, and in praise,
400 If but by labour won, and to endure.
The passing Day should learn to put aside   [395]
Her trappings here, should strip them off, abash'd
Before antiquity, and stedfast truth,
And strong book-mindedness; and over all
405 Should be a healthy, sound simplicity,
A seemly plainness, name it as you will,   [400]
Republican or pious.
                                      If these thoughts
Be a gratuitous emblazonry
That does but mock this recreant age, at least
410 Let Folly and False-seeming, we might say,
Be free to affect whatever formal gait
Of moral or scholastic discipline   [405]
Shall raise them highest in their own esteem;
Let them parade, among the Schools, at will;
415 But spare the House of God. Was ever known
The witless Shepherd who would drive his Flock
With serious repetition to a pool   [409]
Of which 'tis plain to sight they never taste?
A weight must surely hang on days begun
420 And ended with worst mockery: be wise,
Ye Presidents and Deans, and to your Bells
Give seasonable rest; for 'tis a sound   [416]
Hollow as ever vex'd the tranquil air;
And your officious doings bring disgrace

45

425 On the plain Steeples of our English Church,
Whose worship 'mid remotest village trees   [420]
Suffers for this. Even Science, too, at hand
In daily sight of such irreverence,
Is smitten thence with an unnatural taint,

430 Loses her just authority, falls beneath
Collateral suspicion, else unknown.   [425]
This obvious truth did not escape me then,
Unthinking as I was, and I confess
That, having in my native hills given loose

435 To a Schoolboy's dreaming, I had rais'd a pile
Upon the basis of the coming time,
Which now before me melted fast away,
Which could not live, scarcely had life enough
To mock the Builder. Oh! what joy it were   [430]

440 To see a Sanctuary for our Country's Youth,
With such a spirit in it as might be
Protection for itself, a Virgin grove,
Primaeval in its purity and depth;
Where, though the shades were fill'd with chearfulness,

445 Nor indigent of songs, warbled from crowds   [435]
In under-coverts, yet the countenance
Of the whole place should wear a stamp of awe;
A habitation sober and demure
For ruminating creatures, a domain

450 For quiet things to wander in, a haunt   [440]
In which the Heron might delight to feed
By the shy rivers, and the Pelican
Upon the cypress spire in lonely thought
Might sit and sun himself. Alas! alas!

455 In vain for such solemnity we look;   [445]
Our eyes are cross'd by Butterflies, our ears
Hear chattering Popinjays; the inner heart
Is trivial, and the impresses without
Are of a gaudy region.
                            Different sight

460 Those venerable Doctors saw of old   [450]

When all who dwelt within these famous Walls
Led in abstemiousness a studious life,
When, in forlorn and naked chambers coop'd
And crowded, o'er their ponderous Books they sate
465 Like caterpillars eating out their way   [455]
In silence, or with keen devouring noise
Not to be track'd or father'd. Princes then
At matins froze, and couch'd at curfew-time,
Train'd up, through piety and zeal, to prize
470 Spare diet, patient labour, and plain weeds.   [460]
O Seat of Arts! renown'd throughout the world,
Far different service in those homely days
The Nurslings of the Muses underwent
From their first childhood; in that glorious time,
475 When Learning, like a Stranger come from far,   [465]
Sounding through Christian Lands her Trumpet, rouz'd
The Peasant and the King; when Boys and Youths,
The growth of ragged villages and huts,
Forsook their homes, and, errant in the quest
480 Of Patron, famous School or friendly Nook,   [470]
Where, pension'd, they in shelter might sit down,
From Town to Town and through wide-scatter'd Realms
Journeyed with their huge folios in their hands;
And often, starting from some covert place,
485 Saluted the chance-comer on the road,   [475]
Crying, 'an obolus, a penny give
To a poor Scholar'; when illustrious Men,
Lovers of truth, by penury constrain'd,
Bucer, Erasmus, or Melancthon read
490 Before the doors or windows of their Cells   [480]
By moonshine, through mere lack of taper light.

But peace to vain regrets! We see but darkly
Even when we look behind us; and best things
Are not so pure by nature that they needs
495 Must keep to all, as fondly all believe,   [485]
Their highest promise. If the Mariner,

When at reluctant distance he hath pass'd
Some fair enticing Island, did but know
What fate might have been his, could he have brought
His Bark to land upon the wished-for spot,   [490]
Good cause full often would he have to bless
The belt of churlish Surf that scared him thence,
Or haste of the inexorable wind.
For me, I grieve not; happy is the man,
Who only misses what I miss'd, who falls   [495]
No lower than I fell.

                I did not love,
As hath been noticed heretofore, the guise
Of our scholastic studies; could have wish'd
The river to have had an ampler range,
And freer pace; but this I tax not; far   [500]
Far more I griev'd to see among the Band
Of those who in the field of contest stood
As combatants, passions that did to me
Seem low and mean; from ignorance of mine,
In part, and want of just forbearance, yet
My wiser mind grieves now for what I saw.
Willingly did I part from these, and turn
Out of their track, to travel with the shoal   [506]
Of more unthinking Natures; easy Minds
And pillowy; and not wanting love that makes
The day pass lightly on, when foresight sleeps,
And wisdom, and the pledges interchanged   [510]
With our own inner being are forgot.

    To Books, our daily fare prescrib'd, I turn'd
With sickly appetite, and when I went,
At other times, in quest of my own food,
I chaced not steadily the manly deer,
But laid me down to any casual feast
Of wild wood-honey; or, with truant eyes
Unruly, peep'd about for vagrant fruit.
And, as for what pertains to human life,

500

505

510

515

520

525

530

48

The deeper passions working round me here,
Whether of envy, jealousy, pride, shame,
Ambition, emulation, fear, or hope,
535 Or those of dissolute pleasure, were by me
Unshar'd; and only now and then observ'd,
So little was their hold upon my being,
As outward things that might administer
To knowledge or instruction. Hush'd, meanwhile,
540 Was the under soul, lock'd up in such a calm,
That not a leaf of the great nature stirr'd.

Yet was this deep vacation not given up
To utter waste. Hitherto I had stood
In my own mind remote from human life,
545 At least from what we commonly so name,   [515]
Even as a shepherd on a promontory,
Who, lacking occupation, looks far forth
Into the endless sea, and rather makes
Than finds what he beholds. And sure it is
550 That this first transit from the smooth delights,   [520]
And wild outlandish walks of simple youth,
To something that resembled an approach
Towards mortal business; to a privileg'd world
Within a world, a midway residence
555 With all its intervenient imagery,   [525]
Did better suit my visionary mind,
Far better, than to have been bolted forth,
Thrust out abruptly into Fortune's way
Among the conflicts of substantial life;
560 By a more just gradation did lead on   [530]
To higher things, more naturally matur'd,
For permanent possession, better fruits
Whether of truth or virtue, to ensue.

In playful zest of fancy did we note,   [535]
565 (How could we less?) the manners and the ways
Of those who in the livery were array'd

49

Of good or evil fame; of those with whom
By frame of academic discipline
Perforce we were connected, men whose sway [540]
570 And whose authority of Office serv'd
To set our minds on edge, and did no more.
Nor wanted we rich pastime of this kind,
Found everywhere; but chiefly, in the ring
Of the grave Elders, Men unscour'd, grotesque [545]
575 In character; trick'd out like aged trees
Which, through the lapse of their infirmity,
Give ready place to any random seed
That chuses to be rear'd upon their trunks.

Here on my view, confronting as it were [550]
580 Those Shepherd Swains whom I had lately left,
Did flash a different image of old age;
How different! yet both withal alike,
A Book of rudiments for the unpractis'd sight,
Objects emboss'd! and which with sedulous care [554]
585 Nature holds up before the eye of Youth
In her great School; with further view, perhaps,
To enter early on her tender scheme
Of teaching comprehension with delight, [560]
And mingling playful with pathetic thoughts.

590 The surfaces of artificial life
And manners finely spun, the delicate race
Of colours, lurking, gleaming up and down
Through that state arras woven with silk and gold; [565]
This wily interchange of snaky hues,
595 Willingly and unwillingly reveal'd
I had not learn'd to watch, and at this time
Perhaps, had such been in my daily sight
I might have been indifferent thereto
As Hermits are to tales of distant things.
600 Hence for these rarities elaborate
Having no relish yet, I was content

With the more homely produce, rudely pil'd
In this our coarser warehouse. At this day   [570]
I smile in many a mountain solitude
605 At passages and fragments that remain
Of that inferior exhibition, play'd
By wooden images, a theatre
For Wake or Fair. And oftentimes do flit   [576]
Remembrances before me of old Men,
610 Old Humourists who have been long in their graves,
And having almost in my mind put off
Their human names, have into Phantoms pass'd   [580]
Of texture midway betwixt life and books.

I play the Loiterer: 'tis enough to note
615 That here, in dwarf proportions, were express'd
The limbs of the great world, its goings-on
Collaterally pourtray'd, as in mock fight,   [585]
A Tournament of blows, some hardly dealt,
Though short of mortal combat; and whate'er
620 Might of this pageant be suppos'd to hit
A simple Rustic's notice, this way less,
More that way, was not wasted upon me.   [590]
—And yet this spectacle may well demand
A more substantial name, no mimic shew,
625 Itself a living part of a live whole,
A creek of the vast sea. For all Degrees
And Shapes of spurious fame and short-liv'd praise   [595]
Here sate in state, and fed with daily alms
Retainers won away from solid good;
630 And here was Labour, his own Bond-slave, Hope
That never set the pains against the prize,
Idleness, halting with his weary clog,   [600]
And poor misguided Shame, and witless Fear,
And simple Pleasure, foraging for Death,
635 Honour misplaced, and Dignity astray;
Feuds, Factions, Flatteries, Enmity, and Guile;
Murmuring Submission, and bald Government;   [605]

51

The Idol weak as the Idolater;
And Decency and Custom starving Truth;
640 And blind Authority, beating with his Staff
The Child that might have led him; Emptiness
Followed, as of good omen; and meek Worth [610]
Left to itself unheard of, and unknown.

Of these and other kindred notices
645 I cannot say what portion is in truth
The naked recollection of that time,
And what may rather have been call'd to life [615]
By after-meditation. But delight,
That, in an easy temper lull'd asleep,
650 Is still with innocence its own reward,
This surely was not wanting. Carelessly
I gaz'd, roving as through a Cabinet [620]
Or wide Museum (throng'd with fishes, gems,
Birds, crocodiles, shells) where little can be seen
655 Well understood, or naturally endear'd,
Yet still does every step bring something forth
That quickens, pleases, stings; and here and there
A casual rarity is singled out,
And has its brief perusal, then gives way
660 To others, all supplanted in their turn.
Meanwhile, amid this gaudy Congress, framed
Of things, by nature, most unneighbourly, [625]
The head turns round, and cannot right itself;
And, though an aching and a barren sense
665 Of gay confusion still be uppermost,
With few wise longings and but little love,
Yet something to the memory sticks at last, [630]
Whence profit may be drawn in times to come.

Thus in submissive idleness, my Friend,
670 The labouring time of Autumn, Winter, Spring,
Nine months, roll'd pleasingly away; the tenth [635]
Return'd me to my native hills again.

52

BOOK FOURTH

SUMMER VACATION

A PLEASANT sight it was when, having clomb
The Heights of Kendal, and that dreary Moor
Was cross'd, at length, as from a rampart's edge,
I overlook'd the bed of Windermere.   [5]
5   I bounded down the hill, shouting amain
A lusty summons to the farther shore
For the old Ferryman; and when he came   [13]
I did not step into the well-known Boat
Without a cordial welcome. Thence right forth
10 I took my way, now drawing towards home,
To that sweet Valley where I had been rear'd;
'Twas but a short hour's walk ere, veering round,   [20]
I saw the snow-white Church upon its hill
Sit like a thronèd Lady, sending out
15 A gracious look all over its domain.
Glad greetings had I, and some tears, perhaps,   [27]
From my old Dame, so motherly and good;
While she perus'd me with a Parent's pride.
The thoughts of gratitude shall fall like dew   [30]
20 Upon thy grave, good Creature! While my heart
Can beat I never will forget thy name.
Heaven's blessing be upon thee where thou liest,
After thy innocent and busy stir
In narrow cares, thy little daily growth   [35]
25 Of calm enjoyments, after eighty years,
And more than eighty, of untroubled life,
Childless, yet by the strangers to thy blood
Honour'd with little less than filial love.
Great joy was mine to see thee once again,   [40]
30 Thee and thy dwelling; and a throng of things
About its narrow precincts all belov'd,
And many of them seeming yet my own.
Why should I speak of what a thousand hearts

Have felt, and every man alive can guess? [45]
35 The rooms, the court, the garden were not left
Long unsaluted, and the spreading Pine
And broad stone Table underneath its boughs,
Our summer seat in many a festive hour;
And that unruly Child of mountain birth, [50]
40 The froward Brook, which soon as he was box'd
Within our Garden, found himself at once,
As if by trick insidious and unkind,
Stripp'd of his voice, and left to dimple down
Without an effort and without a will, [55]
45 A channel paved by the hand of man.
I look'd at him, and smil'd, and smil'd again,
And in the press of twenty thousand thoughts,
'Ha,' quoth I, 'pretty Prisoner, are you there!' [59]
And now, reviewing soberly that hour,
50 I marvel that a fancy did not flash
Upon me, and a strong desire, straitway,
At sight of such an emblem that shew'd forth
So aptly my late course of even days
And all their smooth enthralment, to pen down
55 A satire on myself. My aged Dame
Was with me, at my side: She guided me; [65]
I willing, nay—nay—wishing to be led.
—The face of every neighbour whom I met
Was as a volume to me; some I hail'd
60 Far off, upon the road, or at their work,
Unceremonious greetings, interchang'd [70]
With half the length of a long field between.
Among my Schoolfellows I scatter'd round
A salutation that was more constrain'd,
65 Though earnest, doubtless with a little pride,
But with more shame, for my habiliments, [75]
The transformation, and the gay attire.

Delighted did I take my place again
At our domestic Table: and, dear Friend!

70 Relating simply as my wish hath been
A Poet's history, can I leave untold   [80]
The joy with which I laid me down at night
In my accustomed bed, more welcome now
Perhaps, than if it had been more desir'd
75 Or been more often thought of with regret?
That bed whence I had heard the roaring wind   [85]
And clamorous rain, that Bed where I, so oft,
Had lain awake, on breezy nights, to watch
The moon in splendour couch'd among the leaves
80 Of a tall Ash, that near our Cottage stood,
And watch'd her with fix'd eyes, while to and fro   [90]
In the dark summit of the moving Tree
She rock'd with every impulse of the wind.

    Among the faces which it pleas'd me well
85 To see again, was one, by ancient right
Our Inmate, a rough Terrier of the hills,   [95]
By birth and call of Nature pre-ordain'd
To hunt the badger, and unearth the fox,
Among the impervious crags; but, having been
90 From youth our own adopted, he had pass'd
Into a gentler service. And when first   [100]
The boyish spirit flagg'd, and day by day
Along my veins I kindled with the stir,
The fermentation and the vernal heat
95 Of Poesy, affecting private shades
Like a sick lover, then this Dog was used   [105]
To watch me, an attendant and a friend
Obsequious to my steps, early and late,
Though often of such dilatory walk
100 Tired, and uneasy at the halts I made.
A hundred times when, in these wanderings,   [110]
I have been busy with the toil of verse,
Great pains and little progress, and at once
Some fair enchanting image in my mind
105 Rose up, full-form'd, like Venus from the sea

Have I sprung forth towards him, and let loose   [115]
My hand upon his back with stormy joy,
Caressing him again, and yet again.
And when, in the public roads at eventide
110 I saunter'd, like a river murmuring
And talking to itself, at such a season   {120]
It was his custom to jog on before;
But, duly, whensoever he had met
A passenger approaching, would he turn
115 To give me timely notice, and straitway,
Punctual to such admonishment, I hush'd   [125]
My voice, compos'd my gait, and shap'd myself
To give and take a greeting that might save
My name from piteous rumours, such as wait
120 On men suspected to be craz'd in brain.   [130]

     Those walks, well worthy to be priz'd and lov'd,
Regretted! that word, too, was on my tongue,
But they were richly laden with all good,
And cannot be remember'd but with thanks
125 And gratitude, and perfect joy of heart,   [135]
Those walks did now, like a returning spring,
Come back on me again. When first I made
Once more the circuit of our little Lake
If ever happiness hath lodg'd with man,
130 That day consummate happiness was mine,   [140]
Wide-spreading, steady, calm, contemplative.
The sun was set, or setting, when I left
Our cottage door, and evening soon brought on
A sober hour, not winning or serene,
135 For cold and raw the air was, and untun'd: [145]
But, as a face we love is sweetest then
When sorrow damps it, or, whatever look
It chance to wear is sweetest if the heart
Have fulness in itself, even so with me
140 It fared that evening. Gently did my soul   [150]
Put off her veil, and, self-transmuted, stood

56

Naked as in the presence of her God.
As on I walked, a comfort seem'd to touch
A heart that had not been disconsolate
145 Strength came where weakness was not known to be, [155]
At least not felt; and restoration came,
Like an intruder, knocking at the door
Of unacknowledg'd weariness. I took
The balance in my hand and weigh'd myself.
150 I saw but little, and thereat was pleas'd; [161]
Little did I remember, and even this
Still pleas'd me more; but I had hopes and peace
And swellings of the spirits, was rapt and soothed,
Convers'd with promises, had glimmering views
155 How Life pervades the undecaying mind, [165]
How the immortal Soul with God-like power
Informs, creates, and thaws the deepest sleep
That time can lay upon her; how on earth,
Man, if he do but live within the light
160 Of high endeavours, daily spreads abroad [170]
His being with a strength that cannot fail.
Nor was there want of milder thoughts, of love,
Of innocence, and holiday repose;
And more than pastoral quiet, in the heart
165 Of amplest projects; and a peaceful end [175]
At last, or glorious, by endurance won.
Thus musing, in a wood I sate me down,
Alone, continuing there to muse: meanwhile
The mountain heights were slowly overspread
170 With darkness, and before a rippling breeze [180]
The long Lake lengthen'd out its hoary line;
And in the shelter'd coppice where I sate,
Around me, from among the hazel leaves,
Now here, now there, stirr'd by the straggling wind,
175 Came intermittingly a breath-like sound, [185]
A respiration short and quick, which oft,
Yea, might I say, again and yet again,
Mistaking for the panting of my Dog,

The off-and-on Companion of my walk,
180   I turned my head, to look if he were there.   [189]

A freshness also found I at this time
In human Life, the life I mean of those
Whose occupations really I lov'd.
The prospect often touch'd me with surprize,
185   Crowded and full, and chang'd, as seem'd to me,
Even as a garden in the heat of Spring,   [195]
After an eight-days' absence. For (to omit
The things which were the same and yet appear'd
So different) amid this solitude,
190   The little Vale where was my chief abode,
'Twas not indifferent to a youthful mind   [200]
To note, perhaps, some shelter'd Seat in which
An old Man had been used to sun himself,
Now empty; pale-fac'd Babes whom I had left
195   In arms, known children of the neighbourhood,
Now rosy prattlers, tottering up and down;   [205]
And growing Girls whose beauty, filch'd away
With all its pleasant promises, was gone
To deck some slighted Playmate's homely cheek.

200   Yes, I had something of another eye,
And often, looking round, was mov'd to smiles,   [210]
Such as a delicate work of humour breeds.
I read, without design, the opinions, thoughts
Of those plain-living people, in a sense
205   Of love and knowledge; with another eye
I saw the quiet Woodman in the Woods,   [215]
The Shepherd on the Hills. With new delight,
This chiefly, did I view my grey-hair'd Dame,
Saw her go forth to Church, or other work
210   Of state, equipp'd in monumental trim,
Short Velvet Cloak (her Bonnet of the like)   [220]
A Mantle such as Spanish Cavaliers
Wore in old time. Her smooth domestic life,
Affectionate without uneasiness,

215 Her talk, her business pleas'd me, and no less
Her clear though shallow stream of piety, [225]
That ran on Sabbath days a fresher course.
With thoughts unfelt till now, I saw her read
Her Bible on the Sunday afternoons;
220 And lov'd the book, when she had dropp'd asleep,
And made of it a pillow for her head. [230]

Nor less do I remember to have felt
Distinctly manifested at this time
A dawning, even as of another sense,
225 A human-heartedness about my love
For objects hitherto the gladsome air
Of my own private being, and no more; [235]
Which I had loved, even as a blessed Spirit
Or Angel, if he were to dwell on earth,
230 Might love, in individual happiness.
But now there open'd on me other thoughts,
Of change, congratulation, and regret, [240]
A new-born feeling. It spread far and wide;
The trees, the mountains shared it, and the brooks;
235 The stars of Heaven, now seen in their old haunts,
White Sirius, glittering o'er the southern crags,
Orion with his belt, and those fair Seven, [245]
Acquaintances of every little child,
And Jupiter, my own beloved Star.
240 Whatever shadings of mortality
Had fallen upon these objects heretofore [250]
Were different in kind; not tender: strong,
Deep, gloomy were they and severe; the scatterings
Of Childhood; and, moreover, had given way,
245 In later youth, to beauty, and to love
Enthusiastic, to delight and joy. [255]

As one who hangs down-bending from the side
Of a slow-moving Boat, upon the breast
Of a still water, solacing himself
250 With such discoveries as his eye can make,

Beneath him, in the bottom of the deeps, [260]
Sees many beauteous sights, weeds, fishes, flowers,
Grots, pebbles, roots of trees, and fancies more;
Yet often is perplex'd, and cannot part
255 The shadow from the substance, rocks and sky,
Mountains and clouds, from that which is indeed [265]
The region, and the things which there abide
In their true dwelling; now is cross'd by gleam
Of his own image, by a sunbeam now,
260 And motions that are sent he knows not whence,
Impediments that make his task more sweet; [270]
—Such pleasant office have we long pursued
Incumbent o'er the surface of past time
With like success; nor have we often look'd
265 On more alluring shows (to me, at least,)
More soft, or less ambiguously descried,
Than those which now we have been passing by, [275]
And where we still are lingering. Yet, in spite
Of all these new employments of the mind,
270 There was an inner falling-off. I loved,
Loved deeply, all that I had loved before,
More deeply even than ever; but a swarm [280]
Of heady thoughts jostling each other, gawds,
And feast, and dance, and public revelry,
275 And sports and games (less pleasing in themselves,
Than as they were a badge glossy and fresh [285]
Of manliness and freedom) these did now
Seduce me from the firm habitual quest
Of feeding pleasures, from that eager zeal,
280 Those yearnings which had every day been mine,
A wild, unworldly-minded Youth, given up [290]
To Nature and to Books, or, at the most,
From time to time, by inclination shipp'd,
One among many, in societies,
285 That were, or seem'd, as simple as myself.
But now was come a change; it would demand
Some skill, and longer time than may be spared,

To paint, even to myself, these vanities,
And how they wrought. But, sure it is that now
290 Contagious air did oft environ me
Unknown among these haunts in former days.
The very garments that I wore appear'd   [295]
To prey upon my strength, and stopp'd the course
And quiet stream of self-forgetfulness.
295 Something there was about me that perplex'd
Th' authentic sight of reason, press'd too closely
On that religious dignity of mind,
That is the very faculty of truth;
Which wanting, either, from the very first,
300 A function never lighted up, or else
Extinguish'd, Man, a creature great and good,
Seems but a pageant plaything with wild claws
And this great frame of breathing elements
A senseless Idol.
                           That vague heartless chace
305 Of trivial pleasures was a poor exchange
For Books and Nature at that early age.
'Tis true, some casual knowledge might be gain'd   [300]
Of character or life; but at that time
Of manners put to school I took small note;
310 And all my deeper passions lay elsewhere.
Far better had it been to exalt the mind
By solitary study; to uphold   [305]
Intense desire by thought and quietness.
And yet, in chastisement of these regrets,
315 The memory of one particular hour
Doth here rise up against me. In a throng,
A festal company of Maids and Youths,
Old Men, and Matrons staid, promiscuous rout,   [310]
A medley of all tempers, I had pass'd
320 The night in dancing, gaiety and mirth;
With din of instruments, and shuffling feet,
And glancing forms, and tapers glittering,
And unaim'd prattle flying up and down,

Spirits upon the stretch, and here and there   [316]
325 Slight shocks of young love-liking interspers'd,
That mounted up like joy into the head,
And tingled through the veins. Ere we retired,
The cock had crow'd, the sky was bright with day.   [320]
Two miles I had to walk along the fields
330 Before I reached my home. Magnificent
The morning was, a memorable pomp,
More glorious than I ever had beheld.   [325]
The Sea was laughing at a distance; all
The solid Mountains were as bright as clouds,
335 Grain-tinctured, drench'd in empyrean light;
And, in the meadows and the lower grounds,
Was all the sweetness of a common dawn,   [330]
Dews, vapours, and the melody of birds,
And Labourers going forth into the fields.
340 —Ah! need I say, dear Friend, that to the brim
My heart was full; I made no vows, but vows
Were then made for me; bond unknown to me   [335]
Was given, that I should be, else sinning greatly,
A dedicated Spirit. On I walk'd
345 In blessedness, which even yet remains.

Strange rendezvous my mind was at that time,
A party-colour'd shew of grave and gay,   [340]
Solid and light, short-sighted and profound,
Of inconsiderate habits and sedate,
350 Consorting in one mansion unreprov'd.
I knew the worth of that which I possess'd,
Though slighted and misus'd. Besides, in truth,   [345]
That Summer, swarming as it did with thoughts
Transient and loose, yet wanted not a store
355 Of primitive hours, when, by these hindrances
Unthwarted, I experienc'd in myself
Conformity as just as that of old   [350]
To the end and written spirit of God's works,
Whether held forth in Nature or in Man.

360   From many wanderings that have left behind
Remembrances not lifeless, I will here
Single out one, then pass to other themes.

    A favourite pleasure hath it been with me,
From time of earliest youth, to walk alone
365 Along the public Way, when, for the night
Deserted, in its silence it assumes
A character of deeper quietness
Than pathless solitudes. At such an hour
Once, ere these summer months were pass'd away,   [370]
370 I slowly mounted up a steep ascent
Where the road's watery surface, to the ridge   [380]
Of that sharp rising, glitter'd in the moon,
And seem'd before my eyes another stream
Creeping with silent lapse to join the brook
375 That murmur'd in the valley. On I went   [384]
Tranquil, receiving in my own despite
Amusement, as I slowly pass'd along,
From such near objects as from time to time
Perforce intruded on the listless sense
380 Quiescent, and dispos'd to sympathy,
With an exhausted mind, worn out by toil,
And all unworthy of the deeper joy
Which waits on distant prospect, cliff, or sea,
The dark blue vault, and universe of stars.
385 Thus did I steal along that silent road,
My body from the stillness drinking in
A restoration like the calm of sleep,
But sweeter far. Above, before, behind,
Around me, all was peace and solitude,
390 I look'd not round, nor did the solitude
Speak to my eye; but it was heard and felt.
O happy state! what beauteous pictures now
Rose in harmonious imagery—they rose
As from some distant region of my soul
395 And came along like dreams; yet such as left

63

Obscurely mingled with their passing forms
A consciousness of animal delight,
A self-possession felt in every pause
And every gentle movement of my frame.
400   While thus I wander'd, step by step led on,
It chanced a sudden turning of the road   [388]
Presented to my view an uncouth shape   [387]
So near, that, slipping back into the shade
Of a thick hawthorn, I could mark him well,   [390]
405 Myself unseen. He was of stature tall,
A foot above man's common measure tall,
Stiff in his form, and upright, lank and lean;
A man more meagre, as it seem'd to me,
Was never seen abroad by night or day.
410 His arms were long, and bare his hands; his mouth   [395]
Shew'd ghastly in the moonlight: from behind
A milestone propp'd him, and his figure seem'd
Half-sitting, and half-standing. I could mark
That he was clad in military garb,
415 Though faded, yet entire. He was alone,
Had no attendant, neither Dog, nor Staff,   [400]
Nor knapsack; in his very dress appear'd
A desolation, a simplicity
That seem'd akin to solitude. Long time
420 Did I peruse him with a mingled sense
Of fear and sorrow. From his lips, meanwhile,
There issued murmuring sounds, as if of pain   [405]
Or of uneasy thought; yet still his form
Kept the same steadiness; and at his feet
425 His shadow lay, and mov'd not. In a Glen
Hard by, a Village stood, whose roofs and doors
Were visible among the scatter'd trees,
Scarce distant from the spot an arrow's flight;
I wish'd to see him move; but he remain'd
430 Fix'd to his place, and still from time to time
Sent forth a murmuring voice of dead complaint,
Groans scarcely audible. Without self-blame

I had not thus prolong'd my watch; and now,
Subduing my heart's specious cowardise   [410]
435 I left the shady nook where I had stood,
And hail'd him. Slowly from his resting-place
He rose, and with a lean and wasted arm
In measur'd gesture lifted to his head,
Return'd my salutation; then resum'd   [415]
440 His station as before: and when, erelong,
I ask'd his history, he in reply
Was neither slow nor eager; but unmov'd,
And with a quiet, uncomplaining voice,
A stately air of mild indifference,   [420]
445 He told, in simple words, a Soldier's tale,
That in the Tropic Islands he had serv'd,
Whence he had landed, scarcely ten days past,
That on his landing he had been dismiss'd,
And now was travelling to his native home.   [425]
450 At this, I turn'd and looked towards the Village
But all were gone to rest; the fires all out;
And every silent window to the Moon
Shone with a yellow glitter. 'No one there,'
Said I, 'is waking, we must measure back
455 The way which we have come: behind yon wood
A Labourer dwells; and, take it on my word
He will not murmur should we break his rest;
And with a ready heart will give you food
And lodging for the night.' At this he stoop'd,
460 And from the ground took up an oaken Staff,   [428]
By me yet unobserv'd, a Traveller's Staff;
Which, I suppose, from his slack hand had dropp'd,
And lain till now neglected in the grass.   [430]

Towards the Cottage without more delay
465 We shap'd our course; as it appear'd to me,
He travell'd without pain, and I beheld   [432]
With ill-suppress'd astonishment his tall
And ghastly figure moving at my side;

65

Nor, while we journey'd thus could I forbear [435]
470 To question him of what he had endured
From hardship, battle, or the pestilence.
He, all the while, was in demeanour calm, [440]
Concise in answer; solemn and sublime
He might have seem'd, but that in all he said
475 There was a strange half-absence, and a tone
Of weakness and indifference, as of one
Remembering the importance of his theme [444]
But feeling it no longer. We advanced
Slowly, and, ere we to the wood were come
480 Discourse had ceas'd. Together on we pass'd, [445–6]
In silence, through the shades, gloomy and dark;
Then, turning up along an open field
We gain'd the Cottage. At the door I knock'd, [449]
Calling aloud 'my Friend, here is a Man
485 By sickness overcome; beneath your roof
This night let him find rest, and give him food,
If food he need, for he is faint and tired.'
Assured that now my Comrade would repose
In comfort, I entreated that henceforth
490 He would not linger in the public ways [455]
But ask for timely furtherance and help
Such as his state requir'd. At this reproof,
With the same ghastly mildness in his look
He said 'my trust is in the God of Heaven
495 And in the eye of him that passes me.' [460]
The Cottage door was speedily unlock'd,
And now the Soldier touch'd his hat again
With his lean hand; and in a voice that seem'd
To speak with a reviving interest,
500 Till then unfelt, he thank'd me; I return'd [465]
The blessing of the poor unhappy Man;
And so we parted. Back I cast a look,
And linger'd near the door a little space;
Then sought with quiet heart my distant home.

66

BOOK FIFTH

BOOKS

Even in the steadiest mood of reason, when
All sorrow for thy transitory pains
Goes out, it grieves me for thy state, O Man,
Thou paramount Creature! and thy race, while ye
5   Shall sojourn on this planet; not for woes   [5]
Which thou endur'st; that weight, albeit huge,
I charm away; but for those palms atchiev'd
Through length of time, by study and hard thought,   [10]
The honours of thy high endowments, there
10   My sadness finds its fuel. Hitherto,
In progress through this Verse, my mind hath look'd
Upon the speaking face of earth and heaven
As her prime Teacher, intercourse with man
Establish'd by the sovereign Intellect,   [15]
15   Who through that bodily Image hath diffus'd
A soul divine which we participate,
A deathless spirit. Thou also, Man, hast wrought,
For commerce of thy nature with itself,
Things worthy of unconquerable life;   [20]
20   And yet we feel, we cannot chuse but feel
That these must perish. Tremblings of the heart
It gives, to think that the immortal being
No more shall need such garments; and yet Man,
As long as he shall be the Child of Earth,   [25]
25   Might almost 'weep to have' what he may lose,
Nor be himself extinguish'd; but survive
Abject, depress'd, forlorn, disconsolate.
A thought is with me sometimes, and I say,
Should earth by inward throes be wrench'd throughout,
30   Or fire be sent from far to wither all
Her pleasant habitations, and dry up
Old Ocean in his bed left sing'd and bare,

Yet would the living Presence still subsist
Victorious; and composure would ensue, [35]
35 And kindlings like the morning; presage sure,
Though slow, perhaps, of a returning day.
But all the meditations of mankind,
Yea, all the adamantine holds of truth,
By reason built, or passion, which itself [40]
40 Is highest reason in a soul sublime;
The consecrated works of Bard and Sage,
Sensuous or intellectual, wrought by men,
Twin labourers and heirs of the same hopes,
Where would they be? Oh! why hath not the mind [45]
45 Some element to stamp her image on
In nature somewhat nearer to her own?
Why, gifted with such powers to send abroad
Her spirit, must it lodge in shrines so frail?

One day, when in the hearing of a Friend, [50]
50 I had given utterance to thoughts like these,
He answer'd with a smile that, in plain truth
'Twas going far to seek disquietude;
But on the front of his reproof, confess'd
That he, at sundry seasons, had himself [55]
55 Yielded to kindred hauntings. And forthwith
Added, that once upon a summer's noon,
While he was sitting in a rocky cave
By the sea-side, perusing, as it chanced,
The famous History of the Errant Knight [60]
60 Recorded by Cervantes, these same thoughts
Came to him; and to height unusual rose
While listlessly he sate, and having closed
The Book, had turned his eyes towards the Sea.
On Poetry and geometric Truth, [65]
65 The knowledge that endures, upon these two,
And their high privilege of lasting life,
Exempt from all internal injury,
He mused: upon these chiefly: and at length,

His senses yielding to the sultry air,
70 Sleep seiz'd him, and he pass'd into a dream.   [70]
He saw before him an Arabian Waste,
A Desert; and he fancied that himself
Was sitting there in the wide wilderness,
Alone, upon the sands. Distress of mind
75 Was growing in him when, behold! at once
To his great joy a Man was at his side,
Upon a dromedary, mounted high.   [76]
He seem'd an Arab of the Bedouin Tribes,
A Lance he bore, and underneath one arm
80 A Stone; and, in the opposite hand, a Shell
Of a surpassing brightness. Much rejoic'd   [80]
The dreaming Man that he should have a Guide
To lead him through the Desert; and he thought,
While questioning himself what this strange freight
85 Which the Newcomer carried through the Waste   [85]
Could mean, the Arab told him that the Stone,
To give it in the language of the Dream,
Was Euclid's Elements; 'and this,' said he,
'This other,' pointing to the Shell, 'this Book
90 Is something of more worth.' And, at the word,
The Stranger, said my Friend continuing,
Stretch'd forth the Shell towards me, with command   [90]
That I should hold it to my ear; I did so,
And heard that instant in an unknown Tongue,
95 Which yet I understood, articulate sounds,
A loud prophetic blast of harmony,   [95]
An Ode, in passion utter'd, which foretold
Destruction to the Children of the Earth,
By deluge now at hand. No sooner ceas'd
100 The Song, but with calm look, the Arab said
That all was true; that it was even so
As had been spoken; and that he himself   [100]
Was going then to bury those two Books:
The one that held acquaintance with the stars.
105 And wedded man to man by purest bond

Of nature, undisturbed by space or time;   [105]
Th' other that was a God, yea many Gods,
Had voices more than all the winds, and was
A joy, a consolation, and a hope.
110 My friend continued, 'strange as it may seem,   [110]
I wonder'd not, although I plainly saw
The one to be a Stone, th' other a Shell,
Nor doubted once but that they both were Books,
Having a perfect faith in all that pass'd.
115 A wish was now ingender'd in my fear
To cleave unto this Man, and I begg'd leave   [115]
To share his errand with him. On he pass'd
Not heeding me; I follow'd, and took note
That he look'd often backward with wild look,
120 Grasping his twofold treasure to his side.
—Upon a Dromedary, Lance in rest,   [120]
He rode, I keeping pace with him, and now
I fancied that he was the very Knight
Whose Tale Cervantes tells, yet not the Knight,
125 But was an Arab of the Desart, too;
Of these was neither, and was both at once.   [125]
His countenance, meanwhile, grew more disturb'd,
And, looking backwards when he look'd, I saw
A glittering light, and ask'd him whence it came.
130 'It is,' said he, 'the waters of the deep   [130]
Gathering upon us,' quickening then his pace
He left me: I call'd after him aloud;
He heeded not; but with his twofold charge
Beneath his arm, before me full in view   [135]
135 I saw him riding o'er the Desart Sands,
With the fleet waters of the drowning world
In chace of him, whereat I wak'd in terror,
And saw the Sea before me; and the Book,
In which I had been reading, at my side.   [140]

140   Full often, taking from the world of sleep
   This Arab Phantom, which my Friend beheld,

This Semi-Quixote, I to him have given
A substance, fancied him a living man,
A gentle Dweller in the Desart, craz'd   [145]
145 By love and feeling and internal thought,
Protracted among endless solitudes;
Have shap'd him, in the oppression of his brain,
Wandering upon this quest, and thus equipp'd.
And I have scarcely pitied him; have felt
150 A reverence for a Being thus employ'd;   [150]
And thought that in the blind and awful lair
Of such a madness, reason did lie couch'd.
Enow there are on earth to take in charge
Their Wives, their Children, and their virgin Loves,
155 Or whatsoever else the heart holds dear;   [155]
Enow to think of these; yea, will I say,
In sober contemplation of the approach
Of such great overthrow, made manifest
By certain evidence, that I, methinks,
160 Could share that Maniac's anxiousness, could go   [160]
Upon like errand. Oftentimes, at least,
Me hath such deep entrancement half-possess'd,
When I have held a volume in my hand
Poor earthly casket of immortal Verse!
165 Shakespeare, or Milton, Labourers divine!   [165]

    Mighty indeed, supreme must be the power
Of living Nature, which could thus so long
Detain me from the best of other thoughts.
Even in the lisping time of Infancy,   [170]
170 And later down, in prattling Childhood, even
While I was travelling back among those days,
How could I ever play an ingrate's part?
Once more should I have made those bowers resound,
And intermingled strains of thankfulness   [175]
175 With their own thoughtless melodies; at least,
It might have well beseem'd me to repeat
Some simply fashion'd tale; to tell again,

71

In slender accents of sweet Verse, some tale
That did bewitch me then, and soothes me now.   [180]
180 O Friend! O Poet! Brother of my soul,
Think not that I could ever pass along
Untouch'd by these remembrances; no, no,
But I was hurried forward by a stream,
And could not stop. Yet wherefore should I speak,
185 Why call upon a few weak words to say
What is already written in the hearts   [185]
Of all that breathe? what in the path of all
Drops daily from the tongue of every child,
Wherever Man is found. The trickling tear
190 Upon the cheek of listening Infancy
Tells it, and the insuperable look   [190]
That drinks as if it never could be full.

    That portion of my story I shall leave
There register'd: whatever else there be
195 Of power or pleasure, sown or fostered thus,
Peculiar to myself, let that remain   [195]
Where it lies hidden in its endless home
Among the depths of time. And yet it seems
That here, in memory of all books which lay
200 Their sure foundations in the heart of Man;
Whether by native prose or numerous verse,   [200]
That in the name of all inspired Souls,
From Homer, the great Thunderer; from the voice
Which roars along the bed of Jewish Song;
205 And that, more varied and elaborate,
Those trumpet-tones of harmony that shake   [205]
Our Shores in England; from those loftiest notes
Down to the low and wren-like warblings, made
For Cottagers and Spinners at the wheel,
210 And weary Travellers when they rest themselves
By the highways and hedges; ballad tunes,   [210]
Food for the hungry ears of little Ones,
And of old Men who have surviv'd their joy;

72

It seemeth, in behalf of these, the works
215 And of the Men who fram'd them, whether known,
Or sleeping nameless in their scatter'd graves,   [215]
That I should here assert their rights, attest
Their honours; and should, once for all, pronounce
Their benediction; speak of them as Powers
220 For ever to be hallowed; only less,
For what we may become, and what we need,   [220]
Than Nature's self, which is the breath of God.

Rarely, and with reluctance, would I stoop
To transitory themes; yet I rejoice,
225 And, by these thoughts admonish'd, must speak out   [225]
Thanksgivings from my heart, that I was rear'd
Safe from an evil which these days have laid
Upon the Children of the Land, a pest
That might have dried me up, body and soul.
230 This Verse is dedicate to Nature's self,   [230]
And things that teach as Nature teaches, then
Oh where had been the Man, the Poet where?
Where had we been, we two, beloved Friend,
If we, in lieu of wandering, as we did,   [235]
235 Through heights and hollows, and bye-spots of tales
Rich with indigenous produce, open ground
Of Fancy, happy pastures rang'd at will!
Had been attended, follow'd, watch'd, and noos'd,
Each in his several melancholy walk
240 String'd like a poor man's Heifer, at its feed   [240]
Led through the lanes in forlorn servitude;
Or rather like a stallèd ox shut out
From touch of growing grass; that may not taste
A flower till it have yielded up its sweets
245 A prelibation to the mower's scythe.   [245]

Behold the Parent Hen amid her Brood,
Though fledged and feather'd, and well pleased to part
And straggle from her presence, still a Brood,

And she herself from the maternal bond
250 Still undischarged; yet doth she little more   [250]
Than move with them in tenderness and love,
A centre of the circle which they make;
And, now and then, alike from need of theirs,
And call of her own natural appetites,
255 She scratches, ransacks up the earth for food   [255]
Which they partake at pleasure. Early died
My honour'd Mother; she who was the heart
And hinge of all our learnings and our loves:
She left us destitute, and as we might
260 Trooping together. Little suits it me   [260]
To break upon the sabbath of her rest
With any thought that looks at others' blame,
Nor would I praise her but in perfect love.
Hence am I check'd: but I will boldly say,
265 In gratitude, and for the sake of truth,   [265]
Unheard by her, that she, not falsely taught,
Fetching her goodness rather from times past
Than shaping novelties from those to come,
Had no presumption, no such jealousy;
270 Nor did by habit of her thoughts mistrust   [270]
Our Nature; but had virtual faith that he,
Who fills the Mother's breasts with innocent milk,
Doth also for our nobler part provide,
Under his great correction and controul,
275 As innocent instincts, and as innocent food.   [275]
This was her creed, and therefore she was pure
From feverish dread of error or mishap   [280]
And evil, overweeningly so call'd;
Was not puff'd up by false unnatural hopes;
280 Nor selfish with unnecessary cares;
Nor with impatience from the season ask'd
More than its timely produce; rather lov'd   [285]
The hours for what they are than from regards
Glanced on their promises in restless pride.
285 Such was she; not from faculties more strong

Than others have, but from the times, perhaps,
And spot in which she liv'd, and through a grace   [290]
Of modest meekness, simple-mindedness,
A heart that found benignity and hope,
290 Being itself benign.
                              My drift hath scarcely,
I fear, been obvious; for I have recoil'd
From showing as it is the monster birth
Engender'd by these too industrious times.
Let few words paint it: 'tis a Child, no Child,
295 But a dwarf Man; in knowledge, virtue, skill;
In what he is not, and in what he is,
The noontide shadow of a man complete;
A worshipper of worldly seemliness,
Not quarrelsome; for that were far beneath   [300]
300 His dignity; with gifts he bubbles o'er
As generous as a fountain; selfishness
May not come near him, gluttony or pride;
The wandering Beggars propagate his name,   [305]
Dumb creatures find him tender as a nun.
305 Yet deem him not for this a naked dish
Of goodness merely, he is garnish'd out.
Arch are his notices, and nice his sense
Of the ridiculous; deceit and guile
Meanness and falsehood he detects, can treat
310 With apt and graceful laughter; nor is blind
To the broad follies of the licens'd world;   [312]
Though shrewd, yet innocent himself withal
And can read lectures upon innocence.
He is fenc'd round, nay arm'd, for aught we know
315 In panoply complete; and fear itself,
Natural or supernatural alike,   [307]
Unless it leap upon him in a dream,
Touches him not. Briefly, the moral part
Is perfect, and in learning and in books
320 He is a prodigy. His discourse moves slow,
Massy and ponderous as a prison door,

Tremendously emboss'd with terms of art;
Rank growth of propositions overruns
The Stripling's brain; the path in which he treads
925 Is chok'd with grammars; cushion of Divine
Was never such a type of thought profound
As is the pillow where he rests his head.
The Ensigns of the Empire which he holds,
The globe and sceptre of his royalties
330 Are telescopes, and crucibles, and maps.
Ships he can guide across the pathless sea,   [316]
And tell you all their cunning; he can read
The inside of the earth, and spell the stars;
He knows the policies of foreign Lands;
335 Can string you names of districts, cities, towns,   [320]
The whole world over, tight as beads of dew
Upon a gossamer thread; he sifts, he weighs;
Takes nothing upon trust: his Teachers stare
The Country People pray for God's good grace,
340 And tremble at his deep experiments.
All things are put to question; he must live
Knowing that he grows wiser every day,
Or else not live at all; and seeing, too,   [325]
Each little drop of wisdom as it falls
345 Into the dimpling cistern of his heart;   [327]
Meanwhile old Grandame Earth is grieved to find   [337]
The playthings, which her love design'd for him,
Unthought of: in their woodland beds the flowers
Weep, and the river sides are all forlorn.   [340]

350   Now this is hollow, 'tis a life of lies
From the beginning, and in lies must end.
Forth bring him to the air of common sense,
And, fresh and shewy as it is, the Corps
Slips from us into powder. Vanity
355 That is his soul, there lives he, and there moves;
It is the soul of every thing he seeks;
That gone, nothing is left which he can love.

Nay, if a thought of purer birth should rise
To carry him towards a better clime
360 Some busy helper still is on the watch
To drive him back and pound him like a Stray   [335]
Within the pinfold of his own conceit;
Which is his home, his natural dwelling place.
Oh! give us once again the Wishing-Cap
365 Of Fortunatus, and the invisible Coat
Of Jack the Giant-killer, Robin Hood,
And Sabra in the forest with St. George!
The child, whose love is here, at least, doth reap   [345]
One precious gain, that he forgets himself.

370   These mighty workmen of our later age
Who with a broad highway have overbridged
The froward chaos of futurity,
Tamed to their bidding; they who have the art   [350]
To manage books, and things, and make them work
375 Gently on infant minds, as does the sun
Upon a flower; the Tutors of our Youth
The Guides, the Wardens of our faculties,
And Stewards of our labour, watchful men
And skilful in the usury of time,
380 Sages, who in their prescience would controul   [355]
All accidents, and to the very road
Which they have fashion'd would confine us down,
Like engines, when will they be taught
That in the unreasoning progress of the world
385 A wiser Spirit is at work for us,   [360]
A better eye than theirs, most prodigal
Of blessings, and most studious of our good,
Even in what seem our most unfruitful hours?

There was a Boy, ye knew him well, ye Cliffs
390 And Islands of Winander! many a time   [365]
At evening, when the stars had just begun
To move along the edges of the hills,

Rising or setting, would he stand alone
Beneath the trees, or by the glimmering Lake,
395 And there, with fingers interwoven, both hands   [370]
Press'd closely, palm to palm, and to his mouth
Uplifted, he, as through an instrument,
Blew mimic hootings to the silent owls
That they might answer him.—And they would shout
400 Across the watry Vale, and shout again,   [375]
Responsive to his call, with quivering peals,
And long halloos, and screams, and echoes loud
Redoubled and redoubled; concourse wild
Of mirth and jocund din! And when it chanced
405 That pauses of deep silence mock'd his skill,   [380]
Then sometimes, in that silence, while he hung
Listening, a gentle shock of mild surprize
Has carried far into his heart the voice
Of mountain torrents; or the visible scene
410 Would enter unawares into his mind   [385]
With all its solemn imagery, its rocks,
Its woods, and that uncertain Heaven, receiv'd
Into the bosom of the steady Lake.

    This Boy was taken from his Mates, and died
415 In childhood, ere he was full ten years old.   [390]
—Fair are the woods, and beauteous is the spot,
The Vale where he was born; the Churchyard hangs
Upon a Slope above the Village School,
And there, along that bank, when I have pass'd
420 At evening, I believe that oftentimes   [395]
A full half-hour together I have stood
Mute—looking at the Grave in which he lies.

    Even now, methinks, before my sight I have
That self-same Village Church; I see her sit,
425 The thronèd Lady spoken of erewhile,   [400]
On her green hill; forgetful of this Boy
Who slumbers at her feet; forgetful, too,
Of all her silent neighbourhood of graves,

And listening only to the gladsome sounds
430 That, from the rural School ascending, play   [405]
Beneath her and about her. May she long
Behold a race of young Ones like to those
With whom I herded! (easily, indeed,
We might have fed upon a fatter soil
435 Of Arts and Letters, but be that forgiven)   [410]
A race of real children, not too wise,
Too learned, or too good; but wanton, fresh,
And bandied up and down by love and hate,
Fierce, moody, patient, venturous, modest, shy;   [415]
440 Mad at their sports like wither'd leaves in winds;
Though doing wrong, and suffering, and full oft
Bending beneath our life's mysterious weight
Of pain and fear; yet still in happiness
Not yielding to the happiest upon earth.   [420]
445 Simplicity in habit, truth in speech,
Be these the daily strengtheners of their minds!
May books and nature be their early joy!
And knowledge, rightly honor'd with that name,
Knowledge not purchas'd with the loss of power!   [425]

450   Well do I call to mind the very week
When I was first entrusted to the care
Of that sweet Valley; when its paths, its shores,
And brooks, were like a dream of novelty
To my half-infant thoughts; that very week   [430]
455 While I was roving up and down alone,
Seeking I knew not what, I chanced to cross
One of those open fields, which, shaped like ears,
Make green peninsulas on Esthwaite's Lake:
Twilight was coming on; yet through the gloom,   [435]
460 I saw distinctly on the opposite Shore
A heap of garments, left, as I suppos'd,
By one who there was bathing; long I watch'd,
But no one own'd them; meanwhile the calm Lake
Grew dark, with all the shadows on its breast,

465 And, now and then, a fish up-leaping, snapp'd
     The breathless stillness. The succeeding day,
     (Those unclaimed garments telling a plain Tale)   [443]
     Went there a Company, and, in their Boat
     Sounded with grappling irons, and long poles.   [447]
470 At length, the dead Man, 'mid that beauteous scene
     Of trees, and hills and water, bolt upright
     Rose with his ghastly face; a spectre shape   [450]
     Of terror even! and yet no vulgar fear,
     Young as I was, a Child not nine years old,
475 Possess'd me; for my inner eye had seen
     Such sights before, among the shining streams
     Of Fairy Land, the Forests of Romance: [455]
     Thence came a spirit hallowing what I saw
     With decoration and ideal grace;
480 A dignity, a smoothness, like the works
     Of Grecian Art, and purest Poesy.

     I had a precious treasure at that time   [460]
     A little, yellow canvas-cover'd Book,
     A slender abstract of the Arabian Tales;
485 And when I learn'd, as now I first did learn,
     From my Companions in this new abode,
     That this dear prize of mine was but a block
     Hewn from a mighty quarry; in a word,   [465]
     That there were four large Volumes, laden all
490 With kindred matter, 'twas, in truth, to me
     A promise scarcely earthly. Instantly
     I made a league, a covenant with a Friend
     Of my own age, that we should lay aside   [470]
     The monies we possess'd, and hoard up more,
495 Till our joint savings had amass'd enough
     To make this Book our own. Through several months
     Religiously did we preserve that vow,
     And spite of all temptation, hoarded up
     And hoarded up; but firmness fail'd at length   [475]
500 Nor were we ever masters of our wish.

And afterwards, when to my Father's House
Returning at the holidays, I found
That golden store of books which I had left
Open to my enjoyment once again
505 What heart was mine! Full often through the course [480]
Of those glad respites in the summer-time
When, arm'd with rod and line we went abroad
For a whole day together, I have lain
Down by thy side, O Derwent! murmuring Stream,
510 On the hot stones and in the glaring sun, [485]
And there have read, devouring as I read,
Defrauding the day's glory, desperate!
Till, with a sudden bound of smart reproach,
Such as an Idler deals with in his shame,
515 I to my sport betook myself again. [490]

A gracious Spirit o'er this earth presides,
And o'er the heart of man: invisibly
It comes, directing those to works of love
Who care not, know not, think not what they do: [495]
520 The Tales that charm away the wakeful night
In Araby, Romances, Legends, penn'd
For solace, by the light of monkish Lamps;
Fictions for Ladies, of their Love, devis'd
By youthful Squires; adventures endless, spun [500]
525 By the dismantled Warrior in old age,
Out of the bowels of those very thoughts
In which his youth did first extravagate,
These spread like day, and something in the shape
Of these, will live till man shall be no more. [505]
530 Dumb yearnings, hidden appetites are ours,
And they must have their food: our childhood sits,
Our simple childhood sits upon a throne
That hath more power than all the elements.
I guess not what this tells of Being past, [510]
535 Nor what it augurs of the life to come;
But so it is; and in that dubious hour,

That twilight when we first begin to see
This dawning earth, to recognise, expect;
And in the long probation that ensues, [515]
540 The time of trial, ere we learn to live
In reconcilement with our stinted powers,
To endure this state of meagre vassalage;
Unwilling to forego, confess, submit,
Uneasy and unsettled, yoke-fellows [520]
545 To custom, mettlesome, and not yet tam'd
And humbled down, oh! then we feel, we feel,
We know when we have Friends. Ye dreamers, then,
Forgers of lawless tales! we bless you then,
Impostors, drivellers, dotards, as the ape [525]
550 Philosophy will call you: then we feel
With what, and how great might ye are in league,
Who make our wish our power, our thought a deed,
An empire, a possession; Ye whom Time
And Seasons serve; all Faculties; to whom [530]
555 Earth crouches, th' elements are potter's clay,
Space like a Heaven fill'd up with Northern lights;
Here, nowhere, there, and everywhere at once.

     It might demand a more impassion'd strain
To tell of later pleasures, link'd to these, [535]
560 A tract of the same isthmus which we cross
In progress from our native continent
To earth and human life; I mean to speak
Of that delightful time of growing youth
When cravings for the marvellous relent, [540]
565 And we begin to love what we have seen;
And sober truth, experience, sympathy,
Take stronger hold of us; and words themselves
Move us with conscious pleasure. [545]
                         I am sad
At thought of raptures, now for ever flown,
570 Even unto tears, I sometimes could be sad
To think of, to read over, many a page,

Poems withal of name, which at that time
Did never fail to entrance me, and are now   [550]
Dead in my eyes as is a theatre
575 Fresh emptied of spectators. Thirteen years
Or haply less, I might have seen, when first
My ears began to open to the charm
Of words in tuneful order, found them sweet   [555]
For *their own sakes*, a passion and a power;
580 And phrases pleas'd me, chosen for delight,
For pomp, or love. Oft in the public roads,
Yet unfrequented, while the morning light
Was yellowing the hill-tops, with that dear Friend   [560]
The same whom I have mention'd heretofore,
585 I went abroad, and for the better part
Of two delightful hours we stroll'd along
By the still borders of the misty Lake,
Repeating favourite verses with one voice,
Or conning more; as happy as the birds   [565]
590 That round us chaunted. Well might we be glad,
Lifted above the ground by airy fancies
More bright than madness or the dreams of wine,
And, though full oft the objects of our love
Were false, and in their splendour overwrought,   [570]
595 Yet, surely, at such time no vulgar power
Was working in us, nothing less, in truth,
Than that most noble attribute of man,
Though yet untutor'd and inordinate,
That wish for something loftier, more adorn'd,   [575]
600 Than is the common aspect, daily garb
Of human life. What wonder then if sounds
Of exultation echoed through the groves!
For images, and sentiments, and words,
And everything with which we had to do   [580]
605 In that delicious world of poesy,
Kept holiday; a never-ending show,
With music, incense, festival, and flowers!

Here must I pause: this only will I add,
From heart-experience, and in humblest sense   [585]
610 Of modesty, that he, who, in his youth
A wanderer among the woods and fields,
With living Nature hath been intimate,
Not only in that raw unpractis'd time
Is stirr'd to ecstasy, as others are,   [590]
615 By glittering verse; but, he doth furthermore,
In measure only dealt out to himself,
Receive enduring touches of deep joy
From the great Nature that exists in works
Of mighty Poets. Visionary Power   [595]
620 Attends upon the motions of the winds
Embodied in the mystery of words.
There darkness makes abode, and all the host
Of shadowy things do work their changes there,
As in a mansion like their proper home;   [600]
625 Even forms and substances are circumfus'd
By that transparent veil with light divine;
And through the turnings intricate of Verse,
Present themselves as objects recognis'd,
In flashes, and with a glory scarce their own.   [605]

630   Thus far a scanty record is deduced
Of what I owed to Books in early life;
Their later influence yet remains untold;
But as this work was taking in my thoughts
Proportions that seem'd larger than had first
635 Been meditated, I was indisposed
To any further progress at a time
When these acknowledgements were left unpaid.

BOOK SIXTH

CAMBRIDGE AND THE ALPS

The leaves were yellow when to Furness Fells,
The haunt of Shepherds, and to cottage life
I bade adieu; and, one among the Flock
Who by that season are conven'd, like birds
5   Trooping together at the Fowler's lure,   [5]
Went back to Granta's cloisters; not so fond,
Or eager, though as gay and undepress'd
In spirit, as when I thence had taken flight
A few short months before. I turn'd my face
10   Without repining from the mountain pomp   [10]
Of Autumn, and its beauty enter'd in
With calmer Lakes, and louder Streams; and You,
Frank-hearted Maids of rocky Cumberland,
You and your not unwelcome days of mirth   [15]
15   I quitted, and your nights of revelry,
And in my own unlovely Cell sate down
In lightsome mood; such privilege has Youth,
That cannot take long leave of pleasant thoughts.

We need not linger o'er the ensuing time,
20   But let me add at once that, now the bonds
Of indolent and vague society   [20]
Relaxing in their hold, I liv'd henceforth
More to myself, read more, reflected more,
Felt more, and settled daily into habits
25   More promising. Two winters may be pass'd
Without a separate notice; many books
Were read in process of this time, devour'd,
Tasted or skimm'd, or studiously perus'd,
Yet with no settled plan. I was detached   [25]
30   Internally from academic cares,
From every hope of prowess and reward,

And wish'd to be a lodger in that house
Of Letters, and no more: and should have been
Even such, but for some personal concerns
35 That hung about me in my own despite
Perpetually, no heavy weight, but still
A baffling and a hindrance, a controul
Which made the thought of planning for myself
A course of independent study seem
40 An act of disobedience towards them
Who lov'd me, proud rebellion and unkind.
This bastard virtue, rather let it have   [30]
A name it more deserves, this cowardise,
Gave treacherous sanction to that overlove
45 Of freedom planted in me from the very first
And indolence, by force of which I turn'd
From regulations even of my own,
As from restraints and bonds. And who can tell,   [35]
Who knows what thus may have been gain'd both then
50 And at a later season, or preserv'd;
What love of nature, what original strength
Of contemplation, what intuitive truths
The deepest and the best, and what research   [40]
Unbiass'd, unbewilder'd, and unaw'd?

55   The Poet's soul was with me at that time,
Sweet meditations, the still overflow
Of happiness and truth. A thousand hopes
Were mine, a thousand tender dreams, of which   [45]
No few have since been realiz'd, and some
60 Do yet remain, hopes for my future life.
Four years and thirty, told this very week,
Have I been now a sojourner on earth,
And yet the morning gladness is not gone
Which then was in my mind. Those were the days
65 Which also first encourag'd me to trust
With firmness, hitherto but lightly touch'd
With such a daring thought, that I might leave   [55]

86

Some monument behind me which pure hearts
Should reverence. The instinctive humbleness,
70 Upheld even by the very name and thought
Of printed books and authorship, began
To melt away, and further, the dread awe   [60]
Of mighty names was soften'd down, and seem'd
Approachable, admitting fellowship
75 Of modest sympathy. Such aspect now,
Though not familiarly, my mind put on;
I lov'd, and I enjoy'd, that was my chief
And ruling business, happy in the strength
And loveliness of imagery and thought.
80 All winter long, whenever free to take
My choice, did I at night frequent our Groves
And tributary walks, the last, and oft
The only one, who had been lingering there
Through hours of silence, till the Porter's Bell,   [70]
85 A punctual follower on the stroke of nine,
Rang with its blunt unceremonious voice,
Inexorable summons. Lofty Elms,
Inviting shades of opportune recess,
Did give composure to a neighbourhood   [75]
90 Unpeaceful in itself. A single Tree
There was, no doubt yet standing there, an Ash
With sinuous trunk, boughs exquisitely wreath'd;
Up from the ground and almost to the top   [80]
The trunk and master branches everywhere
95 Were green with ivy; and the lightsome twigs
And outer spray profusely tipp'd with seeds
That hung in yellow tassels and festoons,
Moving or still, a Favourite trimm'd out
By Winter for himself, as if in pride,
100 And with outlandish grace. Oft have I stood   [85]
Foot-bound, uplooking at this lovely Tree
Beneath a frosty moon. The hemisphere
Of magic fiction, verse of mine perhaps
May never tread; but scarcely Spenser's self

105 Could have more tranquil visions in his youth,   [90]
More bright appearances could scarcely see
Of human Forms and superhuman Powers,
Than I beheld, standing on winter nights
Alone, beneath this fairy work of earth.
110 'Twould be a waste of labour to detail
The rambling studies of a truant Youth,   [95]
Which further may be easily divin'd,
What, and what kind they were. My inner knowledge,
(This barely will I note) was oft in depth
115 And delicacy like another mind
Sequester'd from my outward taste in books,
And yet the books which then I lov'd the most
Are dearest to me now; for, being vers'd   [100]
In living Nature, I had there a guide
120 Which open'd frequently my eyes, else shut,
A standard which was usefully applied,
Even when unconsciously, to other things
Which less I understood. In general terms,
I was a better judge of thoughts than words,   [106]
125 Misled as to these latter, not alone
By common inexperience of youth
But by the trade in classic niceties,
Delusion to young Scholars incident
And old ones also, by that overpriz'd
130 And dangerous craft of picking phrases out   [110]
From languages that want the living voice
To make of them a nature to the heart,
To tell us what is passion, what is truth,
What reason, what simplicity and sense.

135   Yet must I not entirely overlook   [115]
The pleasure gather'd from the elements
Of geometric science. I had stepp'd
In these inquiries but a little way,
No farther than the threshold; with regret   [119]
140 Sincere I mention this; but there I found

Enough to exalt, to chear me and compose.
With Indian awe and wonder, ignorance
Which even was cherish'd, did I meditate
Upon the alliance of those simple, pure
145 Proportions and relations with the frame
And laws of Nature, how they could become   [126]
Herein a leader to the human mind,
And made endeavours frequent to detect
The process by dark guesses of my own.
150 Yet from this source more frequently I drew
A pleasure calm and deeper, a still sense   [130]
Of permanent and universal sway
And paramount endowment in the mind,
An image not unworthy of the one
155 Surpassing Life, which out of space and time,   [135]
Nor touched by welterings of passion, is
And hath the name of God. Transcendent peace
And silence did await upon these thoughts   [140]
That were a frequent comfort to my youth.

160   And as I have read of one by shipwreck thrown
With fellow Sufferers whom the waves had spar'd
Upon a region uninhabited
An island of the Deep, who having brought
To land a single Volume and no more,   [145]
165 A treatise of Geometry, was used,
Although of food and clothing destitute,
And beyond common wretchedness depress'd,
To part from company and take this book,
Then first a self-taught pupil in those truths,   [150]
170 To spots remote and corners of the Isle
By the sea side, and draw his diagrams
With a long stick upon the sand, and thus
Did oft beguile his sorrow, and almost
Forget his feeling; even so, if things
175 Producing like effect, from outward cause   [155]
So different, may rightly be compar'd,

So was it with me then, and so will be
With Poets ever. Mighty is the charm
Of those abstractions to a mind beset
180 With images, and haunted by itself;   [160]
And specially delightful unto me
Was that clear Synthesis built up aloft
So gracefully, even then when it appear'd
No more than as a plaything, or a toy
185 Embodied to the sense, not what it is   [165]
In verity, an independent world
Created out of pure Intelligence.

Such dispositions then were mine, almost
Through grace of Heaven and inborn tenderness.   [170]
190 And not to leave the picture of that time
Imperfect, with these habits I must rank
A melancholy from humours of the blood
In part, and partly taken up, that lov'd
A pensive sky, sad days, and piping winds,
195 The twilight more than dawn, Autumn than Spring;   [175]
A treasur'd and luxurious gloom, of choice
And inclination mainly, and the mere
Redundancy of youth's contentedness.
Add unto this a multitude of hours
200 Pilfer'd away by what the Bard who sang   [180]
Of the Enchanter Indolence hath call'd
'Good-natured lounging,' and behold a map
Of my Collegiate life, far less intense
Than Duty call'd for, or without regard
205 To Duty, might have sprung up of itself   [185]
By change of accidents, or even, to speak
Without unkindness, in another place.

In summer among distant nooks I rov'd
Dovedale, or Yorkshire Dales, or through bye-tracts
210 Of my own native region, and was blest   [195]
Between these sundry wanderings with a joy

    Above all joys, that seem'd another morn
    Risen on mid noon, the presence, Friend, I mean
    Of that sole Sister, she who hath been long
215 Thy Treasure also, thy true friend and mine,   [200]
    Now, after separation desolate
    Restor'd to me, such absence that she seem'd
    A gift then first bestow'd. The gentle Banks
    Of Emont, hitherto unnam'd in Song,
220 And that monastic Castle, on a Flat   [205]
    Low-standing by the margin of the Stream,
    A Mansion not unvisited of old
    By Sidney, where, in sight of our Helvellyn,
    Some snatches he might pen, for aught we know,
225 Of his Arcadia, by fraternal love   [210]
    Inspir'd; that River and that mouldering Dome
    Have seen us sit in many a summer hour,
    My sister and myself, when having climb'd
    In danger through some window's open space,
230 We look'd abroad, or on the Turret's head
    Lay listening to the wild flowers and the grass,
    As they gave out their whispers to the wind.
    Another Maid there was, who also breath'd
    A gladness o'er that season, then to me   [225]
235 By her exulting outside look of youth
    And placid under-countenance, first endear'd,
    That other Spirit, Coleridge, who is now
    So near to us, that meek confiding heart,
    So reverenced by us both. O'er paths and fields   [230]
240 In all that neighbourhood, through narrow lanes
    Of eglantine, and through the shady woods,
    And o'er the Border Beacon, and the Waste
    Of naked Pools, and common Crags that lay
    Expos'd on the bare Fell, was scatter'd love,   [235]
245 A spirit of pleasure and youth's golden gleam.
    O Friend! we had not seen thee at that time;
    And yet a power is on me and a strong
    Confusion, and I seem to plant thee there.

Far art Thou wander'd now in search of health, [240]
250 And milder breezes, melancholy lot!
But Thou art with us, with us in the past,
The present, with us in the times to come:
There is no grief, no sorrow, no despair,
No languor, no dejection, no dismay, [245]
255 No absence scarcely can there be for those
Who love as we do. Speed thee well! divide
Thy pleasure with us, thy returning strength
Receive it daily as a joy of ours;
Share with us thy fresh spirits, whether gift [250]
260 Of gales Etesian, or of loving thoughts.

I, too, have been a Wanderer; but, alas!
How different is the fate of different men
Though Twins almost in genius and in mind!
Unknown unto each other, yea, and breathing
265 As if in different elements, we were framed [255]
To bend at last to the same discipline,
Predestin'd, if two Beings ever were,
To seek the same delights, and have one health,
One happiness. Throughout this narrative,
270 Else sooner ended, I have known full well [260]
For whom I thus record the birth and growth
Of gentleness, simplicity, and truth,
And joyous loves that hallow innocent days
Of peace and self-command. Of Rivers, Fields,
275 And Groves, I speak to thee, my Friend; to thee, [265]
Who, yet a liveried School-Boy, in the depths
Of the huge City, on the leaded Roof
Of that wide Edifice, thy home and School,
Wast used to lie and gaze upon the clouds
280 Moving in Heaven; or haply, tired of this, [270]
To shut thine eyes, and by internal light
See trees, and meadows, and thy native Stream
Far distant, thus beheld from year to year
Of thy long exile. Nor could I forget

285 In this late portion of my argument   [275]
    That scarcely had I finally resign'd
    My rights among those academic Bowers
    When Thou wert thither guided. From the heart
    Of London, and from Cloisters there Thou cam'st,
290 And didst sit down in temperance and peace,   [280]
    A rigorous Student. What a stormy course
    Then follow'd. Oh! it is a pang that calls
    For utterance, to think how small a change
    Of circumstances might to Thee have spared
295 A world of pain, ripen'd ten thousand hopes   [285]
    For ever wither'd. Through this retrospect
    Of my own College life I still have had
    Thy after sojourn in the self-same place
    Present before my eyes; I have play'd with times,
300 (I speak of private business of the thought)
    And accidents as children do with cards,   [290]
    Or as a man, who, when his house is built,
    A frame lock'd up in wood and stone, doth still,
    In impotence of mind, by his fireside
305 Rebuild it to his liking. I have thought
    Of Thee, thy learning, gorgeous eloquence   [295]
    And all the strength and plumage of thy Youth,
    Thy subtle speculations, toils abstruse
    Among the Schoolmen, and platonic forms
310 Of wild ideal pageantry, shap'd out
    From things well-match'd, or ill, and words for things, [300]
    The self-created sustenance of a mind
    Debarr'd from Nature's living images,
    Compell'd to be a life unto itself,
315 And unrelentingly possess'd by thirst
    Of greatness, love, and beauty. Not alone,   [305]
    Ah! surely not in singleness of heart
    Should I have seen the light of evening fade
    Upon the silent Cam, if we had met,
320 Even at that early time; I needs must hope,
    Must feel, must trust, that my maturer age,   [310]

And temperature less willing to be mov'd,
My calmer habits and more steady voice
Would with an influence benign have sooth'd
325 Or chas'd away the airy wretchedness
That batten'd on thy youth. But thou hast trod,
In watchful meditation thou hast trod
A march of glory, which doth put to shame   [315]
These vain regrets; health suffers in thee; else
330 Such grief for thee would be the weakest thought
That ever harbour'd in the breast of man.

A passing word erewhile did lightly touch
On wanderings of my own; and now to these   [320]
My Poem leads me with an easier mind.
335 The employments of three winters when I wore
A student's gown have been already told,
Or shadow'd forth, as far as there is need.
When the third Summer brought its liberty
A Fellow Student and myself, he, too,
340 A Mountaineer, together sallied forth
And, Staff in hand, on foot pursu'd our way   [325]
Towards the distant Alps. An open slight
Of College cares and study was the scheme,
Nor entertain'd without concern for those
345 To whom my worldly interests were dear: [332]
But Nature then was sovereign in my heart,
And mighty forms seizing a youthful Fancy
Had given a charter to irregular hopes.   [335]
In any age, without an impulse sent
350 From work of Nations, and their goings-on,
I should have been possessed by like desire:
But 'twas a time when Europe was rejoiced,
France standing on the top of golden hours,   [340]
And human nature seeming born again.
355 Bound, as I said, to the Alps, it was our lot
To land at Calais on the very eve   [345]
Of that great federal Day; and there we saw,

94

In a mean City, and among a few,
How bright a face is worn when joy of one
360 Is joy of tens of millions. Southward thence
We took our way direct through Hamlets, Towns, [350]
Gaudy with reliques of that Festival,
Flowers left to wither on triumphal Arcs,
And window-Garlands. On the public roads,
365 And, once, three days successively, through paths
By which our toilsome journey was abridg'd, [355]
Among sequester'd villages we walked,
And found benevolence and blessedness
Spread like a fragrance everywhere, like Spring
370 That leaves no corner of the Land untouch'd.
Where Elms, for many and many a league, in files, [360]
With their thin umbrage, on the stately roads
Of that great Kingdom, rustled o'er our heads,
For ever near us as we paced along,
375 'Twas sweet at such a time, with such delights
On every side, in prime of youthful strength, [365]
To feed a Poet's tender melancholy
And fond conceit of sadness, to the noise
And gentle undulations which they made.
380 Unhous'd, beneath the Evening Star we saw [370]
Dances of Liberty, and, in late hours
Of darkness, dances in the open air.
Among the vine-clad Hills of Burgundy, [375]
Upon the bosom of the gentle Soane
385 We glided forward with the flowing stream:
Swift Rhone, thou wert the wings on which we cut
Between thy lofty rocks! Enchanting show [380]
Those woods, and farms, and orchards did present,
And single Cottages, and lurking Towns,
390 Reach after reach, procession without end
Of deep and stately Vales. A lonely Pair
Of Englishmen we were, and sail'd along [385]
Cluster'd together with a merry crowd
Of those emancipated, with a host

395   Of Travellers, chiefly Delegates, returning
      From the great Spousals newly solemniz'd
      At their chief City in the sight of Heaven.   [390]
      Like bees they swarm'd, gaudy and gay as bees;
      Some vapour'd in the unruliness of joy
400   And flourish'd with their swords, as if to fight
      The saucy air. In this blithe Company
      We landed, took with them our evening Meal,   [395]
      Guests welcome almost as the Angels were
      To Abraham of old. The Supper done,
405   With flowing cups elate, and happy thoughts,
      We rose at signal given, and form'd a ring
      And, hand in hand, danced round and round the [400]
          Board;
      All hearts were open, every tongue was loud
      With amity and glee; we bore a name
410   Honour'd in France, the name of Englishmen,
      And hospitably did they give us Hail
      As their forerunners in a glorious course,   [405]
      And round, and round the board they danced again.
      With this same Throng our voyage we pursu'd
415   At early dawn; the Monastery Bells
      Made a sweet jingling in our youthful ears;
      The rapid River flowing without noise,   [410]
      And every Spire we saw among the rocks
      Spake with a sense of peace, at intervals
420   Touching the heart amid the boisterous Crew   [413]
      With which we were environ'd. Having parted
      From this glad Rout, the Convent of Chartreuse
      Received us two days afterwards, and there
      We rested in an awful Solitude;   [419]
425   Thence onward to the Country of the Swiss.

     'Tis not my present purpose to retrace
      That variegated journey step by step: [490]
      A march it was of military speed,
      And earth did change her images and forms

430 Before us, fast as clouds are chang'd in Heaven.
  Day after day, up early and down late,
  From vale to vale, from hill to hill we went   [495]
  From Province on to Province did we pass,
  Keen Hunters in a chace of fourteen weeks
435 Eager as birds of prey, or as a Ship
  Upon the stretch when winds are blowing fair.
  Sweet coverts did we cross of pastoral life,   [500]
  Enticing Vallies, greeted them, and left
  Too soon, while yet the very flash and gleam
440 Of salutation were not pass'd away.
  Oh! sorrow for the Youth who could have seen
  Unchasten'd, unsubdu'd, unaw'd, unrais'd   [505]
  To patriarchal dignity of mind,
  And pure simplicity of wish and will,
445 Those sanctified abodes of peaceful Man.
  My heart leap'd up when first I did look down
  On that which was first seen of those deep haunts,
  A green recess, an aboriginal vale
  Quiet, and lorded over and possess'd   [520]
450 By naked huts, wood-built, and sown like tents
  Or Indian cabins over the fresh lawns,
  And by the river side. That day we first
  Beheld the summit of Mont Blanc, and griev'd   [525]
  To have a soulless image on the eye
455 Which had usurp'd upon a living thought
  That never more could be: the wondrous Vale
  Of Chamouny did, on the following dawn,
  With its dumb cataracts and streams of ice,   [530]
  A motionless array of mighty waves,
460 Five rivers broad and vast, make rich amends,
  And reconcil'd us to realities.
  There small birds warble from the leafy trees,
  The Eagle soareth in the element;   [535]
  There doth the Reaper bind the yellow sheaf,
465 The Maiden spread the haycock in the sun,
  While Winter like a tamed Lion walks

Descending from the mountain to make sport
Among the cottages by beds of flowers.   [540]

    Whate'er in this wide circuit we beheld,
470 Or heard, was fitted to our unripe state
Of intellect and heart. By simple strains
Of feeling, the pure breath of real life,
We were not left untouch'd. With such a book
Before our eyes, we could not chuse but read
475 A frequent lesson of sound tenderness,   [545]
The universal reason of mankind,
The truth of Young and Old. Nor, side by side
Pacing, two brother Pilgrims, or alone
Each with his humour, could we fail to abound
480 (Craft this which hath been hinted at before)
In dreams and fictions pensively compos'd,   [550]
Dejection taken up for pleasure's sake,
And gilded sympathies; the willow wreath,
Even among those solitudes sublime,
485 And sober posies of funereal flowers,
Cull'd from the gardens of the Lady Sorrow,   [555]
Did sweeten many a meditative hour.

    Yet still in me, mingling with these delights
Was something of stern mood, an under-thirst
490 Of vigour, never utterly asleep.   [559]
Far different dejection once was mine,
A deep and genuine sadness then I felt;
The circumstances I will here relate
Even as they were. Upturning with a Band
495 Of Travellers, from the Valais we had clomb
Along the road that leads to Italy;
A length of hours, making of these our Guides
Did we advance, and having reach'd an Inn
Among the mountains, we together ate
500 Our noon's repast, from which the Travellers rose,

Leaving us at the Board. Ere long we follow'd,
Descending by the beaten road that led
Right to a rivulet's edge, and there broke off.
The only track now visible was one   [570]
505 Upon the further side, right opposite,
And up a lofty Mountain. This we took
After a little scruple, and short pause,
And climb'd with eagerness, though not, at length   [575]
Without surprise, and some anxiety
510 On finding that we did not overtake
Our Comrades gone before. By fortunate chance,
While every moment now encreas'd our doubts,
A Peasant met us, and from him we learn'd
That to the place which had perplex'd us first   [580]
515 We must descend, and there should find the road
Which in the stony channel of the Stream
Lay a few steps, and then along its Banks;
And further, that thenceforward all our course
Was downwards, with the current of that Stream.   [585]
520 Hard of belief, we question'd him again,
And all the answers which the Man return'd
To our inquiries, in their sense and substance,
Translated by the feelings which we had   [590]
Ended in this; that we had cross'd the Alps.

525   Imagination! lifting up itself
Before the eye and progress of my Song
Like an unfather'd vapour; here that Power,
In all the might of its endowments, came
Athwart me; I was lost as in a cloud,
530 Halted, without a struggle to break through.   [597]
And now recovering, to my Soul I say
I recognise thy glory; in such strength
Of usurpation, in such visitings
Of awful promise, when the light of sense   [600]
535 Goes out in flashes that have shewn to us
The invisible world, doth Greatness make abode,

There harbours whether we be young or old.
Our destiny, our nature, and our home
Is with infinitude, and only there;   [605]
540   With hope it is, hope that can never die,
Effort, and expectation, and desire,
And something evermore about to be.
The mind beneath such banners militant
Thinks not of spoils or trophies, nor of aught   [610]
545   That may attest its prowess, blest in thoughts
That are their own perfection and reward,
Strong in itself, and in the access of joy
Which hides it like the overflowing Nile.

     The dull and heavy slackening that ensued   [617]
550   Upon those tidings by the Peasant given
Was soon dislodg'd; downwards we hurried fast,
And enter'd with the road which we had miss'd   [620]
Into a narrow chasm; the brook and road
Were fellow-travellers in this gloomy Pass,
555   And with them did we journey several hours
At a slow step. The immeasurable height
Of woods decaying, never to be decay'd,   [625]
The stationary blasts of water-falls,
And every where along the hollow rent
560   Winds thwarting winds, bewilder'd and forlorn,
The torrents shooting from the clear blue sky,
The rocks that mutter'd close upon our ears,   [630]
Black drizzling crags that spake by the way-side
As if a voice were in them, the sick sight
565   And giddy prospect of the raving stream,
The unfetter'd clouds, and region of the heavens,
Tumult and peace, the darkness and the light   [635]
Were all like workings of one mind, the features
Of the same face, blossoms upon one tree,
570   Characters of the great Apocalypse,
The types and symbols of Eternity,
Of first and last, and midst, and without end.   [640]

That night our lodging was an Alpine House,
An Inn, or Hospital, as they are named,
575 Standing in that same valley by itself,
And close upon the confluence of two Streams;
A dreary Mansion, large beyond all need, [645]
With high and spacious rooms, deafen'd and stunn'd
By noise of waters, making innocent Sleep
580 Lie melancholy among weary bones.

Upris'n betimes, our journey we renew'd,
Led by the Stream, ere noon-day magnified [650]
Into a lordly River, broad and deep,
Dimpling along in silent majesty,
585 With mountains for its neighbours, and in view
Of distant mountains and their snowy tops,
And thus proceeding to Locarno's Lake, [655]
Fit resting-place for such a Visitant.
—Locarno, spreading out in width like Heaven,
590 And Como, thou, a treasure by the earth [660]
Kept to itself, a darling bosom'd up
In Abyssinian privacy, I spake
Of thee, thy chestnut woods, and garden plots
Of Indian corn tended by dark-eyed Maids,
595 Thy lofty steeps, and pathways roof'd with vines [665]
Winding from house to house, from town to town,
Sole link that binds them to each other, walks
League after league, and cloistral avenues
Where silence is, if music be not there:
600 While yet a Youth, undisciplin'd in Verse, [670]
Through fond ambition of my heart, I told
Your praises; nor can I approach you now
Ungreeted by a more melodious Song,
Where tones of learned Art and Nature mix'd
605 May frame enduring language. Like a breeze [675]
Or sunbeam over your domain I pass'd
In motion without pause; but Ye have left
Your beauty with me, an impassion'd sight

Of colours and of forms, whose power is sweet [680]
610 And gracious, almost might I dare to say,
As virtue is, or goodness, sweet as love
Or the remembrance of a noble deed,
Or gentlest visitations of pure thought
When God, the Giver of all joy, is thank'd
615 Religiously, in silent blessedness, [686]
Sweet as this last herself; for such it is.

Through those delightful pathways we advanc'd,
Two days, and still in presence of the Lake,
Which, winding up among the Alps, now chang'd [690]
620 Slowly its lovely countenance, and put on
A sterner character. The second night
(In eagerness, and by report misled
Of those Italian Clocks that speak the time
In fashion different from ours) we rose
625 By moonshine, doubting not that day was near, [695]
And that, meanwhile, coasting the Water's edge
As hitherto, and with as plain a track
To be our guide, we might behold the scene
In its most deep repose.—We left the Town
630 Of Gravedona with this hope; but soon [700]
Were lost, bewilder'd among woods immense,
Where, having wander'd for a while, we stopp'd
And on a rock sate down, to wait for day.
An open place it was, and overlook'd,
635 From high, the sullen water underneath,
On which a dull red image of the moon [705]
Lay bedded, changing oftentimes its form
Like an uneasy snake: long time we sate,
For scarcely more than one hour of the night.
640 Such was our error, had been gone, when we
Renew'd our journey. On the rock we lay
And wish'd to sleep but could not, for the stings [711]
Of insects, which with noise like that of noon
Fill'd all the woods; the cry of unknown birds,

645 The mountains, more by darkness visible
    And their own size, than any outward light,   [715]
    The breathless wilderness of clouds, the clock
    That told with unintelligible voice
    The widely-parted hours, the noise of streams
650 And sometimes rustling motions nigh at hand
    Which did not leave us free from personal fear,   [720]
    And lastly the withdrawing Moon, that set
    Before us, while she still was high in heaven,
    These were our food, and such a summer's night
655 Did to that pair of golden days succeed,
    With now and then a doze and snatch of sleep,
    On Como's Banks, the same delicious Lake.   [725]

        But here I must break off, and quit at once,   [727]
    Though loth, the record of these wanderings,
660 A theme which may seduce me else beyond
    All reasonable bounds. Let this alone
    Be mention'd as a parting word, that not
    In hollow exultation, dealing forth
    Hyperboles of praise comparative,
665 Not rich one moment to be poor for ever,   [735]
    Not prostrate, overborn, as if the mind
    Itself were nothing, a mean pensioner
    On outward forms, did we in presence stand
    Of that magnificent region. On the front
670 Of this whole Song is written that my heart   [740]
    Must in such temple needs have offer'd up
    A different worship. Finally whate'er
    I saw, or heard, or felt, was but a stream
    That flow'd into a kindred stream, a gale   [744]
675 That help'd me forwards, did administer
    To grandeur and to tenderness, to the one
    Directly, but to tender thoughts by means
    Less often instantaneous in effect;   [750]
    Conducted me to these along a path
680 Which in the main was more circuitous.

Oh! most beloved Friend, a glorious time
A happy time that was; triumphant looks   [755]
Were then the common language of all eyes:
As if awak'd from sleep, the Nations hail'd
685 Their great expectancy: the fife of War
Was then a spirit-stirring sound indeed,
A blackbird's whistle in a vernal grove.   [760]
We left the Swiss exulting in the fate
Of their near Neighbours, and when shortening fast
690 Our pilgrimage, nor distant far from home,
We cross'd the Brabant Armies on the fret
For battle in the cause of Liberty.   [765]
A Stripling, scarcely of the household then
Of social life, I look'd upon these things
695 As from a distance, heard, and saw, and felt,
Was touch'd, but with no intimate concern;
I seem'd to move among them as a bird   [770]
Moves through the air, or as a fish pursues
Its business, in its proper element;
700 I needed not that joy, I did not need
Such help; the ever-living Universe,   [774]
And independent spirit of pure youth
Were with me at that season, and delight
Was in all places spread around my steps
705 As constant as the grass upon the fields.

BOOK SEVENTH

RESIDENCE IN LONDON

FIVE years are vanish'd since I first pour'd out
Saluted by that animating breeze
Which met me issuing from the City's Walls,
A glad preamble to this Verse: I sang
5   Aloud, in Dythyrambic fervour, deep   [5]
But short-liv'd uproar, like a torrent sent
Out of the bowels of a bursting cloud
Down Scawfell, or Blencathara's rugged sides,
A water-spout from Heaven. But 'twas not long
10 Ere the interrupted stream broke forth once more,
And flowed awhile in strength, then stopp'd for years; [10]
Not heard again until a little space
Before last primrose-time. Beloved Friend,
The assurances then given unto myself,
15 Which did beguile me of some heavy thoughts
At thy departure to a foreign Land,
Have fail'd; for slowly doth this work advance.   [15]
Through the whole summer have I been at rest,
Partly from voluntary holiday
20 And part through outward indolence. But I heard,
After the hour of sunset yester even,
Sitting within doors betwixt light and dark,   [20]
A voice that stirr'd me. 'Twas a little Band,
A Quire of Redbreasts gather'd somewhere near
25 My threshold, Minstrels from the distant woods
And dells, sent in by Winter to bespeak
For the Old Man a welcome, to announce,
With preparation artful and benign,
Yea the most gentle music of the year,
30 That their rough Lord had left the surly North   [25]
And hath begun his journey. A delight,
At this unthought of greeting, unawares

Smote me, a sweetness of the coming time,
And listening, I half whispered, 'We will be
35 Ye heartsome Choristers, ye and I will be
Brethren, and in the hearing of bleak winds [30]
Will chaunt together.' And, thereafter, walking
By later twilight on the hills, I saw
A Glow-worm from beneath a dusky shade
40 Or canopy of the yet unwithered fern,
Clear-shining, like a Hermit's taper seen [35]
Through a thick forest; silence touch'd me here
No less than sound had done before; the Child
Of Summer, lingering, shining by itself,
45 The voiceless Worm on the unfrequented hills,
Seem'd sent on the same errand with the Quire [40]
Of Winter that had warbled at my door,
And the whole year seem'd tenderness and love.

The last Night's genial feeling overflow'd
50 Upon this morning, and my favourite Grove,
Now tossing its dark boughs in sun and wind [45]
Spreads through me a commotion like its own,
Something that fits me for the Poet's task,
Which we will now resume with chearful hope,
55 Nor check'd by aught of tamer argument [50]
That lies before us, needful to be told.

Return'd from that excursion, soon I bade
Farewell for ever to the private Bowers
Of gownèd Students, quitted these, no more [54]
60 To enter them, and pitch'd my vagrant tent,
A casual dweller and at large, among
The unfenced regions of society.

Yet undetermined to what plan of life
I should adhere, and seeming thence to have
65 A little space of intermediate time [60]
Loose and at full command, to London first

I turn'd, if not in calmness, nevertheless
In no disturbance of excessive hope,
At ease from all ambition personal,
70 Frugal as there was need, and though self-will'd,   [64]
Yet temperate and reserv'd, and wholly free
From dangerous passions. 'Twas at least two years
Before this season when I first beheld
That mighty place, a transient visitant:
75 And now it pleas'd me my abode to fix   [69]
Single in the wide waste, to have a house
It was enough (what matter for a home?)
That own'd me; living chearfully abroad,
With fancy on the stir from day to day,   [75]
80 And all my young affections out of doors.

There was a time when whatsoe'er is feign'd
Of airy Palaces, and Gardens built
By Genii of Romance, or hath in grave
Authentic History been set forth of Rome,   [80]
85 Alcairo, Babylon, or Persepolis,
Or given upon report by Pilgrim-Friars
Of golden Cities ten months' journey deep
Among Tartarean Wilds, fell short, far short,
Of that which I in simpleness believed   [85]
90 And thought of London; held me by a chain
Less strong of wonder, and obscure delight.
I know not that herein I shot beyond
The common mark of childhood; but I well
Remember that among our flock of Boys   [90]
95 Was one, a Cripple from his birth, whom chance
Summon'd from School to London, fortunate
And envied Traveller! and when he return'd,
After short absence, and I first set eyes
Upon his person, verily, though strange
100 The thing may seem, I was not wholly free   [95]
From disappointment to behold the same
Appearance, the same body, not to find

Some change, some beams of glory brought away
From that new region. Much I question'd him,
105 And every word he utter'd, on my ears
Fell flatter than a cagèd Parrot's note,   [100]
That answers unexpectedly awry,
And mocks the Prompter's listening. Marvellous things
My fancy had shap'd forth, of sights and shows,
110 Processions, Equipages, Lords and Dukes,
The King, and the King's Palace, and not last
Or least, heaven bless him! the renown'd Lord Mayor:
Dreams hardly less intense than those which wrought
A change of purpose in young Whittington,
115 When he in friendlessness, a drooping Boy,
Sate on a Stone, and heard the Bells speak out
Articulate music. Above all, one thought   [115]
Baffled my understanding, how men lived
Even next-door neighbours, as we say, yet still
120 Strangers, and knowing not each other's names.

Oh wond'rous power of words, how sweet they are
According to the meaning which they bring!   [120]
Vauxhall and Ranelagh, I then had heard
Of your green groves, and wilderness of lamps,
125 Your gorgeous Ladies, fairy cataracts,   [124]
And pageant fireworks; nor must we forget
Those other wonders different in kind,
Though scarcely less illustrious in degree,
The River proudly bridged, the giddy Top
130 And whispering Gallery of St. Paul's, the Tombs   [130]
Of Westminster, the Giants of Guildhall,
Bedlam, and the two figures at its Gates,
Streets without end, and Churches numberless,
Statues, with flowery gardens in vast Squares,   [135]
135 The Monument, and Armoury of the Tower.

These fond imaginations of themselves   [142]
Had long before given way in season due,

Leaving a throng of others in their stead;
And now I look'd upon the real scene,
140 Familiarly perused it day by day   [145]
With keen and lively pleasure even there
Where disappointment was the strongest, pleased
Through courteous self-submission, as a tax
Paid to the object by prescriptive right,   [148]
145 A thing that ought to be. Shall I give way,
Copying the impression of the memory,
Though things remembered idly do half seem
The work of Fancy, shall I, as the mood
Inclines me, here describe, for pastime's sake
150 Some portion of that motley imagery,
A vivid pleasure of my youth, and now
Among the lonely places that I love
A frequent day-dream for my riper mind?
—And first the look and aspect of the place
155 The broad high-way appearance, as it strikes
On Strangers of all ages, the quick dance
Of colours, lights and forms, the Babel din   [155]
The endless stream of men, and moving things,
From hour to hour the illimitable walk
160 Still among streets with clouds and sky above,
The wealth, the bustle and the eagerness,
The glittering Chariots with their pamper'd Steeds,
Stalls, Barrows, Porters; midway in the Street
The Scavenger, who begs with hat in hand,
165 The labouring Hackney Coaches, the rash speed
Of Coaches travelling far, whirl'd on with horn
Loud blowing, and the sturdy Drayman's Team,
Ascending from some Alley of the Thames
And striking right across the crowded Strand
170 Till the fore Horse veer round with punctual skill:
Here there and everywhere a weary throng
The Comers and the Goers face to face,   [156]
Face after face; the string of dazzling Wares,
Shop after shop, with Symbols, blazon'd Names,

175 And all the Tradesman's honours overhead;
Here, fronts of houses, like a title-page   [160]
With letters huge inscribed from top to toe;
Station'd above the door, like guardian Saints,
There, allegoric shapes, female or male;
180 Or physiognomies of real men,
Land-Warriors, Kings, or Admirals of the Sea,   [165]
Boyle, Shakspear, Newton, or the attractive head
Of some Scotch doctor, famous in his day.

Meanwhile the roar continues, till at length,
185 Escaped as from an enemy, we turn
Abruptly into some sequester'd nook   [170]
Still as a shelter'd place when winds blow loud:
At leisure thence, through tracts of thin resort,
And sights and sounds that come at intervals,
190 We take our way: a raree-show is here
With Children gather'd round, another Street   [175]
Presents a company of dancing Dogs,
Or Dromedary, with an antic pair
Of Monkies on his back, a minstrel Band
195 Of Savoyards, or, single and alone,
An English Ballad-singer. Private Courts,   [180]
Gloomy as Coffins, and unsightly Lanes
Thrill'd by some female Vender's scream, belike
The very shrillest of all London Cries,
200 May then entangle us awhile,
Conducted through those labyrinths unawares   [185]
To privileg'd Regions and inviolate,
Where from their airy lodges studious Lawyers
Look out on waters, walks, and gardens green.

205 Thence back into the throng, until we reach,
Following the tide that slackens by degrees,   [190]
Some half-frequented scene where wider Streets
Bring straggling breezes of suburban air;
Here files of ballads dangle from dead walls,
210 Advertisements of giant-size, from high

Press forward in all colours on the sight; [195]
These, bold in conscious merit; lower down
That, fronted with a most imposing word,
Is, peradventure, one in masquerade.
215 As on the broadening Causeway we advance,
Behold a Face turn'd up toward us, strong [200]
In lineaments, and red with over-toil;
'Tis one perhaps, already met elsewhere,
A travelling Cripple, by the trunk cut short,
220 And stumping with his arms: in Sailor's garb
Another lies at length beside a range [205]
Of written characters, with chalk inscrib'd
Upon the smooth flat stones: the Nurse is here,
The Bachelor that loves to sun himself,
225 The military Idler, and the Dame,
That field-ward takes her walk in decency. [210]

Now homeward through the thickening hubbub, where
See, among less distinguishable shapes,
The Italian, with his Frame of Images [215]
230 Upon his head; with Basket at his waist
The Jew; the stately and slow-moving Turk
With freight of slippers piled beneath his arm.
Briefly, we find, if tired of random sights
And haply to that search our thoughts should turn,
235 Among the crowd, conspicuous less or more, [221]
As we proceed, all specimens of man
Through all the colours which the sun bestows,
And every character of form and face,
The Swede, the Russian; from the genial South,
240 The Frenchman and the Spaniard; from remote [225]
America, the Hunter-Indian; Moors,
Malays, Lascars, the Tartar and Chinese,
And Negro Ladies in white muslin gowns.

At leisure let us view, from day to day,
245 As they present themselves, the Spectacles
Within doors, troops of wild Beasts, birds and beasts [230]

    Of every nature, from all climes convened;
    And, next to these, those mimic sights that ape
    The absolute presence of reality,
250 Expressing, as in mirror, sea and land,
    And what earth is, and what she has to shew;   [235]
    I do not here allude to subtlest craft,
    By means refin'd attaining purest ends,
    But imitations fondly made in plain
255 Confession of man's weakness, and his loves.
    Whether the Painter fashioning a work   [240]
    To Nature's circumambient scenery,
    And with his greedy pencil taking in
    A whole horizon on all sides, with power,
260 Like that of Angels or commission'd Spirits,
    Plant us upon some lofty Pinnacle,
    Or in a Ship on Waters, with a world   [245]
    Of life, and life-like mockery, to East,
    To West, beneath, behind us, and before:
265 Or more mechanic Artist represent
    By scale exact, in Model, wood or clay,
    From shading colours also borrowing help,   [250]
    Some miniature of famous spots and things
    Domestic, or the boast of foreign Realms;
270 The Firth of Forth, and Edinburgh throned
    On crags, fit empress of that mountain Land;
    St. Peter's Church; or, more aspiring aim,
    In microscopic vision, Rome itself;
    Or, else perhaps, some rural haunt, the Falls
275 Of Tivoli,
    And high upon the steep, that mouldering Fane   [255]
    The Temple of the Sibyl, every tree
    Through all the landscape, tuft, stone, scratch minute,
    And every Cottage, lurking in the rocks,
280 All that the Traveller sees when he is there.

    Add to these exhibitions mute and still   [260]
    Others of wider scope, where living men,

Music, and shifting pantomimic scenes,
Together join'd their multifarious aid
285 To heighten the allurement. Need I fear
To mention by its name, as in degree
Lowest of these, and humblest in attempt,   [265]
Though richly graced with honours of its own,
Half-rural Sadler's Wells? Though at that time
290 Intolerant, as is the way of Youth
Unless itself be pleased, I more than once
Here took my seat, and, maugre frequent fits   [270]
Of irksomeness, with ample recompense
Saw Singers, Rope-dancers, Giants and Dwarfs,
295 Clowns, Conjurors, Posture-masters, Harlequins,
Amid the uproar of the rabblement,
Perform their feats. Nor was it mean delight
To watch crude nature work in untaught minds,   [275]
To note the laws and progress of belief;
300 Though obstinate on this way, yet on that
How willingly we travel, and how far!
To have, for instance, brought upon the scene
The Champion Jack the Giant-killer, Lo!
He dons his Coat of Darkness; on the Stage   [281]
305 Walks, and atchieves his wonders from the eye
Of living mortal safe as is the moon
'Hid in her vacant interlunar cave'.
Delusion bold! and faith must needs be coy;   [285]
How is it wrought? His garb is black, the word
310 INVISIBLE flames forth upon his chest.

Nor was it unamusing here to view
Those samples as of ancient Comedy
And Thespian times, dramas of living Men,
And recent things, yet warm with life; a Sea-fight,
315 Shipwreck, or some domestic incident
The fame of which is scatter'd through the Land;
Such as this daring brotherhood of late
Set forth, too holy theme for such a place,   [295]

And doubtless treated with irreverence
320 Albeit with their very best of skill,
I mean, O distant Friend! a Story drawn
From our own ground, the Maid of Buttermere,
And how the Spoiler came, 'a bold bad Man'
To God unfaithful, Children, Wife, and Home,
325 And wooed the artless Daughter of the hills,   [300]
And wedded her, in cruel mockery
Of love and marriage bonds. O Friend! I speak
With tender recollection of that time
When first we saw the Maiden, then a name
330 By us unheard of; in her cottage Inn   [305]
Were welcomed, and attended on by her,
Both stricken with one feeling of delight,
An admiration of her modest mien,
And carriage, mark'd by unexampled grace.
335 Not unfamiliarly we since that time
Have seen her; her discretion have observ'd,   [310]
Her just opinions, female modesty,
Her patience, and retiredness of mind
Unsoil'd by commendation, and the excess
340 Of public notice. This memorial Verse
Comes from the Poet's heart, and is her due.
For we were nursed, as almost might be said,
On the same mountains; Children at one time
Must haply often on the self-same day
345 Have from our several dwellings gone abroad
To gather daffodils on Coker's Stream.

These last words utter'd, to my argument
I was returning, when, with sundry Forms
Mingled, that in the way which I must tread
350 Before me stand, thy image rose again,
Mary of Buttermere! She lives in peace   [320]
Upon the ground where she was born and rear'd;
Without contamination does she live
In quietness, without anxiety:

114

355   Beside the mountain-Chapel sleeps in earth
      Her new-born Infant, fearless as a lamb   [325]
      That thither comes, from some unsheltered place,
      To rest beneath the little rock-like Pile
      When storms are blowing. Happy are they both
360   Mother and Child! These feelings, in themselves
      Trite, do yet scarcely seem so when I think   [330]
      Of those ingenuous moments of our youth,
      Ere yet by use we have learn'd to slight the crime
      And sorrows of the world. Those days are now
365   My theme; and, mid the numerous scenes which they [334]
      Have left behind them, foremost I am cross'd
      Here by remembrance of two figures, One
      A rosy Babe, who, for a twelvemonth's space
      Perhaps, had been of age to deal about
370   Articulate prattle, Child as beautiful
      As ever sate upon a Mother's knee;
      The other was the Parent of that Babe;
      But on the Mother's cheek the tints were false,
      A painted bloom. 'Twas at a Theatre
375   That I beheld this Pair; the Boy had been
      The pride and pleasure of all lookers-on
      In whatsoever place; but seem'd in this
      A sort of Alien scatter'd from the clouds.   [350]
      Of lusty vigour, more than infantine,
380   He was in limbs, in face a Cottage rose
      Just three parts blown; a Cottage Child, but ne'er
      Saw I, by Cottage or elsewhere, a Babe   [355]
      By Nature's gifts so honor'd. Upon a Board
      Whence an attendant of the Theatre
385   Serv'd out refreshments, had this Child been placed,
      And there he sate, environ'd with a Ring
      Of chance Spectators, chiefly dissolute men   [360]
      And shameless women; treated and caress'd,
      Ate, drank, and with the fruit and glasses play'd,
390   While oaths, indecent speech, and ribaldry
      Were rife about him as are songs of birds

In spring-time after showers. The Mother, too,　　　[365]
Was present! but of her I know no more
Than hath been said, and scarcely at this time
395　Do I remember her. But I behold
The lovely Boy as I beheld him then,
Among the wretched and the falsely gay,
Like one of those who walk'd with hair unsinged
Amid the fiery furnace. He hath since　　　　　[370]
400　Appear'd to me oft times as if embalm'd
By Nature; through some special privilege,　　　[375]
Stopp'd at the growth he had; destined to live,
To be, to have been, come and go, a Child
And nothing more, no partner in the years
405　That bear us forward to distress and guilt,
Pain and abasement, beauty in such excess
Adorn'd him in that miserable place.
So have I thought of him a thousand times,
And seldom otherwise. But he perhaps
410　Mary! may now have liv'd till he could look
With envy on thy nameless Babe that sleeps　　　[380]
Beside the mountain Chapel, undisturb'd!

It was but little more than three short years
Before the season which I speak of now
415　When first, a Traveller from our pastoral hills,
Southward two hundred miles I had advanced,
And for the first time in my life did hear
The voice of Woman utter blasphemy;　　　　[385]
Saw Woman as she is to open shame
420　Abandon'd and the pride of public vice.
Full surely from the bottom of my heart
I shuddered; but the pain was almost lost,
Absorb'd and buried in the immensity
Of the effect: a barrier seemed at once
425　Thrown in, that from humanity divorced
The human Form, splitting the race of Man　　　[390]
In twain, yet leaving the same outward shape.

Distress of mind ensued upon this sight
And ardent meditation; afterwards
430 A milder sadness on such spectacles
Attended; thought, commiseration, grief [395]
For the individual, and the overthrow
Of her soul's beauty; farther at that time
Than this I was but seldom led; in truth
435 The sorrow of the passion stopp'd me here.

I quit this painful theme; enough is said [400]
To shew what thoughts must often have been mine
At theatres, which then were my delight,
A yearning made more strong by obstacles
440 Which slender funds imposed. Life then was new,
The senses easily pleased; the lustres, lights,
The carving and the gilding, paint and glare,
And all the mean upholstery of the place,
Wanted not animation in my sight: [410]
445 Far less the living Figures on the Stage,
Solemn or gay: whether some beauteous Dame
Advanced in radiance through a deep recess
Of thick-entangled forest, like the Moon [415]
Opening the clouds; or sovereign King, announced
450 With flourishing Trumpets, came in full-blown State
Of the world's greatness, winding round with Train
Of Courtiers, Banners, and a length of Guards;
Or Captive led in abject weeds, and jingling [420]
His slender manacles; or romping Girl
455 Bounced, leapt, and paw'd the air; or mumbling Sire,
A scare-crow pattern of old Age, patch'd up
Of all the tatters of infirmity,
All loosely put together, hobbled in, [425]
Stumping upon a Cane, with which he smites,
460 From time to time, the solid boards, and makes them
Prate somewhat loudly of the whereabout
Of one so overloaded with his years.
But what of this! the laugh, the grin, grimace, [430]

And all the antics and buffoonery,
465 The least of them not lost, were all received
With charitable pleasure. Through the night,
Between the show, and many-headed mass
Of the Spectators, and each little nook   [435]
That had its fray or brawl, how eagerly,
470 And with what flashes, as it were, the mind
Turn'd this way, that way! sportive and alert
And watchful, as a kitten when at play,
While winds are blowing round her, among grass   [440]
And rustling leaves. Enchanting age and sweet!
475 Romantic almost, looked at through a space,
How small of intervening years! For then,
Though surely no mean progress had been made
In meditations holy and sublime,   [445]
Yet something of a girlish child-like gloss
480 Of novelty surviv'd for scenes like these;
Pleasure that had been handed down from times
When, at a Country-Playhouse, having caught,   [449]
In summer, through the fractured wall, a glimpse
Of daylight, at the thought of where I was
485 I gladden'd more than if I had beheld
Before me some bright cavern of Romance,   [455]
Or than we do, when on our beds we lie
At night, in warmth, when rains are beating hard.

The matter that detains me now will seem,
490 To many neither dignified enough
Nor arduous; and is, doubtless, in itself   [460]
Humble and low; yet not to be despised
By those who have observed the curious props
By which the perishable hours of life
495 Rest on each other, and the world of thought
Exists and is sustain'd. More lofty Themes,   [465]
Such as, at least, do wear a prouder face,
Might here be spoken of; but when I think
Of these, I feel the imaginative Power

118

500 Languish within me; even then it slept
 When, wrought upon by tragic sufferings,   [470]
 The heart was full; amid my sobs and tears
 It slept, even in the season of my youth:
 For though I was most passionately moved
505 And yielded to the changes of the scene
 With most obsequious feeling, yet all this   [475]
 Pass'd not beyond the suburbs of the mind:
 If aught there were of real grandeur here
 'Twas only then when gross realities,
510 The incarnation of the Spirits that mov'd
 Amid the Poet's beauteous world, call'd forth,   [480]
 With that distinctness which a contrast gives
 Or opposition, made me recognize
 As by a glimpse, the things which I had shaped
515 And yet not shaped, had seen, and scarcely seen,
 Had felt, and thought of in my solitude.   [485]

 Pass we from entertainments that are such
 Professedly to others titled higher,
 Yet in the estimate of Youth at least,
520 More near akin to those than names imply,
 I mean the brawls of Lawyers in their Courts   [490]
 Before the ermined Judge, or that great Stage
 Where Senators, tongue-favor'd Men, perform,
 Admired and envied. Oh! the beating heart!
525 When one among the prime of these rose up,
 One, of whose name from Childhood we had heard   [495]
 Familiarly, a household term, like those,
 The Bedfords, Glocesters, Salisburys of old,
 Which the fifth Harry talks of. Silence! hush!
530 This is no trifler, no short-flighted Wit,
 No stammerer of a minute, painfully   [500]
 Deliver'd. No! the Orator hath yoked
 The Hours, like young Aurora, to his Car;
 O Presence of delight, can patience e'er
535 Grow weary of attending on a track

That kindles with such glory? Marvellous!   [505]
The enchantment spreads and rises; all are rapt
Astonish'd; like a Hero in Romance
He winds away his never-ending horn,
540 Words follow words, sense seems to follow sense;
What memory and what logic! till the Strain
Transcendent, superhuman as it is,   [510]
Grows tedious even in a young man's ear.

These are grave follies: other public Shows
545 The capital City teems with, of a kind
More light, and where but in the holy Church?
There have I seen a comely Bachelor,   [551]
Fresh from a toilette of two hours, ascend
The Pulpit, with seraphic glance look up,
550 And, in a tone elaborately low
Beginning, lead his voice through many a maze,   [555]
A minuet course, and winding up his mouth,
From time to time into an orifice
Most delicate, a lurking eyelet, small
555 And only not invisible, again
Open it out, diffusing thence a smile   [560]
Of rapt irradiation exquisite.
Meanwhile the Evangelists, Isaiah, Job,
Moses, and he who penn'd the other day
560 The Death of Abel, Shakspear, Doctor Young,
And Ossian, (doubt not, 'tis the naked truth)
Summon'd from streamy Morven, each and all
Must in their turn lend ornament and flowers
To entwine the Crook of eloquence with which   [570]
565 This pretty Shepherd, pride of all the Plains,
Leads up and down his captivated Flock.

I glance but at a few conspicuous marks,
Leaving ten thousand others, that do each,
In Hall or Court, Conventicle, or Shop,   [575]
570 In public Room or private, Park or Street,

With fondness rear'd on his own Pedestal,
Look out for admiration. Folly, vice,
Extravagance in gesture, mien, and dress,
And all the strife of singularity, [580]
575 Lies to the ear, and lies to every sense,
Of these, and of the living shapes they wear,
There is no end. Such Candidates for regard,
Although well pleased to be where they were found,
I did not hunt after, or greatly prize, [585]
580 Nor made unto myself a secret boast
Of reading them with quick and curious eye;
But as a common produce, things that are
To-day, to-morrow will be, took of them
Such willing note as, on some errand bound [590]
585 Of pleasure or of Love some Traveller might,
Among a thousand other images,
Of sea-shells that bestud the sandy beach,
Or daisies swarming through the fields in June.

But foolishness, and madness in parade,
590 Though most at home in this their dear domain, [595]
Are scatter'd everywhere, no rarities,
Even to the rudest novice of the Schools. [597]
O Friend! one feeling was there which belong'd
To this great City, by exclusive right;
595 How often in the overflowing Streets, [626]
Have I gone forward with the Crowd, and said
Unto myself, the face of every one
That passes by me is a mystery.
Thus have I look'd, nor ceas'd to look, oppress'd [630]
600 By thoughts of what, and whither, when and how,
Until the shapes before my eyes became
A second-sight procession, such as glides
Over still mountains, or appears in dreams;
And all the ballast of familiar life,
605 The present, and the past; hope, fear; all stays,
All laws of acting, thinking, speaking man

Went from me, neither knowing me, nor known.
And once, far-travell'd in such mood, beyond   [635]
The reach of common indications, lost
610   Amid the moving pageant, 'twas my chance
Abruptly to be smitten with the view
Of a blind Beggar, who, with upright face,
Stood propp'd against a Wall, upon his Chest   [640]
Wearing a written paper, to explain
615   The story of the Man, and who he was.
My mind did at this spectacle turn round
As with the might of waters, and it seemed
To me that in this Label was a type,
Or emblem, of the utmost that we know,   [645]
620   Both of ourselves and of the universe;
And, on the shape of the unmoving man,
His fixèd face and sightless eyes, I look'd
As if admonish'd from another world.

Though rear'd upon the base of outward things,   [650]
625   These, chiefly, are such structures as the mind
Builds for itself. Scenes different there are,
Full-form'd, which take, with small internal help,
Possession of the faculties; the peace
Of night, for instance, the solemnity   [655]
630   Of nature's intermediate hours of rest,
When the great tide of human life stands still,
The business of the day to come unborn,
Of that gone by, lock'd up as in the grave;
The calmness, beauty, of the spectacle,   [660]
635   Sky, stillness, moonshine, empty streets, and sounds
Unfrequent as in desarts; at late hours
Of winter evenings when unwholesome rains
Are falling hard, with people yet astir,
The feeble salutation from the voice   [665]
640   Of some unhappy Woman, now and then
Heard as we pass; when no one looks about,
Nothing is listen'd to. But these, I fear,

Are falsely catalogu'd, things that are, are not,
Even as we give them welcome, or assist,   [670]
645 Are prompt, or are remiss. What say you then,
To times, when half the City shall break out
Full of one passion, vengeance, rage, or fear,
To executions, to a Street on fire,
Mobs, riots, or rejoicings? From these sights   [675]
650 Take one, an annual Festival, the Fair
Holden where Martyrs suffer'd in past time,
And named of Saint Bartholomew; there see
A work that's finish'd to our hands, that lays,
If any spectacle on earth can do,   [680]
655 The whole creative powers of man asleep!
For once the Muse's help will we implore,
And she shall lodge us, wafted on her wings,
Above the press and danger of the Crowd,
Upon some Showman's platform: what a hell   [685]
660 For eyes and ears! what anarchy and din
Barbarian and infernal! 'tis a dream,
Monstrous in colour, motion, shape, sight, sound.
Below, the open space, through every nook
Of the wide area, twinkles, is alive   [690]
665 With heads; the midway region and above
Is throng'd with staring pictures, and huge scrolls,
Dumb proclamations of the prodigies;
And chattering monkeys dangling from their poles,
And children whirling in their roundabouts;   [695]
670 With those that stretch the neck, and strain the eyes,
And crack the voice in rivalship, the crowd
Inviting; with buffoons against buffoons
Grimacing, writhing, screaming; him who grinds
The hurdy-gurdy, at the fiddle weaves;   [700]
675 Rattles the salt-box, thumps the kettle-drum,
And him who at the trumpet puffs his cheeks,
The silver-collar'd Negro with his timbrel,
Equestrians, Tumblers, Women, Girls, and Boys,
Blue-breech'd, pink-vested, and with towering plumes.

123

680 —All moveables of wonder from all parts,   [706]
Are here, Albinos, painted Indians, Dwarfs,
The Horse of Knowledge, and the learned Pig,
The Stone-eater, the Man that swallows fire,
Giants, Ventriloquists, the Invisible Girl,   [710]
685 The Bust that speaks, and moves its goggling eyes,
The Wax-work, Clock-work, all the marvellous craft
Of modern Merlins, wild Beasts, Puppet-shows,
All out-o'-th'-way, far-fetch'd, perverted things,
All freaks of Nature, all Promethean thoughts   [715]
690 Of man; his dulness, madness, and their feats,
All jumbled up together to make up
This Parliament of Monsters. Tents and Booths
Meanwhile, as if the whole were one vast Mill,
Are vomiting, receiving, on all sides,   [720]
695 Men, Women, three-years' Children, Babes in arms.

Oh, blank confusion! and a type not false
Of what the mighty City is itself
To all except a Straggler here and there,
To the whole swarm of its inhabitants;
700 An undistinguishable world to men,
The slaves unrespited of low pursuits,
Living amid the same perpetual flow   [725]
Of trivial objects, melted and reduced
To one identity, by differences
705 That have no law, no meaning, and no end;
Oppression under which even highest minds
Must labour, whence the strongest are not free;   [730]
But though the picture weary out the eye,
By nature an unmanageable sight,
710 It is not wholly so to him who looks
In steadiness, who hath among least things
An under-sense of greatest; sees the parts   [735]
As parts, but with a feeling of the whole.
This, of all acquisitions first, awaits
715 On sundry and most widely different modes

124

Of education; nor with least delight
On that through which I pass'd. Attention comes,   [740]
And comprehensiveness and memory,
From early converse with the works of God
720 Among all regions; chiefly where appear
Most obviously simplicity and power.   [744]
By influence habitual to the mind
The mountain's outline and its steady form
Gives a pure grandeur, and its presence shapes
725 The measure and the prospect of the soul   [755]
To majesty; such virtue have the forms
Perennial of the ancient hills; nor less
The changeful language of their countenances
Gives movement to the thoughts, and multitude,
730 With order and relation. This, if still,   [761]
As hitherto, with freedom I may speak,
And the same perfect openness of mind,
Not violating any just restraint,
As I would hope, of real modesty,
735 This did I feel in that vast receptacle.   [765]
The Spirit of Nature was upon me here;
The Soul of Beauty and enduring life
Was present as a habit, and diffused,
Through meagre lines and colours, and the press
740 Of self-destroying, transitory things   [770]
Composure and ennobling harmony.

BOOK EIGHTH

RETROSPECT.—LOVE OF NATURE LEADING TO LOVE OF MANKIND

WHAT sounds are those, Helvellyn, which are heard
Up to thy summit? Through the depth of air
Ascending, as if distance had the power
To make the sounds more audible: what Crowd
5 Is yon, assembled in the gay green Field?   [5]
Crowd seems it, solitary Hill! to thee,
Though but a little Family of Men,
Twice twenty, with their Children and their Wives,
And here and there a Stranger interspersed.   [10]
10 It is a summer festival, a Fair,
Such as, on this side now, and now on that,
Repeated through his tributary Vales,
Helvellyn, in the silence of his rest,
Sees annually, if storms be not abroad,   [15]
15 And mists have left him an unshrouded head.
Delightful day it is for all who dwell
In this secluded Glen, and eagerly
They give it welcome. Long ere heat of noon   [20]
Behold the cattle are driven down; the sheep
20 That have for traffic been cull'd out are penn'd
In cotes that stand together on the Plain
Ranged side by side; the chaffering is begun.
The Heifer lows uneasy at the voice
Of a new Master, bleat the Flocks aloud;
25 Booths are there none; a Stall or two is here,   [25]
A lame Man, or a blind, the one to beg,
The other to make music; hither, too,
From far, with Basket, slung upon her arm,
Of Hawker's Wares, books, pictures, combs, and pins,
30 Some aged Woman finds her way again,   [30]
Year after year a punctual visitant!

The Showman with his Freight upon his Back,
And once, perchance, in lapse of many years
Prouder Itinerant, Mountebank, or He   [35]
35   Whose Wonders in a cover'd Wain lie hid.
But One is here, the loveliest of them all,
Some sweet Lass of the Valley, looking out
For gains, and who that sees her would not buy?
Fruits of her Father's Orchard, apples, pears,   [40]
40   (On that day only to such office stooping)
She carries in her Basket, and walks round
Among the crowd, half pleas'd with, half ashamed
Of her new calling, blushing restlessly.
The Children now are rich, the Old Man now
45   Is generous; so gaiety prevails   [45]
Which all partake of, Young and Old. Immense   [55]
Is the Recess, the circumambient World
Magnificent, by which they are embraced.
They move about upon the soft green field:
50   How little They, they and their doings seem,
Their herds and flocks about them, they themselves,
And all that they can further or obstruct!   [60]
Through utter weakness pitiably dear
As tender Infants are: and yet how great!
55   For all things serve them; them the Morning light
Loves as it glistens on the silent rocks,
And them the silent Rocks, which now from high   [65]
Look down upon them; the reposing Clouds,
The lurking Brooks from their invisible haunts,
60   And Old Helvellyn, conscious of the stir,
And the blue Sky that roofs their calm abode.

With deep devotion, Nature, did I feel   [70]
In that great City what I owed to thee,
High thoughts of God and Man, and love of Man,
65   Triumphant over all those loathsome sights
Of wretchedness and vice; a watchful eye,
Which with the outside of our human life

127

Not satisfied, must read the inner mind;
For I already had been taught to love
70 My Fellow-beings, to such habits train'd
Among the woods and mountains, where I found
In thee a gracious Guide, to lead me forth
Beyond the bosom of my Family,
My Friends and youthful Playmates. 'Twas thy power
75 That rais'd the first complacency in me,
And noticeable kindliness of heart,   [124]
Love human to the Creature in himself
As he appear'd, a Stranger in my path,
Before my eyes a Brother of this world;
80 Thou first didst with those motions of delight
Inspire me.—I remember, far from home
Once having stray'd, while yet a very Child,
I saw a sight, and with what joy and love!
It was a day of exhalations, spread
85 Upon the mountains, mists and steam-like fogs
Redounding everywhere, not vehement,
But calm and mild, gentle and beautiful,
With gleams of sunshine on the eyelet spots
And loop-holes of the hills, wherever seen,
90 Hidden by quiet process, and as soon
Unfolded, to be huddled up again:
Along a narrow Valley and profound
I journey'd, when, aloft above my head,
Emerging from the silvery vapours, lo!
95 A Shepherd and his Dog! in open day:
Girt round with mists they stood and look'd about
From that enclosure small, inhabitants
Of an aerial Island floating on,
As seem'd, with that Abode in which they were,
100 A little pendant area of grey rocks,
By the soft wind breath'd forward. With delight
As bland almost, one Evening I beheld,
And at as early age (the spectacle
Is common, but by me was then first seen)

128

105 A Shepherd in the bottom of a Vale
Towards the centre standing, who with voice,
And hand waved to and fro as need required
Gave signal to his Dog, thus teaching him
To chace along the mazes of steep crags
110 The Flock he could not see: and so the Brute
Dear Creature! with a Man's intelligence
Advancing, or retreating on his steps,
Through every pervious strait, to right or left,
Thridded a way unbaffled; while the Flock
115 Fled upwards from the terror of his Bark
Through rocks and seams of turf with liquid gold
Irradiate, that deep farewell light by which
The setting sun proclaims the love he bears
To mountain regions.
                  Beauteous the domain
120 Where to the sense of beauty first my heart
Was open'd, tract more exquisitely fair   [75]
Than is that Paradise of ten thousand Trees,
Or Gehol's famous Gardens, in a Clime
Chosen from widest Empire, for delight
125 Of the Tartarian Dynasty composed;
(Beyond that mighty Wall, not fabulous,
China's stupendous mound!) by patient skill   [80]
Of myriads, and boon Nature's lavish help;
Scene link'd to scene, an evergrowing change,
130 Soft, grand, or gay! with Palaces and Domes
Of Pleasure spangled over, shady Dells   [85]
For Eastern Monasteries, sunny Mounds
With Temples crested, Bridges, Gondolas,
Rocks, Dens, and Groves of foliage taught to melt
135 Into each other their obsequious hues
Going and gone again, in subtile chace,   [90]
Too fine to be pursued; or standing forth
In no discordant opposition, strong
And gorgeous as the colours side by side
140 Bedded among the plumes of Tropic Birds:

And mountains over all embracing all; [95]
And all the landscape endlessly enrich'd
With waters running, falling, or asleep.

But lovelier far than this the Paradise
145 Where I was rear'd; in Nature's primitive gifts
Favor'd no less, and more to every sense [100]
Delicious, seeing that the sun and sky,
The elements and seasons in their change
Do find their dearest Fellow-labourer there,
150 The heart of Man, a district on all sides
The fragrance breathing of humanity,
Man free, man working for himself, with choice
Of time, and place, and object; by his wants, [105]
His comforts, native occupations, cares,
155 Conducted on to individual ends
Or social, and still follow'd by a train
Unwoo'd, unthought-of even, simplicity,
And beauty, and inevitable grace. [110]

Yea, doubtless, at an age when but a glimpse
160 Of those resplendent Gardens, with their frame
Imperial, and elaborate ornaments,
Would to a Child be transport over-great,
When but a half-hour's roam through such a place
Would leave behind a dance of images
165 That shall break in upon his sleep for weeks; [115]
Even then the common haunts of the green earth,
With the ordinary human interests
Which they embosom, all without regard
As both may seem, are fastening on the heart
170 Insensibly, each with the other's help, [120]
So that we love, not knowing that we love,
And feel, not knowing whence our feeling comes.

Such league have these two principles of joy
In our affections. I have singled out

175 Some moments, the earliest that I could, in which
Their several currents blended into one,
Weak yet, and gathering imperceptibly,
Flow'd in by gushes. My first human love,
As hath been mention'd, did incline to those
180 Whose occupations and concerns were most
Illustrated by Nature and adorn'd,   [127]
And Shepherds were the men who pleas'd me first.
Not such as in Arcadian Fastnesses
Sequester'd, handed down among themselves,
185 So ancient Poets sing, the golden Age;
Nor such, a second Race, allied to these,
As Shakespeare in the Wood of Arden placed
Where Phoebe sigh'd for the false Ganymede,   [141]
Or there where Florizel and Perdita
190 Together danced, Queen of the Feast and King
Nor such as Spenser fabled. True it is,
That I had heard what he perhaps had seen   [145]
Of maids at sunrise bringing in from far
Their Maybush, and along the Streets, in flocks,
195 Parading with a Song of taunting Rhymes,
Aim'd at the Laggards slumbering within doors;
Had also heard, from those who yet remember'd,   [150]
Tales of the May-pole Dance, and flowers that deck'd
The Posts and the Kirk-pillars, and of Youths,
200 That each one with his Maid, at break of day,
By annual custom issued forth in troops,
To drink the waters of some favorite Well,
And hang it round with Garlands. This, alas.
Was but a dream; the times had scatter'd all
205 These lighter graces, and the rural custom
And manners which it was my chance to see   [160]
In childhood were severe and unadorn'd,
The unluxuriant produce of a life
Intent on little but substantial needs,
210 Yet beautiful, and beauty that was felt.
But images of danger and distress,
And suffering, these took deepest hold of me,

131

Man suffering among awful Powers, and Forms;   [165]
Of this I heard and saw enough to make
215 The imagination restless; nor was free
Myself from frequent perils; nor were tales
Wanting, the tragedies of former times,
Or hazards and escapes, which in my walks   [170]
I carried with me among crags and woods
220 And mountains; and of these may here be told
One, as recorded by my Household Dame.

At the first falling of autumnal snow
A Shepherd and his Son one day went forth
(Thus did the Matron's Tale begin) to seek
225 A Straggler of their Flock. They both had rang'd
Upon this service the preceding day
All over their own pastures and beyond,
And now, at sun-rise sallying out again
Renew'd their search begun where from Dove Crag,
230 Ill home for bird so gentle, they look'd down
On Deep-dale Head, and Brothers-water, named
From those two Brothers that were drown'd therein.
Thence, northward, having pass'd by Arthur's Seat,
To Fairfield's highest summit; on the right
235 Leaving St. Sunday's Pike, to Grisedale Tarn
They shot, and over that cloud-loving Hill,
Seat Sandal, a fond lover of the clouds;
Thence up Helvellyn, a superior Mount
With prospect underneath of Striding-Edge,
240 And Grisdale's houseless Vale, along the brink
Of Russet Cove, and those two other Coves,
Huge skeletons of crags, which from the trunk
Of old Helvellyn spread their arms abroad,
And make a stormy harbour for the winds.
245 Far went those Shepherds in their devious quest.
From mountain ridges peeping as they pass'd
Down into every Glen: at length the Boy
Said, 'Father, with your leave I will go back,

And range the ground which we have search'd before.'
250 So speaking, southward down the hill the Lad
Sprang like a gust of wind, crying aloud
'I know where I shall find him.' 'For take note,
Said here my grey-hair'd Dame, that tho' the storm
Drive one of these poor Creatures miles and miles.
255 If he can crawl he will return again
To his own hills, the spots where, when a Lamb,
He learn'd to pasture at his Mother's side.'
After so long a labour, suddenly
Bethinking him of this, the Boy
260 Pursued his way towards a brook whose course
Was through that unfenced tract of mountain-ground
Which to his Father's little Farm belong'd,
The home and ancient Birth-right of their Flock.
Down the deep channel of the Stream he went,
265 Prying through every nook; meanwhile the rain
Began to fall upon the mountain tops,
Thick storm and heavy which for three hours' space
Abated not; and all that time the Boy
Was busy in his search until at length
270 He spied the Sheep upon a plot of grass,
An Island in the Brook. It was a place
Remote and deep, piled round with rocks where foot
Of man or beast was seldom used to tread;
But now, when everywhere the summer grass
275 Had fail'd, this one Adventurer, hunger-press'd,
Had left his Fellows, and made his way alone
To the green plot of pasture in the Brook.
Before the Boy knew well what he had seen
He leapt upon the Island with proud heart
280 And with a Prophet's joy. Immediately
The Sheep sprang forward to the further Shore
And was borne headlong by the roaring flood.
At this the Boy look'd round him, and his heart
Fainted with fear; thrice did he turn his face
285 To either brink; nor could he summon up

The courage that was needful to leap back
Cross the tempestuous torrent; so he stood,
A Prisoner on the Island, not without
More than one thought of death and his last hour:
290 Meanwhile the Father had return'd alone
To his own house; and now at the approach
Of evening he went forth to meet his Son,
Conjecturing vainly for what cause the Boy
Had stay'd so long. The Shepherd took his way
295 Up his own mountain grounds, where, as he walk'd
Along the Steep that overhung the Brook,
He seem'd to hear a voice, which was again
Repeated, like the whistling of a kite.
At this, not knowing why, as oftentimes
300 Long afterwards he has been heard to say,
Down to the Brook he went, and track'd its course
Upwards among the o'erhanging rocks; nor thus
Had he gone far, ere he espied the Boy
Where on that little plot of ground he stood
305 Right in the middle of the roaring Stream,
Now stronger every moment and more fierce.
The sight was such as no one could have seen
Without distress and fear. The Shepherd heard
The outcry of his Son, he stretch'd his Staff
310 Towards him, bade him leap, which word scarce said
The Boy was safe within his Father's arms.

Smooth life had Flock and Shepherd in old time,
Long Springs and tepid Winters on the Banks
Of delicate Galesus; and no less   [175]
315 Those scatter'd along Adria's myrtle Shores:
Smooth life the Herdsman and his snow-white Herd
To Triumphs and to sacrificial Rites
Devoted, on the inviolable Stream
Of rich Clitumnus; and the Goatherd liv'd   [180]
320 As sweetly, underneath the pleasant brows
Of cool Lucretilis, where the Pipe was heard

Of Pan, the invisible God, thrilling the rocks
With tutelary music, from all harm
The Fold protecting. I myself, mature   [185]
325 In manhood then, have seen a pastoral Tract
Like one of these, where Fancy might run wild,
Though under skies less generous and serene;
Yet there, as for herself, had Nature fram'd
A Pleasure-ground, diffused a fair expanse   [190]
330 Of level Pasture, islanded with Groves
And bank'd with woody Risings; but the Plain
Endless; here opening widely out, and there
Shut up in lesser lakes or beds of lawn
And intricate recesses, creek or bay   [195]
335 Shelter'd within a shelter, where at large
The Shepherd strays, a rolling hut his home:
Thither he comes with spring-time, there abides
All summer, and at sunrise ye may hear
His flute or flagelet resounding far;
340 There's not a Nook or Hold of that vast space,
Nor Strait where passage is, but it shall have
In turn its Visitant, telling there his hours
In unlaborious pleasure, with no task   [205]
More toilsome than to carve a beechen bowl
345 For Spring or Fountain, which the Traveller finds
When through the region he pursues at will
His devious course. A glimpse of such sweet life
I saw when, from the melancholy Walls   [210]
Of Goslar, once Imperial! I renew'd
350 My daily walk along that chearful Plain,
Which, reaching to her Gates, spreads East and West
And Northwards, from beneath the mountainous verge
Of the Hercynian forest. Yet hail to You,   [215]
Your rocks and precipices, Ye that seize
355 The heart with firmer grasp! your snows and streams
Ungovernable, and your terrifying winds,   [220]
That howl'd so dismally when I have been
Companionless, among your solitudes.

There 'tis the Shepherd's task the winter long
360 To wait upon the storms: of their approach
Sagacious, from the height he drives his Flock   [225]
Down into sheltering coves, and feeds them there
Through the hard time, long as the storm is lock'd,
(So do they phrase it) bearing from the stalls
365 A toilsome burden up the craggy ways,
To strew it on the snow. And when the Spring
Looks out, and all the mountains dance with lambs,   [230]
He through the enclosures won from the steep Waste,
And through the lower Heights hath gone his rounds;
370 And when the Flock with warmer weather climbs
Higher and higher, him his office leads
To range among them, through the hills dispers'd,
And watch their goings, whatsoever track
Each Wanderer chuses for itself; a work
375 That lasts the summer through. He quits his home
At day-spring, and no sooner doth the sun   [235]
Begin to strike him with a fire-like heat
Than he lies down upon some shining place
And breakfasts with his Dog; when he hath stay'd,
380 As for the most he doth, beyond his time,   [239]
He springs up with a bound, and then away!
Ascending fast with his long Pole in hand,
Or winding in and out among the crags.
What need to follow him through what he does   [250]
385 Or sees in his day's march? He feels himself
In those vast regions where his service is
A Freeman; wedded to his life of hope
And hazard, and hard labour interchanged
With that majestic indolence so dear   [255]
390 To native Man. A rambling school-boy, thus
Have I beheld him, without knowing why
Have felt his presence in his own domain,
As of a Lord and Master; or a Power
Or Genius, under Nature, under God,
395 Presiding; and severest solitude   [260]

136

Seem'd more commanding oft when he was there.
Seeking the Raven's Nest, and suddenly
Surpriz'd with vapours, or on rainy days
When I have angled up the lonely brooks
400 Mine eyes have glanced upon him, few steps off, [265]
In size a Giant, stalking through the fog,
His Sheep like Greenland Bears; at other times
When round some shady promontory turning,
His Form hath flash'd upon me, glorified
405 By the deep radiance of the setting sun: [270]
Or him have I descried in distant sky,
A solitary object and sublime,
Above all height! like an aerial Cross,
As it is station'd on some spiry Rock
410 Of the Chartreuse, for worship. Thus was Man [275]
Ennobled outwardly before mine eyes,
And thus my heart at first was introduced
To an unconscious love and reverence
Of human nature; hence the human form
415 To me was like an index of delight, [280]
Of grace and honour, power and worthiness.
Meanwhile, this Creature, spiritual almost
As those of Books; but more exalted far,
Far more of an imaginative form,
420 Was not a Corin of the groves, who lives [285]
For his own fancies, or to dance by the hour
In coronal, with Phillis in the midst,
But, for the purposes of kind, a Man
With the most common; Husband, Father; learn'd,
425 Could teach, admonish, suffer'd with the rest [290]
From vice and folly, wretchedness and fear;
Of this I little saw, cared less for it,
But something must have felt.
                              Call ye these appearances
Which I beheld of Shepherds in my youth,
430 This sanctity of nature given to man [295]
A shadow, a delusion, ye who are fed

By the dead letter, not the spirit of things,
Whose truth is not a motion or a shape
Instinct with vital functions, but a Block
435 Or waxen Image which yourselves have made,   [300]
And ye adore. But blessed be the God
Of Nature and of Man that this was so,
That Men did at the first present themselves
Before my untaught eyes thus purified,
440 Remov'd, and at a distance that was fit.   [305]
And so we all of us in some degree
Are led to knowledge, whencesoever led,
And howsoever; were it otherwise,
And we found evil fast as we find good
445 In our first years, or think that it is found,   [310]
How could the innocent heart bear up and live!
But doubly fortunate my lot; not here
Alone, that something of a better life
Perhaps was round me than it is the privilege
450 Of most to move in, but that first I look'd   [315]
At Man through objects that were great and fair,
First communed with him by their help. And thus
Was founded a sure safeguard and defence
Against the weight of meanness, selfish cares,
455 Coarse manners, vulgar passions, that beat in   [320]
On all sides from the ordinary world
In which we traffic. Starting from this point,
I had my face towards the truth, began
With an advantage; furnish'd with that kind
460 Of prepossession without which the soul   [325]
Receives no knowledge that can bring forth good,
No genuine insight ever comes to her:
Happy in this, that I with nature walk'd,   [330]
Not having a too early intercourse
465 With the deformities of crowded life,
And those ensuing laughters and contempts
Self-pleasing, which if we would wish to think
With admiration and respect of man   [335]

Will not permit us; but pursue the mind
470 That to devotion willingly would be rais'd
Into the Temple and the Temple's heart.

Yet do not deem, my Friend, though thus I speak
Of Man as having taken in my mind   [340]
A place thus early which might almost seem
475 Preeminent, that this was really so.
Nature herself was at this unripe time,
But secondary to my own pursuits
And animal activities, and all
Their trivial pleasures; and long afterwards   [345]
480 When these had died away, and Nature did
For her own sake become my joy, even then
And upwards through late youth, until not less
Than three and twenty summers had been told
Was man in my affections and regards   [350]
485 Subordinate to her; her awful forms
And viewless agencies: a passion, she!
A rapture often, and immediate joy,
Ever at hand; he distant, but a grace
Occasional, an accidental thought,   [355]
490 His hour being not yet come. Far less had then
The inferior Creatures, beast or bird, attun'd
My spirit to that gentleness of love,
Won from me those minute obeisances   [360]
Of tenderness, which I may number now
495 With my first blessings. Nevertheless, on these
The light of beauty did not fall in vain,
Or grandeur circumfuse them to no end.   [364]

Why should I speak of Tillers of the soil?
The Ploughman and his Team; or Men and Boys
500 In festive summer busy with the rake,
Old Men and ruddy Maids, and Little Ones
All out together, and in sun and shade
Dispers'd among the hay-grounds alder-fringed,

The Quarry-man, far heard! that blasts the rock,
505 The Fishermen in pairs, the one to row,
And one to drop the Net, plying their trade
''Mid tossing lakes and tumbling boats' and winds
Whistling; the Miner, melancholy Man!
That works by taper light, while all the hills
510 Are shining with the glory of the day.

But when that first poetic Faculty [365]
Of plain imagination and severe,
No longer a mute Influence of the soul,
An Element of the nature's inner self,
515 Began to have some promptings to put on
A visible shape, and to the works of art,
The notions and the images of books [370]
Did knowingly conform itself, by these
Enflamed, and proud of that her new delight,
520 There came among those shapes of human life
A wilfulness of fancy and conceit
Which gave them new importance to the mind;
And Nature and her objects beautified
These fictions, as in some sort in their turn [375]
525 They burnish'd her. From touch of this new power
Nothing was safe: the Elder-tree that grew
Beside the well-known Charnel-house had then
A dismal look; the Yew-tree had its Ghost, [380]
That took its station there for ornament:
530 Then common death was none, common mishap,
But matter for this humour everywhere,
The tragic super-tragic, else left short.
Then, if a Widow, staggering with the blow
Of her distress, was known to have made her way
535 To the cold grave in which her Husband slept, [385]
One night, or haply more than one, through pain
Or half-insensate impotence of mind
The fact was caught at greedily, and there
She was a Visitant the whole year through, [390]

540 Wetting the turf with never-ending tears,
And all the storms of Heaven must beat on her.

Through wild obliquities could I pursue
Among all objects of the fields and groves
These cravings; when the Fox-glove, one by one,
545 Upwards through every stage of its tall stem,
Had shed its bells, and stood by the wayside   [395]
Dismantled, with a single one, perhaps,
Left at the ladder's top, with which the Plant
Appeared to stoop, as slender blades of grass   [398]
550 Tipp'd with a bead of rain or dew, behold!
If such a sight were seen, would Fancy bring
Some Vagrant thither with her Babes, and seat her
Upon the Turf beneath the stately Flower
Drooping in sympathy, and making so
555 A melancholy Crest above the head
Of the lorn Creature, while her Little-Ones,
All unconcern'd with her unhappy plight,
Were sporting with the purple cups that lay   [405]
Scatter'd upon the ground.
                                There was a Copse
560 An upright bank of wood and woody rock
That opposite our rural Dwelling stood,
In which a sparkling patch of diamond light
Was in bright weather duly to be seen
On summer afternoons, within the wood
565 At the same place. 'Twas doubtless nothing more
Than a black rock, which, wet with constant springs
Glister'd far seen from out its lurking-place
As soon as ever the declining sun
Had smitten it. Beside our cottage hearth,   [410]
570 Sitting with open door, a hundred times
Upon this lustre have I gaz'd, that seem'd
To have some meaning which I could not find:
And now it was a burnish'd shield, I fancied,
Suspended over a Knight's Tomb, who lay   [415]

575 Inglorious, buried in the dusky wood;
An entrance now into some magic cave
Or Palace for a Fairy of the rock;
Nor would I, though not certain whence the cause
Of the effulgence, thither have repair'd
580 Without a precious bribe, and day by day
And month by month I saw the spectacle,
Nor ever once have visited the spot   [420]
Unto this hour. Thus sometimes were the shapes
Of wilful fancy grafted upon feelings
585 Of the imagination, and they rose
In worth accordingly. My present Theme
Is to retrace the way that led me on
Through nature to the love of human Kind;
Nor could I with such object overlook
590 The Influence of this Power which turn'd itself
Instinctively to human passions, things   [425]
Least understood; of this adulterate Power,
For so it may be call'd, and without wrong,
When with that first compared. Yet in the midst
595 Of these vagaries, with an eye so rich
As mine was, through the chance, on me not wasted
Of having been brought up in such a grand
And lovely region, I had forms distinct
To steady me; these thoughts did oft revolve   [430]
600 About some centre palpable, which at once
Incited them to motion, and control'd,
And whatsoever shape the fit might take,
And whencesoever it might come, I still
At all times had a real solid world
605 Of images about me; did not pine
As one in cities bred might do; as Thou,
Beloved Friend! hast told me that thou didst,
Great Spirit as thou art, in endless dreams   [435]
Of sickliness, disjoining, joining things
610 Without the light of knowledge. Where the harm,
If, when the Woodman languish'd with disease

From sleeping night by night among the woods
Within his sod-built Cabin, Indian-wise,   [440]
I call'd the pangs of disappointed love
615 And all the long Etcetera of such thought
To help him to his grave? Meanwhile the Man,
If not already from the woods retired
To die at home, was haply, as I knew,   [445]
Pining alone among the gentle airs,
620 Birds, running streams, and hills so beautiful
On golden evenings, while the charcoal Pile
Breath'd up its smoke, an image of his ghost
Or spirit that was soon to take its flight.   [450]

There came a time of greater dignity
625 Which had been gradually prepar'd, and now
Rush'd in as if on wings, the time in which
The pulse of Being everywhere was felt,   [480]
When all the several frames of things, like stars
Through every magnitude distinguishable,
630 Were half confounded in each other's blaze,
One galaxy of life and joy. Then rose   [485]
Man, inwardly contemplated, and present
In my own being, to a loftier height;
As of all visible natures crown; and first
635 In capability of feeling what
Was to be felt; in being rapt away   [490]
By the divine effect of power and love,
As, more than anything we know instinct
With Godhead, and by reason and by will
640 Acknowledging dependency sublime.

Erelong transported hence as in a dream   [495]
I found myself begirt with temporal shapes
Of vice and folly thrust upon my view,
Objects of sport, and ridicule, and scorn,
545 Manners and characters discriminate,
And little busy passions that eclipsed,   [500]

As well they might, the impersonated thought,
The idea or abstraction of the Kind.
An Idler among academic Bowers,
650 Such was my new condition, as at large
Hath been set forth; yet here the vulgar light   [505]
Of present actual superficial life,
Gleaming through colouring of other times,
Old usages and local privilege,
655 Thereby was soften'd, almost solemniz'd,
And render'd apt and pleasing to the view;
This notwithstanding, being brought more near   [510]
As I was now, to guilt and wretchedness,
I trembled, thought of human life at times
660 With an indefinite terror and dismay
Such as the storms and angry elements
Had bred in me, but gloomier far, a dim   [515]
Analogy to uproar and misrule,
Disquiet, danger, and obscurity.

665   It might be told (but wherefore speak of things
Common to all?) that seeing, I essay'd
To give relief, began to deem myself
A moral agent, judging between good   [520]
And evil, not as for the mind's delight
670 But for her safety, one who was to *act*,
As sometimes, to the best of my weak means,
I did, by human sympathy impell'd;
And through dislike and most offensive pain   [525]
Was to the truth conducted; of this faith
675 Never forsaken, that by acting well
And understanding, I should learn to love
The end of life and every thing we know.

Preceptress stern, that didst instruct me next,   [530]
London! to thee I willingly return.
680 Erewhile my Verse play'd only with the flowers
Enwrought upon thy mantle; satisfied

With this amusement, and a simple look   [535]
Of child-like inquisition, now and then
Cast upwards on thine eye to puzzle out
685 Some inner meanings, which might harbour there.
Yet did I not give way to this light mood   [539]
Wholly beguiled, as one incapable
Of higher things, and ignorant that high things
Were round me. Never shall I forget the hour
690 The moment rather say when having thridded
The labyrinth of suburban Villages,
At length I did unto myself first seem
To enter the great City. On the Roof
Of an itinerant Vehicle I sate
695 With vulgar men about me, vulgar forms   [545]
Of houses, pavement, streets, of men and things,
Mean shapes on every side: but, at the time,
When to myself it fairly might be said,
The very moment that I seem'd to know
700 The threshold now is overpass'd, Great God!
That aught *external* to the living mind   [550]
Should have such mighty sway! yet so it was
A weight of Ages did at once descend
Upon my heart; no thought embodied, no
705 Distinct remembrances; but weight and power,
Power growing with the weight: alas! I feel   [555]
That I am trifling: 'twas a moment's pause.
All that took place within me, came and went
As in a moment, and I only now
710 Remember that it was a thing divine.

As when a traveller hath from open day   [560]
With torches pass'd into some Vault of Earth,
The Grotto of Antiparos, or the Den
Of Yordas among Craven's mountain tracts;
715 He looks and sees the Cavern spread and grow,
Widening itself on all sides, sees, or thinks   [565]
He sees, erelong, the roof above his head.

145

Which instantly unsettles and recedes
Substance and shadow, light and darkness, all
720 Commingled, making up a Canopy
Of Shapes and Forms and Tendencies to Shape   [570]
That shift and vanish, change and interchange
Like Spectres, ferment quiet and sublime;
Which, after a short space, works less and less,
725 Till every effort, every motion gone,
The scene before him lies in perfect view,   [575]
Exposed and lifeless, as a written book.
But let him pause awhile, and look again
And a new quickening shall succeed, at first
730 Beginning timidly, then creeping fast
Through all which he beholds; the senseless mass,   [580]
In its projections, wrinkles, cavities,
Through all its surface, with all colours streaming,
Like a magician's airy pageant, parts
735 Unites, embodying everywhere some pressure
Or image, recognis'd or new, some type
Or picture of the world; forests and lakes,
Ships, rivers, towers, the Warrior clad in Mail,   [585]
The prancing Steed, the Pilgrim with his Staff,
740 The mitred Bishop and the throned King,
A Spectacle to which there is no end.

No otherwise had I at first been mov'd   [590]
With such a swell of feeling, follow'd soon
By a blank sense of greatness pass'd away
745 And afterwards continu'd to be mov'd
In presence of that vast Metropolis,
The Fountain of my Country's destiny
And of the destiny of Earth itself,
That great Emporium, Chronicle at once
750 And Burial-place of passions and their home   [595]
Imperial, and chief living residence.

With strong Sensations, teeming as it did
Of past and present, such a place must needs

Have pleas'd me, in those times; I sought not then
755 Knowledge; but craved for power, and power I found [600]
In all things; nothing had a circumscribed
And narrow influence; but all objects, being
Themselves capacious, also found in me [605]
Capaciousness and amplitude of mind;
760 Such is the strength and glory of our Youth.
The Human nature unto which I felt
That I belong'd, and which I lov'd and reverenced,
Was not a punctual Presence, but a Spirit [610]
Living in time and space, and far diffus'd.
765 In this my joy, in this my dignity
Consisted; the external universe,
By striking upon what is found within,
Had given me this conception, with the help
Of Books, and what they picture and record. [616]

770   'Tis true the History of my native Land,
With those of Greece compared and popular Rome,
Events not lovely nor magnanimous,
But harsh and unaffecting in themselves
And in our high-wrought modern narratives
775 Stript of their harmonising soul, the life
Of manners and familiar incidents, [621]
Had never much delighted me. And less
Than other minds I had been used to owe
The pleasure which I found in place or thing
780 To extrinsic transitory accidents,
To records or traditions; but a sense [625]
Of what had been here done, and suffer'd here
Through ages, and was doing, suffering, still
Weigh'd with me, could support the test of thought,
785 Was like the enduring majesty and power [631]
Of independent nature; and not seldom
Even individual remembrances,
By working on the Shapes before my eyes,
Became like vital functions of the soul;

790 And out of what had been, what was, the place
Was throng'd with impregnations, like those wilds
In which my early feelings had been nurs'd,
And naked valleys, full of caverns, rocks,   [635]
And audible seclusions, dashing lakes,
795 Echoes and Waterfalls, and pointed crags
That into music touch the passing wind.

  Thus here imagination also found
An element that pleased her, tried her strength,   [640]
Among new objects simplified, arranged,
800 Impregnated my knowledge, made it live,
And the result was elevating thoughts
Of human Nature. Neither guilt nor vice,   [645]
Debasement of the body or the mind,
Nor all the misery forced upon my sight,
805 Which was not lightly pass'd, but often scann'd
Most feelingly, could overthrow my trust
In what we may become, induce belief   [650]
That I was ignorant, had been falsely taught,
A Solitary, who with vain conceits
810 Had been inspired, and walk'd about in dreams.
When from that awful prospect overcast
And in eclipse, my meditations turn'd,
Lo! everything that was indeed divine   [655]
Retain'd its purity inviolate
815 And unencroach'd upon, nay, seem'd brighter far
For this deep shade in counterview, that gloom
Of opposition, such as shew'd itself
To the eyes of Adam, yet in Paradise,
Though fallen from bliss, when in the East he saw   [660]
820 Darkness ere day's mid course, and morning light
More orient in the western cloud, that drew
'O'er the blue firmament a radiant white,
Descending slow with something heavenly fraught.'

  Add also, that among the multitudes   [665]
825 Of that great City, oftentimes was seen

148

Affectingly set forth, more than elsewhere
Is possible, the unity of man,
One spirit over ignorance and vice
Predominant, in good and evil hearts   [670]
830 One sense for moral judgements, as one eye
For the sun's light. When strongly breath'd upon
By this sensation, whencesoe'er it comes
Of union or communion doth the soul
Rejoice as in her highest joy: for there,
835 There chiefly, hath she feeling whence she is,
And, passing through all Nature rests with God.

And is not, too, that vast Abiding-place
Of human Creatures, turn where'er we may,
Profusely sown with individual sights
840 Of courage, and integrity, and truth,   [VII. 600]
And tenderness, which, here set off by foil,
Appears more touching. In the tender scenes   [VII. 600]
Chiefly was my delight, and one of these
Never will be forgotten. 'Twas a Man,
845 Whom I saw sitting in an open Square
Close to an iron paling that fenced in   [VII. 605]
The spacious Grass-plot; on the corner stone
Of the low wall in which the pales were fix'd
Sate this one Man, and with a sickly Babe
850 Upon his knee, whom he had thither brought
For sunshine, and to breathe the fresher air.   [VII. 610]
Of those who pass'd, and me who look'd at him,
He took no note; but in his brawny Arms
(The Artificer was to the elbow bare,
855 And from his work this moment had been stolen)
He held the Child, and, bending over it,   [VII. 615]
As if he were afraid both of the sun
And of the air which he had come to seek,
He eyed it with unutterable love.

860   Thus were my thoughts attracted more and more   [676]
By slow gradations towards human Kind

149

And to the good and ill of human life;
Nature had led me on, and now I seem'd
To travel independent of her help,   [681]
865 As if I had forgotten her; but no,
My Fellow beings still were unto me
Far less than she was, though the scale of love
Were filling fast, 'twas light, as yet, compared   [685]
With that in which her mighty objects lay.

BOOK NINTH

RESIDENCE IN FRANCE

As oftentimes a River, it might seem,
Yielding in part to old remembrances,
Part sway'd by fear to tread an onward road
That leads direct to the devouring sea
Turns, and will measure back his course, far back,   [5]
Towards the very regions which he cross'd
In his first outset; so have we long time
Made motions retrograde, in like pursuit
Detain'd. But now we start afresh; I feel
An impulse to precipitate my Verse.
Fair greetings to this shapeless eagerness,
Whene'er it comes, needful in work so long,   [20]
Thrice needful to the argument which now
Awaits us; Oh! how much unlike the past!
One which though bright the promise, will be found
Ere far we shall advance, ungenial, hard
To treat of, and forbidding in itself.

    Free as a colt at pasture on the hill,
I ranged at large, through the Metropolis
Month after month. Obscurely did I live,   [25]
Not courting the society of Men
By literature, or elegance, or rank
Distinguish'd; in the midst of things, it seem'd,
Looking as from a distance on the world
That mov'd about me; yet insensibly
False preconceptions were corrected thus
And errors of the fancy rectified,
Alike with reference to men and things,
And sometimes from each quarter were pour'd in
Novel imaginations and profound.
A year thus spent, this field (with small regret

5

10

15

20

25

30

Save only for the Book-stalls in the streets, [32]
Wild produce, hedge-row fruit, on all sides hung
To lure the sauntering traveller from his track)
35 I quitted, and betook myself to France,
Led thither chiefly by a personal wish
To speak the language more familiarly,
With which intent I chose for my abode
A City on the Borders of the Loire. [41]

40   Through Paris lay my readiest path, and there
I sojourn'd a few days, and visited
In haste each spot of old and recent fame
The latter chiefly, from the Field of Mars [45]
Down to the Suburbs of St. Anthony,
45 And from Mont Martyr southward, to the Dome
Of Geneviève. In both her clamorous Halls,
The National Synod and the Jacobins
I saw the revolutionary Power [50]
Toss like a Ship at anchor, rock'd by storms;
50 The Arcades I traversed in the Palace huge
Of Orleans, coasted round and round the line
Of Tavern, Brothel, Gaming-house, and Shop,
Great rendezvous of worst and best, the walk [55]
Of all who had a purpose, or had not;
55 I star'd and listen'd with a stranger's ears
To Hawkers and Haranguers, hubbub wild!
And hissing Factionists with ardent eyes,
In knots, or pairs, or single, ant-like swarms [60]
Of Builders and Subverters, every face
60 That hope or apprehension could put on,
Joy, anger, and vexation in the midst
Of gaiety and dissolute idleness. [66]

   Where silent zephyrs sported with the dust
Of the Bastille, I sate in the open sun,
65 And from the rubbish gather'd up a stone
And pocketed the relick in the guise [70]
Of an Enthusiast, yet, in honest truth

Though not without some strong incumbences;
And glad, (could living man be otherwise)
70 I look'd for something that I could not find,
Affecting more emotion than I felt,
For 'tis most certain that the utmost force   [74]
Of all these various objects which may shew
The temper of my mind as then it was
75 Seem'd less to recompense the Traveller's pains,
Less mov'd me, gave me less delight than did,
A single picture merely hunted out
Among other sights, the Magdalene of le Brun,
A Beauty exquisitely wrought, fair face
80 And rueful, with its ever-flowing tears.   [80]

But hence to my more permanent residence
I hasten; there, by novelties in speech,
Domestic manners, customs, gestures, looks,
And all the attire of ordinary life,
85 Attention was at first engross'd; and thus,   [85]
Amused and satisfied, I scarcely felt
The shock of these concussions, unconcerned,
Tranquil, almost, and careless as a flower
Glassed in a Green-house, or a Parlour shrub
90 When every bush and tree, the country through,   [90]
Is shaking to the roots; indifference this
Which may seem strange; but I was unprepared
With needful knowledge, had abruptly pass'd
Into a theatre, of which the stage
95 Was busy with an action far advanced.   [95]
Like others I had read, and eagerly
Sometimes, the master Pamphlets of the day;
Nor wanted such half-insight as grew wild
Upon that meagre soil, help'd out by Talk
100 And public News; but having never chanced   [100]
To see a regular Chronicle which might shew,
(If any such indeed existed then)
Whence the main Organs of the public Power

153

Had sprung, their transmigrations when and how
105 Accomplish'd, giving thus unto events
A form and body, all things were to me [105]
Loose and disjointed, and the affections left
Without a vital interest. At that time,
Moreover, the first storm was overblown,
110 And the strong hand of outward violence
Lock'd up in quiet. For myself, I fear [110]
Now in connection with so great a Theme
To speak (as I must be compell'd to do)
Of one so unimportant; a short time
115 I loiter'd, and frequented night by night
Routs, card-tables, the formal haunts of Men,
Whom in the City privilege of birth [115]
Sequester'd from the rest, societies
Where, through punctilios of elegance
120 And deeper causes, all discourse, alike
Of good and evil in the time, was shunn'd
With studious care; but 'twas not long ere this [120]
Proved tedious, and I gradually withdrew
Into a noisier world; and thus did soon
125 Become a Patriot, and my heart was all
Given to the People, and my love was theirs.

A knot of military Officers, [125]
That to a Regiment appertain'd which then
Was station'd in the City, were the chief
130 Of my associates: some of these wore Swords
Which had been seasoned in the Wars, and all
Were men well-born, at least laid claim to such
Distinction, as the Chivalry of France.
In age and temper differing, they had yet [130]
135 One spirit ruling in them all, alike
(Save only one, hereafter to be named)
Were bent upon undoing what was done:
This was their rest, and only hope, therewith
No fear had they of bad becoming worse, [135]

140 For worst to them was come, nor would have stirr'd,
Or deem'd it worth a moment's while to stir,
In anything, save only as the act
Look'd thitherward. One, reckoning by years,
Was in the prime of manhood, and erewhile   [140]
145 He had sate Lord in many tender hearts,
Though heedless of such honours now, and changed:
His temper was quite master'd by the times,
And they had blighted him, had eat away
The beauty of his person, doing wrong   [145]
150 Alike to body and to mind: his port,
Which once had been erect and open, now
Was stooping and contracted, and a face,
By nature lovely in itself, express'd   [150]
As much as any that was ever seen,
155 A ravage out of season, made by thoughts
Unhealthy and vexatious. At the hour,
The most important of each day, in which
The public News was read, the fever came,   [155]
A punctual visitant, to shake this Man,
160 Disarm'd his voice, and fann'd his yellow cheek
Into a thousand colours; while he read,
Or mused, his sword was haunted by his touch
Continually, like an uneasy place   [160]
In his own body. 'Twas in truth an hour
165 Of universal ferment; mildest men
Were agitated; and commotions, strife
Of passion and opinion fill'd the walls
Of peaceful houses with unquiet sounds.   [165]
The soil of common life was at that time
170 Too hot to tread upon; oft said I then,
And not then only, 'what a mockery this
Of history, the past and that to come!
Now do I feel how I have been deceived,   [170]
Reading of Nations and their works, in faith,
175 Faith given to vanity and emptiness;
Oh! laughter for the Page that would reflect

To future times the face of what now is!'
The land all swarm'd with passion, like a Plain   [175]
Devour'd by locusts, Carra, Gorsas, add
180 A hundred other names, forgotten now,
Nor to be heard of more, yet were they Powers,
Like earthquakes, shocks repeated day by day,
And felt through every nook of town and field.   [180]

The Men already spoken of as chief
185 Of my Associates were prepared for flight
To augment the band of Emigrants in Arms
Upon the borders of the Rhine, and leagued
With foreign Foes mustered for instant war.   [185]
This was their undisguis'd intent, and they
190 Were waiting with the whole of their desires
The moment to depart.
               An Englishman,
Born in a Land, the name of which appear'd
To license some unruliness of mind,   [190]
A Stranger, with Youth's further privilege,
195 And that indulgence which a half-learn'd speech
Wins from the courteous, I who had been else
Shunn'd and not tolerated freely lived
With these Defenders of the Crown, and talk'd   [195]
And heard their notions, nor did they disdain
200 The wish to bring me over to their cause.

But though untaught by thinking or by books
To reason well of polity or law
And nice distinctions, then on every tongue,   [200]
Of natural rights and civil, and to acts
205 Of Nations, and their passing interests,
(I speak comparing these with other things)
Almost indifferent, even the Historian's Tale
Prizing but little otherwise than I prized   [205]
Tales of the Poets, as it made my heart
210 Beat high and fill'd my fancy with fair forms,
Old Heroes and their sufferings and their deeds;

156

Yet in the regal Sceptre, and the pomp
Of Orders and Degrees, I nothing found   [210]
Then, or had ever, even in crudest youth,
215 That dazzled me; but rather what my soul
Mourn'd for, or loath'd, beholding that the best
Rul'd not, and feeling that they ought to rule.

For, born in a poor District, and which yet   [215]
Retaineth more of ancient homeliness,
220 Manners erect, and frank simplicity,
Than any other nook of English Land,
It was my fortune scarcely to have seen
Through the whole tenor of my School-day time
The face of one, who, whether Boy or Man,   [220]
225 Was vested with attention or respect
Through claims of wealth or blood; nor was it least
Of many debts which afterwards I owed
To Cambridge, and an academic life
That something there was holden up to view   [225]
230 Of a Republic, where all stood thus far
Upon equal ground, that they were brothers all
In honour, as in one community,
Scholars and Gentlemen, where, furthermore,
Distinction lay open to all that came,   [230]
235 And wealth and titles were in less esteem
Than talents and successful industry.
Add unto this, subservience from the first
To God and Nature's single sovereignty,   [235]
Familiar presences of awful Power
240 And fellowship with venerable books
To sanction the proud workings of the soul,
And mountain liberty. It could not be
But that one tutor'd thus, who had been form'd
To thought and moral feeling in the way
245 This story hath described, should look with awe
Upon the faculties of Man, receive   [240]
Gladly the highest promises, and hail

As best the government of equal rights
And individual worth. And hence, O Friend!
250 If at the first great outbreak I rejoiced
Less than might well befit my youth, the cause   [245]
In part lay here, that unto me the events
Seem'd nothing out of nature's certain course,
A gift that rather was come late than soon.
255 No wonder, then, if advocates like these   [249]
Whom I have mention'd, at this riper day
Were impotent to make my hopes put on
The shape of theirs, my understanding bend
In honour to their honour, zeal which yet
260 Had slumber'd, now in opposition burst   [255]
Forth like a polar summer; every word
They utter'd was a dart, by counter-winds
Blown back upon themselves, their reason seem'd
Confusion-stricken by a higher power
265 Than human understanding, their discourse   [260]
Maim'd, spiritless, and in their weakness strong
I triumph'd.
          Meantime, day by day, the roads
(While I consorted with these Royalists)
Were crowded with the bravest Youth of France,
270 And all the promptest of her Spirits, link'd
In gallant Soldiership, and posting on   [265]
To meet the War upon her Frontier Bounds.
Yet at this very moment do tears start
Into mine eyes; I do not say I weep,
275 I wept not then, but tears have dimm'd my sight,
In memory of the farewells of that time,   [270]
Domestic severings, female fortitude
At dearest separation, patriot love
And self-devotion, and terrestrial hope
280 Encouraged with a martyr's confidence;
Even files of Strangers merely, seen but once,   [275]
And for a moment, men from far with sound
Of music, martial tunes, and banners spread

Entering the City, here and there a face
285 Or person singled out among the rest,
Yet still a stranger and beloved as such,   [280]
Even by these passing spectacles my heart
Was oftentimes uplifted, and they seem'd
Like arguments from Heaven, that 'twas a cause
290 Good, and which no one could stand up against
Who was not lost, abandon'd, selfish, proud,   [285]
Mean, miserable, wilfully deprav'd,
Hater perverse of equity and truth.
　　Among that band of Officers was one
295 Already hinted at, of other mold,
A Patriot, thence rejected by the rest
And with an oriental loathing spurn'd,   [290]
As of a different Cast. A meeker Man
Than this liv'd never, or a more benign
300 Meek, though enthusiastic to the height
Of highest expectation. Injuries
Made him more gracious, and his nature then   [295]
Did breathe its sweetness out most sensibly
As aromatic flowers on alpine turf
305 When foot hath crush'd them. He thro' the events
Of that great change wander'd in perfect faith,
As through a Book, an old Romance or Tale   [300]
Of Fairy, or some dream of actions wrought
Behind the summer clouds. By birth he rank'd
310 With the most noble, but unto the poor
Among mankind he was in service bound
As by some tie invisible, oaths profess'd   [305]
To a religious Order. Man he lov'd
As Man; and to the mean and the obscure
315 And all the homely in their homely works
Transferr'd a courtesy which had no air
Of condescension, but did rather seem   [310]
A passion and a gallantry, like that
Which he, a Soldier, in his idler day
320 Had payed to Woman; somewhat vain he was,

Or seem'd so, yet it was not vanity
But fondness, and a kind of radiant joy   [315]
That cover'd him about when he was bent
On works of love or freedom, or revolved
325 Complacently the progress of a cause,
Whereof he was a part; yet this was meek
And placid, and took nothing from the Man   [320]
That was delightful: oft in solitude
With him did I discourse about the end
330 Of civil government, and its wisest forms,
Of ancient prejudice, and chartered rights,
Allegiance, faith, and laws by time matured,
Custom and habit, novelty and change,   [325]
Of self-respect, and virtue in the Few
335 For patrimonial honour set apart,
And ignorance in the labouring Multitude.
For he, an upright Man and tolerant,
Balanced these contemplations in his mind   [330]
And I, who at that time was scarcely dipp'd
340 Into the turmoil, had a sounder judgment
Than afterwards, carried about me yet
With less alloy to its integrity
The experience of past ages, as through help   [335]
Of Books and common life it finds its way
345 To youthful minds, by objects over near
Not press'd upon, nor dazzled or misled
By struggling with the crowd for present ends.

But though not deaf and obstinate to find   [340]
Error without apology on the side
350 Of those who were against us, more delight
We took, and let this freely be confess'd,
In painting to ourselves the miseries
Of royal Courts, and that voluptuous life   [345]
Unfeeling, where the Man who is of soul
355 The meanest thrives the most, where dignity,
True personal dignity, abideth not,

A light and cruel world, cut off from all
The natural inlets of just sentiment,   [350]
From lowly sympathy, and chastening truth,
360 Where good and evil never have that name,
That which they ought to have, but wrong prevails,
And vice at home. We added dearest themes,
Man and his noble nature, as it is   [355]
The gift of God and lies in his own power,
365 His blind desires and steady faculties
Capable of clear truth, the one to break
Bondage, the other to build liberty
On firm foundations, making social life,   [360]
Through knowledge spreading and imperishable,
370 As just in regulation, and as pure
As individual in the wise and good.
We summon'd up the honorable deeds
Of ancient Story, thought of each bright spot   [365]
That could be found in all recorded time
375 Of truth preserv'd and error pass'd away,
Of single Spirits that catch the flame from Heaven,
And how the multitude of men will feed
And fan each other, thought of Sects, how keen   [370]
They are to put the appropriate nature on,
380 Triumphant over every obstacle
Of custom, language, Country, love and hate,
And what they do and suffer for their creed,
How far they travel, and how long endure,   [375]
How quickly mighty Nations have been form'd
385 From least beginnings, how, together lock'd
By new opinions, scatter'd tribes have made
One body spreading wide as clouds in heaven.
To aspirations then of our own minds   [380]
Did we appeal; and finally beheld
390 A living confirmation of the whole
Before us in a People risen up
Fresh as the morning Star: elate we look'd   [385]
Upon their virtues, saw in rudest men

Self-sacrifice the firmest, generous love
395 And continence of mind, and sense of right
Uppermost in the midst of fiercest strife.

   Oh! sweet it is, in academic Groves,   [390]
Or such retirement, Friend! as we have known
Among the mountains, by our Rotha's Stream,
400 Greta or Derwent, or some nameless Rill,
To ruminate with interchange of talk
On rational liberty, and hope in man,   [395]
Justice and peace; but far more sweet such toil,
Toil say I, for it leads to thoughts abstruse
405 If Nature then be standing on the brink
Of some great trial, and we hear the voice
Of One devoted, one whom circumstance   [400]
Hath call'd upon to embody his deep sense
In action, give it outwardly a shape,
410 And that of benediction to the world;
Then doubt is not, and truth is more than truth,
A hope it is and a desire, a creed   [405]
Of zeal by an authority divine
Sanction'd of danger, difficulty or death.
415 Such conversation under Attic shades
Did Dion hold with Plato, ripen'd thus
For a Deliverer's glorious task, and such,   [410]
He, on that ministry already bound,
Held with Eudemus and Timonides,
420 Surrounded by Adventurers in Arms,
When those two Vessels with their daring Freight
For the Sicilian Tyrant's overthrow   [415]
Sail'd from Zacynthus, philosophic war
Led by Philosophers. With harder fate,
425 Though like ambition, such was he, O Friend!
Of whom I speak, so Beaupuis (let the Name
Stand near the worthiest of Antiquity)   [420]
Fashion'd his life, and many a long discourse
With like persuasion honor'd we maintain'd,

430 He on his part accoutred for the worst.
    He perish'd fighting in supreme command
    Upon the Borders of the unhappy Loire   [425]
    For Liberty against deluded Men,
    His Fellow-countrymen, and yet most bless'd
435 In this, that he the fate of later times
    Liv'd not to see, nor what we now behold
    Who have as ardent hearts as he had then.   [430]

    Along that very Loire, with Festivals
    Resounding at all hours, and innocent yet
440 Of civil slaughter was our frequent walk
    Or in wide Forests of the neighbourhood,
    High woods and over-arch'd with open space   [435]
    On every side, and footing many a mile,
    Inwoven roots and moss smooth as the sea,
445 A solemn region. Often in such place
    From earnest dialogues I slipp'd in thought
    And let remembrance steal to other times   [439]
    When Hermits from their sheds and caves forth stray'd
    Walk'd by themselves, so met in shades like these,
450 And if a devious Traveller was heard   [447]
    Approaching from a distance, as might chance,
    With speed and echoes loud of trampling hoofs
    From the hard floor reverberated, then   [450]
    It was Angelica thundering through the woods
455 Upon her Palfrey, or that gentler Maid
    Erminia, fugitive as fair as She.
    Sometimes I saw, methought, a pair of Knights
    Joust underneath the trees, that, as in storm,   [455]
    Did rock above their heads; anon the din
460 Of boisterous merriment and music's roar,
    With sudden Proclamation, burst from haunt
    Of Satyrs in some viewless glade, with dance
    Rejoicing o'er a Female in the midst,   [460]
    A mortal Beauty, their unhappy Thrall;
465 The width of those huge Forests, unto me

A novel scene, did often in this way
Master my fancy, while I wander'd on
With that revered Companion. And sometimes   [465]
When to a Convent in a meadow green
470 By a brook-side we came, a roofless Pile,
And not by reverential touch of Time
Dismantled, but by violence abrupt,
In spite of those heart-bracing colloquies,   [470]
In spite of real fervour, and of that
475 Less genuine and wrought up within myself
I could not but bewail a wrong so harsh,
And for the matin Bell to sound no more
Griev'd, and the evening Taper, and the Cross   [475]
High on the topmost Pinnacle, a sign
480 Admonitory by the Traveller
First seen above the woods.
                              And when my Friend
Pointed upon occasion to the Site   [480]
Of Romorentin, home of ancient Kings,
To the imperial Edifice of Blois
485 Or to that rural Castle, name now slipp'd
From my remembrance, where a Lady lodg'd
By the first Francis wooed, and bound to him   [485]
In chains of mutual passion; from the Tower,
As a tradition of the Country tells,
490 Practis'd to commune with her Royal Knight
By cressets and love-beacons, intercourse
'Twixt her high-seated Residence and his   [490]
Far off at Chambord on the Plain beneath:
Even here, though less than with the peaceful House
495 Religious, 'mid these frequent monuments
Of Kings, their vices and their better deeds,
Imagination, potent to enflame   [495]
At times with virtuous wrath and noble scorn,
Did also often mitigate the force
500 Of civic prejudice, the bigotry,
So call it, of a youthful Patriot's mind,

164

And on these spots with many gleams I look'd [500]
Of chivalrous delight. Yet not the less,
Hatred of absolute rule, where will of One
505 Is law for all, and of that barren pride
In them who, by immunities unjust,
Betwixt the Sovereign and the People stand, [505]
His helper and not theirs, laid stronger hold
Daily upon me, mix'd with pity too
510 And love; for where hope is there love will be
For the abject multitude. And when we chanc'd
One day to meet a hunger-bitten Girl, [510]
Who crept along, fitting her languid self
Unto a Heifer's motion, by a cord
515 Tied to her arm, and picking thus from the lane
Its sustenance, while the Girl with her two hands
Was busy knitting, in a heartless mood [515]
Of solitude, and at the sight my Friend
In agitation said, ' 'Tis against *that*
520 Which we are fighting,' I with him believed
Devoutly that a spirit was abroad
Which could not be withstood, that poverty [520]
At least like this, would in a little time
Be found no more, that we should see the earth
525 Unthwarted in her wish to recompense
The industrious, and the lowly Child of Toil,
All institutes for ever blotted out [525]
That legalised exclusion, empty pomp
Abolish'd, sensual state and cruel power
530 Whether by edict of the one or few,
And finally, as sum and crown of all,
Should see the People having a strong hand [530]
In making their own Laws, whence better days
To all mankind. But, these things set apart,
535 Was not the single confidence enough
To animate the mind that ever turn'd
A thought to human welfare, that henceforth [535]
Captivity by mandate without law

Should cease, and open accusation lead
540 To sentence in the hearing of the world
And open punishment, if not the air
Be free to breathe in, and the heart of Man   [540]
Dread nothing. Having touch'd this argument
I shall not, as my purpose was, take note
545 Of other matters which detain'd us oft
In thought or conversation, public acts,
And public persons, and the emotions wrought
Within our minds by the ever-varying wind   [545]
Of Record and Report which day by day
550 Swept over us; but I will here instead
Draw from obscurity a tragic Tale
Not in its spirit singular indeed
But haply worth memorial, as I heard
The events related by my patriot Friend
555 And others who had borne a part therein.

    Oh! happy time of youthful Lovers! thus
My Story may begin, Oh! balmy time
In which a Love-knot on a Lady's brow   [555]
Is fairer than the fairest Star in heaven!
560 To such inheritance of blessedness   [5]
Young Vaudracour was brought by years that had
A little overstepp'd his stripling prime.
A Town of small repute in the heart of France   [10]
Was the Youth's Birth-place: there he vow'd his love
565 To Julia, a bright Maid, from Parents sprung
Not mean in their condition; but with rights
Unhonour'd of Nobility, and hence
The Father of the young Man, who had place
Among that order, spurn'd the very thought
570 Of such alliance. From their cradles up,
With but a step between their several homes   [20]
The Pair had thriven together year by year,
Friends, Playmates, Twins in pleasure, after strife
And petty quarrels had grown fond again,   [22]

575 Each other's advocate, each other's help,
     Nor ever happy if they were apart:
     A basis this for deep and solid love,
     And endless constancy, and placid truth;
     But whatsoever of such treasures might,
580 Beneath the outside of their youth, have lain
     Reserv'd for mellower years, his present mind
     Was under fascination; he beheld
     A vision, and he lov'd the thing he saw.
     Arabian Fiction never fill'd the world
585 With half the wonders that were wrought for him. [40]
     Earth liv'd in one great presence of the spring,
     Life turn'd the meanest of her implements
     Before his eyes to price above all gold,
     The house she dwelt in was a sainted shrine,
590 Her chamber-window did surpass in glory   [45]
     The portals of the East, all paradise
     Could by the simple opening of a door
     Let itself in upon him, pathways, walks,
     Swarm'd with enchantment till his spirit sank [49]
595 Beneath the burthen, overbless'd for life.
     This state was theirs, till whether through effect
     Of some delirious hour, or that the Youth,
     Seeing so many bars betwixt himself
     And the dear haven where he wish'd to be
600 In honourable wedlock with his love   [60]
     Without a certain knowledge of his own,
     Was inwardly prepared to turn aside
     From law and custom, and entrust himself
     To Nature for a happy end of all;
605 And thus abated of that pure reserve
     Congenial to his loyal heart, with which
     It would have pleas'd him to attend the steps
     Of Maiden so divinely beautiful
     I know not, but reluctantly must add
610 That Julia, yet without the name of Wife   [66]
     Carried about her for a secret grief

The promise of a Mother.

To conceal

The threaten'd shame the Parents of the Maid
Found means to hurry her away by night [70]
615 And unforewarn'd, that in a distant Town
She might remain shrouded in privacy,
Until the Babe was born. When morning came
The Lover thus bereft, stung with his loss
And all uncertain whither he should turn [75]
620 Chafed like a wild beast in the toils; at length,
Following as his suspicions led, he found
O joy! sure traces of the fugitives,
Pursu'd them to the Town where they had stopp'd,
And lastly to the very house itself
625 Which had been chosen for the Maid's retreat.
The sequel may be easily divined, [79]
Walks backwards, forwards, morning, noon and night
When decency and caution would allow
And Julia, who, whenever to herself
630 She happen'd to be left a moment's space,
Was busy at her casement, as a swallow
About its nest, ere long did thus espy
Her Lover, thence a stolen interview [85]
By night accomplish'd, with a ladder's help.

635   I pass the raptures of the Pair; such theme
Hath by a hundred Poets been set forth
In more delightful verse than skill of mine
Could fashion, chiefly by that darling Bard [90]
Who told of Juliet and her Romeo,
640 And of the lark's note heard before its time,
And of the streaks that laced the severing clouds
In the unrelenting East. 'Tis mine to tread [94]
The humbler province of plain history,
And, without choice of circumstance, submissively
645 Relate what I have heard. The Lovers came
To this resolve, with which they parted, pleased

And confident, that Vaudracour should hie
Back to his Father's house, and there employ
Means aptest to obtain a sum of gold,
650 A final portion, even, if that might be,   [106]
Which done, together they could then take flight
To some remote and solitary place
Where they might live with no one to behold   [110]
Their happiness, or to disturb their love.
655 Immediately, and with this mission charged
Home to his Father's House did he return
And there remain'd a time without hint given
Of his design; but if a word were dropp'd
Touching the matter of his passion, still
660 In hearing of his Father, Vaudracour   [115]
Persisted openly that nothing less
Than death should make him yield up hope to be
A blessed Husband of the Maid he loved.

Incensed at such obduracy and slight
665 Of exhortations and remonstrances
The Father threw out threats that by a mandate
Bearing the private signet of the State
He should be baffled in his mad intent,   [120]
And that should cure him. From this time the Youth
670 Conceived a terror, and by night or day
Stirr'd nowhere without Arms. Soon afterwards
His Parents to their Country Seat withdrew   [125]
Upon some feign'd occasion; and the Son
Was left with one Attendant in the house.
675 Retiring to his Chamber for the night,
While he was entering at the door, attempts
Were made to seize him by three armed Men,   [129]
The instruments of ruffian power; the Youth
In the first impulse of his rage, laid one
680 Dead at his feet, and to the second gave
A perilous wound, which done, at sight
Of the dead Man, he peacefully resign'd   [135]

His Person to the Law, was lodged in prison,
And wore the fetters of a Criminal.

685 Through three weeks' space, by means which love devised,
The Maid in her seclusion had received
Tidings of Vaudracour, and how he sped
Upon his enterprize. Thereafter came
A silence, half a circle did the moon
690 Complete, and then a whole, and still the same
Silence; a thousand thousand fears and hopes
Stirr'd in her mind; thoughts waking, thoughts of sleep
Entangled in each other, and at last
Self-slaughter seem'd her only resting-place.
695 So did she fare in her uncertainty.

At length, by interference of a Friend,   [151]
One who had sway at Court, the Youth regain'd
His liberty, on promise to sit down
Quietly in his Father's House, nor take
700 One step to reunite himself with her
Of whom his Parents disapprov'd: hard law
To which he gave consent only because
His freedom else could nowise be procured.
Back to his Father's house he went, remain'd
705 Eight days, and then his resolution fail'd:
He fled to Julia, and the words with which   [155]
He greeted her were these. 'All right is gone,
Gone from me. Thou no longer now art mine,   [160]
I thine; a Murderer, Julia, cannot love
710 An innocent Woman; I behold thy face
I see thee and my misery is complete.'
She could not give him answer; afterwards
She coupled with his Father's name some words   [166]
Of vehement indignation; but the Youth
715 Check'd her, nor would he hear of this; for thought
Unfilial, or unkind, had never once
Found harbour in his breast. The Lovers thus
United once again together lived

For a few days, which were to Vaudracour
720 Days of dejection, sorrow and remorse
For that ill deed of violence which his hand
Had hastily committed: for the Youth
Was of a loyal spirit, a conscience nice
And over tender for the trial which
725 His fate had call'd him to. The Father's mind,
Meanwhile, remain'd unchanged, and Vaudracour
Learn'd that a mandate had been newly issued
To arrest him on the spot. Oh pain it was
To part! he could not—and he linger'd still
730 To the last moment of his time, and then,
At dead of night with snow upon the ground,
He left the City, and in Villages
The most sequester'd of the neighbourhood
Lay hidden for the space of several days
735 Until the horseman bringing back report
That he was nowhere to be found, the search
Was ended. Back return'd the ill-fated Youth,
And from the House where Julia lodged (to which
He now found open ingress, having gain'd
740 The affection of the family, who lov'd him
Both for his own, and for the Maiden's sake)
One night retiring, he was seized—But here
A portion of the Tale may well be left   [177]
In silence, though my memory could add
745 Much how the Youth, and in short space of time,
Was travers'd from without, much, too, of thoughts
By which he was employ'd in solitude
Under privation and restraint, and what   [182]
Through dark and shapeless fear of things to come,
750 And what through strong compunction for the past
He suffer'd breaking down in heart and mind.   [185]
Such grace, if grace it were, had been vouchsafed
Or such effect had through the Father's want
Of power, or through his negligence ensued
755 That Vaudracour was suffered to remain,

Though under guard and without liberty,
In the same City with the unhappy Maid
From whom he was divided. So they fared
Objects of general concern, till, moved
760 With pity for their wrongs, the Magistrate,
The same who had placed the Youth in custody,
By application to the Minister
Obtain'd his liberty upon condition
That to his Father's House he should return.

765   He left his Prison almost on the eve
Of Julia's travail; she had likewise been
As from the time indeed, when she had first
Been brought for secresy to this abode,
Though treated with consoling tenderness,
770 Herself a Prisoner, a dejected one,
Fill'd with a lover's and a Woman's fears,
And whensoe'er the Mistress of the House
Enter'd the Room for the last time at night
And Julia with a low and plaintive voice
775 Said 'You are coming then to lock me up'
The Housewife when these words, always the same,
Were by her Captive languidly pronounced
Could never hear them utter'd without tears.

    A day or two before her child-bed time
780 Was Vaudracour restored to her, and soon
As he might be permitted to return
Into her Chamber after the Child's birth
The Master of the Family begg'd that all
The household might be summon'd, doubting not
785 But that they might receive impressions then
Friendly to human kindness. Vaudracour
(This heard I from one present at the time)
Held up the new-born Infant in his arms
And kiss'd, and bless'd, and cover'd it with tears,
790 Uttering a prayer that he might never be
As wretched as his Father; then he gave

The Child to her who bare it, and she too
Repeated the same prayer, took it again
And muttering something faintly afterwards
795 He gave the Infant to the Standers-by,
And wept in silence upon Julia's neck.

Two months did he continue in the House,
And often yielded up himself to plans
Of future happiness. 'You shall return,   [190]
800 Julia,' said he, 'and to your Father's House
Go with your Child, you have been wretched, yet
It is a town where both of us were born,
None will reproach you, for our loves are known,
With ornaments the prettiest you shall dress
805 Your Boy, as soon as he can run about,
And when he thus is at his play my Father   [205]
Will see him from the window, and the Child
Will by his beauty move his Grandsire's heart,   [210]
So that it will be soften'd, and our loves
810 End happily, as they began.' These gleams
Appear'd but seldom; oftener he was seen
Propping a pale and melancholy face
Upon the Mother's bosom, resting thus   [215]
His head upon one breast, while from the other
815 The Babe was drawing in its quiet food.
At other times, when he, in silence, long
And fixedly had look'd upon her face,
He would exclaim, 'Julia, how much thine eyes
Have cost me!' During day-time when the child
820 Lay in its cradle, by its side he sate,
Not quitting it an instant. The whole Town
In his unmerited misfortunes now
Took part, and if he either at the door
Or window for a moment with his Child
825 Appear'd, immediately the Street was throng'd
While others frequently without reserve
Pass'd and repass'd before the house to steal

173

A look at him. Oft at this time he wrote
Requesting, since he knew that the consent
830 Of Julia's Parents never could be gain'd
To a clandestine marriage, that his Father
Would from the birthright of an eldest Son
Exclude him, giving but, when this was done,
A sanction to his nuptials: vain request,
835 To which no answer was return'd. And now
From her own home the Mother of his Love
Arrived to apprise the Daughter of her fix'd
And last resolve, that, since all hope to move
The old Man's heart prov'd vain, she must retire
840 Into a Convent, and be there immured.
Julia was thunderstricken by these words,
And she insisted on a Mother's rights
To take her Child along with her, a grant
Impossible, as she at last perceived;
845 The Persons of the house no sooner heard
Of this decision upon Julia's fate
Than everyone was overwhelm'd with grief
Nor could they frame a manner soft enough
To impart the tidings to the Youth; but great
850 Was their astonishment when they beheld him
Receive the news in calm despondency,
Composed and silent, without outward sign
Of even the least emotion; seeing this   [230]
When Julia scatter'd some upbraiding words
855 Upon his slackness he thereto return'd
No answer, only took the Mother's hand
Who lov'd him scarcely less than her own Child,
And kissed it, without seeming to be press'd   [235]
By any pain that 'twas the hand of one
860 Whose errand was to part him from his Love
For ever. In the City he remain'd   [241]
A season after Julia had retired
And in the Convent taken up her home
To the end that he might place his infant Babe

865 With a fit Nurse, which done, beneath the roof
      Where now his little One was lodged, he pass'd
      The day entire, and scarcely could at length
      Tear himself from the cradle to return
      Home to his Father's House, in which he dwelt
870 Awhile, and then came back that he might see
      Whether the Babe had gain'd sufficient strength
      To bear removal. He quitted this same Town
      For the last time, attendant by the side   [246]
      Of a close chair, a Litter or Sedan,
875 In which the Child was carried. To a hill,
      Which rose at a League's distance from the Town,
      The Family of the house where he had lodged
      Attended him, and parted from him there,
      Watching below till he had disappear'd
880 On the hill top. His eyes he scarcely took,
      Through all that journey, from the Chair in which   [255]
      The Babe was carried; and at every Inn
      Or place at which they halted or reposed
      Laid him upon his knees, nor would permit   [260]
885 The hands of any but himself to dress
      The Infant or undress. By one of those
      Who bore the Chair these facts, at his return,
      Were told, and in relating them he wept.

      This was the manner in which Vaudracour
890 Departed with his Infant; and thus reach'd
      His Father's House, where to the innocent Child   [265]
      Admittance was denied. The young Man spake
      No words of indignation or reproof,
      But of his Father begg'd, a last request,
895 That a retreat might be assign'd to him,
      A house where in the Country he might dwell   [270]
      With such allowance as his wants required
      And the more lonely that the Mansion was
      'Twould be more welcome. To a lodge that stood
900 Deep in a Forest, with leave given, at the age

Of four and twenty summers he retired;
And thither took with him his Infant Babe,   [275]
And one Domestic for their common needs,
An aged woman. It consoled him here
905 To attend upon the Orphan and perform
The office of a Nurse to his young Child
Which after a short time by some mistake   [280]
Or indiscretion of the Father, died.
The Tale I follow to its last recess
910 Of suffering or of peace, I know not which;
Theirs be the blame who caused the woe, not mine.

From that time forth he never utter'd word   [285]
To any living. An Inhabitant
Of that same Town in which the Pair had left
915 So lively a remembrance of their griefs
By chance of business coming within reach
Of his retirement to the spot repair'd   [290]
With the intent to visit him: he reach'd
The house and only found the Matron there,
920 Who told him that his pains were thrown away,
For that her Master never utter'd word
To living soul—not even to her. Behold   [295]
While they were speaking, Vaudracour approach'd;
But, seeing some one there, just as his hand
925 Was stretch'd towards the garden-gate, he shrunk,
And like a shadow glided out of view.
Shock'd at his savage outside, from the place   [300]
The Visitor retired.
                    Thus liv'd the Youth
Cut off from all intelligence with Man,
930 And shunning even the light of common day;
Nor could the voice of Freedom, which through France
Soon afterwards resounded, public hope,   [305]
Or personal memory of his own deep wrongs,
Rouze him: but in those solitary shades
His days he wasted, an imbecile mind.

BOOK TENTH

RESIDENCE IN FRANCE AND FRENCH REVOLUTION

It was a beautiful and silent day
That overspread the countenance of earth,
Then fading, with unusual quietness,   [3]
When from the Loire I parted, and through scenes
5 Of vineyard, orchard, meadow-ground and tilth,
Calm waters, gleams of sun, and breathless trees
Towards the fierce Metropolis turn'd my steps
Their homeward way to England. From his Throne   [11]
The King had fallen; the congregated Host,
10 Dire cloud upon the front of which was written
The tender mercies of the dismal wind
That bore it, on the Plains of Liberty   [15]
Had burst innocuously, say more, the swarm
That came elate and jocund, like a Band
15 Of Eastern Hunters, to enfold in ring
Narrowing itself by moments and reduce
To the last punctual spot of their despair
A race of victims, so they seem'd, *themselves*
Had shrunk from sight of their own task, and fled
20 In terror; desolation and dismay
Remained for them whose fancies had grown rank
With evil expectations, confidence
And perfect triumph to the better cause.   [30]
The State, as if to stamp the final seal
25 On her security, and to the world
Shew what she was, a high and fearless soul,   [33]
Or rather in a spirit of thanks to those
Who had stirr'd up her slackening faculties
To a new transition, had assumed with joy
30 The body and the venerable name   [40]
Of a Republic: lamentable crimes
'Tis true had gone before this hour, the work

Of massacre, in which the senseless sword
Was pray'd to as a judge; but these were past,
35   Earth free from them for ever, as was thought,   [45]
Ephemeral monsters, to be seen but once;
Things that could only shew themselves and die.

    This was the time in which enflam'd with hope,
To Paris I returned. Again I rang'd
40   More eagerly than I had done before
Through the wide City, and in progress pass'd   [50]
The Prison where the unhappy Monarch lay,
Associate with his Children and his Wife
In bondage; and the Palace lately storm'd
45   With roar of cannon, and a numerous Host.
I cross'd (a blank and empty area then)   [55]
The Square of the Carousel, few weeks back
Heap'd up with dead and dying, upon these
And other sights looking as doth a man
50   Upon a volume whose contents he knows
Are memorable, but from him lock'd up,   [60]
Being written in a tongue he cannot read,
So that he questions the mute leaves with pain
And half upbraids their silence. But that night
55   When on my bed I lay, I was most mov'd
And felt most deeply in what world I was;
My room was high and lonely, near the roof
Of a large Mansion or Hotel, a spot
That would have pleas'd me in more quiet times,
60   Nor was it wholly without pleasure then.
With unextinguish'd taper I kept watch,   [70]
Reading at intervals; the fear gone by
Press'd on me almost like a fear to come;
I thought of those September Massacres,
65   Divided from me by a little month,
And felt and touch'd them, a substantial dread;   [75]
The rest was conjured up from tragic fictions,
And mournful Calendars of true history,

Remembrances and dim admonishments.
70 'The horse is taught his manage, and the wind
Of heaven wheels round and treads in his own steps,
Year follows year, the tide returns again,
Day follows day, all things have second birth;
The earthquake is not satisfied at once.'
75 And in such way I wrought upon myself,   [35]
Until I seem'd to hear a voice that cried,
To the whole City, 'Sleep no more.' To this
Add comments of a calmer mind, from which
I could not gather full security,
80 But at the best it seem'd a place of fear
Unfit for the repose of night [   ],   [92]
Defenceless as a wood where tigers roam.

Betimes next morning to the Palace Walk
Of Orleans I repair'd and entering there
85 Was greeted, among divers other notes,
By voices of the Hawkers in the crowd
Bawling, *Denunciation of the crimes*   [100]
Of Maximilian Robespierre; the speech
Which in their hands they carried was the same
90 Which had been recently pronounced, the day
When Robespierre, well knowing for what mark
Some words of indirect reproof had been   [105]
Intended, rose in hardihood, and dared
The Man who had an ill surmise of him
95 To bring his charge in openness, whereat
When a dead pause ensued, and no one stirr'd,
In silence of all present, from his seat   [110]
Louvet walked singly through the avenue
And took his station in the Tribune, saying,
100 'I, Robespierre, accuse thee!' 'Tis well known
What was the issue of that charge, and how
Louvet was left alone without support
Of his irresolute Friends; but these are things   [120]
Of which I speak, only as they were storm

179

105 Or sunshine to my individual mind,
No further. Let me then relate that now
In some sort seeing with my proper eyes
That Liberty, and Life, and Death would soon   [125]
To the remotest corners of the land
110 Lie in the arbitrement of those who ruled
The capital City, what was struggled for,
And by what combatants victory must be won,
The indecision on their part whose aim   [130]
Seem'd best, and the straightforward path of those
115 Who in attack or in defence alike
Were strong through their impiety, greatly I
Was agitated; yea I could almost
Have pray'd that throughout earth upon all souls   [135]
Worthy of liberty, upon every soul
120 Matured to live in plainness and in truth
The gift of tongues might fall, and men arrive
From the four quarters of the winds to do   [140]
For France what without help she could not do,
A work of honour; think not that to this
125 I added, work of safety; from such thought
And the least fear about the end of things
I was as far as Angels are from guilt.   [145]

Yet did I grieve, nor only griev'd, but thought
Of opposition and of remedies,
130 An insignificant Stranger, and obscure,
Mean as I was, and little graced with power
Of eloquence even in my native speech,   [150]
And all unfit for tumult and intrigue,
Yet would I willingly have taken up
135 A service at this time for cause so great,
However dangerous. Inly I revolved
How much the destiny of man had still   [155]
Hung upon single persons, that there was,
Transcendent to all local patrimony,

140 One Nature as there is one Sun in heaven,
    That objects, even as they are great, thereby
    Do come within the reach of humblest eyes,   [160]
    That Man was only weak through his mistrust
    And want of hope, where evidence divine
145 Proclaim'd to him that hope should be most sure,
    That, with desires heroic and firm sense,
    A Spirit thoroughly faithful to itself,
    Unquenchable, unsleeping, undismay'd,
    Was as an instinct among men, a stream
150 That gather'd up each petty straggling rill
    And vein of water, glad to be roll'd on
    In safe obedience, that a mind whose rest
    Was where it ought to be, in self-restraint,
    In circumspection and simplicity,   [175]
155 Fell rarely in entire discomfiture
    Below its aim, or met with from without
    A treachery that defeated it or foil'd.

    On the other side, I call'd to mind those truths   [191]
    Which are the common-places of the Schools,
160 A theme for Boys, too trite even to be felt,
    Yet, with a revelation's liveliness,
    In all their comprehensive bearings known   [195]
    And visible to Philosophers of old,
    Men who, to business of the world untrain'd,
165 Liv'd in the Shade, and to Harmodius known
    And his Compeer Aristogiton, known
    To Brutus, that tyrannic Power is weak,   [200]
    Hath neither gratitude, nor faith, nor love,
    Nor the support of good or evil men
170 To trust in, that the Godhead which is ours
    Can never utterly be charm'd or still'd,
    That nothing hath a natural right to last   [205]
    But equity and reason, that all else
    Meets foes irreconcilable, and at best
175 Doth live but by variety of disease.

    Well might my wishes be intense, my thoughts
Strong and perturb'd, not doubting at that time,   [210]
Creed which ten shameful years have not annull'd,
But that the virtue of one paramount mind
180 Would have abash'd those impious crests, have quell'd
Outrage and bloody power, and in despite
Of what the People were through ignorance
And immaturity, and, in the teeth   [216]
Of desperate opposition from without,
185 Have clear'd a passage for just government,
And left a solid birthright to the State,
Redeem'd according to example given   [220]
By ancient Lawgivers.
                In this frame of mind,
Reluctantly to England I return'd,
190 Compell'd by nothing less than absolute want
Of funds for my support, else, well assured
That I both was and must be of small worth,
No better than an alien in the Land,
I doubtless should have made a common cause
195 With some who perish'd, haply perish'd, too,   [230]
A poor mistaken and bewilder'd offering,
Should to the breast of Nature have gone back
With all my resolutions, all my hopes,
A Poet only to myself, to Men
200 Useless, and even, beloved Friend! a soul   [235]
To thee unknown.
            When to my native Land
(After a whole year's absence) I return'd
I found the air yet busy with the stir   [246]
Of a contention which had been rais'd up
205 Against the Traffickers in Negro blood,
An effort, which though baffled, nevertheless   [250]
Had call'd back old forgotten principles
Dismiss'd from service, had diffus'd some truths
And more of virtuous feeling through the heart
210 Of the English People. And no few of those

182

So numerous (little less in verity
Than a whole Nation crying with one voice)
Who had been cross'd in this their just intent
And righteous hope, thereby were well prepared
215 To let that journey sleep awhile, and join
Whatever other Caravan appear'd
To travel forward towards Liberty
With more success. For me that strife had ne'er
Fasten'd on my affections, nor did now   [255]
220 Its unsuccessful issue much excite
My sorrow, having laid this faith to heart,
That, if France prosper'd, good Men would not long
Pay fruitless worship to humanity,
And this most rotten branch of human shame,   [260]
225 Object, as seem'd, of a superfluous pains
Would fall together with its parent tree.

Such was my then belief, that there was one,
And only one solicitude for all;
And now the strength of Britain was put forth
230 In league with the confederated Host,   [265]
Not in my single self alone I found,
But in the minds of all ingenuous Youth,
Change and subversion from this hour. No shock
Given to my moral nature had I known
235 Down to that very moment; neither lapse   [270]
Nor turn of sentiment that might be nam'd
A revolution, save at this one time,
All else was progress on the self-same path
On which with a diversity of pace
240 I had been travelling; this a stride at once   [275]
Into another region. True it is,
'Twas not conceal'd with what ungracious eyes
Our native Rulers from the very first
Had look'd upon regenerated France
245 Nor had I doubted that this day would come.
But in such contemplation I had thought

Of general interests only, beyond this
Had [never] once foretasted the event.
Now had I other business for I felt
250 The ravage of this most unnatural strife
In my own heart; there lay it like a weight
At enmity with all the tenderest springs
Of my enjoyments. I, who with the breeze
Had play'd, a green leaf on the blessed tree
255 Of my beloved Country; nor had wish'd   [280]
For happier fortune than to wither there,
Now from my pleasant station was cut off,
And toss'd about in whirlwinds. I rejoiced,
Yea, afterwards, truth painful to record!
260 Exulted in the triumph of my soul   [285]
When Englishmen by thousands were o'erthrown,
Left without glory on the Field, or driven,
Brave hearts, to shameful flight. It was a grief,
Grief call it not, 'twas anything but that,
265 A conflict of sensations without name,   [290]
Of which he only who may love the sight
Of a Village Steeple as I do can judge
When in the Congregation, bending all
To their great Father, prayers were offer'd up,
270 Or praises for our Country's Victories,   [295]
And 'mid the simple worshippers, perchance,
I only, like an uninvited Guest
Whom no one owned sate silent, shall I add,
Fed on the day of vengeance yet to come?

275   Oh! much have they to account for, who could tear [300]
By violence at one decisive rent
From the best Youth in England, their dear pride,
Their joy, in England; this, too, at a time
In which worst losses easily might wear
280 The best of names, when patriotic love   [305]
Did of itself in modesty give way
Like the Precursor when the Deity

Is come, whose Harbinger he is, a time
In which apostacy from ancient faith
285 Seem'd but conversion to a higher creed, [310]
Withal a season dangerous and wild,
A time in which Experience would have plucked
Flowers out of any hedge to make thereof
A Chaplet, in contempt of his grey locks.

290 Ere yet the Fleet of Britain had gone forth [315]
On this unworthy service, whereunto
The unhappy counsel of a few weak men
Had doom'd it, I beheld the Vessels lie,
A brood of gallant creatures, on the Deep
295 I saw them in their rest, a sojourner
Through a whole month of calm and glassy days, [320]
In that delightful Island which protects
Their place of convocation; there I heard
Each evening, walking by the still sea-shore,
300 A monitory sound that never fail'd,
The sunset cannon. While the Orb went down [325]
In the tranquillity of Nature, came
That voice, ill requiem! seldom heard by me
Without a spirit overcast, a deep
305 Imagination, thought of woes to come,
And sorrow for mankind, and pain of heart. [330]

In France, the Men who for their desperate ends
Had pluck'd up mercy by the roots were glad
Of this new enemy. Tyrants, strong before
310 In devilish pleas were ten times stronger now,
And thus beset with Foes on every side [335]
The goaded Land wax'd mad; the crimes of few
Spread into madness of the many, blasts
From hell came sanctified like airs from heaven;
315 The sternness of the Just, the faith of those
Who doubted not that Providence had times [340]
Of anger and of vengeance,—theirs who throned
The human understanding paramount

And made of that their God, the hopes of those
320 Who were content to barter short-lived pangs
For a paradise of ages, the blind rage   [345]
Of insolent tempers, the light vanity
Of intermeddlers, steady purposes
Of the suspicious, slips of the indiscreet,
325 And all the accidents of life were press'd
Into one service, busy with one work;   [350]
The Senate was heart-stricken, not a voice
Uplifted, none to oppose or mitigate;   [355]
Domestic carnage now fill'd all the year
330 With Feast-days; the Old Man from the chimney-nook,
The Maiden from the bosom of her Love,
The Mother from the Cradle of her Babe,
The Warrior from the Field, all perish'd, all,   [360]
Friends, enemies, of all parties, ages, ranks,
335 Head after head, and never heads enough
For those who bade them fall: they found their joy,
They made it, ever thirsty as a Child,
If light desires of innocent little Ones   [365]
May with such heinous appetites be match'd,
340 Having a toy, a wind-mill, though the air
Do of itself blow fresh, and makes the vane   [370]
Spin in his eyesight, he is not content
But with the play-thing at arm's length he sets
His front against the blast, and runs amain,
345 To make it whirl the faster.
                              In the depth
Of those enormities, even thinking minds   [375]
Forgot at seasons whence they had their being,
Forgot that such a sound was ever heard
As Liberty upon earth: yet all beneath
350 Her innocent authority was wrought,
Nor could have been, without her blessed name.   [380]
The illustrious Wife of Roland, in the hour
Of her composure, felt that agony
And gave it vent in her last words. O Friend!

186

355 It was a lamentable time for man
Whether a hope had e'er been his or not,   [385]
A woeful time for them whose hopes did still
Outlast the shock; most woeful for those few,
They had the deepest feeling of the grief,
360 Who still were flatter'd, and had trust in man.
Meanwhile, the Invaders fared as they deserv'd;   [390]
The Herculean Commonwealth had put forth her arms
And throttled with an infant Godhead's might
The snakes about her cradle; that was well
365 And as it should be, yet no cure for those
Whose souls were sick with pain of what would be   [395]
Hereafter brought in charge against mankind;
Most melancholy at that time, O Friend!
Were my day-thoughts, my dreams were miserable;
370 Through months, through years, long after the last beat
Of those atrocities (I speak bare truth,   [400]
As if to thee alone in private talk)
I scarcely had one night of quiet sleep
Such ghastly visions had I of despair
375 And tyranny, and implements of death,
And long orations which in dreams I pleaded   [411]
Before unjust Tribunals, with a voice
Labouring, a brain confounded, and a sense,
Of treachery and desertion in the place
380 The holiest that I knew of, my own soul.   [415]

When I began at first, in early youth
To yield myself to Nature, when that strong
And holy passion overcame me first,
Neither the day nor night, evening or morn
385 Were free from the oppression; but, Great God!   [420]
Who send'st thyself into this breathing world
Through Nature and through every kind of life,
And mak'st Man what he is, Creature divine,
In single or in social eminence   [425]
390 Above all these raised infinite ascents

When reason, which enables him to be,
Is not sequester'd, what a change is here!
How different ritual for this after worship
What countenance to promote this second love   [430]
395 That first was service but to things which lie
At rest, within the bosom of thy will:
Therefore to serve was high beatitude;
The tumult was a gladness, and the fear
Ennobling, venerable; sleep secure,   [435]
400 And waking thoughts more rich than happiest dreams.

But as the ancient Prophets were enflamed
Nor wanted consolations of their own   [440]
And majesty of mind, when they denounced
On Towns and Cities, wallowing in the abyss
405 Of their offences, punishment to come;
Or saw like other men with bodily eyes
Before them in some desolated place   [445]
The consummation of the wrath of Heaven,
So did some portion of that spirit fall
410 On me, to uphold me through those evil times,
And in their rage and dog-day heat I found
Something to glory in, as just and fit,
And in the order of sublimest laws;
And even if that were not, amid the awe
415 Of unintelligible chastisement,   [455]
I felt a kind of sympathy with power,
Motions rais'd up within me, nevertheless,
Which had relationship to highest things.
Wild blasts of music thus did find their way   [461]
420 Into the midst of terrible events,
So that worst tempests might be listen'd to:
Then was the truth received into my heart,
That under heaviest sorrow earth can bring,   [465]
Griefs bitterest of ourselves or of our Kind,
425 If from the affliction somewhere do not grow
Honour which could not else have been, a faith,

An elevation, and a sanctity,
If new strength be not given, or old restored
The blame is ours not Nature's. When a taunt   [470]
430 Was taken up by scoffers in their pride,
Saying, 'behold the harvest which we reap
From popular Government and Equality,'
I saw that it was neither these, nor aught
Of wild belief engrafted on their names   [475]
435 By false philosophy, that caus'd the woe,
But that it was a reservoir of guilt
And ignorance, fill'd up from age to age,
That could no longer hold its loathsome charge,
But burst and spread in deluge through the Land.   [480]

440   And as the desart hath green spots, the sea
Small islands in the midst of stormy waves,
So that disastrous period did not want
Such sprinklings of all human excellence,
As were a joy to hear of. Yet (nor less   [486]
445 For those bright spots, those fair examples given
Of fortitude, and energy, and love,
And human nature faithful to itself
Under worst trials) was I impell'd to think   [490]
Of the glad time when first I traversed France,
450 A youthful pilgrim, above all remember'd
That day when through an Arch that spann'd the street,
A rainbow made of garish ornaments,
Triumphal pomp for Liberty confirm'd,
We walk'd, a pair of weary Travellers,
455 Along the Town of Arras, place from which
Issued that Robespierre, who afterwards
Wielded the sceptre of the atheist crew.   [502]
When the calamity spread far and wide,
And this same City, which had even appear'd
460 To outrun the rest in exultation, groan'd   [505]
Under the vengeance of her cruel Son,
As Lear reproach'd the winds, I could almost

189

Have quarrel'd with that blameless spectacle
For being yet an image in my mind
465 To mock me under such a strange reverse.   [510]

O Friend! few happier moments have been mine
Through my whole life than that when first I heard
That this foul Tribe of Moloch was o'erthrown,
And their chief Regent levell'd with the dust.
470 The day was one which haply may deserve
A separate chronicle. Having gone abroad
From a small Village where I tarried then,
To the same far-secluded privacy
I was returning. Over the smooth Sands
475 Of Leven's ample Æstuary lay   [515]
My journey, and beneath a genial sun;
With distant prospect among gleams of sky
And clouds, and intermingled mountain tops,
In one inseparable glory clad,
480 Creatures of one ethereal substance, met   [520]
In Consistory, like a diadem
Or crown of burning Seraphs, as they sit
In the Empyrean. Underneath this show
Lay, as I knew, the nest of pastoral vales
485 Among whose happy fields I had grown up   [525]
From childhood. On the fulgent spectacle
Which neither changed, nor stirr'd, nor pass'd away,
I gazed, and with a fancy more alive
On this account, that I had chanced to find
490 That morning, ranging thro' the churchyard graves
Of Cartmell's rural Town, the place in which
An honor'd Teacher of my youth was laid.   [534]
While we were Schoolboys he had died among us,
And was borne hither, as I knew, to rest
495 With his own Family. A plain Stone, inscribed
With name, date, office, pointed out the spot,
To which a slip of verses was subjoin'd,
(By his desire, as afterwards I learn'd)

A fragment from the Elegy of Gray.   [536]
500 A week, or little less, before his death
He had said to me, 'my head will soon lie low;'
And when I saw the turf that cover'd him,   [540]
After the lapse of full eight years, those words,
With sound of voice, and countenance of the Man,
505 Came back upon me; so that some few tears
Fell from me in my own despite. And now,
Thus travelling smoothly o'er the level Sands,   [545]
I thought with pleasure of the Verses, graven
Upon his Tombstone, saying to myself
510 He loved the Poets, and if now alive,
Would have loved me, as one not destitute
Of promise, nor belying the kind hope   [550]
Which he had form'd, when I at his command,
Began to spin, at first, my toilsome Songs.

515   Without me and within, as I advanced,
All that I saw, or felt, or communed with
Was gentleness and peace. Upon a small
And rocky Island near, a fragment stood   [555]
(Itself like a sea rock) of what had been
520 A Romish Chapel, where in ancient times
Masses were said at the hour which suited those
Who cross'd the Sands with ebb of morning tide.   [561]
Not far from this still Ruin all the Plain
Was spotted with a variegated crowd
525 Of Coaches, Wains, and Travellers, horse and foot,
Wading, beneath the conduct of their Guide   [565]
In loose procession through the shallow Stream
Of inland water; the great Sea meanwhile
Was at safe distance, far retired. I paused,
530 Unwilling to proceed, the scene appear'd
So gay and chearful, when a Traveller
Chancing to pass, I carelessly inquired
If any news were stirring; he replied
In the familiar language of the day   [572]

191

535 That, *Robespierre was dead.* Nor was a doubt,
On further question, left within my mind
But that the tidings were substantial truth;
That he and his supporters all were fallen. [575]

Great was my glee of spirit, great my joy
540 In vengeance, and eternal justice, thus
Made manifest. 'Come now ye golden times,'
Said I, forth-breathing on those open Sands
A Hymn of triumph, 'as the morning comes [580]
Out of the bosom of the night, come Ye:
545 Thus far our trust is verified; behold!
They who with clumsy desperation brought
Rivers of Blood, and preached that nothing else
Could cleanse the Augean Stable, by the might [585]
Of their own helper have been swept away;
550 Their madness is declared and visible,
Elsewhere will safety now be sought, and Earth
March firmly towards righteousness and peace.'
Then schemes I framed more calmly, when and how [590]
The madding Factions might be tranquillised,
555 And, though through hardships manifold and long,
The mighty renovation would proceed;
Thus, interrupted by uneasy bursts
Of exultation, I pursued my way [595]
Along that very Shore which I had skimm'd
560 In former times, when, spurring from the Vale
Of Nightshade, and St. Mary's mouldering Fane,
And the Stone Abbot, after circuit made
In wantonness of heart, a joyous Crew [600]
Of School-boys, hastening to their distant home,
565 Along the margin of the moonlight Sea,
We beat with thundering hoofs the level Sand.

From this time forth, in France, as is well known,
Authority put on a milder face,
Yet everything was wanting that might give
570 Courage to those who look'd for good by light

Of rational experience, good I mean   [5]
At hand, and in the spirit of past aims.
The same belief I, nevertheless, retain'd;
The language of the Senate and the acts
575 And public measures of the Government,
Though both of heartless omen, had not power   [10]
To daunt me; in the People was my trust
And in the vertues which mine eyes had seen,
And to the ultimate repose of things
580 I look'd with unabated confidence;
I knew that wound external could not take
Life from the young Republic, that new foes
Would only follow in the path of shame   [15]
Their brethren, and her triumphs be in the end
585 Great, universal, irresistible.
This faith, which was an object in my mind
Of passionate intuition, had effect
Not small in dazzling me; for thus, thro' zeal,
Such victory I confounded in my thoughts
590 With one far higher and more difficult,
Triumphs of unambitious peace at home   [20]
And noiseless fortitude. Beholding still
Resistance strong as heretofore, I thought
That what was in degree the same, was likewise
595 The same in quality, that, as the worse
Of the two spirits then at strife remain'd   [25]
Untired, the better surely would preserve
The heart that first had rouzed him, never dreamt
That transmigration could be undergone
600 A fall of being suffer'd, and of hope
By creature that appear'd to have received
Entire conviction what a great ascent
Had been accomplish'd, what high faculties
It had been call'd to. Youth maintains, I knew,
605 In all conditions of society,
Communion more direct and intimate
With Nature, and the inner strength she has,   [30]

And hence, oft-times, no less, with Reason too,
Than Age or Manhood, even. To Nature then,
610 Power had reverted: habit, custom, law,
Had left an interregnum's open space
For her to stir about in, uncontrol'd.
The warmest judgments and the most untaught
Found in events which every day brought forth
615 Enough to sanction them, and far, far more
To shake the authority of canons drawn
From ordinary practice. I could see
How Babel-like the employment was of those   [35]
Who, by the recent Deluge stupefied,
620 With their whole souls went culling from the day
Its petty promises to build a tower
For their own safety; laugh'd at gravest heads,
Who, watching in their hate of France for signs   [40]
Of her disasters, if the stream of rumour
625 Brought with it one green branch, conceited thence
That not a single tree was left alive
In all her forests. How could I believe
That wisdom could in any shape come near   [45]
Men clinging to delusions so insane?
630 And thus, experience proving that no few
Of my opinions had been just, I took
Like credit to myself where less was due,
And thought that other notions were as sound,   [50]
Yea, could not but be right, because I saw
635 That foolish men opposed them.

                          To a strain
More animated I might here give way,
And tell, since juvenile errors are my theme,
What in those days through Britain was perform'd   [55]
To turn *all* judgments out of their right course;
640 But this is passion over-near ourselves,
Reality too close and too intense,
And mingled up with something, in my mind,
Of scorn and condemnation personal,   [60]

That would profane the sanctity of verse.
645 Our Shepherds (this say merely) at that time
Thirsted to make the guardian Crook of Law
A tool of Murder; they who ruled the State,   [65]
Though with such awful proof before their eyes
That he who would sow death, reaps death, or worse,
650 And can reap nothing better, child-like long'd
To imitate, not wise enough to avoid,   [69]
Giants in their impiety alone,
But, in their weapons and their warfare base
As vermin working out of reach, they leagued
655 Their strength perfidiously, to undermine
Justice, and make an end of Liberty.

    But from these bitter truths I must return
To my own History. It hath been told   [75]
That I was led to take an eager part
660 In arguments of civil polity
Abruptly, and indeed before my time:
I had approach'd, like other Youth, the Shield
Of human nature from the golden side   [80]
And would have fought, even to the death, to attest
665 The quality of the metal which I saw.
What there is best in individual Man,
Of wise in passion, and sublime in power,
What there is strong and pure in household love,
Benevolent in small societies,   [85]
670 And great in large ones also, when call'd forth
By great occasions, these were things of which
I something knew, yet even these themselves,
Felt deeply, were not thoroughly understood
By Reason; nay, far from it, they were yet,
675 As cause was given me afterwards to learn,
Not proof against the injuries of the day,   [90]
Lodged only at the Sanctuary's door,
Not safe within its bosom. Thus prepared,
And with such general insight into evil,

680 And of the bounds which sever it from good,
  As books and common intercourse with life   [95]
  Must needs have given; to the noviciate mind,
  When the world travels in a beaten road,
  Guide faithful as is needed, I began
685 To think with fervour upon management
  Of Nations, what it is and ought to be,   [100]
  And how their worth depended on their Laws
  And on the Constitution of the State.

  O pleasant exercise of hope and joy!   [105]
690 For great were the auxiliars which then stood
  Upon our side, we who were strong in love;
  Bliss was it in that dawn to be alive,
  But to be young was very heaven; O times,
  In which the meagre, stale, forbidding ways   [110]
695 Gf custom, law, and statute took at once
  The attraction of a Country in Romance;
  When Reason seem'd the most to assert her rights
  When most intent on making of herself
  A prime Enchanter to assist the work,   [115]
700 Which then was going forwards in her name.
  Not favour'd spots alone, but the whole earth
  The beauty wore of promise, that which sets,
  To take an image which was felt, no doubt,
  Among the bowers of paradise itself,   [120]
705 The budding rose above the rose full blown.
  What temper at the prospect did not wake
  To happiness unthought of? The inert
  Were rouz'd, and lively natures rapt away:
  They who had fed their childhood upon dreams,   [125]
710 The Play-fellows of Fancy, who had made
  All powers of swiftness, subtlety, and strength
  Their ministers, used to stir in lordly wise
  Among the grandest objects of the sense,
  And deal with whatsoever they found there   [130]
715 As if they had within some lurking right

To wield it; they too, who, of gentle mood
Had watch'd all gentle motions, and to these
Had fitted their own thoughts, schemers more mild,
And in the region of their peaceful selves,   [135]
720 Did now find helpers to their hearts' desire,
And stuff at hand, plastic as they could wish,
Were call'd upon to exercise their skill,
Not in Utopia, subterraneous Fields,   [140]
Or some secreted Island, Heaven knows where,
725 But in the very world which is the world
Of all of us, the place on which, in the end,
We find our happiness, or not at all.

Why should I not confess that earth was then   [145]
To me what an inheritance new-fallen
730 Seems, when the first time visited, to one
Who thither comes to find in it his home?
He walks about and looks upon the place
With cordial transport, moulds it, and remoulds,   [150]
And is half pleased with things that are amiss,
735 'Twill be such joy to see them disappear.

An active partisan, I thus convoked
From every object pleasant circumstance
To suit my ends; I moved among mankind   [155]
With genial feelings still predominant;
740 When erring, erring on the better part,
And in the kinder spirit; placable,
Indulgent oft-times to the worst desires
As on one side not uninform'd that men
See as it hath been taught them, and that time
745 Gives rights to error; on the other hand   [161]
That throwing off oppression must be work
As well of license as of liberty;
And above all, for this was more than all,
Not caring if the wind did now and then   [165]
750 Blow keen upon an eminence that gave
Prospect so large into futurity;

In brief, a child of nature, as at first,
Diffusing only those affections wider
That from the cradle had grown up with me,   [170]
755 And losing, in no other way than light
Is lost in light, the weak in the more strong.

In the main outline, such, it might be said,
Was my condition, till with open war
Britain opposed the Liberties of France;   [175]
760 This threw me first out of the pale of love;
Sour'd and corrupted upwards to the source
My sentiments, was not, as hitherto,
A swallowing up of lesser things in great;
But change of them into their opposites,   [180]
765 And thus a way was opened for mistakes
And false conclusions of the intellect,
As gross in their degree and in their kind
Far, far more dangerous. What had been a pride
Was now a shame; my likings and my loves
770 Ran in new channels, leaving old ones dry,   [185]
And thus a blow which, in maturer age,
Would but have touch'd the judgment struck more deep
Into sensations near the heart: meantime,
As from the first, wild theories were afloat,
775 Unto the subtleties of which, at least,   [190]
I had but lent a careless ear, assured
Of this, that time would soon set all things right,
Prove that the multitude had been oppress'd,
And would be so no more.
                                   But when events
780 Brought less encouragement, and unto these   [195]
The immediate proof of principles no more
Could be entrusted, while the events themselves,
Worn out in greatness, and in novelty,
Less occupied the mind, and sentiments
785 Could through my understanding's natural growth   [200]
No longer justify themselves through faith

Of inward consciousness, and hope that laid
Its hand upon its object, evidence
Safer, of universal application, such
790 As could not be impeach'd, was sought elsewhere.   [205]

And now, become oppressors in their turn,
Frenchmen had changed a war of self-defence
For one of conquest, losing sight of all
Which they had struggled for; and mounted up,
795 Openly, in the view of earth and heaven,   [210]
The scale of Liberty. I read her doom,
Vex'd inly somewhat, it is true, and sore;
But not dismay'd, nor taking to the shame
Of a false Prophet; but, rouz'd up I stuck   [214]
800 More firmly to old tenets, and to prove
Their temper, strain'd them more, and thus in heat
Of contest did opinions every day
Grow into consequence, till round my mind   [220]
They clung, as if they were the life of it.

805 This was the time when all things tending fast
To depravation, the Philosophy
That promised to abstract the hopes of man   [225]
Out of his feelings, to be fix'd thenceforth
For ever in a purer element
810 Found ready welcome. Tempting region that
For Zeal to enter and refresh herself,
Where passions had the privilege to work,   [230]
And never hear the sound of their own names;
But, speaking more in charity, the dream
815 Was flattering to the young ingenuous mind
Pleas'd with extremes, and not the least with that
Which makes the human Reason's naked self
The object of its fervour. What delight!   [235]
How glorious! in self-knowledge and self-rule,
820 To look through all the frailties of the world,
And, with a resolute mastery shaking off
The accidents of nature, time, and place,

That make up the weak being of the past,
Build social freedom on its only basis,
825 The freedom of the individual mind,   [240]
Which, to the blind restraint of general laws
Superior, magisterially adopts
One guide, the light of circumstances, flash'd
Upon an independent intellect.   [244]

830   For howsoe'er unsettled, never once
Had I thought ill of human kind, or been
Indifferent to its welfare, but, enflam'd
With thirst of a secure intelligence
And sick of other passion, I pursued   [250]
835 A higher nature, wish'd that Man should start
Out of the worm-like state in which he is,
And spread abroad the wings of Liberty,
Lord of himself, in undisturb'd delight—
A noble aspiration, yet I feel   [255]
840 The aspiration, but with other thoughts
And happier; for I was perplex'd and sought
To accomplish the transition by such means
As did not lie in nature, sacrificed
The exactness of a comprehensive mind
845 To scrupulous and microscopic views
That furnish'd out materials for a work
Of false imagination, placed beyond
The limits of experience and of truth.

    Enough, no doubt, the advocates themselves   [259]
850 Of ancient institutions had perform'd
To bring disgrace upon their very names,
Disgrace of which custom and written law
And sundry moral sentiments as props
And emanations of these institutes   [265]
855 Too justly bore a part. A veil had been
Uplifted; why deceive ourselves? 'Twas so,
'Twas even so, and sorrow for the Man
Who either had not eyes wherewith to see,

Or seeing hath forgotten. Let this pass,   [270]
860 Suffice it that a shock had then been given
To old opinions; and the minds of all men
Had felt it; that my mind was both let loose,
Let loose and goaded. After what hath been
Already said of patriotic love,   [274]
865 And hinted at in other sentiments
We need not linger long upon this theme.
This only may be said, that from the first
Having two natures in me, joy the one
The other melancholy, and withal
870 A happy man, and therefore bold to look
On painful things, slow, somewhat, too, and stern
In temperament, I took the knife in hand
And stopping not at parts less sensitive,
Endeavoured with my best of skill to probe
875 The living body of society   [281]
Even to the heart; I push'd without remorse
My speculations forward; yea, set foot
On Nature's holiest places. Time may come
When some dramatic Story may afford
880 Shapes livelier to convey to thee, my Friend,
What then I learn'd, or think I learn'd, of truth,   [286]
And the errors into which I was betray'd
By present objects, and by reasonings false
From the beginning, inasmuch as drawn
885 Out of a heart which had been turn'd aside   [290]
From nature by external accidents,
And which was thus confounded more and more,
Misguiding and misguided. Thus I fared,
Dragging all passions, notions, shapes of faith,
890 Like culprits to the bar, suspiciously   [295]
Calling the mind to establish in plain day
Her titles and her honours, now believing,
Now disbelieving, endlessly perplex'd
With impulse, motive, right and wrong, the ground
895 Of moral obligation, what the rule   [300]

And what the sanction, till, demanding *proof,*
And seeking it in everything, I lost
All feeling of conviction, and, in fine,
Sick, wearied out with contrarieties,
900   Yielded up moral questions in despair,   [305]
And for my future studies, as the sole
Employment of the enquiring faculty,
Turn'd towards mathematics, and their clear
And solid evidence—Ah! then it was
905   That Thou, most precious Friend! about this time
First known to me, didst lend a living help
To regulate my Soul, and then it was
That the belovèd Woman in whose sight   [335]
Those days were pass'd, now speaking in a voice
910   Of sudden admonition, like a brook
That does but cross a lonely road, and now
Seen, heard and felt, and caught at every turn,
Companion never lost through many a league,   [340]
Maintain'd for me a saving intercourse
915   With my true self; for, though impair'd and changed
Much, as it seem'd, I was no further changed
Than as a clouded, not a waning moon: [344]
She, in the midst of all, preserv'd me still
A Poet, made me seek beneath that name
920   My office upon earth, and nowhere else,
And lastly, Nature's self, by human love   [350]
Assisted, through the weary labyrinth
Conducted me again to open day,
Revived the feelings of my earlier life,
925   Gave me that strength and knowledge full of peace,
Enlarged, and never more to be disturb'd,
Which through the steps of our degeneracy,
All degradation of this age, hath still
Upheld me, and upholds me at this day
930   In the catastrophe (for so they dream,
And nothing less), when finally, to close
And rivet up the gains of France, a Pope

Is summon'd in to crown an Emperor; [360]
This last opprobrium, when we see the dog
935 Returning to his vomit, when the sun
That rose in splendour, was alive, and moved [365]
In exultation among living clouds
Hath put his function and his glory off,
And, turned into a gewgaw, a machine,
940 Sets like an opera phantom. [370]
                          Thus, O Friend!
Through times of honour, and through times of shame,
Have I descended, tracing faithfully
The workings of a youthful mind, beneath
The breath of great events, its hopes no less
945 Than universal, and its boundless love;
A Story destined for thy ear, who now, [375]
Among the basest and the lowest fallen
Of all the race of men, dost make abode
Where Etna looketh down on Syracuse,
950 The city of Timoleon! Living God!
How are the Mighty prostrated! they first, [380]
They first of all that breathe should have awaked
When the great voice was heard out of the tombs
Of ancient Heroes. If for France I have griev'd
955 Who, in the judgment of no few, hath been
A trifler only, in her proudest day, [385]
Have been distress'd to think of what she once
Promised, now is, a far more sober cause
Thine eyes must see of sorrow, in a Land
960 Strew'd with the wreck of loftiest years, a Land [388]
Glorious indeed, substantially renown'd
Of simple vertue once, and manly praise,
Now without one memorial hope, not even
A hope to be deferr'd; for that would serve
965 To chear the heart in such entire decay.

But indignation works where hope is not,
And thou, O Friend! wilt be refresh'd. There is

One great Society alone on earth,
The noble Living and the noble Dead: [395]
970 Thy consolation shall be there, and Time
And Nature shall before thee spread in store
Imperishable thoughts, the Place itself
Be conscious of thy presence, and the dull
Sirocco air of its degeneracy
975 Turn as thou mov'st into a healthful breeze
To cherish and invigorate thy frame.

    Thine be those motions strong and sanative,
A ladder for thy Spirit to reascend
To health and joy and pure contentedness;
980 To me the grief confined that Thou art gone
From this last spot of earth where Freedom now   [400]
Stands single in her only sanctuary,
A lonely wanderer, art gone, by pain
Compell'd and sickness, at this latter day,
985 This heavy time of change for all mankind;
I feel for Thee, must utter what I feel: [405]
The sympathies, erewhile, in part discharg'd,
Gather afresh, and will have vent again:
My own delights do scarcely seem to me
990 My own delights; the lordly Alps themselves,
Those rosy Peaks, from which the Morning looks   [410]
Abroad on many Nations, are not now
Since thy migration and departure, Friend,
The gladsome image in my memory
995 Which they were used to be; to kindred scenes,
On errand, at a time how different!
Thou tak'st thy way, carrying a heart more ripe   [415]
For all divine enjoyment, with the soul
Which Nature gives to Poets, now by thought
1000 Matured, and in the summer of its strength.
Oh! wrap him in your Shades, ye Giant Woods,
On Etna's side, and thou, O flowery Vale
Of Enna! is there not some nook of thine,   [420]

From the first playtime of the infant earth
1005 Kept sacred to restorative delight?

    Child of the mountains, among Shepherds rear'd,
Even from my earliest school-day time, I loved
To dream of Sicily; and now a sweet
And vital promise wafted from that Land
1010 Comes o'er my heart; there's not a single name
Of note belonging to that honor'd isle,
Philosopher or Bard, Empedocles,
Or Archimedes, deep and tranquil Soul!   [435]
That is not like a comfort to my grief:
1015 And, O Theocritus, so far have some
Prevail'd among the Powers of heaven and earth,
By force of graces which were their's, that they
Have had, as thou reportest, miracles   [440]
Wrought for them in old time: yea, not unmov'd,
1020 When thinking of my own beloved Friend,
I hear thee tell how bees with honey fed
Divine Comates, by his tyrant lord
Within a chest imprison'd impiously   [445]
How with their honey from the fields they came
1025 And fed him there, alive, from month to month,
Because the Goatherd, blessed Man! had lips
Wet with the Muses' Nectar.
                     Thus I soothe
The pensive moments by this calm fire side,   [450]
And find a thousand fancied images
1030 That chear the thoughts of those I love, and mine.
Our prayers have been accepted; Thou wilt stand
Not as an Exile but a Visitant
On Etna's top; by pastoral Arethuse   [465]
Or, if that fountain be indeed no more,
1035 Then near some other Spring, which by the name
Thou gratulatest, willingly deceived,
Shalt linger as a gladsome Votary,
And not a Captive, pining for his home.   [470]

IMAGINATION, HOW IMPAIRED AND RESTORED

LONG time hath Man's unhappiness and guilt
Detain'd us; with what dismal sights beset
For the outward view, and inwardly oppress'd
With sorrow, disappointment, vexing thoughts,
5 Confusion of opinion, zeal decay'd,   [5]
And lastly, utter loss of hope itself,
And things to hope for. Not with these began
Our Song, and not with these our Song must end:
Ye motions of delight, that through the fields
10 Stir gently, breezes and soft airs that breathe   [10]
The breath of paradise, and find your way
To the recesses of the soul! Ye Brooks
Muttering along the stones, a busy noise
By day, a quiet one in silent night,   [20]
15 And you, ye Groves, whose ministry it is
To interpose the covert of your shades,   [25]
Even as a sleep, betwixt the heart of man
And the uneasy world, 'twixt man himself,
Not seldom, and his own unquiet heart,
20 Oh! that I had a music and a voice,
Harmonious as your own, that I might tell   [30]
What ye have done for me. The morning shines,
Nor heedeth Man's perverseness; Spring returns,
I saw the Spring return, when I was dead
25 To deeper hope, yet had I joy for her,
And welcomed her benevolence, rejoiced
In common with the Children of her Love,
Plants, insects, beasts in field, and birds in bower.   [35]
So neither were complacency nor peace
30 Nor tender yearnings wanting for my good

Through those distracted times; in Nature still [40]
Glorying, I found a counterpoise in her,
Which, when the spirit of evil was at height
Maintain'd for me a secret happiness;
35 Her I resorted to, and lov'd so much
I seem'd to love as much as heretofore;
And yet this passion, fervent as it was,
Had suffer'd change; how could there fail to be
Some change, if merely hence, that years of life
40 Were going on, and with them loss or gain
Inevitable, sure alternative.

This History, my Friend, hath chiefly told
Of intellectual power, from stage to stage [45]
Advancing, hand in hand with love and joy,
45 And of imagination teaching truth
Until that natural graciousness of mind [50]
Gave way to over-pressure of the times
And their disastrous issues. What avail'd,
When Spells forbade the Voyager to land,
50 The fragrance which did ever and anon
Give notice of the Shore, from arbours breathed [55]
Of blessed sentiment and fearless love?
What did such sweet remembrances avail,
Perfidious then, as seem'd, what served they then?
55 My business was upon the barren sea,
My errand was to sail to other coasts.
Shall I avow that I had hope to see,
I mean that future times would surely see
The man to come parted as by a gulph,
60 From him who had been, that I could no more [60]
Trust the elevation which had made me one
With the great Family that here and there
Is scatter'd through the abyss of ages past,
Sage, Patriot, Lover, Hero; for it seem'd
65 That their best virtues were not free from taint [65]
Of something false and weak, which could not stand

207

The open eye of Reason. Then I said,
Go to the Poets; they will speak to thee
More perfectly of purer creatures, yet
70   If Reason be nobility in man,   [70]
Can aught be more ignoble than the man
Whom they describe, would fasten if they may
Upon our love by sympathies of truth.

    Thus strangely did I war against myself;   [76]
75   A Bigot to a new Idolatry
Did like a Monk who hath forsworn the world
Zealously labour to cut off my heart
From all the sources of her former strength;   [80]
And, as by simple waving of a wand
80   The wizard instantaneously dissolves
Palace or grove, even so did I unsoul
As readily by syllogistic words
Some Charm of Logic, ever within reach,
Those mysteries of passion which have made,   [85]
85   And shall continue evermore to make,
(In spite of all that Reason hath perform'd
And shall perform to exalt and to refine)
One brotherhood of all the human race
Through all the habitations of past years
90   And those to come, and hence an emptiness
Fell on the Historian's Page, and even on that
Of Poets, pregnant with more absolute truth.
The works of both wither'd in my esteem,
Their sentence was, I thought, pronounc'd; their rights
95   Seem'd mortal, and their empire pass'd away.

    What then remain'd in such eclipse? what light
To guide or chear? The laws of things which lie
Beyond the reach of human will or power;
The life of nature, by the God of love
100 Inspired, celestial presence ever pure;
These left, the soul of Youth must needs be rich,

    Whatever else be lost, and these were mine.
    Not a deaf echo, merely, of the thought
    Bewilder'd recollections, solitary,
105 But living sounds. Yet in despite of this,
    This feeling, which howe'er impair'd or damp'd,
    Yet having been once born can never die.
    'Tis true that Earth with all her appanage
    Of elements and organs, storm and sunshine,
110 With its pure forms and colours, pomp of clouds
    Rivers and mountains, objects among which
    It might be thought that no dislike or blame,
    No sense of weakness or infirmity
    Or aught amiss could possibly have come,
115 Yea, even the visible universe was scann'd
    With something of a kindred spirit, fell
    Beneath the domination of a taste   [90]
    Less elevated, which did in my mind
    With its more noble influence interfere,
120 Its animation and its deeper sway.

     There comes (if need be now to speak of this
    After such long detail of our mistakes)
    There comes a time when Reason, not the grand
    And simple Reason, but that humbler power
125 Which carries on its no inglorious work
    By logic and minute analysis
    Is of all Idols that which pleases most
    The growing mind. A Trifler would he be
    Who on the obvious benefits should dwell
130 That rise out of this process; but to speak
    Of all the narrow estimates of things
    Which hence originate were a worthy theme
    For philosophic Verse; suffice it here
    To hint that danger cannot but attend
135 Upon a Function rather proud to be
    The enemy of falsehood, than the friend
    Of truth, to sit in judgment than to feel.

Oh! soul of Nature, excellent and fair,
That didst rejoice with me, with whom I too
140 Rejoiced, through early youth before the winds   [95]
And powerful waters, and in lights and shades
That march'd and countermarch'd about the hills
In glorious apparition, now all eye
And now all ear; but ever with the heart   [100]
145 Employ'd, and the majestic intellect,
Oh! Soul of Nature! that dost overflow
With passion and with life, what feeble men
Walk on this earth! how feeble have I been   [105]
When thou wert in thy strength! Nor this through stroke
150 Of human suffering, such as justifies
Remissness and inaptitude of mind,
But through presumption, even in pleasure pleased
Unworthily, disliking here, and there,   [110]
Liking, by rules of mimic art transferr'd
155 To things above all art. But more, for this,
Although a strong infection of the age,
Was never much my habit, giving way
To a comparison of scene with scene,   [115]
Bent overmuch on superficial things,
160 Pampering myself with meagre novelties
Of colour and proportion, to the moods
Of time or season, to the moral power
The affections, and the spirit of the place,   [120]
Less sensible. Nor only did the love
165 Of sitting thus in judgment interrupt
My deeper feelings, but another cause
More subtle and less easily explain'd
That almost seems inherent in the Creature,   [125]
Sensuous and intellectual as he is,
170 A twofold Frame of body and of mind;
The state to which I now allude was one
In which the eye was master of the heart,
When that which is in every stage of life
The most despotic of our senses gain'd

175 Such strength in me as often held my mind   [130]
      In absolute dominion. Gladly here,
      Entering upon abstruser argument,
      Would I endeavour to unfold the means
      Which Nature studiously employs to thwart
180 This tyranny, summons all the senses each   [135]
      To counteract the other and themselves,
      And makes them all, and the objects with which all
      Are conversant, subservient in their turn
      To the great ends of Liberty and Power.
185 But this is matter for another Song;
      Here only let me add that my delights,   [140]
      Such as they were, were sought insatiably,
      Though 'twas a transport of the outward sense,
      Not of the mind, vivid but not profound:
190 Yet was I often greedy in the chace,
      And roam'd from hill to hill, from rock to rock,
      Still craving combinations of new forms,
      New pleasure, wider empire for the sight,   [145]
      Proud of its own endowments, and rejoiced
195 To lay the inner faculties asleep.
      Amid the turns and counterturns, the strife
      And various trials of our complex being,
      As we grow up, such thraldom of that sense   [150]
      Seems hard to shun; and yet I knew a Maid,
200 Who, young as I was then, conversed with things
      In higher style, from appetites like these
      She, gentle Visitant, as well she might
      Was wholly free, far less did critic rules
      Or barren intermeddling subtleties   [155]
205 Perplex her mind; but, wise as Women are
      When genial circumstance hath favor'd them,
      She welcom'd what was given, and craved no more.
      Whatever scene was present to her eyes,
      That was the best, to that she was attuned   [160]
210 Through her humility and lowliness,
      And through a perfect happiness of soul

Whose variegated feelings were in this
Sisters, that they were each some new delight: [164]
For she was Nature's inmate. Her the birds
215   And every flower she met with, could they but
Have known her, would have lov'd. Methought such charm
Of sweetness did her presence breathe around
That all the trees, and all the silent hills
And every thing she look'd on, should have had
220   An intimation how she bore herself   [170]
Towards them and to all creatures. God delights
In such a being; for her common thoughts
Are piety, her life is blessedness.

Even like this Maid before I was call'd forth
225   From the retirement of my native hills   [175]
I lov'd whate'er I saw; nor lightly loved,
But fervently, did never dream of aught
More grand, more fair, more exquisitely framed
Than those few nooks to which my happy feet
230   Were limited. I had not at that time   [180]
Liv'd long enough, nor in the least survived
The first diviner influence of this world,
As it appears to unaccustom'd eyes;
I worshipp'd then among the depths of things
235   As my soul bade me; could I then take part   [185]
In aught but admiration, or be pleased
With any thing but humbleness and love;
I felt, and nothing else; I did not judge,
I never thought of judging, with the gift
240   Of all this glory fill'd and satisfied.   [190]
And afterwards, when through the gorgeous Alps
Roaming, I carried with me the same heart:
In truth, this degradation, howsoe'er
Induced, effect in whatsoe'er degree
245   Of custom, that prepares such wantonness   [195]
As makes the greatest things give way to least,
Or any other cause which hath been named;

Or lastly, aggravated by the times,
Which with their passionate sounds might often make
250 The milder minstrelsies of rural scenes   [200]
Inaudible, was transient; I had felt
Too forcibly, too early in my life,
Visitings of imaginative power
For this to last: I shook the habit off
255 Entirely and for ever, and again   [205]
In Nature's presence stood, as I stand now,
A sensitive, and a creative soul.

     There are in our existence spots of time,
Which with distinct pre-eminence retain
260 A vivifying Virtue, whence, depress'd   [210]
By false opinion and contentious thought,
Or aught of heavier and more deadly weight
In trivial occupations, and the round
Of ordinary intercourse, our minds
265 Are nourish'd and invisibly repair'd,   [215]
A virtue by which pleasure is enhanced
That penetrates, enables us to mount
When high, more high, and lifts us up when fallen.
This efficacious spirit chiefly lurks
270 Among those passages of life in which   [220]
We have had deepest feeling that the mind
Is lord and master, and that outward sense
Is but the obedient servant of her will.
Such moments worthy of all gratitude,
275 Are scatter'd everywhere, taking their date
From our first childhood: in our childhood even   [225]
Perhaps are most conspicuous. Life with me,
As far as memory can look back, is full
Of this beneficent influence. At a time
280 When scarcely (I was then not six years old)
My hand could hold a bridle, with proud hopes
I mounted, and we rode towards the hills:
We were a pair of Horsemen; honest James

Was with me, my encourager and guide. [230]
285 We had not travell'd long, ere some mischance
Disjoin'd me from my Comrade, and, through fear
Dismounting, down the rough and stony Moor
I led my Horse, and stumbling on, at length
Came to a bottom, where in former times [235]
290 A Murderer had been hung in iron chains.
The Gibbet-mast was moulder'd down, the bones
And iron case were gone; but on the turf,
Hard by, soon after that fell deed was wrought
Some unknown hand had carved the Murderer's name. [240]
295 The monumental writing was engraven
In times long past, and still, from year to year,
By superstition of the neighbourhood,
The grass is clear'd away; and to this hour
The letters are all fresh and visible. [245]
300 Faltering, and ignorant where I was, at length
I chanced to espy those characters inscribed
On the green sod: forthwith I left the spot
And, reascending the bare Common, saw
A naked Pool that lay beneath the hills,
305 The Beacon on the summit, and more near, [250]
A Girl who bore a Pitcher on her head
And seem'd with difficult steps to force her way
Against the blowing wind. It was, in truth,
An ordinary sight; but I should need
310 Colours and words that are unknown to man [255]
To paint the visionary dreariness
Which, while I look'd all round for my lost guide,
Did at that time invest the naked Pool,
The Beacon on the lonely Eminence,
315 The Woman, and her garments vex'd and toss'd [260]
By the strong wind. When, in a blessed season
With those two dear Ones, to my heart so dear,
When in the blessed time of early love,
Long afterwards, I roam'd about
320 In daily presence of this very scene,

Upon the naked pool and dreary crags,
And on the melancholy Beacon, fell   [265]
The spirit of pleasure and youth's golden gleam;
And think ye not with radiance more divine
325 From these remembrances, and from the power
They left behind? So feeling comes in aid
Of feeling, and diversity of strength   [270]
Attends us, if but once we have been strong.
Oh! mystery of Man, from what a depth
330 Proceed thy honours! I am lost, but see
In simple childhood something of the base   —
On which thy greatness stands, but this I feel,   [275]
That from thyself it is that thou must give,
Else never canst receive. The days gone by
335 Come back upon me from the dawn almost
Of life: the hiding-places of my power
Seem open; I approach, and then they close;   [280]
I see by glimpses now; when age comes on,
May scarcely see at all, and I would give,
340 While yet we may, as far as words can give,
A substance and a life to what I feel:
I would enshrine the spirit of the past   [285]
For future restoration. Yet another
Of these to me affecting incidents
345 With which we will conclude.
                              One Christmas-time,
The day before the Holidays began,
Feverish and tired, and restless, I went forth
Into the fields, impatient for the sight   [290]
Of those two Horses which should bear us home·
350 My Brothers and myself. There was a crag,
An Eminence, which from the meeting-point
Of two highways ascending, overlook'd
At least a long half-mile of those two roads,
By each of which the expected Steeds might come,
355 The choice uncertain. Thither I repair'd   [296]
Up to the highest summit; 'twas a day

Stormy, and rough, and wild, and on the grass
I sate, half-shelter'd by a naked wall;
Upon my right hand was a single sheep, [300]
360 A whistling hawthorn on my left, and there,
With those companions at my side, I watch'd,
Straining my eyes intensely, as the mist
Gave intermitting prospect of the wood
And plain beneath. Ere I to School return'd [305]
365 That dreary time, ere I had been ten days
A dweller in my Father's House, he died,
And I and my two Brothers, Orphans then,
Followed his Body to the Grave. The event
With all the sorrow which it brought appear'd [310]
370 A chastisement; and when I call'd to mind
That day so lately pass'd, when from the crag
I look'd in such anxiety of hope,
With trite reflections of morality,
Yet in the deepest passion, I bow'd low [315]
375 To God, who thus corrected my desires;
And afterwards, the wind and sleety rain
And all the business of the elements,
The single sheep, and the one blasted tree,
And the bleak music of that old stone wall, [320]
380 The noise of wood and water, and the mist
Which on the line of each of those two Roads
Advanced in such indisputable shapes,
All these were spectacles and sounds to which
I often would repair and thence would drink, [325]
385 As at a fountain; and I do not doubt
That in this later time, when storm and rain
Beat on my roof at midnight, or by day
When I am in the woods, unknown to me
The workings of my spirit thence are brought. [331]

390 Thou wilt not languish here, O Friend, for whom
I travel in these dim uncertain ways
Thou wilt assist me as a pilgrim gone

In quest of highest truth. Behold me then
Once more in Nature's presence, thus restored
395 Or otherwise, and strengthened once again
(With memory left of what had been escaped)
To habits of devoutest sympathy.

SAME SUBJECT (*continued*)

From nature doth emotion come, and moods
Of calmness equally are nature's gift,
This is her glory; these two attributes
Are sister horns that constitute her strength;   [4]
5   This twofold influence is the sun and shower
Of all her bounties, both in origin
And end alike benignant. Hence it is,
That Genius which exists by interchange   [5]
Of peace and excitation, finds in her
10 His best and purest Friend, from her receives
That energy by which he seeks the truth,
Is rouzed, aspires, grasps, struggles, wishes, craves,
From her that happy stillness of the mind
Which fits him to receive it, when unsought.   [10]

15   Such benefit may souls of humblest frame
Partake of, each in their degree; 'tis mine
To speak of what myself have known and felt
Sweet task! for words find easy way, inspired
By gratitude and confidence in truth.   [15]
20 Long time in search of knowledge desperate,
I was benighted heart and mind; but now
On all sides day began to reappear,
And it was proved indeed that not in vain
I had been taught to reverence a Power   [20]
25 That is the very quality and shape
And image of right reason, that matures
Her processes by steady laws, gives birth
To no impatient or fallacious hopes,
No heat of passion or excessive zeal,   [25]
30 No vain conceits, provokes to no quick turns

Of self-applauding intellect, but lifts
The Being into magnanimity;
Holds up before the mind, intoxicate
With present objects and the busy dance   [30]
35 Of things that pass away, a temperate shew
Of objects that endure, and by this course
Disposes her, when over-fondly set
On leaving her incumbrances behind
To seek in Man, and in the frame of life,   [35]
40 Social and individual, what there is
Desireable, affecting, good or fair
Of kindred permanence, the gifts divine
And universal, the pervading grace
That hath been, is, and shall be. Above all   [39]
45 Did Nature bring again that wiser mood
More deeply re-established in my soul,
Which, seeing little worthy or sublime
In what we blazon with the pompous names
Of power and action, early tutor'd me
50 To look with feelings of fraternal love   [45]
Upon those unassuming things, that hold
A silent station in this beauteous world.

Thus moderated, thus composed, I found
Once more in Man an object of delight
55 Of pure imagination, and of love;   [50]
And, as the horizon of my mind enlarged,
Again I took the intellectual eye
For my instructor, studious more to see
Great Truths, than touch and handle little ones.
60 Knowledge was given accordingly; my trust   [55]
Was firmer in the feelings which had stood
The test of such a trial; clearer far
My sense of what was excellent and right;
The promise of the present time retired
65 Into its true proportion; sanguine schemes,   [60]
Ambitious virtues pleased me less, I sought

For good in the familiar race of life
And built thereon my hopes of good to come.

With settling judgments now of what would last
70 And what would disappear, prepared to find [65]
Ambition, folly, madness in the men
Who thrust themselves upon this passive world
As Rulers of the world, to see in these,
Even when the public welfare is their aim,
75 Plans without thought, or bottom'd on false thought [70]
And false philosophy: having brought to test
Of solid life and true result the Books
Of modern Statists, and thereby perceiv'd
The utter hollowness of what we name
80 The wealth of Nations, where alone that wealth
Is lodged, and how encreased, and having gain'd
A more judicious knowledge of what makes [80]
The dignity of individual Man,
Of Man, no composition of the thought,
85 Abstraction, shadow, image, but the man
Of whom we read, the man whom we behold
With our own eyes; I could not but inquire,
Not with less interest than heretofore, [85]
But greater, though in spirit more subdued,
90 Why is this glorious Creature to be found
One only in ten thousand? What one is,
Why may not many be? What bars are thrown
By Nature in the way of such a hope? [90]
Our animal wants and the necessities
95 Which they impose, are these the obstacles?
If not, then others vanish into air.
Such meditations bred an anxious wish
To ascertain how much of real worth
And genuine knowledge, and true power of mind [95]
100 Did at this day exist in those who liv'd
By bodily labour, labour far exceeding
Their due proportion, under all the weight

Of that injustice which upon ourselves
By composition of society
105 Ourselves entail. To frame such estimate   [100]
I chiefly look'd (what need to look beyond?)
Among the natural abodes of men,
Fields with their rural works, recall'd to mind
My earliest notices, with these compared
110 The observations of my later youth,   [105]
Continued downwards to that very day.

   For time had never been in which the throes
And mighty hopes of Nations, and the stir
And tumult of the world to me could yield,
115 How far soe'er transported and possess'd,
Full measure of content; but still I craved   [110]
An intermixture of distinct regards
And truths of individual sympathy
Nearer ourselves. Such often might be glean'd
120 From that great City, else it must have been
A heart-depressing wilderness indeed,   [115]
Full soon to me a wearisome abode;
But much was wanting; therefore did I turn
To you, ye Pathways, and ye lonely Roads
125 Sought you enrich'd with everything I prized,
With human kindness and with Nature's joy.

   Oh! next to one dear state of bliss, vouchsafed   [120]
Alas! to few in this untoward world,
The bliss of walking daily in Life's prime
130 Through field or forest with the Maid we love,
While yet our hearts are young, while yet we breathe
Nothing but happiness, living in some place,   [125]
Deep Vale, or anywhere, the home of both,
From which it would be misery to stir;
135 Oh! next to such enjoyment of our youth,
In my esteem, next to such dear delight
Was that of wandering on from day to day   [130]
Where I could meditate in peace, and find

The knowledge which I love, and teach the sound
140   Of Poet's music to strange fields and groves,   [135]
Converse with men, where if we meet a face
We almost meet a friend, on naked Moors
With long, long ways before, by Cottage Bench   [140]
Or Well-spring where the weary Traveller rests.

145   I love a public road: few sights there are
That please me more; such object hath had power
O'er my imagination since the dawn   [145]
Of childhood, when its disappearing line,
Seen daily afar off, on one bare steep
150   Beyond the limits which my feet had trod
Was like a guide into eternity,   [151]
At least to things unknown and without bound.
Even something of the grandeur which invests
The Mariner who sails the roaring sea
155   Through storm and darkness early in my mind
Surrounded, too, the Wanderers of the Earth,   [155]
Grandeur as much, and loveliness far more;
Awed have I been by strolling Bedlamites,
From many other uncouth Vagrants pass'd
160   In fear, have walk'd with quicker step; but why
Take note of this? When I began to inquire,   [160]
To watch and question those I met, and held
Familiar talk with them, the lonely roads
Were schools to me in which I daily read
165   With most delight the passions of mankind,   [164]
There saw into the depth of human souls,
Souls that appear to have no depth at all
To vulgar eyes. And now convinced at heart
How little that to which alone we give
170   The name of education hath to do   [171]
With real feeling and just sense, how vain
A correspondence with the talking world
Proves to the most, and call'd to make good search
If man's estate, by doom of Nature yoked   [175]

175 With toil, is therefore yoked with ignorance,
     If virtue be indeed so hard to rear,
     And intellectual strength so rare a boon
     I prized such walks still more; for there I found
     Hope to my hope, and to my pleasure peace,   [180]
180 And steadiness; and healing and repose
     To every angry passion. There I heard,
     From mouths of lowly men and of obscure
     A tale of honour; sounds in unison
     With loftiest promises of good and fair.   [185]

185   There are who think that strong affections, love
     Known by whatever name, is falsely deem'd
     A gift, to use a term which they would use,
     Of vulgar Nature, that its growth requires
     Retirement, leisure, language purified   [190]
190 By manners thoughtful and elaborate,
     That whoso feels such passion in excess
     Must live within the very light and air
     Of elegances that are made by man.
     True is it, where oppression worse than death   [195]
195 Salutes the Being at his birth, where grace
     Of culture hath been utterly unknown,
     And labour in excess and poverty
     From day to day pre-occupy the ground
     Of the affections, and to Nature's self   [200]
200 Oppose a deeper nature, there indeed,
     Love cannot be; nor does it easily thrive
     In cities, where the human heart is sick,
     And the eye feeds it not, and cannot feed: [205]
     Thus far, no further, is that inference good.

205   Yes, in those wanderings deeply did I feel
     How we mislead each other, above all
     How Books mislead us, looking for their fame
     To judgments of the wealthy Few, who see
     By artificial lights, how they debase   [210]
210 The Many for the pleasure of those few

Effeminately level down the truth
To certain general notions for the sake
Of being understood at once, or else
Through want of better knowledge in the men   [215]
215 Who frame them, flattering thus our self-conceit
With pictures that ambitiously set forth
The differences, the outside marks by which
Society has parted man from man,
Neglectful of the universal heart.   [220]

220   Here calling up to mind what then I saw
A youthful Traveller, and see daily now
Before me in my rural neighbourhood,
Here might I pause, and bend in reverence
To Nature, and the power of human minds,   [225]
225 To men as they are men within themselves.
How oft high service is perform'd within,
When all the external man is rude in shew,
Not like a temple rich with pomp and gold
But a mere mountain-Chapel such as shields   [230]
230 Its simple worshippers from sun and shower.
Of these, said I, shall be my Song; of these,
If future years mature me for the task,
Will I record the praises, making Verse
Deal boldly with substantial things, in truth   [235]
235 And sanctity of passion, speak of these
That justice may be done, obeisance paid
Where it is due: thus haply shall I teach,
Inspire, through unadulterated ears
Pour rapture, tenderness, and hope, my theme   [240]
240 No other than the very heart of man
As found among the best of those who live
Not unexalted by religious hope,
Nor uninformed by books, good books though few,
In Nature's presence: thence may I select   [245]
245 Sorrow that is not sorrow, but delight,
And miserable love that is not pain

To hear of, for the glory that redounds
Therefrom to human kind and what we are.
Be mine to follow with no timid step   [250]
250 Where knowledge leads me; it shall be my pride
That I have dared to tread this holy ground,
Speaking no dream but things oracular,
Matter not lightly to be heard by those
Who to the letter of the outward promise   [255]
255 Do read the invisible soul, by men adroit
In speech and for communion with the world
Accomplish'd, minds whose faculties are then
Most active when they are most eloquent
And elevated most when most admired.   [260]
260 Men may be found of other mold than these,
Who are their own upholders, to themselves
Encouragement, and energy and will,
Expressing liveliest thoughts in lively words
As native passion dictates. Others, too,   [265]
265 There are among the walks of homely life
Still higher, men for contemplation framed,
Shy, and unpractis'd in the strife of phrase,
Meek men, whose very souls perhaps would sink
Beneath them, summon'd to such intercourse: [270]
270 Theirs is the language of the heavens, the power,
The thought, the image, and the silent joy;
Words are but under-agents in their souls;
When they are grasping with their greatest strength
They do not breathe among them: this I speak   [275]
275 In gratitude to God, who feeds our hearts
For his own service, knoweth, loveth us
When we are unregarded by the world.

Also about this time did I receive
Convictions still more strong than heretofore   [280]
280 Not only that the inner frame is good,
And graciously composed, but that no less
Nature through all conditions hath a power

225

To consecrate, if we have eyes to see,   [285]
The outside of her creatures, and to breathe
285   Grandeur upon the very humblest face
Of human life. I felt that the array
Of outward circumstance and visible form
Is to the pleasure of the human mind
What passion makes it, that meanwhile the forms   [290]
290   Of Nature have a passion in themselves
That intermingles with those works of man
To which she summons him, although the works
Be mean, have nothing lofty of their own;
And that the genius of the Poet hence   [295]
295   May boldly take his way among mankind
Wherever Nature leads, that he hath stood
By Nature's side among the men of old,
And so shall stand for ever. Dearest Friend,
Forgive me if I say that I, who long
300   Had harbour'd reverentially a thought
That Poets, even as Prophets, each with each   [301]
Connected in a mighty scheme of truth,
Have each for his peculiar dower, a sense
By which he is enabled to perceive
305   Something unseen before; forgive me, Friend,   [305]
If I, the meanest of this Band, had hope
That unto me had also been vouchsafed
An influx, that in some sort I possess'd
A privilege, and that a work of mine,
310   Proceeding from the depth of untaught things,   [310]
Enduring and creative, might become
A power like one of Nature's. To such mood,
Once above all, a Traveller at that time
Upon the Plain of Sarum was I raised;
315   There on the pastoral Downs without a track   [315]
To guide me, or along the bare white roads
Lengthening in solitude their dreary line,
While through those vestiges of ancient times
I ranged, and by the solitude oercome,

320 I had a reverie and saw the past,
Saw multitudes of men, and here and there,   [321]
A single Briton in his wolf-skin vest
With shield and stone-axe, stride across the Wold;
The voice of spears was heard, the rattling spear
325 Shaken by arms of mighty bone, in strength   [325]
Long moulder'd of barbaric majesty.
I called upon the darkness; and it took,
A midnight darkness seem'd to come and take
All objects from my sight; and lo! again
330 The desart visible by dismal flames!   [330]
It is the sacrificial Altar, fed
With living men, how deep the groans, the voice
Of those in the gigantic wicker thrills
Throughout the region far and near, pervades
335 The monumental hillocks; and the pomp
Is for both worlds, the living and the dead.   [335]
At other moments, for through that wide waste
Three summer days I roam'd, when 'twas my chance
To have before me on the downy Plain
340 Lines, circles, mounts, a mystery of shapes
Such as in many quarters yet survive,
With intricate profusion figuring o'er
The untill'd ground, the work, as some divine,
Of infant science, imitative forms
345 By which the Druids covertly express'd
Their knowledge of the heavens, and imaged forth   [341]
The constellations, I was gently charm'd,
Albeit with an antiquarian's dream,
I saw the bearded Teachers, with white wands   [345]
350 Uplifted, pointing to the starry sky
Alternately, and Plain below, while breath
Of music seem'd to guide them, and the Waste
Was chear'd with stillness and a pleasant sound.

        This for the past, and things that may be view'd   [350]
355 Or fancied, in the obscurities of time.

Nor is it, Friend, unknown to thee, at least
Thyself delighted, who for my delight
Hast said, perusing some imperfect verse
Which in that lonesome journey was composed,
That also then I must have exercised   [355]
Upon the vulgar forms of present things
And actual world of our familiar days,
A higher power, have caught from them a tone,
An image, and a character, by books
Not hitherto reflected. Call we this   [360]
But a persuasion taken up by thee
In friendship; yet the mind is to herself
Witness and judge, and I remember well
That in life's every-day appearances
I seem'd about this period to have sight
Of a new world, a world, too, that was fit   [370]
To be transmitted and made visible
To other eyes, as having for its base
That whence our dignity originates,
That which both gives it being and maintains
A balance, an ennobling interchange   [375]
Of action from within and from without,
The excellence, pure spirit, and best power
Both of the object seen, and eye that sees.

360

365

370

375

BOOK THIRTEENTH

CONCLUSION

In one of these excursions, travelling then
Through Wales on foot, and with a youthful Friend,
I left Bethkelet's huts at couching-time,
And westward took my way to see the sun   [5]
5   Rise from the top of Snowdon. Having reach'd
The Cottage at the Mountain's foot, we there
Rouz'd up the Shepherd, who by ancient right
Of office is the Stranger's usual Guide;
And after short refreshment sallied forth.   [10]

10   It was a Summer's night, a close warm night,
Wan, dull and glaring, with a dripping mist
Low-hung and thick that cover'd all the sky,
Half threatening storm and rain; but on we went
Uncheck'd, being full of heart and having faith
15   In our tried Pilot. Little could we see
Hemm'd round on every side with fog and damp,
And, after ordinary travellers' chat   [16]
With our Conductor, silently we sank
Each into commerce with his private thoughts:
20   Thus did we breast the ascent, and by myself
Was nothing either seen or heard the while   [20]
Which took me from my musings, save that once
The Shepherd's Cur did to his own great joy
Unearth a hedgehog in the mountain crags
25   Round which he made a barking turbulent.
This small adventure, for even such it seemed   [25]
In that wild place and at the dead of night,
Being over and forgotten, on we wound
In silence as before. With forehead bent
30   Earthward, as if in opposition set
Against an enemy, I panted up   [30]

229

With eager pace, and no less eager thoughts.
Thus might we wear perhaps an hour away,
Ascending at loose distance each from each,
35 And I, as chanced, the foremost of the Band;
     When at my feet the ground appear'd to brighten,   [35]
     And with a step or two seem'd brighter still;
     Nor had I time to ask the cause of this,
     For instantly a Light upon the turf
40 Fell like a flash: I look'd about, and lo!
     The Moon stood naked in the Heavens, at height   [40]
     Immense above my head, and on the shore
     I found myself of a huge sea of mist,
     Which, meek and silent, rested at my feet:
45 A hundred hills their dusky backs upheaved
     All over this still Ocean, and beyond,
     Far, far beyond, the vapours shot themselves,   [45]
     In headlands, tongues, and promontory shapes,
     Into the Sea, the real Sea, that seem'd
50 To dwindle, and give up its majesty,
     Usurp'd upon as far as sight could reach.
     Meanwhile, the Moon look'd down upon this shew
     In single glory, and we stood, the mist
     Touching our very feet; and from the shore
55 At distance not the third part of a mile
     Was a blue chasm; a fracture in the vapour,
     A deep and gloomy breathing-place thro' which
     Mounted the roar of waters, torrents, streams
     Innumerable, roaring with one voice.   [60]
60 The universal spectacle throughout
     Was shaped for admiration and delight,
     Grand in itself alone, but in that breach
     Through which the homeless voice of waters rose,
     That dark deep thoroughfare had Nature lodg'd
65 The Soul, the Imagination of the whole.

     A meditation rose in me that night
     Upon the lonely Mountain when the scene

Had pass'd away, and it appear'd to me
The perfect image of a mighty Mind, [70]
70 Of one that feeds upon infinity,
That is exalted by an underpresence,
The sense of God, or whatsoe'er is dim
Or vast in its own being, above all
One function of such mind had Nature there
75 Exhibited by putting forth, and that
With circumstance most awful and sublime, [80]
That domination which she oftentimes
Exerts upon the outward face of things,
So moulds them, and endues, abstracts, combines,
80 Or by abrupt and unhabitual influence
Doth make one object so impress itself
Upon all others, and pervade them so
That even the grossest minds must see and hear [85]
And cannot chuse but feel. The Power which these
85 Acknowledge when thus moved, which Nature thus
Thrusts forth upon the senses, is the express
Resemblance, in the fulness of its strength
Made visible, a genuine Counterpart
And Brother of the glorious faculty
90 Which higher minds bear with them as their own. [90]
This is the very spirit in which they deal
With all the objects of the universe;
They from their native selves can send abroad
Like transformations, for themselves create
95 A like existence, and, whene'er it is [95]
Created for them, catch it by an instinct;
Them the enduring and the transient both [100]
Serve to exalt; they build up greatest things
From least suggestions, ever on the watch,
100 Willing to work and to be wrought upon,
They need not extraordinary calls
To rouze them, in a world of life they live, [105]
By sensible impressions not enthrall'd,
But quicken'd, rouz'd, and made thereby more fit

231

105　To hold communion with the invisible world.
　　　Such minds are truly from the Deity,
　　　For they are Powers; and hence the highest bliss
　　　That can be known is theirs, the consciousness
　　　Of whom they are habitually infused　　　　　　　[115]
110　Through every image, and through every thought,
　　　And all impressions; hence religion, faith,
　　　And endless occupation for the soul
　　　Whether discursive or intuitive　　　　　　　　　[120]
　　　Hence chearfulness in every act of life
115　Hence truth in moral judgements and delight
　　　That fails not in the external universe.

　　　Oh! who is he that hath his whole life long　　　[130]
　　　Preserved, enlarged, this freedom in himself?
　　　For this alone is genuine Liberty:
120　Witness, ye Solitudes! where I received
　　　My earliest visitations, careless then　　　　　　[141]
　　　Of what was given me, and where now I roam,
　　　A meditative, oft a suffering Man,　　　　　　　[143]
　　　And yet, I trust, with undiminish'd powers,
125　Witness, whatever falls my better mind,
　　　Revolving with the accidents of life,
　　　May have sustain'd, that, howsoe'er misled,
　　　I never, in the quest of right and wrong,　　　　[150]
　　　Did tamper with myself from private aims;
130　Nor was in any of my hopes the dupe
　　　Of selfish passions; nor did wilfully
　　　Yield ever to mean cares and low pursuits;
　　　But rather did with jealousy shrink back　　　　　[155]
　　　From every combination that might aid
135　The tendency, too potent in itself,
　　　Of habit to enslave the mind, I mean
　　　Oppress it by the laws of vulgar sense,
　　　And substitute a universe of death,　　　　　　　[160]
　　　The falsest of all worlds, in place of that
140　Which is divine and true. To fear and love,

232

To love as first and chief, for there fear ends,
Be this ascribed; to early intercourse,
In presence of sublime and lovely forms, [165]
With the adverse principles of pain and joy,
145 Evil as one is rashly named by those
Who know not what they say. From love, for here
Do we begin and end, all grandeur comes,
All truth and beauty, from pervading love,
That gone, we are as dust. Behold the fields [170]
150 In balmy spring-time, full of rising flowers
And happy creatures; see that Pair, the Lamb
And the Lamb's Mother, and their tender ways
Shall touch thee to the heart; thou call'st this love
And so it is, but there is higher love [175]
155 Than this, a love that comes into the heart
With awe and a diffusive sentiment;
Thy love is human merely; this proceeds
More from the brooding Soul, and is divine.

    This love more intellectual cannot be
160 Without Imagination, which, in truth,
Is but another name for absolute strength [190]
And clearest insight, amplitude of mind,
And reason in her most exalted mood.
This faculty hath been the moving soul
165 Of our long labour: we have traced the stream
From darkness, and the very place of birth
In its blind cavern, whence is faintly heard [195]
The sound of waters; follow'd it to light
And open day, accompanied its course
170 Among the ways of Nature, afterwards
Lost sight of it bewilder'd and engulph'd,
Then given it greeting, as it rose once more [200]
With strength, reflecting in its solemn breast
The works of man and face of human life,
175 And lastly, from its progress have we drawn
The feeling of life endless, the great thought

By which we live, Infinity and God. [205]
Imagination having been our theme,
So also hath that intellectual love,
180 For they are each in each, and cannot stand
Dividually.—Here must thou be, O Man!
Strength to thyself; no Helper hast thou here; [210]
Here keepest thou thy individual state:
No other can divide with thee this work,
185 No secondary hand can intervene
To fashion this ability; 'tis thine,
The prime and vital principle is thine [215]
In the recesses of thy nature, far
From any reach of outward fellowship,
190 Else 'tis not thine at all. But joy to him,
Oh, joy to him who here hath sown, hath laid
Here the foundations of his future years! [220]
For all that friendship, all that love can do,
All that a darling countenance can look
195 Or dear voice utter to complete the man,
Perfect him, made imperfect in himself,
All shall be his: and he whose soul hath risen [225]
Up to the height of feeling intellect
Shall want no humbler tenderness, his heart
200 Be tender as a nursing Mother's heart;
Of female softness shall his life be full,
Of little loves and delicate desires, [230]
Mild interests and gentlest sympathies.

Child of my Parents! Sister of my Soul!
205 Elsewhere have strains of gratitude been breath'd
To thee for all the early tenderness
Which I from thee imbibed. And true it is [235]
That later seasons owed to thee no less;
For, spite of thy sweet influence and the touch
210 Of other kindred hands that open'd out
The springs of tender thought in infancy,
And spite of all which singly I had watch'd [240]

234

Of elegance, and each minuter charm
In nature and in life, still to the last
215 Even to the very going out of youth,
The period which our Story now hath reach'd,
I too exclusively esteem'd that love,
And sought that beauty, which, as Milton sings,   [245]
Hath terror in it. Thou didst soften down
220 This over-sternness; but for thee, sweet Friend,
My soul, too reckless of mild grace, had been
Far longer what by Nature it was framed,
Longer retain'd its countenance severe,   [250]
A rock with torrents roaring, with the clouds
225 Familiar, and a favourite of the Stars:
But thou didst plant its crevices with flowers,
Hang it with shrubs that twinkle in the breeze,
And teach the little birds to build their nests   [255]
And warble in its chambers. At a time
230 When Nature, destined to remain so long
Foremost in my affections, had fallen back
Into a second place, well pleas'd to be
A handmaid to a nobler than herself,   [260]
When every day brought with it some new sense
235 Of exquisite regard for common things,
And all the earth was budding with these gifts
Of more refined humanity, thy breath,
Dear Sister, was a kind of gentler spring   [265]
That went before my steps.
                              With such a theme,   [275]
240 Coleridge! with this my argument, of thee
Shall I be silent? O most loving Soul!
Placed on this earth to love and understand,
And from thy presence shed the light of love,
Shall I be mute ere thou be spoken of?   [280]
245 Thy gentle Spirit to my heart of hearts
Did also find its way; and thus the life
Of all things and the mighty unity
In all which we behold, and feel, and are,

Admitted more habitually a mild [288]
250 Interposition, and closelier gathering thoughts
Of man and his concerns, such as become [290]
A human Creature, be he who he may!
Poet, or destined for a humbler name;
And so the deep enthusiastic joy,
255 The rapture of the Hallelujah sent
From all that breathes and is, was chasten'd, stemm'd
And balanced by a Reason which indeed [296]
Is reason; duty and pathetic truth;
And God and Man divided, as they ought,
260 Between them the great system of the world
Where Man is sphered, and which God animates.

And now, O Friend! this History is brought
To its appointed close: the discipline
And consummation of the Poet's mind,
265 In everything that stood most prominent, [305]
Have faithfully been pictured; we have reach'd
The time (which was our object from the first)
When we may, not presumptuously, I hope,
Suppose my powers so far confirm'd, and such
270 My knowledge, as to make me capable [310]
Of building up a work that should endure.
Yet much hath been omitted, as need was;
Of Books how much! and even of the other wealth
Which is collected among woods and fields,
275 Far more: for Nature's secondary grace, [315]
That outward illustration which is hers,
Hath hitherto been barely touch'd upon,
The charm more superficial, and yet sweet
Which from her works finds way, contemplated
280 As they hold forth a genuine counterpart
And softening mirror of the moral world.

Yes, having track'd the main essential Power,
Imagination, up her way sublime,

In turn might Fancy also be pursued
285 Through all her transmigrations, till she too
Was purified, had learn'd to ply her craft
By judgment steadied. Then might we return
And in the Rivers and the Groves behold
Another face, might hear them from all sides
290 Calling upon the more instructed mind
To link their images with subtle skill
Sometimes, and by elaborate research
With forms and definite appearances
Of human life, presenting them sometimes
295 To the involuntary sympathy
Of our internal being, satisfied
And soothed with a conception of delight
Where meditation cannot come, which thought
Could never heighten. Above all how much
300 Still nearer to ourselves we overlook
In human nature and that marvellous world
As studied first in my own heart, and then   [324]
In life among the passions of mankind
And qualities commix'd and modified
305 By the infinite varieties and shades
Of individual character. Herein
It was for me (this justice bids me say)
No useless preparation to have been
The pupil of a public School, and forced
310 In hardy independence, to stand up
Among conflicting passions, and the shock
Of various tempers, to endure and note   [335]
What was not understood though known to be;
Among the mysteries of love and hate,
315 Honour and shame, looking to right and left,
Uncheck'd by innocence too delicate
And moral notions too intolerant,   [340]
Sympathies too contracted. Hence, when call'd
To take a station among Men, the step
320 Was easier, the transition more secure,

More profitable also; for the mind
Learns from such timely exercise to keep [345]
In wholesome separation the two natures,
The one that feels, the other that observes.

325   Let one word more of personal circumstance,
Not needless, as it seems, be added here.
Since I withdrew unwillingly from France,
The Story hath demanded less regard
To time and place; and where I lived, and how
330 Hath been no longer scrupulously mark'd.
Three years, until a permanent abode
Receiv'd me with that Sister of my heart
Who ought by rights the dearest to have been
Conspicuous through this biographic Verse,
335 Star seldom utterly conceal'd from view,
I led an undomestic Wanderer's life,
In London chiefly was my home, and thence
Excursively, as personal friendships, chance
Or inclination led, or slender means
340 Gave leave, I roam'd about from place to place
Tarrying in pleasant nooks, wherever found
Through England or through Wales. A Youth (he bore
The name of Calvert; it shall live, if words [355]
Of mine can give it life,) without respect
345 To prejudice or custom, having hope
That I had some endowments by which good
Might be promoted, in his last decay
From his own Family withdrawing part
Of no redundant Patrimony, did
350 By a Bequest sufficient for my needs
Enable me to pause for choice, and walk [360]
At large and unrestrain'd, nor damp'd too soon
By mortal cares. Himself no Poet, yet
Far less a common Spirit of the world,
355 He deem'd that my pursuits and labours lay
Apart from all that leads to wealth, or even [365]

Perhaps to necessary maintenance,
Without some hazard to the finer sense;
He clear'd a passage for me, and the stream
Flowed in the bent of Nature.

360   Having now
Told what best merits mention, further pains   [370]
Our present labour seems not to require,
And I have other tasks. Call back to mind
The mood in which this Poem was begun,
365 O Friend! the termination of my course
Is nearer now, much nearer; yet even then   [375]
In that distraction and intense desire
I said unto the life which I had lived,
Where art thou? Hear I not a voice from thee
370 Which 'tis reproach to hear? Anon I rose
As if on wings, and saw beneath me stretch'd   [380]
Vast prospect of the world which I had been
And was; and hence this Song, which like a lark
I have protracted, in the unwearied Heavens
375 Singing, and often with more plaintive voice
Attemper'd to the sorrows of the earth;   [385]
Yet centring all in love, and in the end
All gratulant if rightly understood.

    Whether to me shall be allotted life,
380 And with life power to accomplish aught of worth
Sufficient to excuse me in men's sight
For having given this Record of myself,   [391]
Is all uncertain: but, beloved Friend,
When, looking back thou seest in clearer view
385 Than any sweetest sight of yesterday
That summer when on Quantock's grassy Hills   [395]
Far ranging, and among the sylvan Coombs,
Thou in delicious words, with happy heart,
Didst speak the Vision of that Ancient Man,
390 The bright-eyed Mariner, and rueful woes   [400]
Didst utter of the Lady Christabel;

And I, associate in such labour, walk'd
Murmuring of him who, joyous hap! was found,
After the perils of his moonlight ride   [405]
395 Near the loud Waterfall; or her who sate
In misery near the miserable Thorn;
When thou dost to that summer turn thy thoughts,
And hast before thee all which then we were,
To thee, in memory of that happiness   [410]
400 It will be known, by thee at least, my Friend,
Felt, that the history of a Poet's mind
Is labour not unworthy of regard:
To thee the work shall justify itself.

The last and later portions of this Gift   [415]
405 Which I for Thee design, have been prepared
In times which have from those wherein we first
Together wanton'd in wild Poesy,
Differ'd thus far, that they have been, my Friend,
Times of much sorrow, of a private grief
410 Keen and enduring, which the frame of mind   [420]
That in this meditative History
Hath been described, more deeply makes me feel;
Yet likewise hath enabled me to bear
More firmly; and a comfort now, a hope,
415 One of the dearest which this life can give,
Is mine; that Thou art near, and wilt be soon   [425]
Restored to us in renovated health;
When, after the first mingling of our tears,
'Mong other consolations we may find
420 Some pleasure from this Offering of my love.

Oh! yet a few short years of useful life,   [430]
And all will be complete, thy race be run,
Thy monument of glory will be raised.
Then, though, too weak to tread the ways of truth,
425 This Age fall back to old idolatry,
Though men return to servitude as fast   [435]

As the tide ebbs, to ignominy and shame
By Nations sink together, we shall still
Find solace in the knowledge which we have,
430 Bless'd with true happiness if we may be
United helpers forward of a day   [440]
Of firmer trust, joint-labourers in a work
(Should Providence such grace to us vouchsafe)
Of their redemption, surely yet to come.
435 Prophets of Nature, we to them will speak
A lasting inspiration, sanctified   [445]
By reason and by truth; what we have loved,
Others will love; and we may teach them how;
Instruct them how the mind of man becomes
440 A thousand times more beautiful than the earth
On which he dwells, above this Frame of things   [450]
(Which, 'mid all revolutions in the hopes
And fears of men, doth still remain unchanged)
In beauty exalted, as it is itself
445 Of substance and of fabric more divine.

NOTES

The Manuscripts. There are five almost complete MSS. of *The Prelude* (A B C D E) covering the years 1805–39, as well as more than a dozen note-books and other MSS. which contain drafts of parts of the poem, and belong to an earlier period. A and B give us the first version of the poem as a whole: they were written, A by Dorothy Wordsworth and B by Sara Hutchinson, in the winter of 1805–6, under the poet's direct supervision. The text of the present edition is printed from A.

C, which can be dated 1817–19, is in the handwriting of Wordsworth's clerk, John Carter.

D was copied by Mrs. Wordsworth about 1827–9 and was much corrected in 1832 and again in 1839.

E was copied by the poet's daughter Dora and Elizabeth Cookson in May 1839. From this copy the edition of 1850 was printed.

For further details of these MSS., and for the variant readings in them and in the earlier drafts, students should consult the Library Edition of *The Prelude* published at the Clarendon Press in 1959, and referred to in these notes as P.

The text of the first printed edition of *The Prelude* is referred to as 1850. A number in square brackets denotes the number of a line in the 1850 edition: e.g. [175]=line 175 in 1850.

Other abbreviations used in the Introduction and notes are as follows:

W. W., D. W., and M. W. = William Wordsworth, Dorothy Wordsworth, and Mary Wordsworth.

S. H. = Sara Hutchinson; S. T. C. = Samuel Taylor Coleridge.

Oxf. W. = The one-volume edition of Wordsworth's poems, ed. by Thomas Hutchinson, Oxford University Press.

Knight = *Poems of W. W.*, ed. by William Knight, 8 vols., 1896 (vol. iii contains *The Prelude*).

Nowell Smith = *Poems of W. W.*, ed. by Nowell Charles Smith, 3 vols., 1896 (vol. iii contains *The Prelude*).

P.W. = *The Poetical Works of W. W.*, Vols. I–V ed. by E. de Selincourt and Helen Darbishire, 1940–9.

Moore Smith = *The Prelude*, ed. by G. C. Moore Smith (Temple Classics).

Worsfold = *The Prelude*, ed. by Basil Worsfold, 1907.

Grosart = *The Prose Works of W. W.*, ed. by Alexander B. Grosart, 3 vols., 1876.

I. F. notes = Notes on the different poems dictated by Wordsworth in later life to Miss Fenwick, and first printed in full in Grosart.

E.Y.; M.Y. (1) = *The Letters of W. W. and D. W.: The Early Years*, ed. by Ernest de Selincourt, revised Chester L. Shaver (Oxford, 1967); *The Middle Years: Volume One*, revised Mary Moorman (Oxford, 1969).

M.Y.; L.Y. = *The Letters of W. W.: Middle Years*, ed. by Ernest de Selincourt (Oxford, 1937); *The Later Years* (Oxford, 1939).

C.R. = *Correspondence of Crabb Robinson and the Wordsworth Circle*, ed. by E. Morley, 1927.

Journals = *The Journals of D. W.*, ed. by E. de Selincourt, 2 vols., 1941.

Memoirs = *Memoirs of W.*, by Christopher Wordsworth, 2 vols., 1851.

Legouis = *The Early Life of W. W., 1770–99*, by Émile Legouis, translated by J. W. Matthews, 1897.

Harper = *W. W., his Life, Works, and Influence*, by George McLean Harper, 2 vols., 1916.

Havens = *The Mind of a Poet, A Study of Wordsworth's Thought*, by Raymond D. Havens, 1941.

Moorman I = *W. W. The Early Years, 1770–1803*, by M. Moorman, 1957.

Moorman II = *W. W. The Later Years, 1803–1850*, by M. Moorman, 1965.

Garrod = *W. W.: Lectures and Essays*, by H. W. Garrod, 1923.

Chronology = Mark L. Reed, *W.: The Chronology of the Early Years 1770–1799* (Harvard, 1967).

Studies = *W.: Bi-Centenary Studies*, ed. Jonathan Wordsworth (Cornell, 1970).

The Prelude was published by Moxon on 20 July 1850, and the statement of accounts, sent to Wordsworth's executors on 3 July 1851, proves that by that date the whole edition of 2,000 copies was exhausted. They received in payment the sum of £414. 15*s*. 8*d*., two-thirds of the profits. A second edition appeared in 1851.

The following 'Advertisement' was prefixed to the Poem:

THE following Poem was commenced in the beginning of the year 1799, and completed in the summer of 1805.

The design and occasion of the work are described by the Author in his Preface to the "EXCURSION," first published in 1814, where he thus speaks:—

"Several years ago, when the Author retired to his native mountains with the hope of being enabled to construct a literary work that might live, it was a reasonable thing that he should take a review of his own mind, and examine how far Nature and Education had qualified him for such an employment.

"As subsidiary to this preparation, he undertook to record, in verse, the origin and progress of his own powers, as far as he was acquainted with them.

"That work, addressed to a dear friend, most distinguished for his knowledge and genius, and to whom the Author's intellect is deeply indebted, has been long finished; and the result of the investigation which gave rise to it, was a determination to compose a philosophical Poem, containing views of Man, Nature, and Society, and to be entitled the "RECLUSE;" as having for its principal subject the sensations and opinions of a poet living in retirement.

"The preparatory poem is biographical, and conducts the history of the Author's mind to the point when he was emboldened to hope that his faculties were sufficiently matured for entering upon the arduous labour which he had proposed to himself; and the two works have the same kind of relation to each other, if he may so express himself, as the Ante-chapel has to the body of a Gothic Church. Continuing this allusion, he may be permitted to add, that his minor pieces, which have been long before the public, when they shall be properly arranged, will be found by the attentive reader to have such connection with the main work as may give them claim to be likened to the little cells, oratories, and sepulchral recesses, ordinarily included in those edifices."

Such was the Author's language in the year 1814.

It will thence be seen, that the present Poem was intended to be introductory to the "RECLUSE," and that the "RECLUSE," if completed, would have consisted of Three Parts. Of these, the Second Part alone, viz. the "EXCURSION," was finished, and given to the world by the Author.

The First Book of the First Part of the "RECLUSE" still [1850] remains in manuscript; but the Third Part was only planned. The materials of which it would have been formed have, however, been incorporated, for the most part, in the Author's other Publications, written subsequently to the "EXCURSION."

The Friend, to whom the present Poem is addressed, was the late SAMUEL TAYLOR COLERIDGE, who was resident in Malta, for the restoration of his health, when the greater part of it was composed.

Mr. Coleridge read a considerable portion of the Poem while he was abroad; and his feelings, on hearing it recited by the Author (after his return to his own country) are recorded in his Verses, addressed to Mr. Wordsworth, which will be found in the "Sibylline Leaves," p. 197, ed. 1817, or "Poetical Works, by S. T. Coleridge," vol. i., p. 206.

RYDAL MOUNT,
July 13th, 1850.

At the end of MS. D is the note: 'The composition of this poem was finished early in 1805—it having been begun about 1798.' To this E adds, 'The Life is brought up to the time of the Composition of the first Edition of the Lyrical Ballads'.

BOOK I

1–54 [1–45]. Garrod (pp. 186–90) has pointed out that these lines are a record of Wordsworth's feelings in September 1795, when, after the distraction of eight months' residence in London, he was about to enter upon a life of freedom, and was on his way from Bristol to Racedown, where he was to take up his abode with his sister Dorothy. Thus, though the city he is actually leaving is Bristol, the 'prison where he hath been long immured' (8), 'the vast city where I long had pined' [7] is London. But the whole passage cannot, as Garrod further states, have been actually written in 1795 in the form in which it appears in the A text. For l. 20, and the first draft of ll. 40–8, are found jotted down in a note-book among other passages which were written in Germany during the winter of 1798–9 (cf. P., p. 608 E). The most probable explanation of the difficulty is that ll. 1–54 are a development, written in 1799 when he was completing Bk. I, of lines which he improvised (or 'sang Aloud, in Dythyrambic fervour, deep But short-liv'd uproar,' VII. 6) as he walked from Bristol to Racedown. It is possible that ll. 1–19 are an almost verbal reproduction of this 'short-liv'd uproar', the rest being a development of its spirit. Hence, perhaps, the alteration of ll. 58–9, which are not literally true of the whole passage, though they may be true of a part of it, to the text of 1850. In the opening lines of Bk. VII (written in 1804) which speak of 'five years' (corrected to 'six' in 1850 text) as having passed since he poured out his 'glad preamble', Wordsworth is obviously confusing the date of his escape from the City with the date at which he actually began to compose *The Prelude*. For a similar confusion and blending of separate occasions into one cf. *note* to VI. 216–45. [The interpretation of the details of the 'glad preamble' and of its date are not as settled as de Selincourt's note suggests. See John Finch's important essay in *Studies*. It will be noted that de Selincourt largely accepted H. W. Garrod's exposition of these lines, and that this resulted in notes at ll. 7, 74, 82, 114, 122 which Wordsworth scholars would now question. S. G.]

1. *Oh there is blessing in this gentle breeze*: It is worth noting how often Wordsworth's imagination conceives of the coming of creative energy to the soul as a 'breeze'. Cf. I. 41–5, II. 245, VII. 2, and *Excursion*, IV. 600, 'The breeze of nature stirring in his soul'.

7. *from yon City's walls set free*: Wordsworth resided in London from January to September 1795. The freedom came from the legacy of £900 left him by Raisley Calvert (*v.* XIII. 342–60).

15. *The earth is all before me*: the first of the many Miltonic echoes in the poem. Cf. *Paradise Lost*, xii. 646: 'The world was all before them, where to choose' (*v. Introduction*, p. xiv).

23–4. *That burthen. . . , weary day*:
Cf. *Lines composed a few miles above Tintern Abbey*, 37–41:

> that blessed mood,
> In which the burthen of the mystery,
> In which the heavy and the weary weight
> Of all this unintelligible world,
> Is lightened.

Tintern Abbey was written on 13 June 1798, and the lines quoted above must have owed something of their form to unconscious reminiscence of the 'preamble' which had lately been adopted for *The Prelude*. So the phrase 'undisturbed delight' (28) recalls *A Night-piece*, composed 25 January 1798, 'Not undisturbed by the delight it feels'. The phrase reappears in X. 838, 'Lord of himself, in undisturb'd delight'.

55–6. *not used to make A present joy the matter of my Song*: 'I have said that poetry is the spontaneous overflow of powerful feelings: it takes its origin from emotion recollected in tranquillity: the emotion is contemplated till by a species of reaction the tranquillity gradually disappears, and an emotion, similar to that which was before the subject of contemplation, is gradually produced, and does itself actually exist in the mind. In this mood successful composition generally begins', *etc*. Preface to *Lyrical Ballads*, 1800. Wordsworth, as Garrod points out, calls special attention here to the fact that ll. 1–54 differed in this respect from his other poetry.

58–9. *Even in the very words which I have here Recorded*: a statement modified in D and E, owing to the changes introduced in the previous lines. In the 'preamble' as written in 1795 there was nothing about 'punctual service high' or 'Matins and vespers'.

74. *'Twas Autumn*: This statement alone should have been enough to convince the early editors of Wordsworth that he is describing neither his departure from Goslar nor his journey to take up his abode at Grasmere. He left Goslar in February 1799, and settled at Dove Cottage, Grasmere, on 20 December of the same year.

82. *one sweet Vale*: Racedown, to which, as Garrod suggests, Wordsworth was now paying a visit of inspection. It was, therefore, not a 'known' vale [72] except by hearsay, as indeed the words 'No picture of mere memory' [75] and 'fancied scene' [76] indicate.

104 [96]. *Eolian visitations*: thoughts that come and go with the breeze, as the Aeolian harp sounds when the wind passes over it. Cf. Coleridge, *The Eolian Harp*, 39–43:

> Full many a thought uncalled and undetained,
> And many idle flitting phantasies,
> Traverse my indolent and passive brain,
> As wild and various as the random gales
> That swell and flutter on this subject lute!

114 [106]. *A pleasant loitering journey, through two days*: 'two' is altered to 'three' as late as the E text. The distance was fifty miles. As Wordsworth only started towards evening he probably took two days more. But the alteration of text was hardly necessary, for 'through two days Continued' might be taken to bear that meaning.

117. *The admiration and the love*: to Wordsworth the true sustenance of the spiritual life. Cf. *Excursion*, IV. 763–5.

122 [113]. *the happiness entire*: This is hardly a true picture of Wordsworth's frame of mind in the *early* days at Racedown, when he had 'given up moral questions in despair'; but looking back over a space of more than two years he speaks rather of the total effect of his life there. And, indeed, he goes on, by a natural transition, to describe his feelings at the present, i.e. the early months of 1798.

143–4 [133–4]. *present gifts Of humbler industry*: In the early months of 1798 he was engaged on the character of the Wanderer (*Excursion*, I), *The Cumberland Beggar*, and *The Discharged Soldier* (*Prelude*, IV). A little later he wrote the simpler poems to be included in the *Lyrical Ballads*, and *Peter Bell*.

151–2 [140–1]. *as the Mother Dove, Sits brooding*: Cf. *Paradise Lost*, i. 21: 'Dove-like satst brooding on the vast Abyss.'

153–4 [142–3]. *goadings on That drive her as in trouble through the groves*: Cf. the portrait which Wordsworth has drawn of himself in *Stanzas written in my pocket copy of Thomson's Castle of Indolence*, 1–36, especially the lines

> Oft could we see him driving full in view . . .
> And his own mind did like a tempest strong
> Come to him thus, and drove the weary wight along.

179–80 [168–9].   *some British theme, some old Romantic tale, by Milton left unsung*:

It is significant that Wordsworth's first ambition is to emulate Milton. In the *Milton* MS. at Trinity, Cambridge, is a list of subjects for a projected epic, in which the history of Britain before the Conquest is divided into thirty-three heads. Cf. also the *Epitaphium Damonis*, in which Milton tells of his project for writing a poem on the subject of king Arthur.

182–3 [171–2].   *Within the groves of Chivalry, I pipe Among the Shepherds, with reposing Knights*:

Spenser: *Faerie Queene*, Book VI. Notice the manner in which Wordsworth develops this passage later, giving it a definite moral turn of which, when he wrote in 1798, he was quite innocent.

186–95. *Mithridates . . . Odin . . . Sertorius*: To these themes Wordsworth was attracted by his reading of Plutarch and Gibbon. 'There were only two provinces of literature', says De Quincey (*Works*, ii. 288 *ed.* Masson) 'in which Wordsworth could be looked upon as decently well read—Poetry and Ancient History. Nor do I believe that he would much have lamented, on his own account, if all books had perished, excepting the entire body of English Poetry, and, perhaps, Plutarch's Lives. . . . His business with Plutarch was not for purposes of research: he was satisfied with his fine moral effects.' This statement, like many of De Quincey's, is fantastically exaggerated, for Wordsworth was more widely read than is often supposed (*v.* pp. xiii–xiv and notes *passim*), but at least it points to two of his three favourite classes of reading. Of Mithridates (131–63 B.C.) he read in Plutarch's *Lives* of *Sulla* and *Pompey*. After his defeat by Pompey in 66 B.C. Mithridates marched into Colchis and thence to the Cimmerian Bosphorus, where he planned to pass round the north and west coasts of the Euxine, through the tribes of Sarmatians and Getae, and invade Italy from the north. The connection of Odin with Mithridates was suggested, as Worsfold points out, by Gibbon (*Decline and Fall of the Roman Empire*, ch. x). 'It is supposed that Odin was the chief of a tribe of barbarians which dwelt on the banks of the lake Maeotis, till the fall of

Mithridates and the arms of Pompey menaced the north with servitude; that Odin, yielding with indignant fury to a power which he was unable to resist, conducted his tribe from the frontiers of the Asiatic Sarmatia into Sweden, with the great design of forming, in that inaccessible retreat of freedom, a religion and a people which, in some remote age, might be subservient to his immortal revenge; when his invincible Goths, armed with martial fanaticism, should issue in numerous swarms from the neighbourhood of the Polar circle, to chastise the oppressors of mankind.' Gibbon appends to this passage a note which, doubtless, suggested the theme to Wordsworth. 'This wonderful expedition of Odin, which, by deducing the enmity of the Goths and Romans from so memorable a cause, might supply the noble groundwork of an Epic poem, cannot safely be received as authentic history.' The identi- fication of Mithridates with Odin is probably Wordsworth's own contribution to the legend.

Sertorius: the famous Roman general who for eight years resisted the tyranny of the Senatorial party and kept the armies of Metellus and Pompey at bay till, in 72 B.C., he was assassinated. Mithridates sent him ships and men to support him against their common enemy. Plutarch relates that on one occasion Sertorius went to north Africa and on his return 'passed the strait of *Gibralter*, and turning on his right hand landed upon the coast of *Spaine*, lying towards the great Westerne sea, a little above the mouth of the river of *Baetis*. There certaine sailers met with him that were newly arrived from the Iles of the *ocean Atlanticum*, which the ancients called, the fortunate ilands. . . . They have raine there very seldome, howbeit a gentle wind commonly that bloweth in a little silver deaw, which moisteneth the earth so finely, that it maketh it fertile and lusty. . . . The weather is faire and pleasant continually and never hurteth the body . . . insomuch as the very barbarous people them- selves do faithfully believe that there are the *Elysian* fields, the aboad of blessed creatures, which Homer hath so much spoken of. *Sertorius* hearing report of these Ilands (upon a certain desire now to live quietly out of tyranny and warres) had straight a marvellous mind to go dwell there.' (Plutarch's *Lives*: *Sertorius*, tr. by North.) Wordsworth seems to have read Plutarch in the French translation of Thevet (1676) of which a copy was in his library.

Miss Darbishire has pointed out to me that in *The Guanches of Teneriffe* by Alonso de Espinosa (first published, in Spanish, in 1594) the story is told that the followers of Sertorius, after his death, in order to escape the tyranny of Rome, fled to the Canary Isles, known to the ancients as The Fortunate Isles: it was their heroic descendants who fought against the invading Spaniards at Teneriffe in 1493: but their final subjugation was due less to the valour of the Spaniards than to a terrible pestilence which attacked them in 1494. Hence, perhaps, the simile in l. 199.

205. *That one Frenchman*: 'Dominique de Gourges, a French gentleman who went in 1568 to Florida to avenge the massacre of the French by the Spaniards there' (note in 1850). In 1562 Jean Ribault, a Huguenot, with a band of French emigrants, landed in Florida and claimed the country for France;

in 1565 Pedro Menendez de Aviles followed him there, with the resolve to uproot the French colony, and hanged all the settlers he could lay hands on— 'not as Frenchmen, but as Lutherans'. The French court received the news with indifference, but Dominique de Gourges, a friend of Ribault, organized an expedition of vengeance, and reached Florida in 1567, 'where he most justly valiantly and sharply revenged the bloody and inhumane massacre committed by the Spaniards upon his countrymen in the yere 1565'. He hanged all his prisoners, saying 'I do not this as unto Spaniards, but as unto Traitors, Robbers, and Murtherers'. De Gourges returned to France in June 1568, but was ill received at court. He died in 1582. Wordsworth owed his knowledge of the incident to Hakluyt's *Voyages, etc.*, from which the above quotations are taken.

211. *Gustavus*: Gustavus I (1496–1560) freed his country from the tyranny of Denmark. Dalecarlia, a mining district in the west midlands of Sweden, is known as 'the cradle of Swedish civil and religious liberty'. Here Gustavus arranged and matured his schemes for the liberation of his country, and the district is full of mementoes of his life there, when he had often to assume the guise of a peasant or miner to escape capture by the Danes.

213. *Wallace*: Knight and Worsfold refer to Dorothy Wordsworth's *Journal* for 21 August 1803: 'Passed two of Wallace's caves. There is scarcely a noted glen in Scotland that has not a cave for Wallace, or some other hero.' [De Selincourt's original suggestion that these lines were 'almost certainly written in 1798' is without foundation. See *Chronology*, 29–31. S. G.]

233–4. *immortal verse Thoughtfully fitted to the Orphean lyre*: Cf. Milton: *L'Allegro*, 137, and *Paradise Lost*, iii. 17. So Coleridge, in his poem, *To a Gentleman, composed on the night after his recitation of a poem on the growth of an individual mind*, speaks of *The Prelude* as

> An Orphic song indeed,
> A song divine of high and passionate thoughts
> To their own music chaunted!

[248 [246]. *Doth lock my functions up*: cf. Pope, *Imit.* of 1st Epistle of 1st Book of Horace, 39, 40:

> So slow the unprofitable moments roll
> That lock up all the functions of my soul.   H. D.]

277. *Derwent*: the river that rises in the heart of the Lake District and flows down Borrowdale, through Derwentwater and Bassenthwaite, joining the Cocker under the walls of Cockermouth Castle.

278. *my 'sweet Birthplace'*: a quotation from Coleridge's *Frost at Midnight*, l. 28. And in his *Sonnet to the River Otter*, Coleridge has told how

so deep imprest
Sink the sweet scenes of childhood, that mine eyes
I never shut amid the sunny ray
But straight with all their tints thy waters rise.

Wordsworth by this quotation subtly associates the reminiscences of his own childhood with those of the friend for whom he writes.

286–7. *the Towers Of Cockermouth*: 'At the end of the garden of my father's house at Cockermouth was a high terrace that commanded a fine view of the river Derwent and Cockermouth Castle. This was our favourite playground.' (I. F. note to *The Sparrow's Nest*.) In Sonnet vii of *Poems . . . of 1833* (*Oxf. W.*, p. 464) Wordsworth tells us that it was in the 'green courts' of the castle that as a boy he chased the butterfly. Cf. *To a Butterfly*. 'Stay near me—do not take thy flight!' *etc.*

308. *that beloved Vale*: Esthwaite, at the north-west end of which is Hawkshead, where Wordsworth spent his school-days. The family account-books prove conclusively that, with his elder brother Richard, he entered the school at Whitsuntide 1779. Whitsuntide falls somewhere near the middle of the summer term, but apparently it was not an unusual time for boys to enter. Thus Mr. Gordon Wordsworth finds the following corroborative note in Sir Daniel Fleming's accounts for 4 June 1683, 'Given to George, Michael, Richard and Roger when they went to Hawkeshead School 4s.' In the autumn following, therefore, Wordsworth had seen *ten* summers, and not *nine*, as stated in l. 311.

315. *the smooth Hollows*: probably, as Knight suggests, on 'the round-headed grassy hills that lead up and on to the moor between Hawkshead and Coniston'.

362–5. *But I believe etc.*: An earlier version of this passage reads:
But I believe
That there are spirits, which, when they would form
A favored being, from his very dawn
Of infancy do open out the clouds *etc.*

It is interesting to notice that when Wordsworth began to write *The Prelude* he still delighted to conceive of Nature not merely as the expression of one divine spirit, but as in its several parts animated by individual spirits who had, like human beings, an independent life and power of action. This was obviously his firm belief in the primitive paganism of his boyhood (*v.* ll. 329–50, 405–27); and long after he had given up definite belief in it, he cherished it as more than mere poetic fancy. The passages which illustrate this are chiefly found in the readings of an earlier MS. (cf. P., *app. crit.* to I. 351, 490), but it is at least suggested in the text of II. 139.

376. *'Twas by the shores of Patterdale*: The scene of this famous boating episode has always been supposed to be Esthwaite, and critics have vainly sought to identify the 'rocky Cave' and the 'craggy Steep' upon its level banks, and to name the 'huge Cliff' that rose above it, when it was viewed at some distance from the shore. Ullswater, now shown to be the lake referred to, is far more suited to the adventure. Stybarrow crag, about 1¼ miles from the inn at Patterdale, well answers to the description of the 'craggy Steep', and where the crag touches the water there are several little inlets, in which a boat might well be moored, answering to the description of 'rocky caves'. The 'huge Cliff' which appears due west behind Stybarrow Crag on rowing out from shore is called Black Crag (2,000 ft.). Mr. Gordon Wordsworth, however, holds the view that the boat was taken from the spot, now occupied by the Patterdale Hall boat-house, where the road from Patterdale first touches the lake. The 'huge Cliff' would then be St. Sunday's Crag. The objection to his view is that the shore is flat at this spot, and there is nothing that by any poetic licence could be regarded as a 'rocky Cave'.

387–8. *Even like a Man, etc.*: an echo of *Paradise Lost*, xii. 1–2. 'As one who on his journey bates at noon, Though bent on speed.'

399 [371]. *for behind*: As Mr. Nowell Smith conjectured, 'far' in the 1850 text should be 'for'. 'Far' is only found in E, where it is clearly a copyist's error.

428–89 [401–63]. *Wisdom and Spirit, etc.*: 'These lines have already been published in the Author's Poetical Works, vol. i, p. 172, ed. 1849—p. 62 of the edition in one volume' (note in 1850). They were first published in *The Friend*, 28 December 1809, and were included in 1815 *ed.* of *Poems*.

468–9 [441–2]. *The leafless trees, and every icy crag Tinkled like iron*: Soon after receiving from D. W. a letter containing this passage, Coleridge wrote to his wife (14 January 1799), 'When very many are skating together the sounds and noises give an impulse to the icy trees, and the woods all round the lake tinkle.' Much of this letter was afterwards adapted for an Essay in *The Friend*, December 1809.

485–6 [459–60]. *as if the earth had roll'd*
                  With visible motion her diurnal round:

Cf. the second stanza of '*A slumber did my spirit seal*' which, like this passage, was written at Goslar in 1799:

> No motion has she now, no force;
> She neither hears nor sees;
> Rolled round in earth's diurnal course
> With rocks and stones and trees.

549 [522]. *plebeian cards*: Wordsworth, who had committed much of Pope to memory (*Memoirs*, ii. 470) could hardly fail, when he wrote this passage, to recall the famous game of cards in *The Rape of the Lock*. As Knight notes, he borrows the phrase from that poem (iii. 54):

> Gained but one trump, and one plebeian card.

563–4 [536–7]. *the frost . . . with keen and silent tooth*: Cf. *As You Like It*, II. vii. 177.

566–70 [539–43]. *the splitting ice, etc.*: Notice the change introduced into the text of this passage, due to a desire for greater scientific accuracy. Wordsworth's own experience of the noise occasioned by the splitting ice may have been reinforced by recollection of Coleridge's vivid description in the *Ancient Mariner*:

> It cracked and growled and roared and howled,
> Like noises in a swound.

571 [544]. *Nor, sedulous as I have been to trace How Nature*: An echo of *Paradise Lost*, ix. 27, 'Not sedulous by nature to indite'.

643 [615]. *birth of spring*: There is no MS. authority for 'breath of spring' (ed. 1850), which is therefore a printer's error.

644 [616]. *Planting my snowdrops among winter snows*: The text of 1850 here follows D and not E, the copy sent to press. Botanically the metaphor is inaccurate, for it implies, at least, that snowdrops are normally 'planted' in the spring, and its meaning is obscure. Garrod (p. 196) interprets it as referring to the time of year (winter) at which Wordsworth began the composition of *The Prelude*. But the poet seems to mean not 'I began my story early in the year'—a remark which would be pointless in this context, and would give to the word 'early' as applied to the second part of the sentence a meaning different from that which it bore in the first, but rather 'I started my story far back in the earliest period of my Life, dealing with incidents of my babyhood of which, I admit, I have no distinct memories'. In the words 'ere the birth of spring planting' *etc.*, he aims at expressing his misgivings at his attempt to go back to days 'disowned by memory'. In his last revision Wordsworth noticed the weakness of the metaphor, for he deleted it, and substituted in its place:

> fancying flowers where none,
> Not even the sweetest, do or can survive
> For him at least whose dawning day they cheered.

There is no doubt that he wished this reading to stand in the final text, but unfortunately his editor did not accept the correction.

BOOK II

[1. In an early manuscript appears an abortive opening of this book (*v. P.*, p. 42):

> Friend of my heart and genius we had reach'd
> A small green island which I was well pleased
> To pass not lightly by for though I felt
> Strength unabated yet I seem'd to need
> Thy cheering voice or ere I could pursue
> My voyage, resting else for ever there.   H. D.]

57. *To beat along the plain of Windermere*: Knight compares *Excursion*, IX. 485–88:

> When on thy bosom, spacious Windermere!
> A Youth, I practised this delightful art:
> Tossed on the waves alone, or 'mid a crew
> Of joyous comrades.

59–65. *an Island etc.*: In the fourth ed. of Wordsworth's *Guide to the Lakes* is the following note on the Islands of Windermere. 'This Lake has seventeen islands. Among those that lie near the largest, formerly called "Great Holm", may be noticed "Lady Holm", so called from the Virgin who had formerly a Chapel or Oratory there. On the road from Kendal to the Ferry Boat, might lately, and perhaps may still be seen, the ruins of the Holy Cross; a place where the pilgrims to this beautifully situated shrine must have been in the habit of offering up their devotions. Two other of these islands are named from the Lily of the Valley, which grows there in profusion.'

83–6. The *little weekly stipend*, paid by Ann Tyson, began at threepence and rose to sixpence as the boys grew older. Sums varying from 5*s*. 3*d*. to one guinea were paid to the boys at the close of some vacations. The half-yearly holidays came at Midsummer and Christmas, lasting approximately from 20 June to 4 August, and from 20 December to 20 January (*v.* 'The Boyhood of Wordsworth' by G. G. Wordsworth, *Cornhill Magazine*, April 1920).

110 [103]. *that large Abbey*: Furness Abbey. Its distance from Hawkshead is twenty-one miles.

139. *that still Spirit of the evening air*: Note the textual alteration of this line, and cf. note to I. 362–5.

144 [137]. *We beat with thundering hoofs the level sand*: The passage in Book X. 566 where this incident is recalled proves that the sands referred to were those of 'Leven's ample estuary', that lie between Cartmel and Ulverston.

147. *an Inn*: The White Lion at Bowness. Part of the bowling-green is still extant. It was this bowling-green that the Jacobite and Whig, described in *Excursion*, VI. 405–521, 'filled with harmless strife' (*ib.* 466).

152 [145]. *or ere*: 'and ere' (1850) is a mistake made by the copyist of E.

155 [148]. *its one bright fire*: 'own' (1850) is a copyist's error for 'one'.

174 [168]. *The Minstrel of our troop*: 'Robert Greenwood, afterwards Senior Fellow of Trinity College, Cambridge.' (*Memoirs*, i. 41.)

219 [214]. *succedaneum*: The only other employment of this word in verse with which I am familiar is in Cowper's humorous *Lines to the Rev. William Bull*:

> Oh for a succedaneum then
> To accelerate a creeping pen!

In Cowper's line the word is more suited to its context than it is here.

232 [228]. *Hard task*: So Raphael speaks of his difficulty in relating the 'invisible exploits of warring spirits' as 'sad task and hard'. *P.L.* v. 564.

246. *Even [in the first trial of its powers]*: This line must have been illegible in the MS. from which A and B were taken. It is supplied from an earlier MS.

263-4. *The gravitation and the filial bond etc.*: In an article on Wordsworth's reading of Addison (*Rev. of Engl. Stud.*, April 1927) Mr. T. E. Casson compares this passage with *Spectator*, No. 571: 'Every particle of matter is actuated by this Almighty Being which passes through it. The heavens and the earth, the stars and planets, move and gravitate by virtue of this great principle within them.' Cf. also *Spectator*, No. 120.

314 [295]. *'best society'*: *Paradise Lost*, ix. 249.
> For solitude sometimes is best society.

338-9 [319-20].   *With growing faculties she doth aspire,*
                   With faculties still growing:
an imitation of one of the most characteristic features of Milton's poetic style, a studied repetition of words or phrases, the repetition both emphasizing the idea and giving a peculiar musical effect.

349 [330]. *hours of School*: 'The daily work in Hawkshead School began—by Archbishop Sandys' ordinance—at 6 a.m. in summer, and 7 a.m. in winter.' (Knight.)

352 [333]. *a Friend*: the late Revd. John Fleming, of Rayrigg, Windermere (*note* in 1850). Knight suggests that the friend was the Revd. Charles Farish, author of *The Minstrels of Windermere* and *Black Agnes*, but he gives no authority for his suggestion.

362 [343]. *some jutting eminence*: Knight has attempted to identify the eminence, but by the word 'some' Wordsworth implies that the same eminence was not chosen every morning. Hence the attempt to identify it is futile.

368-71 [349-52]. *I forgot That I had bodily eyes etc.*: Cf. the I. F. note to the *Ode: Intimations etc.* 'I was often unable to think of external things as having external existence, and I communed with all that I saw as something not apart from, but inherent in, my own immaterial nature. Many times while going to school have I grasped at a wall or tree to recall myself from this abyss of idealism to the reality. At that time I was afraid of such processes. In later periods of life I have deplored, as we all have reason to do, a subjugation of an opposite character, and have rejoiced over the remembrances, as is expressed in the lines "Obstinate questionings *etc.*" To that dreamlike vividness and splendour which invests objects of sight in childhood, every one, I believe, if he would look back, could bear testimony.' Cf. also *Lines composed . . . above Tintern Abbey*, describing the 'serene and blessed mood' in which
> the breath of this corporeal frame,
> And even the motion of our human blood
> Almost suspended, we are laid asleep
> In body, and become a living soul.

and ll. 432-4 *infra*, and VI. 529-42.

380–1 [361–2].   *That by the regular action of the world*
                  My soul was unsubdu'd:

Wordsworth speaks in several places of the danger to the growing soul when the novelty and wonder of the world begins to wear off, and things are taken for granted: cf. *Ode*, 130–2,

> Full soon thy Soul shall have her earthly freight,
> And custom lie upon thee with a weight,
> Heavy as frost, and deep almost as life!

430. *I saw one life, and felt that it was joy*: The definitely Christian explanation of this 'joy' [412–14] is among the latest of the additions to the poem—in MS. E.

448–56 [432–40]. *if in these times of fear etc.*: Legouis was the first to point out that this passage was suggested to Wordsworth by a letter he received from Coleridge in the summer of 1799 (quoted *Memoirs*, i. 159), 'I wish you would write a poem, in blank verse, addressed to those, who, in consequence of the complete failure of the French Revolution, have thrown up all hopes of the amelioration of mankind, and are sinking into an almost epicurean selfishness, disguising the same under the soft titles of domestic attachment and contempt for visionary *philosophes*. It would do great good, and might form a part of *The Recluse*.' At this time Wordsworth intended to make it so, for in the five books which formed the original scheme of *The Prelude* his relations with the French Revolution were not touched upon (v. *Introduction*, p. xxix).

466–7 [451–2]. *Thou . . . wert rear'd In the great City*: Wordsworth here recalls the lines written by Coleridge himself in his *Frost at Midnight*:

> I was reared
> In the great city, pent 'mid cloisters dim.

BOOK III

[For a detailed account of W. W.'s Cambridge years the reader should consult Ben Ross Schneider, *Wordsworth's Cambridge Education* (Cambridge, 1957). S. G.]

44. *The Evangelist St. John*: Wordsworth entered St. John's College on 30 October 1787.

81 *ff*. *But wherefore be cast down? etc.*: It is significant that the almost defiant justification of his life at Cambridge, found in the A text and developed in lines added to A (*v. P. app. crit.*), is toned down to apology in D E. The parenthesis in 1850 text [83–7], however admirable its sentiment, is wholly irrelevant to his feelings in 1787. In the A text he is interpreting his actual feelings as an undergraduate: in 1850 he reflects upon them from the outlook of an elder brother of the Master of Trinity, just as, after l. [110], he interpolates a gloss on 'earth and heaven' quite foreign to the spirit of the A text.

85–8. *To apprehend all passions etc.*: Cf. II. 267–80; 377 *ff.*

102–8. *this first absence etc.*: One of Wordsworth's chief debts to Cambridge was that here first he realized that great source of his poetic inspiration—the 'spiritual presences of absent things'.

113 [117]. *spread my thoughts*: Cf. II. 253.

121 [127]. *A track pursuing not untrod before*: Note that in the A text a fresh paragraph begins here, and the comma after 'subdued' (123) connects lines 121–3 with what follows, and not, as in 1850, with what precedes. This was obviously Wordsworth's intention.

136–7 [140–1].　　　*To the sky's motion; in a kindred sense*
　　　　　　　　　　　Of passion was obedient etc.:
The punctuation of A is correct and that of 1850 obviously wrong.

182. *This is, in truth, heroic argument*: Wordsworth, like Milton, insists on the heroic nature of his theme. Cf. *Paradise Lost*, ix. 13–29

> . . . argument
> Not less but more Heroic than the wrauth
> Of stern Achilles . . .
> Not sedulous by Nature to indite
> Warrs, hitherto the onely Argument
> Heroic deem'd.

Cf. also Wordsworth's *Prospectus to the Excursion*, 25–41. Both there and in this passage he infers that as Milton deemed his subject more 'heroic' (i.e. worthy of epic treatment) than Homer's or Virgil's, so his theme, 'the might of Souls', is more heroic than Milton's.

201. *Uphold . . . my fainting steps*: an echo of Milton: *Samson Agonistes*, 666, 'And fainting spirits uphold'.

218. *than sodden clay On a sea River's bed at ebb of tide*: a simile vividly recalling the sands of Leven and Duddon, known to Wordsworth from boyhood.

259. *the opening act*: rightly altered in D to 'second act'. The first act of his new life had been more significant in his spiritual development, for then it was that he first became conscious of what he owed to the country he had left behind. Cf. *supra*, 102–8 and *note*.

261–2. *print . . . steps*: Cf. Milton, *Arcades*, 85, 'Where no print of step has been'.

269. *nobler*: the correct reading; 'noble' (1850) is a copyist's error in E.

276–81. The punctuation of A is obviously correct (*v.* P. *app. crit.* for its gradual deterioration). For the phrasing cf. Milton, *L'Allegro*, 67–8,

> And every Shepherd tells his tale
> Under the hawthorn in the dale.

'Trumpington, nat fer fro Canterbrigge' was the scene of Chaucer's *Reve's Tale*.

277, 281, 297. *Chaucer . . . Spenser . . . Milton*: 'When I began to give myself up to the profession of a poet for life, I was impressed with a conviction, that there were four poets whom I must have continually before me as examples—Chaucer, Shakespeare, Spenser, and Milton. These I must study, and equal *if I could*; and I need not think of the rest.' *Memoirs*, ii. 470. Spenser was at Pembroke Hall, Milton at Christ's.

284–5. *who, in his later day, Stood almost single, uttering odious truth*: So Milton, depicting under the figure of Abdiel his own position at the Restoration, insists on the same point:

> Nor number, nor example with him wrought
> To swerve from truth, or change his constant mind
> Though single. *P.L.* v. 901–3.

> well hast thou fought
> The better fight, who single hast maintaind
> Against revolted multitudes the cause
> Of truth *P.L.* vi. 29–32.

286. *Darkness before, and danger's voice behind*: Cf. *Paradise Lost*, vii. 27. 'In darkness, and with dangers compast round.'

305. *Within my private thoughts*: It is significant that Wordsworth does not impart to his companions, who would be in no mood to understand it, what was passing in his mind. The reading of A in the next line, too, is suggestive, and his various modifications of the A text (*v. P. app. crit.*) a little amusing.

326–8.
> *Ye will forgive the weakness of that hour*
> *In some of its unworthy vanities,*
> *Brother of many more:*

The punctuation of neither A nor 1850 is correct. There should be a comma after 'hour', but not after 'vanities'.

340–1. *A floating island . . . of spungy texture*: Cf. *Guide to Lakes* (present editor's reprint, p. 38). 'There occasionally appears above the surface of Derwentwater, and always in the same place, a considerable tract of spongy ground covered with aquatic plants, which is called the Floating, but with more propriety might be named the Buoyant, Island; and on one of the pools near the Lake of Esthwaite, may sometimes be seen a mossy Islet, with trees upon it, shifting about before the wind, a *lusus naturae* frequent on the great rivers of America, and not unknown in other parts of the world.' Cf. also D. W.'s poem 'Harmonious Powers with Nature work' *etc.*

400–1 [394–5]. *and to endure. The passing Day*: The punctuation of A, which had been conjectured by Professor Garrod as an emendation of 1850, is clearly correct. All MSS. before E have the full stop after 'endure'.

410–27 [404–21]. It is interesting to notice that this attack upon compulsory attendance at College Chapel was toned down in later texts; in an earlier MS. (*v. P. app. crit.*) it was far stronger than in A. It speaks eloquently for

Wordsworth's independence of mind that in his most conventional days it was not altogether deleted.

442–54. *a Virgin grove etc.*: Professor Lane Cooper has called attention to the fact that this passage is a striking example of Wordsworth's debt to that literature of travel and adventure, which, next to poetry and ancient history, was his favourite reading:

'I ascended this beautiful river on whose fruitful banks the generous and true sons of liberty securely dwell, fifty miles above the white settlements. . . . My progress was rendered delightful by the sylvan elegance of the groves, cheerful meadows, and high distant forests, which in grand order presented themselves to view. The winding banks of the rivers, and the high projecting promontories, unfolded fresh scenes of grandeur and sublimity. The deep forests and distant hills re-echoed the cheering social lowings of domestic herds. The air was filled with the loud and shrill hooping of the wary sharp-sighted crane. Behold, on yon decayed, defoliated cypress tree, the solitary wood pelican, dejectedly perched upon its utmost elevated spire; he there, like an ancient venerable sage, sets himself up as a mark of derision, for the safety of his kindred tribes.' Bartram: *Travels through North and South Carolina, etc.* 1794, pp. 47–8.

486–7 [476–7]. *'an obolus, a penny give To a poor Scholar'*: The allusion is to Belisarius, the general of the Byzantine Empire, who according to the popular story (dismissed by Gibbon as an idle fable), after he had been disgraced and his eyes put out, begged in the streets of Constantinople, saying 'Date obolum Belisario'. Wordsworth owed his knowledge of the story to Coleridge; for in a letter to him, dated 29 March 1804, he writes 'I ought to have asked your permission for the scholars and their obolus *etc.*'. Perhaps the '*etc.*' is meant to include the references to Bucer and Melanchthon also, which are more in Coleridge's line of reading than Wordsworth's. Bucer (1491–1551) was a German Greek scholar brought over to England on Cranmer's invitation. He taught theology at Cambridge, and died there. Erasmus came to England in 1497 and taught for some time at Oxford. Melanchthon (1497–1560) Professor of Greek at Wittenberg, friend and associate of Martin Luther.

511–16 [500–5]. *Far more I griev'd etc.*: On these lines Mrs. Davy's report of a conversation with Wordsworth, 5 June 1846 (*quoted* Grosart: iii. 456) provides an interesting commentary. 'Some talk concerning school led Mr. Wordsworth into a discourse, which, in relation to himself, I thought very interesting, on the dangers of emulation, as used in the way of help to school progress. Mr. Wordsworth thinks that envy is too likely to go along with this, and therefore would hold it to be unsafe. "In my own case," he said, "I never felt emulation with another man but once, and that was accompanied by envy. This once was in the study of Italian, which I entered on at College along with ——. I never engaged in the proper studies of the university, so that in these I had no temptation to envy anyone; but I remember with pain that I *had* envious feelings when my fellow student in Italian got before me.

I was his superior in many departments of mind, but he was the better Italian scholar, and I envied him. The annoyance this gave me made me feel that emulation was dangerous for *me*, and it made me very thankful that as a boy I never experienced it. I felt very early the force of the words 'Be ye perfect even as your Father in heaven is perfect,' and as a teacher, or friend, or counsellor of youth, I would hold forth no other motive to exertion than this. . . . There must always be a danger of incurring the passion of vanity by emulation. Oh! one other time," he added, smiling, "one other time in my life I felt envy. It was when my brother was nearly certain of success in a foot race with me. I tripped up his heels. This *must* have been envy." '

So in his College days Wordsworth annoyed his uncle by declining to compete for the prize offered for elegiac stanzas on the late master of his College. Cf. ll. 533–6 *infra*.

535. *dissolute pleasure*: Cf. Wordsworth's statement in a letter to De Quincey, written 6 March 1804, just after completing this book of *The Prelude*, that when he was at Cambridge 'the manners of the young men were very frantic and dissolute'.

546–9. Oswald Doughty suggests a debt in these lines to Thomson's *Castle of Indolence*, I. 30.

592–4.
> *Of colours, lurking, gleaming up and down*
> *Through that state arras woven with silk and gold;*
> *This wily interchange of snaky hues*:

A reminiscence of Spenser, *F.Q.* III. xi. 28:
> For, round about, the walls yclothed were
> With goodly arras of great majesty,
> Woven with gold and silke so close and nere
> That the rich metall lurked privily,
> As faining to be hid from envious eye;
> Yet here, and there, and every where, unwares
> It shewd itselfe and shone unwillingly;
> Like a discolourd snake, whose hidden snares
> Through the greene gras his long bright burnisht back declares.

616. *goings-on*: a favourite word of both Coleridge and Wordsworth. Cf. VI. 350, a fragment of *Michael* (*P.W.*, II. 482) 'the goings-on Of earth and sky' and *Gipsies* (1807), l. 23, 'The silent Heavens have goings on', of which W. W. wrote to Barron Field in October 1828, ' "Goings-on" is precisely the word wanted, but it makes a weak and apparently prosaic line so near the end of a poem.' So also in Preface 1802 Wordsworth speaks of the Poet as 'a man pleased with his own passions and volitions . . . delighting to contemplate similar volitions and passions as manifested in the goings-on of the Universe' *etc*. Cf. Coleridge: *Frost at Midnight*, 11–12,
> Sea, and hill, and wood,
> With all the numberless goings-on of life.

and *The Friend*, where he translates Bruno's 'ex visibilium aeterno immenso et innumerabili effectu' as 'the perpetual immense and innumerable goings-on of the visible world'. The word is not found in the final text of any poem of Wordsworth's.

636–7 [604–5]. *Guile; Murmuring Submission*: The punctuation of 1850 is obviously an improvement, but it is not likely that Wordsworth is responsible for it, for it only occurs in E, which is throughout careless in its punctuation.

BOOK IV

1–15 [1–26]. These lines describe the walk from Kendal, which Wordsworth reached by coach, over to the Ferry on Windermere, and after crossing the lake, up through Sawrey, past Esthwaite, to Hawkshead.

11 [19]. *that sweet Valley*: Esthwaite (*note* in 1850).

17 [28]. *my old Dame*: There was no boarding-house at Hawkshead School; boys living at a distance were housed with various cottagers in the village. The Wordsworth boys lodged with Anne Tyson and her husband, first in a cottage in Hawkshead, and afterwards in a cottage called Green-end, half a mile east of the town. The family account-books record a payment for each boy of £10 per half year.

26 [37]. *more than eighty*: Anne Tyson died on 25 May 1796, aged eighty-three.

35–7 [46–8].
> *the court, the garden were not left*
> *Long unsaluted, and the spreading Pine*
> *And broad stone Table*:

Dr. Cradock (quoted by Knight) calls attention to the reminiscence of *Peter Bell*, 155–6.

> To the stone table in my garden
> Loved haunt of many a summer hour.

40 [51]. *The froward Brook*: So all MSS. before E. 'Famous' for 'froward' is a copyist's error in E, which thus found its way into 1850. The brook, now as then, flows in a stone-built channel through the garden, under the square and main street and appears again on the other side of the village, whence it takes its course through fields into Esthwaite.

75 [84]. *regret?*: All MSS. read 'regret;' which is clearly wrong. Knight suggests reading 'nor' for 'and' in l. 69, which gives the required sense, but it is safer to alter a stop than a word.

110–11 [119–20]. *like a river murmuring And talking to itself*: 'Though the accompaniment of a musical instrument be dispensed with, the true Poet does not therefore abandon his privilege distinct from that of the mere Proseman:

He murmurs near the running brooks
A music sweeter than their own.'   (*Preface to Poems*, 1815.)

140–1. *my soul Put off her veil*: Cf. Exod. 34: 33–5; 2 Cor. 3: 13–16.

148 [157]. *weariness*: 'weakness', the reading of A, is clearly a copyist's error which at first escaped detection, but can never have been written by Wordsworth. I have therefore substituted 'weariness' in the text. Similarly 'rapt' in 153, which is copied 'wrapped' as late as the D text.

199 [208]. *To deck some slighted Playmate's homely cheek*: a curious echo of Milton: *Lycidas* 65: 'To tend the homely slighted shepherd's trade.'

296. *Th' authentic sight of reason*: Cf. *The Friend* (ed. 1818, i. 268) where Coleridge defines reason as 'the mind's eye', 'an organ bearing the same relation to spiritual objects . . . as the eye bears to material and contingent phenomena'.

335 [327]. *Grain-tinctured, drench'd in empyrean light*: a Miltonic line. 'Grain-tinctured' is a reminiscence of Milton's 'sky-tinctured grain' (*P.L.* v. 285). On its meaning cf. a long and interesting note in Masson's edition (III. 465–7). The word 'grain', now used as equivalent to 'texture' or 'fibre' as of wood or stone (cf. the phrase 'hard in grain'), originally implied colour (cf. *Il Penseroso*, 33 'All in a robe of darkest grain'); and not merely colour, but a particular colour, i.e. a clear red (*granum*, a seed or kernel, applied to the seed-like bodies of insects of the Coccus genus, from which dark-red dye was procured). The literary associations of the word, which would influence Wordsworth in his use of it, are with scarlet or crimson. Cf. Chaucer, *Sir Thopas*, 'His rode is lyk scarlet in grayn', and Spenser, *Epithalamion*, 226–8:

> How the red roses flush up in her cheekes,
> And the pure snow, with goodly vermill stayne,
> Like crimsin dyde in grayne.

Thus in the word 'grain-tinctured' Wordsworth describes the mountains as drenched in the crimson of the sky at dawn.

The phrase 'melody of birds' (338) is also found in Milton (*P.L.* viii. 528). Many conjectures have been made as to the possible route of this memorable walk, for Wordsworth has given no clue as to the situation of the house from which he was coming. If he had spent the evening at a farm in Yewdale, High Arnside, or in the region of Skelwith and Elterwater, he would strike across the high ground which lies between the Oxenfell and Barn Gates roads from Coniston to Ambleside. The mountain panorama here is magnificent, but the views of the sea, which can be obtained in one or two places, are so slight and distant that they hardly can be said to form a real feature of the view. Moreover, the distance from Hawkshead of any house in these directions would be considerably greater than the two miles mentioned in the A text.

If he was coming from High Wray, or the west bank of Windermere, he might cross Claife Heights, and at the top of Latterbarrow Crag obtain a really magnificent view of the sea in front, but rather to the left of him; but the mountains could hardly be described as 'near'.

Robertson (*Wordsworthshire*, pp. 142–3) suggests that the poet was walking from a farm at Grisedale, about three miles SSW. from Hawkshead. On the height known as Sans Keldin, to the right of the road thence, a fine view of the sea can be obtained. The objections to this suggestion are that it would be distinctly off the route to ascend Sans Keldin, that the mountains are rather too distant, and that the sea would be behind him and not in front. A final possibility is that he was coming from the head of Coniston Lake or from Atkinson Ground. The direct route would be through meadow and copse near the lake and up on to Hawkshead Moor. His direction would be ENE. and the track would naturally take him over a high point known as Ligging Shaw. As he reached this point he would have a view of the sea in front, somewhat to his right. The sea is rather more distant than in the last-mentioned route, but the mountains are nearer, and the total length of the walk would be little over two miles. I incline to agree with Mr. Gordon Wordsworth that this last route answers best to the description.

346 [339]. *Strange rendezvous my mind was at that time,*: There is no manuscript authority for the punctuation of 1850, which makes nonsense of the passage. Wordsworth would hardly describe this greatest moment of his life, in which he received his poetic baptism, as 'a strange rendezvous'. The meaning of the A text is clear enough. The mistake arose through E's omission of the comma after 'time', whence 1850, finding the line unpunctuated, interpolated the note of exclamation.

363–5. *A favourite pleasure etc.*: Cf. XII. 145 *ff.*: 'I love a public road' *etc.*

[400–504. The Discharged Soldier episode was originally composed independently of *The Prelude* and not, as de Selincourt implied in a note, as part of the early design. S. G.]

468. *ghastly*: 1850 reads 'ghostly' which is a copyist's error in E. The 'o's' and 'a's' in D are often indistinguishable, and here E took for an 'o' what was meant for an 'a'.

BOOK V

16. *A soul divine which we participate*: The later reading of this line removes from it all trace of Wordsworth's early Pantheism.

25. *Might almost 'weep to have' what he may lose*: a quotation from Shakespeare' *Sonnet* lxiv:

> This thought is as a death, which cannot choose
> But weep to have that which it fears to lose.

This sonnet is among those which Wordsworth singled out 'for their various merits of thought and language' (*Essay, supplementary to Preface*, 1815).

55–139. In his articles on Wordsworth in *Tait's Magazine* for January, February, and April 1839 (*v. Collected Works*, ed. Masson, ii. 268), De Quincey writes: 'in a great philosophical poem of Wordsworth's, which is still in manuscript, there is, at the opening of one of the books, a dream, which reaches the very *ne plus ultra* of sublimity, in my opinion, expressly framed to illustrate the eternity, and the independence of all social modes or fashions of existence, conceded to those two hemispheres, as it were, that compose the total world of human power—mathematics on the one hand, poetry on the other.' He proceeds to give, with quotations, 'though not refreshed by a sight of the poem for more than twenty years,' an interesting critical account of this passage—a striking proof of the impression it had made upon him.

[It has been generally assumed that the dream was dreamt or at least invented by W. W. himself. In the first manuscripts he gives the dream to 'a Philosophic Friend', but in the final text attributes it to himself. Mrs. J. W. Smyser (*PMLA*, March 1956) shows that the dream was dreamt by Descartes on 10 November 1619 (*v.* Baillet's *Life of Descartes*, 1691). The 'Philosophic Friend' is probably Coleridge. H. D.]

106. *undisturbed by space or time*: Cf. VI. 155 and [XI. 330–3].

164. *immortal Verse*: From Milton, *L'Allegro*, 137.

166–72 [166–73]. Mr. Nowell Smith has already called attention to the punctuation of 1850, which makes nonsense of the passage: in A the meaning is quite clear. The development of the text (*v.* P. *app. crit.*) shows how the error arose.

178–9. *some tale That did bewitch me then*: The reading of Wordsworth's boyhood may be conjectured from his reference to Fortunatus, Jack the Giant-killer, and Robin Hood, and Sabra and St. George in ll. 364–9, to the Arabian Nights (484), to Fairy Land and the Forests of Romance (477), and from the following statement in his Autobiographical Memoranda (*Memoirs*, i. 10): 'Of my earliest days at school I have little to say, but that they were very happy ones, chiefly because I was left at liberty, then and in the vacations, to read whatever books I liked. For example, I read all Fielding's works, Don Quixote, Gil Blas, and any part of Swift that I liked; Gulliver's Travels and the Tale of a Tub, being both much to my taste.' From *Memoirs* (i. 34) we learn 'that the poet's father set him very early to learn portions of the works of the best English poets by heart, so that at an early age he could repeat large portions of Shakespeare, Milton, and Spenser.'

201. *Whether by native prose or numerous verse*: *Paradise Lost*, v. 150.

205–6.   *And that, more varied and elaborate,*
                       Those trumpet-tones of harmony:

i.e. Milton; cf. 'Scorn not the sonnet', ll. 11–14.

209. *For Cottagers and Spinners at the wheel*: Cf. the words of the Duke in *Twelfth Night* of the 'old and plain song' which

> The spinsters and the sitters in the sun
> Do use to chant.

219–22. *speak of them as Powers . . . only less . . . Than Nature's self*: Cf. XII. 309–12, where Wordsworth expresses the hope

> that a work of mine,
> Proceeding from the depth of untaught things,
> Enduring and creative, might become
> A power like one of Nature's.

It was by this power, which Wordsworth always insisted was the distinctive mark of great literature, that he wished his own work to be judged. Crabb Robinson (ed. E. J. Morley, p. 53) records a conversation in which a friend of his 'estimated Wordsworth's poems chiefly for the purity of their morals. Wordsworth, on the other hand, valued them only according to the power of mind they presupposed in the writer, or excited in the hearer'. Cf. *Essay suppl. to Pref.* 1815 (Oxf. *W.*, p. 952.) The clearest statement of Wordsworth's position is found in De Quincey's Essay on Pope: 'There is', says De Quincey, 'first the literature of *knowledge*; and secondly the literature of *power*. The function of the first is to *teach*; of the second is to *move*. The first speaks to the *mere* discursive understanding; the second speaks ultimately to the higher understanding or reason, but always *through* the affections of pleasure and sympathy. . . . There is a rarer thing than truth, namely *power* or deep sympathy with truth. . . . What you owe to Milton is not any knowledge, what you owe is *power*, i.e. exercise and expansion to your own latent capacity of sympathy with the infinite, where every pulse and each separate influx is a step upwards.' Elsewhere he writes: 'The true antithesis to knowledge is not pleasure but *power*. All that is literature seeks to communicate power; all that is not literature, to communicate knowledge', and he adds in a note, 'For which distinction, as for most of the sound criticism on poetry, or any subject connected with it that I have ever met with, I must acknowledge my obligations to many years conversation with Mr. Wordsworth.' (De Q. *Works*, ed. Masson, xi. 55; x. 48.)

In the earlier scheme of *The Prelude*, which was to consist of five books only, the last book was to be devoted in part to illustrating this 'power' as gained from Nature and Books, and to showing by examples the kinship of the emotion aroused by both of them.

226 *ff.* *I was rear'd Safe from an evil*: Much has been written on the influence of Rousseau on Wordsworth's theories of education, but though he had certainly read *Émile*, and as a young man was surrounded by warm advocates of Rousseau, he based his views solely on his own experience, and only seems to refer to Rousseau when he differs from him. Like Rousseau he held that Nature was fundamentally good and her creatures pure until they had been

perverted by society, that education, therefore, must be directed to the development rather than the repression of natural instinct, and that much harm was done by premature appeals to the reason; but whilst Rousseau, not trusting Nature to do her work unaided, advocates the close guidance of the child in the path of Nature, Wordsworth is content to stand aside, and leave Nature and the child to themselves. The praise he accords his mother in this respect (ll. 270–85) is an implicit criticism of Rousseau's 'tutor', with his artificial manipulation of Nature's lessons. In contrast, too, to Rousseau's attack on books, and especially on tales of wonder and magic, as the bane of childhood, Wordsworth insists on their value as the firmest ally of Nature in educating the child, stimulating his imagination, saving him from vanity and self-consciousness (354–69), keeping alive his sense of wonder when it tends to lose its hold upon him (*v.* MSS. lines quoted in P., p. 555), and softening the effects of Nature's sterner lessons (ll. 473–81 *infra*). Moreover, Wordsworth raises no protest against the school tasks which fell to his lot at an age long before Rousseau would admit any formal instruction, and instead of advocating a childhood free from contamination with his fellows, pays special tribute to his debt to the rough and tumble of public school life (XIII. 306–24).

His chief protests, however, are not against Rousseau, but against those who, stimulated by the enthusiasm for education kindled by Rousseau, but without his genius, devoted their lives to 'child study', substituted for the old-time classics of the nursery, such as *Robin Hood* and the *Arabian Nights etc.*, edifying tales designed to inculcate scientific information or moral truth, and invented systems which, under a show of developing the latent powers of the child, fettered that development at every turn, and produced not the child of Nature, but the self-conscious prig. It is interesting to note D. W.'s account of the training that she and her brother gave to little Basil Montagu, of whom they had charge in 1796–7. 'You ask to be informed of our system respecting Basil. It is a very simple one; so simple that, in this age of systems, you will hardly be likely to follow it. We teach him nothing at present, but what he learns he learns from the evidence of his senses. He has an insatiable curiosity, which we are always careful to satisfy to the best of our ability. He is directed to everything he sees, the sky, the fields, trees, shrubs, corn, the making of tools, carts, etc. He knows his letters, but we have not attempted any further step in the path of *book-learning*.' (*E.Y.*, 180.) [See Moorman, I. 332–7 for an amusing account of Thomas Wedgwood's plans for a nursery for genius and the effect this probably had on W. W.'s own thoughts on ideal education. S. G.]

235. *bye-spots*: a word not found in *The Oxford Dictionary*, but recorded in Wright's *Dialect Dictionary* as peculiar to Cumberland (= lonely spots). It is interesting to find Wordsworth using, and then deleting, a dialect word.

256–7. *Early died My honour'd Mother*: i.e. in March 1778, at Penrith, her former home.

268. *shaping novelties from those to come*: The reading 'from', which persists through several MSS., was probably a scribal error for 'for', due to the 'from' in the line above.

290–1. *My drift hath scarcely, I fear, been obvious*: It is strange that though the poem underwent such continued revision, Wordsworth did not improve this prosaic and unnecessary statement.

303 [305]. *The wandering Beggars propagate his name*: Legouis points out (p. 62) that here Wordsworth is in agreement with Rousseau, who protested in *Émile* (Book II) against Locke's opinion that the child should be incited to liberality.

315–18 [307–9]. *fear itself . . . Touches him not*: To Wordsworth 'the discipline of fear' was among the most educative of Nature's agencies. Cf. I. 329–441, and the passage from the MS. quoted in P.'s note to VIII. 159–72.

384–6. *in the unreasoning . . . better eye than theirs*: These lines were first published as a quotation in the *Postscript to the Poems* of 1835, where Wordsworth gives them a significance and a moral of which he was quite innocent when he wrote them in 1804.

389–422 [364–97]. *There was a boy etc.*: written in Germany, October–December 1798, and sent to Coleridge, who acknowledged it in a letter dated 10 December 1798: 'The blank lines gave me as much direct pleasure as was possible in the general bustle of pleasure with which I received and read your letter. I observed, I remember, that the "fingers interwoven" etc. only puzzled me; and though I liked the twelve or fourteen first lines very well, yet I liked the remainder much better. Well, now I have read them again, they are very beautiful, and leave an affecting impression. That

> Uncertain heaven received
> Into the bosom of the steady lake

I should have recognized anywhere; and had I met these lines running wild in the deserts of Arabia, I should instantly have screamed out "Wordsworth".' Dykes Campbell has suggested that l. 396, which is not found in an early manuscript, was added later 'in deference to S. T. C.'s expression of puzzlement'.

In the first extant version of ll. 389–413 the first personal pronoun is used throughout in place of the third, indicating that W. W. was himself the boy who 'blew mimic hootings to the silent owls'. ll. 414–22 were added after the change had been made.

The lines were first published in the *Lyrical Ballads*, 1800, and afterwards included in the *Poems* (1815). At different times slight changes were introduced into the text. Thus, ed. 1800 reads 'a wild scene' for 'concourse wild' (403), omits ll. 414–15, and at l. 422 reads:

> Mute—for he died when he was ten years old.

Ed. 1827 reads in ll. 416–17:

> Pre-eminent in beauty is that Vale
> Where he was born and bred. The churchyard hangs

and ed. 1836 reads in ll. 404–5:

> and when there came a pause
> Of silence such as baffled his best skill.

In 1815 it stands first among the *Poems of the Imagination* and is referred to in the Preface in the following passage (omitted in 1845):

'I dismiss this subject with observing—that in the series of Poems placed under the head of Imagination, I have begun with one of the earliest processes of Nature in the development of this faculty. Guided by one of my own primary consciousnesses, I have represented a commutation and transfer of internal feelings, co-operating with external accidents to plant, for immortality, images of sound and sight, in the celestial soil of the Imagination. The Boy, there introduced, is listening, with something of a feverish and restless anxiety, for the recurrence of the riotous sounds which he had previously excited; and, at the moment when the intenseness of his mind is beginning to remit, he is surprized into a perception of the solemn and tranquillizing images which the Poem describes.'

397–8 [372–3]. *he, as through an instrument, Blew mimic hootings*: 'This practice of making an instrument of their own fingers is known to most boys, though some are more skilful at it than others. William Raincock of Rayrigg, a fine spirited lad, took the lead of all my school-fellows in this art' (I. F. note).

450–81 [426–59]. *Well do I call to mind etc.*: probably written in Germany in the winter of 1798–9. On the date when Wordsworth went to school *v.* I. 308 *note*.

465–6 [441–2]. *a fish up-leaping, snapp'd The breathless stillness*: Cf. *Fidelity* (written 1805):

> There sometimes doth a leaping fish
> Send through the tarn a lonely cheer.

513 [488]. *a sudden bound of smart reproach*: It is characteristic of Wordsworth and the hold that Nature had upon him, that he reproaches himself on what most boys would regard as a matter of congratulation.

532–3 [508–9].
> Our simple childhood sits upon a throne
> That hath more power than all the elements:

Cf. *Personal Talk*, 23–5:

> Children are blest, and powerful; their world lies
> More justly balanced; partly at their feet,
> And part far from them.

552 [528]. *Who make our wish our power, our thought a deed*: The punctuation of A is obviously right; that of 1850 has no manuscript authority.

554 [530]. *And Seasons serve; all Faculties; to whom*: Again A's punctuation is correct, and its significance is still further emphasized by D, which reads 'all Faculties;—'. But E omits all stops, and 1850, while restoring the semicolon after 'serve', omits the equally important one after 'Faculties'.

556. *Northern lights*: Cf. note to *The Complaint etc.* (*Oxf. W.*, p. 113).

560. *A tract of the same isthmus*: Mr. Oswald Doughty compares Pope's *Essay on Man*, II. 3, 'Plac'd on this isthmus of a middle state.'

575–6 [552–3]. *Thirteen years Or haply less*: More probably correct than the reading of 1850. 'Less than twice five years' would mean on his entrance to Hawkshead school.

583–4 [561].   *with that dear Friend*
         The same whom I have mention'd heretofore:

The reading of 1850 'with a dear friend' has left room for speculation as to who the friend was. Text A makes this clear (*v.* II. 352 and *note*).

630–7. There is no manuscript authority for the omission of these lines in 1850. They are found unerased in both D and E. The lines might justly be omitted on poetic grounds, but they are valuable biographically, as probably written a few days after Wordsworth had given up the idea of completing the poem in five books, i.e. after 6 March, when the opening of XIV was headed 'Fifth Book', and before the 'nearly three weeks idleness' which ended on 29 March.

BOOK VI

Among the notes on this Book will be found, marked 'S. T. C.', the annotations made by Coleridge in MS. B, which had been specially copied by Sara Hutchinson for him.

[25 [22]. *Two winters may be pass'd*: the winters of 1788–9 and 1789–90. H. D.]

26–8 [23–4]. *many ,books . . . devour'd, Tasted or skimm'd, or studiously perus'd*: Because Wordsworth himself lays stress on the less studious side of his life at Cambridge, and speaking of himself as 'an Idler among academic Bowers' (VIII. 649) and of reading with 'no settled plan', accepts in later years that apologetic attitude to his undergraduate days common enough to mature graduates, the extent of his reading has often been absurdly minimized and its whole character misconceived. As a matter of fact he read more widely and with better result than many students who win unqualified approval from their tutors. As to mathematics he himself explains (*Memoirs*, i. 14) that he did so much at school that 'I had a full twelve months' start of the freshmen of my year, and accordingly got into rather an idle way'. 'William', wrote Dorothy, 26 June 1791, 'lost the chance (indeed the certainty) of a fellowship, by not combating his inclinations. He gave way to his natural dislike to studies so dry as many parts of Mathematics, consequently could not succeed at Cambridge. He reads Italian, Spanish, French, Greek, Latin, and English, but never opens a mathematical book. . . . He has a great attachment to poetry, . . . which is not the most likely thing to produce his advancement in the world. His pleasures are chiefly of the imagination. He is never so happy as in a beautiful country. Do not think from what I have said that he reads not at all, for he does read a great deal, and not only poetry, and other languages he is acquainted with, but history *etc., etc.*' It is true that he writes himself to Mathews (Nov. 1791) that he knows 'little of Latin and scarce anything of Greek, . . . a pretty confession for a young gentleman whose whole life ought to have been devoted to study', but though he was not in any technical sense a scholar he 'read classic authors according to my fancy' and he knew enough, at least, of the classics to be able to appreciate Virgil, Horace, and Theocritus (cf. VIII. 312–24, X. 1014–27).

43 [31]. *more*: The reading of 1850, 'now', has no manuscript authority and is obviously a misprint.

55 [42]. *The Poet's soul was with me at that time*: It was in his first long vacation that he was dedicated a poet. Cf. IV. 340–5.

61 [48]. *Four years and thirty, told this very week*: i.e. the first week in April 1804. Thursday, 7 April 1804 was the anniversary of his birthday.

66 [54]. *lightly*: So all MSS. and 1850: 'slightly', the reading of Hutchinson, Nowell Smith, and Moore Smith, has no authority.

77–9. *I lov'd, and I enjoy'd etc.*: Cf. the description of the poet in *A Poet's Epitaph*, ll. 53–6.

90 [76]. *A single Tree*: In August 1808 Dorothy Wordsworth, then on a visit to Cambridge, wrote to Lady Beaumont: 'We walked in groves all the morning and visited the Colleges. I sought out a favourite ash tree which my brother speaks of in his poem on his own life—a tree covered with ivy.' It was, perhaps, of this tree that Wordsworth was thinking in the *Ode*: *Intimations etc.*, 51–3.

> But there's a tree, of many, one,
> A single field that I have looked upon,
> Both of them speak of something that is gone.

He may, however, be there referring to another tree, also an ash, which particularly impressed his imagination as he watched it from his bed at Anne Tyson's cottage in Hawkshead. Cf. IV. 79–83.

124–34 [106–14]. An interesting passage which should be read in connection with the *Appendix* 'on what is usually called Poetic Diction' (1802), and with XII. 253–74. It is evident that Wordsworth's later views on the subject of poetic style were a strong reaction from the taste of his undergraduate days. For if, as he says in ll. 117–18, the books which he 'then lov'd the most' are dearest to him now, as he writes *The Prelude* in 1804 (i.e. Spenser, Shakespeare, and Milton), his outward taste (l. 116) was for the most artificial and elaborate of the eighteenth-century poets, for it was they whom he strove to imitate and overgo in *An Evening Walk* (written at Cambridge). On the style of his early poems, *v.* the acute criticism in Legouis, trs. pp. 127–57. Wordsworth was doubtless attracted to this style of writing, as he himself suggests in the *Appendix*, by its 'influence in impressing a notion of the peculiarity and exaltation of the Poet's character, and in flattering the Reader's self-love by bringing him nearer to a sympathy with that character'. As a child, poetry had appealed to him, as to most children, from a love of fine language and rhythm for their own sakes (V. 567–81).

On the 'delusion to young scholars incident', cf. the remarks of Coleridge, *Biographia Literaria*, ch. i.

135–87. For Wordsworth's interest in mathematics v. *note* to ll. 26–8, V. 71–139, and X. 901 *ff.*

[160–74. *as I have read of one by shipwreck thrown*: The source of these lines is a passage from *An Authentic Narrative of some remarkable and interesting particulars in the life of * * ** , 1764, by John Newton, the friend of Cowper. *v.* Havens p. 412. The passage, closely followed here, has been copied out by D. W. in a notebook used in 1798–9. H. D.]

192. *A melancholy from humours of the blood*: It is worth noting that in the A text Wordsworth definitely connects this melancholy with his physical health (cf. X. 869 and *note*). Both here and in Book X the text is altered.

194. *piping winds*: Cf. *Il Penseroso*, 126, 'While rocking winds are piping loud'.

195 [175]. *Autumn than Spring*: His sister Dorothy shared this youthful taste. Cf. her letter to Jane Pollard, August 1793: 'I grant that the sensations autumn excites are not so cheerful as those excited by the burst of Nature's beauties in the spring months, yet they are more congenial to my taste. The melancholy pleasure of walking in a grove or wood, while the yellow leaves are showering around me, is grateful to my mind beyond even the exhilarating charms of the budding trees.'

200–2 [180–2]. *the Bard who sang etc.*: James Thomson in *The Castle of Indolence*, I. xv:

> Here nought but candour reigns, indulgent ease,
> Good-natured lounging, sauntering up and down.

208 [190]. *In summer*: i.e. the long vacation of 1789. The 'works of art', i.e. of architecture, were not sought in Dovedale or his 'own native region', but in Yorkshire, e.g. Bolton and Fountains Abbeys.

212–13 [197]8. *that seem'd another morn Risen on mid noon*: the words used by Adam to describe the 'presence' of Raphael—*Paradise Lost*, v. 310–11.

214 [199]. *she*: The 'her' of 1850 is a correction not found in any of the MSS.

[215–18. *Thy Treasure also . . . A gift then first bestow'd*: For the play on the meaning of Dorothy's name cf. Coleridge's phrase 'our Sister Gift of God' (Letter to W. W. 23 July 1803). H. D.]

216–45. *Now, after separation desolate Restor'd to me etc.*: The natural interpretation of this passage is that Wordsworth visited Brougham Castle and the Border Beacon with his sister and Mary Hutchinson in his second Long Vacation, i.e. in 1789. But Dorothy had left Penrith in the previous November to take up her abode with her uncle at Forncett in Norfolk, and there is no evidence, other than this passage, that she revisited the North till 1794. Travelling in those days was costly, and the Wordsworths were in straitened circumstances; moreover, it is difficult to believe that if she made this journey, so adventurous for a girl of seventeen, and so momentous in her association with her brother, she would make no subsequent allusion to it. It is true that no letters of hers written in 1789 are extant, but we know that she had not written to Jane Pollard for more than six months before January 1790; hence, when she wrote, she could hardly have passed over so great an event without notice if it had occurred. Indeed, such evidence as can be gathered from subsequent letters tells clearly against her having made the journey.

(1) On 25 January 1790 she writes that she had started a village school at Forncett six months before, i.e. July–August. But if she had been in the North that summer it is highly improbable that she would have returned so soon, before the middle of her brother's Long Vacation.

(2) On 30 March 1790 she writes that she has not seen William 'since my aunt was with us', i.e. at Forncett. This visit of the aunt, and therefore of William, cannot have been in the Christmas vacation, because in January 1790 her aunt was complaining of Dorothy's long silence, which she could not have done had she just seen her. It must, therefore, have been either at the beginning or the end of the previous Long Vacation, and probably at the beginning, because if it had come at the end (i.e. in October) there would certainly have been some mention of it in the letter of the following January, which recounts her chief doings since she wrote last.

(3) In February 1793 Dorothy writes that she had been separated from her brother Christopher 'nearly five years last Christmas', i.e. she had not seen him since he returned to school in the August of 1788. But it is hard to believe that if she had been at Penrith in 1789 she would not have seen him during his summer holidays.

My conclusion, therefore, in which Mr. Gordon Wordsworth concurs, is that Dorothy did not leave Forncett in 1789, and that in this passage Wordsworth is blending in one picture events which took place during three years. It is clear from (2) *supra* that he *did* see Dorothy during this Vacation of 1789, but at Forncett and not at Penrith. It is clear also that he visited Brougham Castle and the Beacon with her in the summers of 1787 and 1788, and that on some of these visits Mary Hutchinson was their companion. It is probable that he took walks with Mary Hutchinson in 1789, for she did not leave

Penrith till that year. And this might explain why, on his revision of the poem, he removed from the passage where he recalls once more his visits to the Beacon (XI. 316–23) all allusion to Dorothy's being his companion.

Since their mother's death in 1778, and Dorothy's departure for Halifax, they had been so little together that in 1794 Dorothy wrote: 'such have been the circumstances of my life that I may be said to have enjoyed his company only for a very few months.' But from childhood it had been their dream to live together, and after their reunion at Racedown in September 1795 they were never parted for more than a few weeks at a time until Wordsworth's death. Those passages in which Wordsworth refers to his companionship with Dorothy and what he owed to it are among the most deeply moving in all his poetry. Cf. X. 907–29, XIII. 204–39, *Lines composed a few miles above Tintern Abbey*, 114–59, *The Sparrow's Nest, To a Butterfly*, 'On nature's invitation do I come' (Oxf. *W.*, p. 621) and *Poems on the Naming of Places*, III. 14–16, in which Dorothy is spoken of as

> She who dwells with me, whom I have loved
> With such communion that no place on earth
> Can ever be a solitude to me.

[See *Chronology* 93–4 for further important discussion of W. W.'s movements at this time. S. G.]

220 [205]. *that monastic Castle*: Brougham Castle, a mile and a half east of Penrith, at the junction of the rivers Lowther and Emont.

223 [208]. *Sidney*: The evidence that Sir Philip Sidney ever visited Brougham Castle is hardly trustworthy, and it will be noticed that the text of 1850 is less confident on the point than the A text. Mr. W. G. Collingwood points out to me that Wordsworth probably got the idea from Clarke, *Survey of the Lakes* (2nd ed. 1789), p. 10, where, speaking of 'the great Countess of Pembroke' Clarke says 'Sir Philip Sidney, whose intelligence was very great, resided with her at Brougham Castle during the time he wrote part of his Arcadia.' 'He didn't,' adds Mr. Collingwood, 'for Sidney died in 1586 and the Countess was only born about 1594, and came to live at Brougham Castle as lady of the place in 1649. She might have had visits from her cousin Sir Philip Musgrave, and that might have started the legend. But her father George, third Earl of Cumberland (1570–1605) lived at Brougham Castle and Sidney might have visited him. There was a tradition that he came to Coniston Hall,' and this, though unauthenticated, strengthens the evidence of his connection with the district. Wordsworth was attracted to the story, and doubtless introduced it here, because, like so much of his own best work, the *Arcadia* was 'by fraternal love inspired'.

As Hutchinson has pointed out (ed. of *Poems of 1807*, I, p. xii), there are many traces in the poems written in the first few years following Wordsworth's settling at Grasmere of a careful study of the Elizabethans; and the poems themselves contain two quotations from Sidney and one from Lord Brooke's *Life of Sidney*.

233 [224]. *Another Maid there was*: Mary Hutchinson.

242 [233]. *the Border Beacon*: a little north-east of Penrith, the scene of the episode described XI. 280–323. The two visits are definitely associated by the repetition, at XI. 323, of l. 245 'A spirit of pleasure and youth's golden gleam'.

276 [266]. *a liveried School-Boy*: i.e. at Christ's Hospital, situated till a few years ago in the heart of the City. The boys still wear a distinctive costume of long dark-blue coat reaching below the knees, yellow stockings, and no hat (cf. II. 466–7 and *note*). Coleridge entered the 'Blue-coat School' in 1782, and almost certainly did not see his Devonshire birthplace again till 1789—hence Christ's Hospital is here spoken of as his 'home and school'. He went to Cambridge in October 1791, Wordsworth having left in the previous January (ll. 286–8).

281. *To shut thine eyes etc.*: 'an allusion to Coleridge's *Sonnet to the River Otter* (*publ.* 1797):

> so deep impres't
> Sink the sweet scenes of childhood, that mine eyes
> I never shut amid the sunny ray
> But straight with all their tints thy waters rise.

291–2 [281–2]. *What a stormy course Then follow'd*: Coleridge's college career began well, and in his first year he gained the Browne Gold Medal for a Sapphic Ode, and was chosen by Porson as one of four to compete for the Craven Scholarship. But his politics became too revolutionary to please the authorities, he was in debt and crossed in love; and in December 1793 he enlisted in the King's Regiment of Light Dragoons under the name of Silas Tomkyn Comberbach. He returned to Cambridge the following April, but left in December without taking a degree. In the intervening summer he had visited Oxford, met Southey and with him evolved his schemes for Pantisocracy, and for emigration to the banks of the Susquehanna. A precarious life in London and at Bristol followed, spent in journalism and in lecturing, but always in financial straits. It was probably in September 1795, at Bristol, that he met Wordsworth for the first time.

308–16 [294–305]. *Thy subtle speculations, toils abstruse etc.*: Cf. the words of Lamb in his essay *Christ's Hospital Five and Thirty Years Ago*: 'How have I seen the casual passer through the cloisters stand still, entranced with admiration (while he weighed the disproportion between the *speech* and the *garb* of the young Mirandula), to hear thee unfold, in thy deep and sweet intonations, the mysteries of Jamblichus, or Plotinus (for even in those years thou waxedst not pale at such philosophic draughts), or reciting Homer in his Greek, or Pindar, while the walls of the old Grey Friars re-echoed to the accents of the *inspired charity boy*!'

339. *A Fellow Student*: Robert Jones, to whom Wordsworth dedicated *Descriptive Sketches*, a poem written in 1792 to commemorate the tour. Wordsworth visited him at his home at Plas-yn-llan, Denbighshire, in the summer of 1791, expected to be joined by him at Blois in May 1792, and was with him again in autumn 1793. He was a guest at Dove Cottage in September 1800. He remained throughout life one of the poet's most intimate and valued friends. Jones took orders, and had a curacy in Wales, and in later life he had a living in Oxfordshire (cf. *Sonnet*, 'A genial hearth, a hospitable board' and I.F. note), but continued spending much of his time in Wales, where Wordsworth visited him in 1824, noting that his 'plumpness, ruddy cheeks and smiling countenance' seemed to those who met him 'little suited to a hermit living in the Vale of Meditation'. This picture of him, and that given by Dorothy when he came to Rydal Mount in 1832, 'fat and roundabout and rosy, and puffing and panting while he climbs the little hill from the road to our house', suggest some of the charm that drew him to his austere friend.

342 [326] *ff. An open slight etc.*: 'to me were obscure, and now appear rather awkwardly expressed. I should wish to trace the classical use of the word "concern". These are the passages, which it is so difficult and fretsome to correct; because, if once amiss, no after genial moment can be pressed into the dull service of emending them. Yet I venture to propose, thinking dilatation better than awkwardness,

> A disregard
> Of College objects was our scheme, say rather,
> A mere slight of the studies and the cares
> Expected from us, we too (? two) being then
> Just at the close of our novitiate:
> Nor was it formed by me without some fears,
> And some uneasy forethought of the pain,
> The censures, and ill-omening of those,
> To whom my worldly interests were dear—' (S. T. C.)

350. *goings-on*: v. *note* to III. 616.

353 [340]. *France standing on the top of golden hours*: A reminiscence of Shakespeare, *Sonnet* xviii: 'Now stand you on the top of happy hours.' The substitution of 'golden' for 'happy' makes the passage no less Shakespearian, for 'golden' is one of Shakespeare's favourite epithets. Cf. 'golden time' in *Sonnet* iii. Wordsworth uses the phrase 'golden days' in l. 655.

355–7 [344–6].   *it was our lot*
> To land at Calais on the very eve
> Of that great federal Day:

i.e. 13 July 1790. 'I set off for the Continent, in companionship with Robert Jones. . . . We went staff in hand, without knapsacks, and carrying each his needments tied up in a pocket handkerchief, with about twenty pounds apiece in our pockets. We crossed from Dover and landed at Calais on the eve of the day when the king was to swear fidelity to the new constitution: an event which was solemnized with due pomp at Calais. On the afternoon of that day we started, and slept at Ardres' (*Memoirs*, i. 14–15). For details of their itinerary, *v.* Harper, i. 90–5. Knight, *Poems*, i. 332–3, and Wordsworth's letter to Dorothy, 6 September 1790 (*E.Y.*, 32–8).

This tour was the subject of *Descriptive Sketches*, which Wordsworth wrote during his second stay in France (1791–2). But the melancholy of *Descriptive Sketches* is far less true to his actual feeling during the tour than this record of it written in 1804, nearly ten years later, for *The Prelude*. Of this the evidence is his letter to Dorothy above referred to, in which he writes: 'I am in excellent health and spirits, and have had no reason to complain of the contrary during our whole tour. My spirits have been kept in a perpetual hurry of delight.' Indeed, the only source of any uneasiness 'during this delightful tour' was the fear that Dorothy might be feeling some anxiety as to his safety. The poet's tender melancholy, and fond conceit of sadness (377–8) was never at this time potent enough to be depressing.

359–60 [348–9].   *How bright a face is worn when joy of one*
                            Is joy of tens of millions:

'We crossed at the time when the whole nation was mad with joy in consequence of the revolution. It was a most interesting period to be in France; and we had many delightful scenes, where the interest of the picture was owing solely to this cause' (letter quoted above). Cf. also *Sonnet*, 'Jones! as from Calais' etc.

378. *to the noise*: If the reading is correct 'to' must mean 'to the accompaniment of'. But perhaps 'to' is a mistake of the copyist, and hence the correction in 1850.

382 [372]. *dances in the open air*: The late addition of ll. [373–4] records a protest at which Wordsworth felt no concern either in 1790 or 1804.

386 [378]. *we cut*: 'May "we cut" be used neutrally in pure language? if so, the "right of the best", if not "we flow" or "we rush'd"' (S. T. C.). Note that in deference to Coleridge's criticism Wordsworth added [379], which makes 'cut' transitive.

396–7. *Spousals newly solemniz'd At their chief City*: Cf. *note* to IX. 41–51.

422 [418]. *Convent of Chartreuse*: Wordsworth reached the Chartreuse on 4 August. Cf. note to VIII. 410.

446. *My heart leap'd up when first I did look down*: ' "leap'd *up*", "look'd down", "leap'd high", or rather "O! my heart leap'd when first"' *etc.* (S. T. C.) In deference to S. T. C. later texts read 'How leap'd my heart' *etc.* The lyric 'My heart leaps up' *etc.* was written in 1802.

[448. *A green recess*: *v.* D. W.'s *Journals*, II. 280. H. D.]

467 [539]. *Descending from the mountain to make sport*: 'This line I would omit; as it clearly carries on the metaphor of the Lion, and yet is contradictory to the idea of a "tamed" Lion. "to make sport" *etc.* is here at once the proof

of his having been "tamed" and the object of his "descending from the mountains", which appear incompatible' (S. T. C.). Wordsworth altered the text in deference to Coleridge, but in D reverted to the previous reading, save that he changed 'tamed' to 'well-tamed'.

489 [558]. *something of stern mood*: Cf. X. 871, XIII. 207–25.

525–48 [592–616]. *Imagination etc.*: No passage illustrates better than this at once Wordsworth's relation with the sensationist, empirical philosophy of the eighteenth century and the manner in which he transcends and spiritualizes it. All intellectual and spiritual growth comes from the reaction of the senses, chiefly of eye and ear, to the external world, which is 'exquisitely fitted to the mind', but the highest vision is superinduced upon this in a state of ecstasy, in which the light of sense goes out and the soul feels its kinship with that which is beyond sense. Cf. *Lines composed . . . above Tintern Abbey*, 35–49. And this great spiritual experience comes generally not immediately after the sense experience which has inspired it, but perhaps years later, when the original emotion, recollected in tranquillity, is rekindled.

Wordsworth made many efforts to give a satisfactory philosophic account of the imagination, but it is hardly surprising that he failed, for it is a faculty that essentially defies exact definition. It was easier to him to say what it was not than what it was. It was a higher quality than fancy; it had nothing to do with the processes of the analytic reason, but rather seemed to have some relation with the affections and the moral nature. But his inability to understand or to define it did not affect his faith in its reality. It was to him 'the vision and the faculty divine', for it was a vital part of his mystical experience, by reason of which, to put it baldly, the poet *is* a poet.

526. *the eye and progress of my Song*: This use of the so-called 'doublet' is suggested by Shakespeare. Cf. *King John*, II. i. 208: 'Before the eye and prospect of your town.' Wordsworth uses it again at VII. 725: 'The measure and the prospect of the soul.'

537 [603]. *There harbours whether we be young or old.*: There is no manuscript authority for the punctuation of the 1850 text: 'harbours; . . . old,' which is due to E's unfortunate habit of omitting the full stop at the end of a line.

544–5. *aught . . . thoughts*: 'aught: thoughts: was a hitch to my ear:
      ? seeks for no trophies, struggles for no spoils
    That may attest' *etc.*   (S. T. C.)
Wordsworth accepts the correction.

548 [616]. *Which hides it like the overflowing Nile*: 'Was it by mere caprice or a beginning of an impulse to alter, from having looked over the latter half of this Book for the purpose of correcting, which I employed myself on for the deadening of a too strong feeling, which the personal Passages, so exquisitely beautiful, had excited—that I wished this faultless line to stand "Spread o'er it, like the fertilizing Nile"? For fear it should be so, I will leave off. Ὕσ(τ)ερον ἄδιον ᾄσω' (S. T. C.). Notice that Wordsworth adopts the idea of the

'fertilizing Nile'. It is significant that this book, written just after Coleridge had left for Malta, and most full of tender affection for him, is the one to which Coleridge turns in his mood of depression.

553–72 [621–40]. *brook and road etc.*: 'See *Poetical Works*, ii. 99—p. 143 of the Edition in One Volume' (*note* in 1850), i.e. ii. 99 of the 1849 edition of the *Poems*, and p. 143 of the 1845 edition. The lines were first published in 1845, with ll. 554 and 556 as A, and l. 559 as 1850. In both editions the passage is dated 1799.

566 [634]. *The unfetter'd clouds, and region of the heavens*: a curiously Shake-spearian line. Shakespeare in several places uses 'region' with the meaning of 'sky' or 'upper air'. Cf. 'the region clouds' (*Sonnet* xxxiii); 'Her eyes in heaven Would through the airy region stream so bright', *Romeo and Juliet*, ii. ii. 21. 573–80.

[573–80. *That night our lodging was an Alpine House*: *v.* D. W.'s *Journals*, II. 258–9. H. D.]

579 [647]. *innocent Sleep*: *Macbeth*, ii. ii. 36.

587 [655]. *Locarno's Lake*: i.e. Maggiore. On the whole description given here Wordsworth's letter to Dorothy, September 1790, affords an interesting commentary: 'After passing two days in the environs of Chamouny, we returned to Martigny, and pursued our mount up the Valais, along the Rhine, to Brig. At Brig we quitted the Valais, and passed the Alps at the Simplon, in order to visit part of Italy. The impressions of three hours of our walk among these Alps will never be effaced. From Duomo d'Ossola, a town of Italy which lay in our route, we proceeded to the Lake of Locarno, to visit the Borromean Islands, and thence to Como. A more charming path was scarcely ever travelled over. The banks of many of the Italian and Swiss lakes are so steep and rocky, as not to admit of roads; that of Como is partly of this character. A small foot-path is all the communication by land between one village and another, on the side along which we passed, for upwards of thirty miles. We entered upon this path about noon, and owing to the steep-ness of the banks, were soon unmolested by the sun, which illuminated the woods, rocks, and villages of the opposite shore. The lake is narrow, and the shadows of the mountains were early thrown across it. It was beautiful to watch them travelling up the side of the hills,—for several hours to remark one half of a village covered with shade, and the other bright with the strongest sunshine. . . .

'The shores of the lake consist of steeps, covered with large sweeping woods of chestnut, spotted with villages; some clinging from the summits of the advancing rocks, and others hiding themselves within their recesses. Nor was the surface of the lake less interesting than its shores; half of it glowing with the richest green and gold, the reflection of the illuminated wood and path, shaded with a soft blue tint. . . . It was impossible not to contrast that repose, that complacency of spirit, produced by these lovely scenes, with the

sensations I had experienced two or three days before, in passing the Alps.
At the lake of Como, my mind ran through a thousand dreams of happiness,
which might be enjoyed upon its banks, if heightened by conversation and the
exercise of the social affections. Among the more awful scenes of the Alps, I
had not a thought of man, or a single created being, my whole soul was
turned to him who produced the terrible majesty before me.'

604–5 [674–5]. *Where tones of learned Art and Nature mix'd*
May frame enduring language:
For this contrast between the verse of his 'undisciplined youth' and of his
maturity when he had realized the part that 'Art' must play in all great
poetry, *v. Introduction*, p. xviii–xix.

667 [737]. *a mean pensioner*: The 'mere' in 1850 is probably due to an
undetected error of the copyist of D.

691 [764]. *We cross'd the Brabant Armies on the fret*: The 'États belgiques unis'
had been declared in January 1790, and had aroused great enthusiasm in
Paris, where, for example, Camille Desmoulins wrote proudly of 'les révolutions
de France et de Brabant'. But this new Republic was soon rent by dissension,
and after the death of Joseph II his successor Leopold saw an opportunity for
enforcing his authority. Through his ambassador in London he pointed out
that 'the general interest of the whole of Europe demands a restitution of the
old constitution', and he gained the sympathy of England, Prussia, and
Holland. Early in October he collected his forces to march on Belgium, but
under the guarantee of the three powers he promised the Belgians to main-
tain the charters of the provinces; and proclaiming an amnesty, invited the
submission of his rebellious subjects before the end of the following month.
The Three Powers advised the Belgians to accept, but they refused, though
their internal quarrels made them powerless to offer any effective resistance.
'The Brabant Armies on the fret', witnessed by Wordsworth in this October,
must have been the republican troops preparing to oppose Leopold.

BOOK VII

3. *issuing from the City's Walls*: 'The city of Goslar in South Saxony' (*note* in 1850).
But this is clearly wrong (*v. I.* 1–54 *note*). [See my note to I. 1–54 above. S. G.]

12–13. *a little space Before last primrose-time*: This is more accurate than the later
reading.

16. *At thy departure to a foreign Land*: Coleridge did not actually leave for Malta
till 9 April, but by the end of the previous November he had already decided
to go abroad, and early in January he paid his farewell visit to Dove Cottage;
after which Wordsworth, 'to beguile his heavy thoughts' at his friend's depar-
ture, and doubtless urged on by Coleridge's entreaties, had restarted on
The Prelude.

35-6 [29-30]. *ye and I will be Brethren*: In 1808 the *Simpliciad* laughed at Words-worth for his habit of expressing fraternity and equality with the humbler creatures; and, in particular, in the couplet:

> With brother lark or brother Robin fly
> And flutter with half-brother butterfly,

had held up to scorn the lines in *The Redbreast and the Butterfly* (1802, *publ.* 1807).

> 'All men who know thee call thee Brother' (the robin)

> 'A brother he seems of thine own' (the butterfly).

This last line Wordsworth omitted in 1815, and doubtless he altered 'Brethren' here to 'Associates' in recollection of the same criticism. Indeed, he seems to have become nervous about using the word brother, for he removes it from the text of VI. 478 and XIII. 89, in both cases with a loss of strength to the line. But in III. 328, where it might well have been altered, for its use con-fuses the sense, he retains it.

50 [44]. *my favourite Grove*: known in the Wordsworth family as 'Brother John's Grove', situated below White Moss Common, in Ladywood. Cf. *Poems on the naming of Places*, VI, 'When to the attractions of the busy world.' *etc.* [See D. W.'s journal entry 29 April 1802: 'We then went to John's grove. . . .' S. G.]

57 [52]. *Return'd from that excursion etc.*: i.e. his foreign tour with Robert Jones, described in the previous Book. He returned to Cambridge early in Novem-ber, spent a six-weeks Christmas vacation at Forncett, Norfolk, in the com-pany of Dorothy, and was at Cambridge again to take his degree on 21 January 1791.

68-72. With what he says here as to his character, cf. III. 531-6.

73-4. *when I first beheld That mighty place*: There is no other record of this early visit to London except the allusion to it in VIII. 689-710. It must have been on one of his journeys to or from Cambridge in 1788, or at Christmas 1789 (*v.* Moorman I, p. 125).

81-88 [77-84], *There was a time etc.*: a passage written in the Miltonic style and with reminiscence, partly of *Paradise Lost*, partly of Purchas, *His Pilgrimes*. Cf. *Paradise Lost*, i. 717-19:

> Not Babilon
> Nor great Alcairo such magnificence
> Equal'd in all thir glories

123. *Vauxhall and Ranelagh*: Fashionable resorts of pleasure in the eighteenth century; *v.* Walpole's *Letters, passim*, and Fanny Burney's *Evelina*: Letters xlvi and xii, and *Cecilia*, ch. xii. Cf. also Austin Dobson, *Eighteenth Century Vignettes*.

131. *the Giants of Guildhall*: Gog and Magog. Cf. Horace Walpole's *Letter to Montague*, 24 September 1761, where he likens Lord Errol to 'one of the Giants in Guildhall, new gilt'.

132. *Bedlam*: the famous hospital for lunatics, situated in Moorfields, and one of the sights of eighteenth-century London. It was pulled down in 1814.

137. *in season due*: a Miltonic phrase. Cf. *Lycidas*, 7.

176–80 [160–4]. The punctuation of 1850 is obviously incorrect, and to elucidate the passage it has been suggested that ll. 178 and 179 are in the wrong order. But Mr. Nowell Smith has already anticipated the true solution, which is found in the punctuation of the A text.

186. *sequester'd nook*: Cf. *Comus*, 500.

200. *May then entangle us awhile*: The incompleteness of this line is explained by an earlier text, where the words 'at length' are deleted, and nothing substituted for them. The mistake was not rectified till the revision of D.

209 [193]. *Here files of ballads dangle from dead walls*: 'The railing adjacent to the gate (i.e. Cumberland Gate, now the Marble Arch) was at that period (about 1812) permitted to be strung with rows of printed old-fashioned ballads, such as *Cruel Barbara Allen, etc.*' Mrs. Cowden Clarke, *My Long Life*, quoted by Nowell Smith.

228. *distinguishable shapes*: *Paradise Lost*, ii. 667–8, 'that shape had none Distinguishable'.

267 [250]. *shading colours*: The 'shading' colours (altered to 'blended' in D) is probably an unconscious echo of *Paradise Lost*, iii. 509, 'By *Model*, or by *shading* Pencil drawn'.

281 [260]. *Add*: In D the word was so indistinctly written that E took it for 'And'. Hence the reading of 1850.

289 [267]. *Half-rural Sadler's Wells*: situated at Islington, then a suburb of London. In the seventeenth and early eighteenth century it consisted of a Tea Garden with a Music House attached, and was a popular resort of entertainment, for rope dancers and tumblers could be seen there. When, in 1765, a Theatre was erected on the site of the Music House, it retained its 'popular' character, and in 1783 Horace Walpole refers to it as 'a place of low buffoonery.'

307 [284]. A quotation from Milton, *Samson Agonistes*, 87–9:

> as the Moon,
> When she deserts the night,
> Hid in her vacant interlunar cave.

322 [297]. *the Maid of Buttermere*: John Hatfield, a vulgar adventurer, came to Keswick in 1802, and giving himself out to be Alexander Augustus Hope, M.P. for Linlithgowshire, and brother to the Earl of Hopetown, imposed upon all the tradesmen of the district. He married Mary, daughter of the innkeeper of the Fish, Buttermere, at Lorton Church on 2 October, but before the end of the month his frauds were detected, and he fled the country, leaving behind him papers which proved that he had another wife living, and several children. He was caught soon afterwards, and tried for forgery at the Carlisle Assizes on the prosecution of the Post Office, for franking letters under the name of Hope. He was hanged at Carlisle on 3 September 1803. Wordsworth and Coleridge were much interested in the incident, and Coleridge contributed three papers upon it to the *Morning Post* of 11 October, 22 October, and 5 November 1802, under the titles of *Romantic Marriage* and *The Fraudulent Marriage*. (They were afterwards collected in *Essays on His Own Times*, 1850.) A further paper on the subject, not from Coleridge's hand, appeared in the *Morning Post* of 6 November. The case caused a considerable stir in the country and was made the subject of a successful melodrama, which was produced at Sadler's Wells (*v.* note to 289) on 25 April 1803, and was described by its author, Charles Dibdin the younger, the manager of the theatre, as an operatic piece in rhyme. It was entitled *Edward and Susan or the Beauty of Buttermere*. It ran till the end of May and was revived towards the end of June. Mary Lamb wrote to Dorothy Wordsworth in the following July: 'We went last week with Southey and Rickman and his sister to Sadler's Wells, the lowest and most London-like of our amusements. The entertainments were Goody Two Shoes, Jack the Giant Killer, and *Mary of Buttermere*! Poor Mary was very happily married at the end of the piece, to a sailor, her former sweetheart. We had a prodigious fine view of her father's house in the vale of Buttermere—mountains very like large haycocks, and a lake like nothing at all. If you had been with us, would you have laughed the whole time like Charles and Miss Rickman, or gone to sleep as Southey and Rickman did?' (Lucas, *Life of Charles Lamb*, i. 241). De Quincey, in his article on Coleridge in *Tait's Magazine* of October 1834, gave a detailed account of the whole story (*Works*, ii. 177–84, ed. Masson), and in 1841 a novel *James Hatfield and the Beauty of Buttermere, a Story of Modern Times*, was published by Henry Colburn. This book was in the library of Rydal Mount, bearing witness to Wordsworth's continued interest in the story.

323. '*a bold bad Man*': a quotation from Spenser: *Faerie Queene*, i. i. 37.

342–3.   *For we were nursed, as almost might be said,*
                 On the same mountains; Children at one time:

a reminiscence of Milton, *Lycidas*, 23, 'For we were nursed upon the self-same hill'. Mary of Buttermere was born in 1772, and was thus only two years younger than Wordsworth: the Coker (345) flows from Buttermere through Crummock Water to Cockermouth.

413 [382]. *little more than three short years*: i.e. on his first journey to Cambridge, in October 1787.

461 [428]. *Prate somewhat loudly of the whereabout*: *Macbeth*, II. i. 58.

472 [43]. *a kitten when at play etc.*: *The Kitten and the Falling Leaves* was written in the same year (1804) as this passage.

487–8. *when on our beds we lie etc.*: Cf. IV. 72–8.

507 [476]. *the suburbs of the mind*: Shakespeare: *Julius Caesar*, II. i. 285–6: 'Dwell I but in the suburbs Of your good pleasure?'

527–8 [496–8].   *Familiarly, a household term, like those,*
                    The Bedfords, Glocesters, Salisburys of old,
                    Which the fifth Harry talks of:

Cf. *Henry V*, IV. iii. 51–5:   Then shall our names
                    Familiar in his mouth as household words
                    Harry the King, Bedford and Exeter,
                    Warwick and Talbot, Salisbury and Gloucester,
                    Be in their flowing cups freshly remember'd.

539. *He winds away his never-ending horn*: an echo of Milton: *Lycidas*, 28: 'What time the gray-fly winds her sultry horn.'

547–66 [551–72]. *There have I seen a comely Bachelor etc.*: Cf. the attack on the 'theatrical clerical coxcomb' made by Cowper in *The Task*, ii. 414–62.

560. *The Death of Abel*: Gessner's *Tod Abels* was written in 1758 and translated into English soon afterwards. It ran through many editions. Its great popularity was due to its 'süsslicher und weinerlicher Ton' which appealed to the sentimentality of the time. Young's *Night Thoughts* (1742–5) appealed to the more morbid and gloomy aspects of the same sentimental tendency. For Wordsworth's views on Macpherson's *Ossian*, v. *Essay, supplementary to Preface* (1815) and *Lines written in a blank leaf of Macpherson's Ossian* (1824).

650–2. *the Fair Holden where Martyrs suffer'd etc.*: St. Bartholomew's Fair, following the alteration in the calendar in 1753, was held in the four days following 3 September at Smithfield, the scene of many of the executions of Protestants under Queen Mary. It was held for the last time in 1855. W. W. and D. W. visited it in 1802 with Charles Lamb.

714 [737]. *This, of all acquisitions first, awaits*: The punctuation of 1850 is obviously incorrect.

725. *The measure and the prospect of the soul*: Cf. VI. 526 *note*.

BOOK VIII

1–61. These lines describing Helvellyn fair were an after-thought; in their place Wordsworth originally wrote that passage which he afterwards adapted for the opening of *Excursion* II.

In a letter dated 1805 Wordsworth sent ll. 1–61 to Sir George Beaumont, in a form which, as quoted by Knight, tallies almost entirely with that of our text.

10 [11]. *It is a summer festival, a Fair*: Cf. D. W.'s *Journal* for 2 September 1800. 'The fair day . . . There seemed very few people and very few stalls, yet I

believe there were many cakes and much beer sold. . . . It was a lovely moon-light night. We talked much about a house on Helvellyn. The moonlight shone only upon the village. It did not eclipse the village lights, and the the sound of dancing and merriment came along the still air.'

116–19: cf. [470, 474–5].

119–45 [74–99]. This passage, in which Wordsworth describes the beauty of 'the Paradise where I was rear'd', is strongly reminiscent in style, construc-tion and phrasing of *Paradise Lost*, iv. 208–47, and other lines in which Milton calls to memory various scenes famed in history or fiction, only to dismiss them as unworthy of comparison with Eden:

> in this pleasant soile
> His farr more pleasant Garden God ordaind.

Cf. also especially 'boon Nature' (128) with 'Nature boon' (*Paradise Lost*, iv. 242) and 129 *ff.*, with

> sweet interchange
> Of Hill and Vallie, Rivers, Woods, and Plaines,
> Now Land, now Sea, and Shores with Forrest crownd,
> Rocks, Dens, and Caves;   (*Paradise Lost*, ix. 115–18.)

For the comparison with Gehol's famous Gardens Wordsworth draws on Lord Macartney's description, quoted by John Barrow (*Travels in China*, 1804, pp. 127–33): 'The Emperor was pleased to give directions to his first minister to shew us his park or garden at Gehol. It is called Chinese Van-shoo-yuen, or the Paradise of ten thousand trees. We rode about three miles through a very beautiful park kept in the highest order . . . the grounds gently undulated and chequered with various groups of well-contrasted trees in the offskip. . . . An extensive lake appeared before us, the extremities of which seemed to lose themselves in distance and obscurity. The shores of the lake have all the varieties of shape which the fancy of a painter can delineate. Nor are islands wanting, but they are situated only where they should be, each in its own proper place and having its proper character: one marked by a pagoda or other building; one quite destitute of ornaments; some smooth and level, some steep and uneven, and others frowning with wood or smiling with culture. . . . In the course of our journey we stopped at forty or fifty different palaces or pavilions. . . . The western garden . . . forms a strong contrast with the other, and exhibits all the sublimer beauties of nature in as high a degree as the part which we saw before possesses the attractions of softness and amenity. It is one of the finest forest scenes in the world; wild, woody, moun-tainous and rocky. . . . In many places immense woods . . . grow on almost perpendicular steeps. There at proper distances you find palaces, banquetting houses, and monasteries, adapted to the situation and peculiar uses of the place; sometimes with a rivulet on one hand, gently stealing through the glade, at others with a cataract tumbling from above raging with foam, and rebounding with a thousand echoes from below, or silently engulphed in a gloomy pool or yawning chasm. . . . On a mound so elevated as perfectly to command the whole surrounding country I saw everything before me as on an illuminated map—palaces, pagodas, towns, villages, plains, vallies watered by innumerable streams, hills waving with woods, meadows covered with cattle of the most beautiful marks and colours.' The 'Domes of Pleasure' (130–1) recall Coleridge's *Kubla Khan*.

[159–172. See *P*. 569–78 for a most important note on W. W.'s early attempts to formulate his thinking on the interrelation of love of man and love of nature. S. G.]

191–203 [144–56]. *Nor such as Spencer fabled etc.*: Cf. *Shepheardes Calender*: *May* 9–14, 19–24, 27–34.

> Yougthes folke now flocken in euery where,
> To gather may buskets and smelling brere:
> And home they hasten the postes to dight,
> And all the Kirk pillours eare day light,
> With Hawthorne buds, and swete Eglantine,
> And girlonds of roses and Sopps in wine.
>
> . . . .
>
> Sicker this morrowe, ne lenger agoe,
> I sawe a shole of shepheardes outgoe,
> With singing, and shouting, and iolly chere:
> Before them yode a lusty Tabrere,
> That to the many a Horne pype playd,
> Whereto they dauncen eche one with his mayd.
>
> . . . .
>
> Tho to the greene Wood they speeden hem all,
> To fetchen home May with their musicall:
> And home they bringen in a royall throne,
> Crowned as king: and his Queene attone
> Was Lady Flora, on whom did attend
> A fayre flocke of Faeries, and a fresh bend
> Of louely Nymphes. (O that I were there,
> To helpen the Ladyes their Maybush beare)

Cf. also *Epithalamion*, 207–8:

> And all the postes adorne as doth behove,
> And all the pillours deck with girlonds trim.

221. *my Household Dame*: i.e. Anne Tyson. Cf. IV. 17, 55, 208–21.

222–311. This story was originally written as an incident in the life of Michael and Luke, and therefore must be the work of October–December 1800, when Wordsworth was occupied with *Michael*. It was first printed, with some errors, in Knight's edition of the *Poems* (VIII. 224–30).

236–7. *that cloud-loving Hill, Seat Sandal etc.*: Wordsworth used these lines more than thirty years later in *Musings near Aquapendente*, April 1837:

> Transported over that cloud-wooing hill,
> Seat Sandal, a fond suitor of the clouds,

241. *Russet Cove*: (printed by Knight 'Sheepcot' Cove). There is no Russet Cove in the neighbourhood of Helvellyn. Mr. Gordon Wordsworth points out to me that the spot referred to is Ruthwaite (pronounced 'Ruthet') Cove, about a mile north of Grisedale Tarn and north-east of Dollywaggon Pike. Wordsworth's mistake is pardonable if we remember that he had settled at Grasmere less than a year before he wrote the line.

312–24 [173–85]. A passage which bears witness to a knowledge and love of Latin poetry with which Wordsworth is not always credited. Galaesus is a river in Calabria, flowing into the bay of Tarentum, celebrated by Virgil and Horace for the sheep that fed upon its banks; cf. *Georgics*, iv. 126 and Horace, *Odes*, II. vi. 10:

> Unde si Parcae prohibent iniquae,
> Dulce pellitis ovibus Galaesi
> Flumen . . . petam.

Clitumnus was a river in Calabria whose waters were so pure that it whitened the coats of the herds that fed upon its banks and made them fit for sacrifice: cf. *Georgics*, ii. 146–8:

> Hinc albi, Clitumne, greges et maxima taurus
> Victima, saepe tuo perfusi flumine sacro,
> Romanos ad templa deum duxere triumphos:

Lucretilis (now Monte Gennaro), a hill overlooking Horace's Sabine farm. Cf. *Odes*, I. xvii:

> Velox amoenum saepe Lucretilem
> Mutat Lycaeo Faunus et igneam
> Defendit aestatem capellis
> Usque meis pluviosque ventos.

Horace identifies Faunus with Pan, the pipe-player, cf. ll. 10–12 (utcumque dulci fistula . . . levia personuere saxa). 'Horace', said Wordsworth in his later life, 'is my great favourite: I love him dearly.'

339. *His flute . . . resounding*: cf. *Sonnet*: 'The fairest brightest' *etc.* 3–4:

> O Friend! thy flute has breathed a harmony
> Softly resounded through this rocky glade.

349 [211]. *Goslar, once Imperial!*: 'In this town the German emperors of the Franconian line were accustomed to keep their court, and it retains vestiges of its ancient splendour. . . . I walked daily on the ramparts, or in a sort of public ground or garden.' (I. F. note to *Lines written in Germany*.)

353. *Hercynian forest*: The Hercynia silva in the time of Julius Caesar stretched over a vast mountainous tract of South and East Germany. The name Hartz is derived from it.

401 [266]. *In size a Giant, stalking through the fog*: Cf. Thomson, *Autumn*, 727–30, where the poet describes how, when 'sits the general fog Unbounded o'er the world,' 'o'er the waste the shepherd stalks gigantic'.

410 [275]. *Chartreuse*: Cf. VI. [482–8], and D. W.'s letter to Crabb Robinson, 21 December 1822, 'My Br. is very sorry that you should have missed the Chartreuse. I do not think that any one spot which he visited during his youthful travels with Robert Jones made so great an impression on his mind: in my young days he used to talk so much of it to me.'

420, 422 [285, 287]. *Corin, Phillis*: Typical names from the classical and Elizabethan pastoral; cf. *As You Like It*, and *L'Allegro*.

428 [293], 449 [314]. Two hypermetric lines. The MSS. suggest no explanation in either case.

442 [307]. *whencesoever*: The reading of 1850 'wheresoever' is clearly a mistake in copying.

483 [349]. The change from 'three' (A) to 'two' (D) 'and twenty' puts the date right. Wordsworth was born in April 1770. The time when 'two and twenty summers had been told' must, therefore, be after the summer of 1791 and before the summer of 1792. Garrod (p. 58) holds that two and twenty summers necessarily points to the autumn of 1791, and adds 'it means that the interest in Man was not first acquired in France, as is commonly supposed, and under the influence of Beaupuy, but that it was this interest, which, acquired in England, took him to France for the second time in 1792'. Against this view it can be argued:

(i) When Wordsworth went to France for the second time (it was in November 1791, not, as Garrod states, in 1792) his chief reason, as he says in the A text, was to learn the language.

(ii) His own account in *The Prelude* makes it clear that Nature was still first with him in the London period (VIII. 860–9) and that the winter of 1791–2 witnessed a shifting of his love from Nature to Man. Even in Paris, though he 'visited each spot of recent fame' (IX. 41–2), he 'affected more emotion than he felt' (*ib.* 71): it was only after he reached the Loire that

> my heart was all
> Given to the people, and my love was theirs (*ib.* 124–5).

If my interpretation is correct, this shifting of interest from Nature to Man would coincide with his plunge into humanitarian politics and the dawning of his love for Annette (December–January 1791–2).

491 [357]. Cf. *Paradise Lost*, iv. 264–6:

> The Birds thir quire apply; aires, vernal aires,
> Breathing the smell of field and grove, attune
> The trembling leaves.

The 'minute obeisances of tenderness' (493–4) Wordsworth owed to the influence of Dorothy at Racedown (*v.* XIII. 219–29).

498–510. These lines were perhaps omitted in later texts because they interrupt the train of thought, but they are well worthy of preservation. They give a vivid picture of the occupations of the men and women among whom the poet grew up, and who were unconsciously leading him from love of nature to love of man.

[559 [406] *ff. There was a Copse etc.* The house Green-end, in which Wordsworth lodged at Colthouse, has a view of Spring Wood on the slope of Claife Heights. H. D.]

584–5 [421–3]. *wilful fancy . . . imagination*: For the relation of fancy to imagination, and the distinction between them cf. XIII. 275–99, and *Preface* to 1815 ed. of *Poems*.

605–7 [433–4]. Cf. II. 466–7 and *note*.

634 [487]. *As of all visible natures crown*: Notice the theological limitation to man's glory added to the 1850 text.

646 [500]. *eclipsed*: eclipse (1850) is probably an uncorrected copyist's error.

680–1 [533–4]. An unconscious echo of Milton, *Lycidas*, 104–6:

> His *mantle* hairy and his bonnet sedge,
> *Inwrought* with figures dim, and on the edge
> Like to that sanguine flower

689–93 [540–3]. i.e. in 1788. Cf. VII. 73.

711 [560] *ff.* Another passage in the Miltonic style ('sees, or thinks He sees' is reminiscent of *Paradise Lost*, i. 783–4, 'sees, or dreams he sees').

713 [562]. *Antiparos*: a small island among the Cyclades.

714 [564]. *Yordas*: near Ingleton, Yorkshire, and visited by Wordsworth with his brother John in May 1800 (*E.Y.*, 298).

735. *pressure*: used in Shakespearian sense; cf. VII. [288].

742–51 [590–6]. Originally written to form part of Book VII.

763 [610]. *punctual*: i.e. confined to one spot, a Miltonic use of the word. Cf. *Paradise Lost*, viii. 23: 'this punctual spot'.

771. *Greece . . . and Rome*: For Wordsworth's interest in ancient history cf. I. 186 (*note*).

775. *Stript of their harmonising soul*: 'their' refers, of course, to 'events' (771). When 771–2 were omitted from the text 'their' should have been altered to 'its'. As it stands in the 1850 text 'their' is ungrammatical.

823 [664]. From Milton, *Paradise Lost*, xi. 204 (*note* in 1850). But the quotation is of more than one line:

> why in the East
> Darkness ere Dayes mid-course, and Morning light
> More orient in yon Western Cloud that draws
> O're the blew Firmament a radiant white,
> And slow descends, with something heav'nly fraught.

BOOK IX

12–17. The reading of A suggests that at the back of Wordsworth's mind was the opening of *Paradise Lost*, ix, where Milton turns from the delineation of sinless Paradise to describe

> foul distrust, and breach
> Disloyal on the part of Man, revolt,
> And disobedience; on the part of Heav'n
> Now alienated, distance and distaste,
> Anger and just rebuke, and judgement giv'n.

24. *Looking as from a distance*: possibly omitted from D E because it repeats the statement made in VI. 695–6 of his feeling towards the Revolution in the previous year. But the A text of this passage (23–30) gives as a whole a more discerning account of what London had contributed to the growth of his mind than the versions in D and E.

31 [28]. *A year thus spent*: 'Scarcely a year' E. The time was really much shorter. Wordsworth went to London in February 1791, and from a letter of his sister's, dated 23 May, we learn that he was then already in Wales; and though he was probably in London again in October, on 23 November he was at Brighton, *en route* for France.

36–7. The reading of A disposes of the view advanced by some critics that Wordsworth was chiefly drawn to France by a newly awakened interest in man, and hence a sympathy with the Revolution. Cf. also ll. 74–80, 86–108, and *note* on VIII. 483.

39 [41]. *A City on the Borders of the Loire*: i.e. Orleans, which Wordsworth reached on 6 October; at some date in the early months of the next year, 1792, he removed to Blois. As Professor Harper has pointed out, Wordsworth does not distinguish in *The Prelude* between his experiences at Orleans and at Blois. He dated a letter to his brother Richard on 19 December from Orleans, and on 17 May following wrote that he was 'overwhelmed by a sense of shame' for leaving so long unanswered a letter from Matthews which had reached him just as he 'was busy preparing to quit Orleans', since when 'day after day, and week after week, have stolen insensibly over my head with inconceivable rapidity'. At the lowest computation this would take us back to

March, and Harper adduces good evidence (*Life*, i. 155) that he was already at Blois in February. The 'knot of military Officers' (127) were certainly stationed there, for Blois, and not Orleans, was at the time a garrison city. Wordsworth was still at Blois when the king was *suspendu* on 10 August (*Memoirs*, i. 15), and on 3 September, when he dates a letter from there, but at Orleans in the next day or two during the September massacres, and also in the following month (v. *Descriptive Sketches*, 1793 ed., 760–3). At the end of October he was again in Paris, where he remained till the end of the year.

41–51. *visited In haste each spot of old and recent fame etc.*: All those 'spots' mentioned here by Wordsworth were 'of recent fame'. The *Field of Mars* (43), in the west of Paris, was the scene of the Federation fête held on 14 July 1790, to commemorate the fall of the Bastille. The Federated States were invited to send delegates, and great preparations were made for the festivities. A huge *arc de triomphe* was erected, and in the middle was placed the *autel de la Patrie*. Fifteen thousand workmen were not enough to complete the work, so that the whole population was invited to volunteer. At the altar a solemn oath was administered to the deputies and to the newly formed National Guards, and here Louis XVI swore fidelity to the new constitution. But in the July following (1791), after the king's flight, a petition asking for the deposition of the monarch was exposed on the altar, to receive signatures. The National Guard under Lafayette was called out to check riotous meetings, and blood flowed even up to the steps of the altar.

44. *The Suburbs of St. Anthony*: The Faubourg Saint-Antoine, in the east of the city, and abutting on the Bastille, was the workmen's quarter, where much of the revolutionary violence was fomented.

45. *Mont Martyr*: i.e. Montmartre, in the north of Paris, where revolutionary meetings were held, possibly in two convents evacuated by the order of the Government in the preceding year.

45–6. *the Dome of Geneviève*: i.e. the Panthéon, in the south of Paris, was a church built to the classic designs of the architect Soufflot on the site of the old Abbey of Ste Geneviève. It was in course of erection at the outbreak of the Revolution. On the death of Mirabeau (April 1791) the Assembly wished for a place of burial, like Westminster Abbey, in which to deposit the remains of those who had deserved well of their country. Soufflot's building seemed well suited for the purpose, and *dans un transport civique* it was baptised, and 'henceforth received a soul and a meaning' (Quinet). It was still called Ste Geneviève, however, as the separation of Church and State had not yet taken place, and at Mirabeau's funeral the clergy officiated. Voltaire's remains were brought there in July of the same year, and when, a few days later, a petition was submitted that the body of Rousseau should be placed there also, the name Panthéon was suggested.

47. *The National Synod*: The National Assembly at this time met in the *salle du Manège* or Riding Hall at the east corner of the Rue de Rivoli. The Hall was demolished in 1810.

the Jacobins: The Jacobin Club met in the library of the convent of the Dominicans, near the Rue Saint-Honoré. The Dominicans were known as Jacobins because their earliest convent in Paris (A.D. 1218) was a hospice bearing the title of St. Jacques, and the name was transferred to the revolutionaries who met there.

50-1. *The Arcades . . . in the Palace huge Of Orleans*: i.e. in the Palais Royal. On three sides of the courtyard arcades of shops had been built (51-2), and this was the chief centre in Paris both for business and for idle lounging (53-4). 'The beauty of the buildings and magnificence of the shops did not impress us', writes a visitor in 1787, 'so much as the crowds of people who flocked there at mid-day. It is the rendez-vous of strangers, of the idle Parisians, and charming women.' (J. Letaconnoux: *La Vie parisienne au xviiime siècle*, p. 55.) Cf. also X. 83-4.

56. *hubbub wild*: cf. *Paradise Lost*, ii. 951-2:

> At length an universal hubbub wild,
> Of stunning sounds and voices all confused.

68. *incumbences*: i.e. spiritual brooding or visitations. Cf. III. 115.

78. *Magdalene of le Brun*: Charles le Brun (1616-90), court painter to Louis XIV, painted this picture for the Carmelite convent in the Rue d'Enfer. 'It was regarded as one of the "sights" of the day. Religious music was played for the benefit of those who came to view it' (Legouis, trs. p. 194). It is now in the Louvre. Wordsworth never acquired any sound taste in pictorial art, and was able later to express a genuine admiration for the canvases of his friends Haydon and Sir George Beaumont.

97. *the master Pamphlets of the day*: Among the many pamphlets issued at this time Aulard (*Hist. pol. rev.*) mentions those of the royalist Peltier, the *constituant* Drouet (*Voilà ce qu'il faut faire*), and the extremists Marat and Robespierre (on universal suffrage); also the anonymous *Grande Visite de Mademoiselle République*, and *Deux Brutus au peuple français*. At the sale of W. W.'s library in 1859 'Lot 405' was 'Pamphlets and Ephemera—French; a bundle'.

108-11. *At the time, . . . Lock'd up in quiet*: On 30 September 1791, the Constituent Assembly had dispersed and on the following day the Legislative Assembly heard from the throne the statement that 'le terme de la Révolution est arrivé. Que la nation reprenne son heureux caractère.' This internal peace was not disturbed till after 29 November, when the strong measures taken against those priests who were not loyal to the new constitution began to embitter good Catholics. Abroad, the *émigrés* (v. *note* to l. 186 *infra*) had as yet achieved no dangerous success with foreign powers, and the king and queen rather feared their zeal than favoured their intrigues. Wordsworth's description of the state of things on his arrival in France is therefore quite accurate.

125. *patriot*: Wordsworth could not be a 'patriot' of France in the ordinary acceptance of the term. But Camille Desmoulins in his *Révolutions de France*

et de Brabant had given the word the special political meaning of 'republican'. Both here and in ll. 296, 554, W. W. uses it in this technical sense.

127. *A knot of military Officers*: Wordsworth's first associates were all anti-revolutionary in their sympathies. Cf. the letter to his brother Richard, 19 December: 'I had imagined . . . there were some people of wealth and circumstance favourers of the Revolution, but here is no one to be found.' He had not yet met Beaupuy.

179. *Carra, Gorsas*: Journalist deputies of Girondist sympathy, who sat at the National Convention. Gorsas was the first Girondist to be guillotined (7 October 1793). In 1840 Wordsworth told Carlyle that he was present at the execution. If this was so, and Carlyle is hardly likely to have misunderstood Wordsworth on a matter which would interest him so deeply, Wordsworth must have paid a flying visit to France at that time. [See *Chronology*, 147 for a fuller presentation of the evidence for W. W.'s hurried visit to France. S. G.]

186. *To augment the band of Emigrants*: The first *émigrés* were the extreme reactionaries who, exasperated by the king's early concessions to the National Assembly, left France with the avowed object of returning to reconquer the country for the *ancien régime*. On the general attack upon the châteaux throughout France they were joined, for reasons of personal safety, by many more of the nobility and gentry; and, after the flight of the king to Varennes (June 1791), by the majority of the army officers. They made their headquarters at Coblenz, and formed later the nucleus of the Royalist armies ranged against France.

294. *Among that band of Officers was one*: Michel Armand Beaupuy (wrongly spelt in l. 426 Beaupuis), born at Mussidan, Périgord, in 1755, and thus fifteen years older than Wordsworth. He was of noble family, and descended on the female side from Montaigne; but his sympathy, and that of his mother and four brothers, was entirely with the revolutionary cause, and he was, moreover, a student, and widely read in the philosophy of the eighteenth century. For a full account of his life and character *v*. Legouis, *Early Life of Wordsworth*, and Bussière and Legouis, *Le Général Michel Beaupuy*. It is clear from M. Legouis's researches that Beaupuy was well worthy of Wordsworth's enthusiastic but discerning praise of him, and that his influence on the poet's mind was only equalled by that exercised later by Coleridge. Before his intimacy with Beaupuy Wordsworth's interest in the Revolution was largely sentimental (cf. ll. 63–80, 201–17): it now became practical, and reasoned, if a little doctrinaire. Harper is surely right in his suggestion that when Wordsworth drew his portrait of *The Happy Warrior* (less than two years after this sketch of Beaupuy was written) his French friend was at the back of his mind.

341. *Than afterwards*: i.e. in 1793–5, the period with which he deals in Book X [X–XI].

370–1. *As just etc.*: the meaning here is not clear and the construction awkward. Wordsworth probably means 'making the life of society as a whole as pure and as well-regulated as is the life of the individual wise and good man'. Cf. the remark made by Dicey (*Statesmanship of Wordsworth*, p. 32): 'Beaupuy and Wordsworth were in 1792 democrats who hoped to obtain every kind of socialistic reform by means which would have met with the approval of zealous individualists.'

415–24 [408–17]. *Such conversation . . . Did Dion hold with Plato etc.*: Wordsworth owed his knowledge of this story to Plutarch (v. *note* to I. 186–95), and the poem which he wrote later (1816) upon Dion is full of reminiscences of Plutarch's *Life of Dion*. Dion was the brother-in-law of Dionysius the elder, tyrant of Syracuse. On Plato's first visit to Sicily Dion became his disciple, and after the accession of Dionysius the younger (367 B.C.), a weak and dissolute tyrant, he induced Plato to return in the hope of influencing his nephew. But his plans for the young man's reformation, though for a time successful, were undermined by flatterers and proved abortive; he was himself banished and retired to Athens, where once more he was associated with Plato and other philosophers. Plato paid a third visit to Syracuse in the hope of effecting the recall of Dion, but Dionysius refused, confiscated Dion's property and married his wife, Arete, to another husband. 'These things went to *Dions* heart, so that shortly after he shewed himselfe an open enemie unto *Dionysius*, but specially when he heard how he handled his wife . . . *Dion* from thenceforth disposed himself altogether unto war, against *Platoes* counsel and advise; . . . Howbeit, on the other side, *Speusippus* and his other friends did provoke him unto it, and perswade him to deliver *Sicile* from the slaverie and bondage of the tyrant, the which held up her hands unto him, and would receive him with great love and goodwill. . . . The philosophers do set forward *Dions* warres; many citizens dealing in the affaires of the commonwealth, did aide him, and divers of them also that only gave their minds to the studie of Philosophie: and among them *Eudemus Cyprian* . . . *Timonides Leucadian*, went with him. . . . The place where they appointed to meete was the *Ile* of *Zacynth* where they leavied all their souldiers. . . . So *Dions* souldiers were embarked into two great ships of burden' (Plutarch: *Dion*: North's *trans.*). Dion succeeded in deposing Dionysius (357 B.C.) but was himself assassinated in 353 B.C.

431 [424]. *He perish'd fighting*: In this statement Wordsworth was mistaken. Beaupuy was dangerously wounded in Vendée, but recovered, and served the republican cause with distinction and unswerving loyalty till 1796, when he fell at the battle of the Elz, on 19 November (*v.* Legouis, trs. p. 214).

442 [435]. *High woods and over-arch'd etc.*: Cf. *Paradise Lost*, ix. 1106–7:

a Pillard shade
High overarch't, and echoing Walks between.

454 [451]. *Angelica*: the heroine of Ariosto's *Orlando Furioso* (*v.* Canto I. 13):

La donna il palafreno addietro volta,
e per la selva a tutta briglia il caccia;

nè per la rara più che per la folta,
la più sicura e miglior via procaccia;
ma pallida, tremando, e di sè tolta,
lascia cura al destrier che la via faccia.

456 [453]. *Erminia*: the heroine of Tasso's *Gerusalemme Liberata* (*v.* Canto VII. 1.)

Intanto Erminia in fra l'ombrose piante
d'antica selva dal cavallo è scorta:
nè più governa il fren la man tremante,
e mezza quasi par tra viva e morta.
Per tante strade si raggira e tante
il corridor che 'n sua balìa la porta
ch'alfin da gli occhi altrui pur si dilegua;
ed è soverchio omai ch'altri la segua.

Wordsworth studied Italian at Cambridge under Isola, who had formerly been Gray's teacher.

462 [459]. *Satyrs in some viewless glade etc.*: Cf. Spenser, *Faerie Queene*, I. vi. 13, where Una is rescued from Sansloy by the satyrs who

lead her forth, about her dauncing round,
Shouting, and singing all a shepheards ryme;
And with greene braunches strowing all the ground,
Do worship her as Queene, with olive girlond cround.

Cf. also the picture of Hellenore among the Satyrs (*F.Q.* III. x. 43–4):

Now when among the thickest woodes they were,
They heard a noyse of many bagpipes shrill,
And shrieking Hububs them approaching nere,
Which all the forest did with horror fill;
. . . .
The jolly Satyres full of fresh delight,
Came dauncing forth, and with them nimbly ledd
Faire Hellenore, with girlonds all bespredd.

The hermits (448) are possibly suggested by Archimago (*F.Q.* I. i. 34).

476 [473]. *I could not but bewail a wrong so harsh etc.*: Cf. his feelings at the Chartreuse, described in VI. [420–87].

483–93. *Romorentin ... Edifice of Blois ... Chambord: Romorantin* (*not* Romorentin), a small château, twenty-five miles from Blois, beloved by Louise de Savoie, the mother of Francis I. Francis spent much time there as a boy with his sister. It was here that Louise saw the comet in the sky which was supposed to presage the first military success of her son at Marignano. *The imperial Edifice of Blois* was reconstructed by Louis XII; here the Emperor Charles V visited Francis in 1539. *Chambord* is on the plain of Sologne, nine miles southeast of Blois, and one of the finest examples of Renaissance architecture. Originally an old *maison de chasse*, Francis began its transformation in 1519, and on his return from captivity in Madrid the building and decoration were his delight, and he lived there at least three years (1526–30). The episode referred to by Wordsworth must belong to this time. In 1526 his mother, hoping to dissociate him from Françoise de Chateaubriant, produced from her suite a young maid of honour, Anne de Pisseleu d'Heilly, who forthwith became his mistress, and was 'in constant company with the king in his daily examination of the progress at Chambord'. Of the three châteaux within a radius of ten miles from Chambord, and on the heights, Chaverney was not built till 1640, and Chaumont, which is on a hill and commands a long view of the Loire, was occupied after 1561 by Diane; and she did not come on the scene till 1537, when Francis's interest in Chambord had waned. The third, Beauregard, was a hunting-lodge built by Francis, 4½ miles from Blois, and on one of the roads to Chambord. This seems therefore the most likely to have been the 'rural Castle' (483) whose name Wordsworth had forgotten, and Anne the lady to whom the king signalled. There seems no trust-worthy source for the suggestion (taken by Nowell Smith from Hachette's *Guide*) that Thoury was the castle and the Comtesse de Thoury the lady —still less for Knight's statement that the lady was Claude, daughter of Louis XII.

538. *mandate without law*: i.e. *lettre de cachet*, or letter expressing the personal will of the sovereign or his government, not a legal decision, and sent *cachetée* to the officer charged with the execution of the order contained in it.

554–5. *related by my patriot Friend And others*: In the 1850 version Wordsworth speaks of the tale simply as 'told by my patriot friend'. In the I.F. note to *Vaudracour and Julia* he stated that it was 'faithfully narrated, though with the omission of many pathetic circumstances, from the mouth of a French lady, who had been an eye and ear witness of all that was done and said. Many long years after, I was told that Dupligne was then a monk in the Convent of La Trappe.' This incompatibility has more than once been commented on, and M. Legouis has suggested that its object was 'to avert suspicion rather than to give information to the public' (*William Wordsworth and Annette Vallon*, 1922). But it is difficult to see why the mouth of a French lady would awaken less suspicion than the mouth of his patriot friend. The read-ing of A perhaps explains the discrepancy. If, as Wordsworth said in 1820 (and his statements of fact can be trusted), 'the facts are true; no invention as to these has been exercised, as none was needed', the events would naturally be much talked of at the time of their occurrence; and it is not unlikely that Wordsworth would hear the story not only from Beaupuy, but from others; among them, with much detail in which Beaupuy would not be interested, from the French lady referred to in the I.F. note. The statement, also made in 1820, that 'the following tale was written as an episode in a work from which its length may perhaps exclude it', does not imply that its length was the only reason of its exclusion. Doubtless he omitted it in part to avert suspicion, just as he included it, in spite of its length, when he wrote *The*

Prelude, that he might not leave without allusion an important episode of his own life in France—i.e. his love for Annette. He has been accused of a reticence amounting to insincerity in tracing 'the growth of a poet's mind' without any reference to an event which must have borne some part in that growth. The explanation is twofold. (1) Quite apart from his own feelings in the matter, it was impossible for him to relate the facts without causing pain to those who had every claim upon his consideration—not only his own wife and family, but also Annette and Caroline: on the other hand, he could hardly pass over the matter without some allusion to it. Consequently he adopts the compromise of telling the story in veiled language through the tale of Vaudracour and Julia. The fates of these two lovers were sufficiently like and sufficiently unlike those of Wordsworth and Annette to tell Coleridge (for whom, it must be remembered, *The Prelude* was specially written) the state of his own feelings at the time. Few students of Wordsworth, realizing how much his genius was dependent for all its greatest manifestations upon actual personal experience, will doubt that in the great passages of *Vaudracour and Julia*, which stand out all the more clearly from the inferiority of the poem as a whole—the account of the ecstasy of young love (582–95), the exciting passion of stolen interviews (626–34) (ed. 1820, 94–101), and the distracted state of mind of the separated lovers (745–51)—Wordsworth is drawing on his own experience. Certainly Coleridge would so understand it. (2) This passion for Annette, overwhelming as it was at the time, could not have left him the same man as he was before. Yet in retrospect it seemed to him to have been transient rather than permanent in its effects upon him, and perhaps to have arrested rather than developed the natural growth of his poetic mind. It had, for example, none of that formative and continually stimulating effect upon his imagination which he recognized in the experiences of his childhood. Consequently, however vital a part of his biography as a man, it seemed less vital in the history of his mind. That it had more influence upon his mind and art than he believed it to have is probable; it can hardly be doubted, for example, that he owed to it that sympathetic penetration into the heart of the deserted woman, and the relations of mother and child, which is a marked feature of his poetry from 1795 to 1805. But it is one thing to differ from Wordsworth as to the importance of the episode in the development of his mind, and another to accuse him of wilfully misrepresenting that development.

[Cf. *Letters written in France in 1790, containing Memoirs of Mons. and Madame F.* by Helen Williams, which tells a story corresponding in its main lines to that of Vaudracour and Julia. H. D.]

584. *Arabian fiction*: For Wordsworth's fondness for the *Arabian Nights* cf. V. 484–99 and MS. quoted in P., p. 573.

596–7. *whether through effect Of some delirious hour*: the obvious psychological explanation, which is ill replaced by the shocked morality of the 1820 version.

912. Altered, doubtless, in later texts to escape odious comparison with *Othello*, v. ii. 303, 'From this time forth I never will speak word.'

934–5. This is an unwitting departure from fact, but it was only years after that Wordsworth learnt that Dupligne (i.e. Vaudracour) was a monk at La Trappe (*v.* I.F. note, quoted p. 295).

BOOK X

9–37. *The King had fallen etc.*: On 25 July 1792, the Duke of Brunswick signed a manifesto inspired by Marie Antoinette, to the effect that if the least violence or outrage were done upon the king the allies would avenge it by a military execution in Paris. Two days later the Princes issued a declaration that not only Paris should suffer the extremity of martial law, but every town to which the king might be removed. These manifestos, intended to terrorize Paris, only strengthened the hands of the more violent section; as a counterstroke, the Revolutionists led by Danton decided to depose the king and hold him as a hostage. On the night of 9 August the Tuileries was stormed by the mob and on the following day the king was deposed and confined in prison 'for his own security'. On 19 August the allied forces entered France and took Longwy (24 August) and Verdun (1 September). In retaliation the committee of the Commune, of whom Marat, Danton, and Robespierre were chief, organized the September massacres (2, 3, and 4 September), in which over 3,000 Royalist suspects were taken from prison and slaughtered. After the poor resistance of the Republican troops at Longwy and Verdun, the allied forces anticipated no difficulty in reaching Paris; but the French troops under Dumouriez made an unexpected stand at Valmy on 20 September, and early in the following month the allies had completely evacuated French territory. The Republic was decreed on the day of the victory of Valmy and was proclaimed on 22 September. In the new assembly, which had just been elected, Paris was represented by Jacobin extremists, but the September massacres had not appealed to the country as a whole, and there was a large majority of moderates who were prepared to follow the Girondists—if the Girondists would lead. Hence Wordsworth's optimism in ll. 34–7.

The changes which Wordsworth introduced into the text of this passage are noteworthy, as showing his increased horror of the Revolution in his later life. The statement that 'in a spirit of thanks' to the victors of Valmy she 'assumed with joy' the name of a Republic is replaced by the assertion that it was an act of defiance and resentment, and prompted by the desire 'to taunt the baffled League'. Similarly he tones down the expression of his own enthusiasm at the time from 'enflam'd with hope' to 'cheered with this hope'.

17. *punctual spot*: a Miltonic phrase, *Paradise Lost*, viii. 23 (cf. *The Prelude*, VIII. 762). It is worth noting that, whilst this phrase goes out in later versions, the simile of the 'eastern hunters' is elaborated in the Miltonic manner, with a definite debt to *Paradise Lost*, xi. 391, 'Agra and Lahor of great Mogul', and i. 776, 'the signal given' (of the narrowing of the giants into pigmies).

19–20 [26–7]. *fled In terror*: a somewhat exaggerated description of the retreat of the allied army from France.

29. *assumed with joy*: 'Wordsworth was probably present on 21 September at the civic feast given at Orleans to celebrate the suppression of monarchy, during which deputy Manuel made a speech before the assembly. As a symbol of the fall of royalty, fire was set to a big wood-pile: "Le feu est solennellement mis à l'énorme bûcher, composé de fagots élevés en une haute pyramide couronnée d'un bouquet d'artifice qui bientôt tombe en mille flammèches étincelantes, et les citoyens se livrent à la joie qu'ils ressentent de l'établissement de la République française: dans leur enthousiasme, avec les élans qui n'appartiennent qu'à des hommes vraiment dignes de la liberté, les cris de 'Vive la République! Vive la nation française!' éclatent de toutes parts." ' Legouis, *William Wordsworth and Annette Vallon*, p. 24 (quoted from *Histoire de la ville d'Orléans* by Bimbenet).

42 [51]. *The Prison where the unhappy Monarch lay*: the 'Temple', in north-east Paris, built in the second half of the twelfth century for the Order of Templars. When they were suppressed in the fourteenth century, it became the seat of the Grand Priory of France. The tower of the 'Temple' was a thick-walled building, square, and flanked with turrets at the four corners. It was demolished in 1811.

44 [53]. *the Palace lately storm'd*: the Tuileries, situated between the Louvre and the Champs Élysées.

47 [56]. *The Square of the Carousel*: a vast square in front of the Tuileries and only separated from it by an iron paling. It was so called because in 1662 Louis XIV gave here a magnificent tourney or 'carrousel'. On 10 August 1792, a mob composed chiefly of the Marseillese and of workmen from the Faubourg Saint-Antoine attacked the Tuileries; they were fired on by the Swiss guards, and many of them fell in the Place du Carrousel before entry was gained into the Palace.

70. *The horse is taught his manage*: Cf. *As You Like It*, I. i. 13: 'His horses are bred better: . . . they are taught their manage.'

76–7. *a voice that cried*, . . . *'Sleep no more'*: *Macbeth*, II. ii. 35.

[81.The last word of this line is illegible in MS. S. G.]

83. *Betimes next morning*: From this passage it is natural to suppose that Wordsworth arrived in Paris on the very day, 29 October, on which Louvet made his accusation, which would be hawked about the streets on the next morning. Louvet accused Robespierre of having 'perverted the Jacobin Club and exercised a despotism of opinion. These bloody men', he said, and he mentioned Marat also by name, 'wished to satiate their cruel eyes with the spectacle of 28,000 bodies sacrificed to their fury. I accuse you of having dispersed and persecuted the Legislative Assembly, of having exhibited yourself as an object of idolatry, of having aimed at supreme power; and in this

accusation your own conduct will speak more strongly than words' (Report in *Morning Chronicle*, 3–6 November). Robespierre was given a week in which to prepare his answer to Louvet, and in the meantime popular feeling ran strong against him, and 'there was a marvellous clamour for the heads of Robespierre, Marat and Danton', who were burnt in effigy on 4 November. But in his speech on Monday, 5 November, he succeeded in turning the tide back in his favour. He denied any hand in the September massacres. 'They were', he said, 'the act of men raised to defend their country after the Verdun disaster. If people will lament, let them lament the patriots massacred by despotism. I am always suspicious of that sensibility which is exclusively excited by the fate of the enemies of the State' (*St. James's Chronicle*, 8–10 November). It is easy to imagine Wordsworth's feelings as he saw 'with my proper eyes' that Robespierre now 'ruled The capital City' (111), and that 'Liberty, and Life, and Death' in the whole land would soon lie in his 'arbitrement' (110).

107–17. The Girondists were idealists whose speeches were full of references to ancient Greece and Rome; but they had no definite policy, and used all their efforts in a vain attempt to discredit the Jacobins. Hence, though they could command a majority they could make no use of it, and the power remained in the hands of the extremist minority. Cf. Coleridge, *Conciones ad Populum* (1795): 'The Girondists . . . were men of enlarged views and great literary attainments; but they seem to have been deficient in that vigour and daring activity, which circumstances made necessary. Men of genius are rarely either prompt in action or consistent in general conduct: their early habits have been those of contemplative indolence; and the day-dreams with which they have been accustomed to amuse their solitude, adapt them for splendid speculation, not temperate and practical counsels. Brissot, the leader of the Gironde party, is entitled to the character of a virtuous man and an eloquent speaker; and his excellences equally with his faults rendered him unfit for the helm in the stormy hour of Revolution. Robespierre, who displaced him, possessed a glowing ardour that still remembered the *end*, and a cool ferocity that never either overlooked or scrupled the means.'

165–6. *Harmodius . . . And his Compeer Aristogiton*: two noble Athenians who raised a conspiracy against the tyranny of the Pisistratae, 514 B.C. They lost their lives, but gained from the later generations of Athenians the character of patriots and deliverers.

178. *Creed which ten shameful years have not annull'd*: Such was Wordsworth's faith in 1804; but evidently he had lost it before 1820, for the line does not appear in C.

179. *one paramount mind*: v. *note* to ll. 107–17.

190–1.   *Compell'd by nothing less than absolute want*
            Of funds for my support:

Both Harper (i. 178) and Garrod (p. 57) have raised doubts whether the 'chain of harsh necessity' [222] was really an empty purse. But the reading of A proves that interpretation to be correct.

195. *some who perish'd*: Brissot and his Girondist followers vainly fought against the growing Jacobin strength, but in the following June they were put under arrest in their own houses, imprisoned in July, and guillotined in October 1793.

201. *To thee unknown*: Wordsworth did not meet Coleridge till nearly three years later, i.e. in the autumn of 1795.

202. *After a whole year's absence*: Wordsworth was in France from November 1791 to December 1792. The reading of A is, therefore, more accurate than the more decorative version of 1850. On his return he went to London, where he stayed till the summer.

205 [249]. *Against the Traffickers in Negro blood*: The Society for the Suppression of the Slave Trade was founded by Clarkson and Wilberforce in 1787. In the following year Wilberforce brought a bill for abolition before Parliament, but without success; in 1792 a bill passed the Commons but was thrown out by the Lords. The Act was finally passed in March 1807. Cf. Wordsworth's *Sonnet*, 'Clarkson! it was an obstinate hill to climb.'

229-30. *Britain . . . In league with the confederated Host*: France declared war on England and Holland, 1 February 1793; England declared war in return, 11 February.

233-41. An important passage. It is too often forgotten that it was not the Revolution, but the definite siding of England *against* the Revolution, that caused the first great moral shock to Wordsworth. The Revolution had seemed to him

> nothing out of nature's certain course,
> A gift that rather was come late than soon.   (IX. 253-4.)

(Cf. Garrod: pp. 59-61.) And the shock was not less because, as he tells us in the A text, he had anticipated it from the hostility of English politicians. But he had never realized what the effect would be upon his own nature.

261 [286]. *When Englishmen by thousands were o'erthrown*: The English troops had some slight success at first, and the Duke of York besieged Dunkirk, but in September he was defeated in the Battle of Hondshoote, and obliged to retreat.

268-9 [293-4]. *bending all To their great Father*: a reminiscence of *The Ancient Mariner*, 607: 'While each to his great Father bends.'

279 [304]. *wear*: Despite Worsfold's eloquent defence of the reading 'wean', it has no MS. authority. But the 'r' in E might easily be mistaken for an 'n'; hence the error in 1850.

292. *The unhappy counsel of a few weak men*: Note the omission in later texts of this attack upon the English government.

297 [321]. *In that delightful Island*: 'During the latter part of the summer of 1793, having passed a month in the Isle of Wight, in view of the fleet which was then preparing for sea off Portsmouth at the commencement of the war, I left the place with melancholy forebodings. The American war was still fresh in memory. The struggle which was beginning, and which many thought would be brought to a speedy close by the irresistible arms of Great Britain being added to those of the allies, I was assured in my own mind would be of long continuance, and productive of distress and misery beyond all calculation. This conviction was pressed upon me by having been a witness, during a long residence in revolutionary France, of the spirit which prevailed in that country.' *Advertisement to Guilt and Sorrow*, 1842. Wordsworth's companion in the Isle of Wight was William Calvert, brother of Raisley Calvert.

[299–306. See *P.W.*, I. 307–8. W. W.'s verses on an evening walk at the Isle of Wight conclude:

> But hark from yon proud fleet in peal profound
> Thunders the sunset cannon; at the sound
> The star of life appears to set in blood,
> And ocean shudders in offended mood,
> Deepening with moral gloom his angry flood.   S. G.]

309–10. *Tyrants, strong before In devilish pleas*: Cf. Milton, *Paradise Lost*, iv. 394–5:

> So spake the Fiend, and with necessitie,
> The Tyrant's plea, excus'd his devilish deeds.

313–14. *blasts From hell came sanctified like airs from heaven*: Cf. *Hamlet*, 1. iv. 41:

> Bring with thee airs from heaven or blasts from hell.

317–18 [341–2]. *who throned The human understanding paramount*: For this Chaumette, 'the glowing patriarch of irreligious belief', was chiefly responsible. On 10 November 1793 'Chaumette opened the Cathedral of Notre Dame to the religion of Reason. The Convention stood aloof, in cold disdain. But an actress, who played the leading part, and was variously described as the Goddess of Reason or the Goddess of Liberty, and who possibly did not know herself which she was, came down from her throne in the church, proceeded to the Assembly, and was admitted to a seat beside the President, who gave her what was known as a friendly accolade, amid loud applause. After that invasion, the hesitating deputies yielded, and about half of them attended the goddess back to her place under the Gothic towers. Chaumette decidedly triumphed. He had already forbidden religious service outside the buildings. He had now turned out the clergy whom the state had appointed, and had filled their place with a Parisian actress.' Acton: *Lectures on the French Revolution*, p. 178.

329–80 [356–415]. *Domestic carnage etc.*: The Reign of Terror may be dated from 25 September, when Robespierre obtained a unanimous vote of confidence against the Dantonists. The 'Reign' was inaugurated by the execution of the Girondist leaders in October and November, and lasted till the fall of Robespierre on 26 July 1794.

338 [365]. *light*: obviously the correct reading, for which 'like' (1850) is a copyist's error. If the 'desires of innocent little Ones' were 'like', there would be no reason to apologize for the comparison; it is only apologized for because they *were* 'light', whereas those of the Jacobins were 'heinous'.

352 [381]. *The illustrious Wife of Roland*: Madame Roland, a leading Girondist, was guillotined on 8 November 1793. Her last words, as she looked on the statue of Liberty, were 'Ô Liberté, que de crimes l'on commet en ton nom!'

455 [498]. *the Town of Arras*: Wordsworth passed through Arras on 16 July 1790, on his tour with Robert Jones, en route from Calais to Switzerland. For his impressions of the state of France at that time *v.* VI. 352-425 and *Sonnet* 'Jones! as from Calais southward you and I' 1-8. Robespierre was born at Arras in 1758, and came as a deputy to Paris, where he sat in the first legislative Assembly. It was by his motion that all those who sat in the first Assembly were excluded from the second. He became the chief speaker in the Jacobin clubs, and a leading spirit in dictating their policy. He was elected President of the Committee of Public Safety in 1793. But though Chaumette carried on his anti-religious policy in the days of Robespierre's supremacy, Robespierre was never, as Wordsworth seems to imply, an atheist, but like his master Rousseau, a worshipper of the Supreme Being. 'He denounced Chaumette's irreligious masquerades, and declared that the Convention never intended to proscribe the Catholic worship.' In March 1792 he had proposed a resolution that the belief in Providence and a future life is a necessary condition of Jacobinism, and in November argued that 'the essential principles of politics might be found in the sublime teaching of Christ . . . and on 7 May 1794, brought forward his famous motion that the Convention acknowledge the existence of a Supreme Being' (Acton, *op. cit.*, pp. 285-6). On 8 June he headed the procession at the Feast of the Supreme Being.

457 [502]. *atheist crew*: a Miltonic phrase. Cf. *Paradise Lost*, vi. 370.

462 [506]. *As Lear reproach'd the winds*: *King Lear*, III. ii. 1-24, iv. 22-32.

468. *this foul Tribe of Moloch*: This description of Robespierre and his crew has an added significance when we realize that Wordsworth had in mind *Paradise Lost*, i. 392-5:

> Moloch, horrid king besmear'd with blood
> Of human sacrifice, and parents tears,
> Though for the noise of Drums and Timbrels loud
> Their childrens cries unheard.

470 [513]. *The day*: Robespierre was guillotined 28 July 1794. Hence Knight states that Wordsworth 'must have made this journey across the Ulverston sands in the first week of August'. But it was certainly not before the third week. On Saturday 16 August the first (inaccurate) account of Robespierre's

fall appeared in *The Times*, announcing that he had been murdered in the Convention with poniards. On the 18th there was a definite statement of his execution and a full report of the events which occurred on 27 July; on the 19th, reports from Paris of what had taken place down to 1 August, when all was quiet again, and a definite statement that on the 28th, at night, Robespierre had been guillotined.

472. *From a small Village*: probably Rampside, a village in Low Furness, Lancashire, opposite Peel Castle, where Wordsworth spent four weeks with his cousin Mrs. Barker. Cf. *Elegiac stanzas suggested by a picture of Peele Castle*, 1805:

> I was thy neighbour once, thou rugged Pile!
> Four summer weeks I dwelt in sight of thee.

Hutchinson (Oxf. *W.*, p. xxvi) has thought that Wordsworth's visit to Rampside was in the long vacation of 1778 or 1779, but 1794 is much more likely. There is no other 'village of far-secluded privacy' at which Wordsworth is known to have stayed at this time, to which he could have returned from this walk over Leven Sands: moreover, the description of the fulgent spectacle

> Which neither changed, nor stirr'd, nor pass'd away (487)

recalls significantly the language in which he describes his impression of Peel Castle as seen from Rampside.

479–86. *In one inseparable glory clad etc.*: These lines ring with Miltonic echoes. 'Ethereal substance', *Paradise Lost*, vi. 330, 'in consistory', *Paradise Regained*, i. 42, 'burning seraphs', *At a Solemn Music*, l. 10 ('Where the bright Seraphim in burning row'), 'the empyrean', *passim*. 'Fulgent' (486) is also a Miltonic word.

492 [534]. *An honor'd Teacher of my youth*: In the churchyard of Cartmel Priory the following epitaph can still be read: 'In memory of the Rev. William Taylor, A.M., son of John Taylor of Outerthwaite who was for some years a Fellow of Emmanuel College Cambridge; Master of the Free School at Hawkshead. He departed this life June the 12th, 1786, aged 32 years 2 months and 13 days.

> His merits, stranger, seek not to disclose,
> Or draw his Frailties from their dread abode;
> There they alike in trembling Hope repose
> The bosom of his Father and his God.'

It was thus 'full eight years' in 1794 from the time when Wordsworth, then a schoolboy, took leave of Taylor on his death-bed. Cf. *Address to the scholars of the village school of——*, *Matthew*, *The two April Mornings*, and *The Fountain*, all of which, as Wordsworth says, are 'composite' pictures, but owed much to his memory of Taylor, though the school-master delineated in these poems is an old man.

514. *my toilsome Songs*: 'The first verses that I wrote were a task imposed by my master, the subject, "The Summer Vacation"; and of my own accord I added

others upon "Return to School". There was nothing remarkable in either poem; but I was called upon, among other scholars, to write verses upon the completion of the second centenary from the foundation of the school, in 1585, by Archbishop Sandys. The verses were much admired, far more than they deserved, for they were but a tame imitation of Pope's versification, and a little in his style. This exercise, however, put it into my head to compose verses from the impulse of my own mind, and I wrote, while yet a schoolboy, a long poem running upon my own adventures, and the scenery of the country in which I was brought up. The only part of it which has been preserved is the conclusion of it.' *Memoirs*, i. 10–13 (*q.v.* for the lines imitative of Pope; for the others, *v. Oxf. W.* p. 1).

518 [555]. *rocky Island*: known as Chapel Island from the remains of a small oratory, still extant in Wordsworth's time, built by the monks of Furness.

559–66 [596–603]. Cf. II. 108–44, and *notes*.

574–82 [XI. 8–14]. The faulty punctuation of this passage in 1850, which has been noticed and corrected by several editors, is explained by a study of the development of the text. C, in omitting 579–80, forgot to change the comma after 'confidence' into a semicolon, and E omitted even the comma after 'seen'. So that 1850 had to reconstruct the punctuation for itself. In this, as often, it was not successful.

598–604. *never dreamt . . . call'd to*: A passage deleted from A, and not appearing in later texts, probably because of its awkwardness of expression. The meaning is 'I never dreamt that men inspired by the spirit of the early Revolutionists, instead of realizing the significance of their achievement and the greatness of their mission, could suffer a change of heart and a fall from their ideal'.

611 [XI. 33]. *an interregnum's . . . space*: i.e. after the fall of Robespierre.

625. *conceited*: an obsolete form of the verb 'conceive' used also by Wordsworth in his adaptation of *Troilus and Cressida* (1801), 104–5,

> All which he of himself conceited wholly
> Out of his weakness and his melancholy.

The whole sentence 'if the stream . . . forests' was altered, doubtless, because of its perversion of an incident in the story of the deluge. The appearance of the green branch would naturally suggest to the plain man, and not only 'to gravest heads', that the tree from which it came was *not* dead, but alive.

645–56 [XI. 62–76]. *Our Shepherds etc.*: Cf. Coleridge, *The Friend*: 'Essay on Party Spirit': 'In order to oppose Jacobinism they imitated it in its worst features: in personal slander, in illegal violence, and even in the thirst for blood.' Early in 1793 the Habeas Corpus Act was suspended, and the law-courts filled with government prosecutions of those who argued for political reform, or seemed in any way to favour a policy sympathetic with France. Muir, Palmer, and others were tried for treason and sent to Botany Bay; and in the next year (i.e. soon after the fall of Robespierre—which Wordsworth has just recounted) the government made an effort to get Hardy, the founder of the Corresponding Society, and the organizer of political movement among the working classes, condemned to death as a traitor. He was defended by Erskine, and London, though anti-Jacobin as a whole, rejoiced at his acquittal. It is to the government attack on Hardy (acquitted 5 November), Horne Tooke, and Thelwall that Wordsworth specially alludes here. With this passage should be compared his remarks in his *Letter to the Bishop of Llandaff, Apology for the French Revolution*, 1793: 'At this moment have we not daily the strongest proofs of the success with which, in what you call the best of monarchical governments, the popular mind may be debauched? Left to the quiet exercise of their own judgements, do you think the people would have thought it necessary to set fire to the house of the philosophic Priestley, and to hunt down his life like that of a traitor or a parricide?' [For a statement of W. W.'s political feelings at this time see his letters to William Mathews, 23 May 1794, 8 June 1794, 24 December 1794, and 7 January 1795. *E.Y.*, 118–20, 123–9, 136–9. S. G.]

657–756 [XI. 74–172]. Wordsworth now reverts from describing the conduct of the English government in 1793–4, to recount his own relation to public events from the time of his arrival in France (November 1791) till his return to England. He is therefore traversing again the ground covered by Books IX and X. 1–226.

689–727 [XI. 105–44]. First published in *The Friend*, 26 October 1809, then in the 1815 and subsequent editions of the *Poems*. The text of *The Friend* shows already some changes towards the final version. As Coleridge was at Grasmere when he wrote *The Friend*, some of the changes may have been his suggestion.

757–9 [XI. 173–94]. Another statement of Wordsworth's feelings after the declaration of war in February 1793, and thus a restatement of ll. 227–306.

774 [XI. 189]. *wild theories were afloat*: In February 1793 William Godwin's *Enquiry Concerning Political Justice* was published, and there can be no doubt that in this passage Wordsworth is referring to its early influence upon him. For a full and connected statement of Godwin's theories, *v*. Legouis trs. (*op. cit.*), Leslie Stephen, *English Thought in the Eighteenth Century*, and Brailsford, *Shelley, Godwin, and their Circle*; it is enough for the present purpose to recall that he was a necessitarian; that he denied the doctrine of innate ideas and insisted that sense-impressions and experience can be the only source of knowledge; that he exalted reason at the expense of the passions, and had boundless faith in the perfectibility of man when his passions had become subordinate to his reason; that he exalted the individual at the expense of the collective reason and hence rejected Rousseau's 'general will', and denied the right of government or society to coerce the individual either in action or opinion. Lastly, that his writing was inspired with a genuine passion for justice and a noble humanitarianism. When Wordsworth says, in the A text, that he 'lent but

a careless ear' to the 'subtleties' of Godwinism, he must be understood to mean that at first he accepted such of Godwin's creed as did not militate against his faith in the Revolution, but that he did not realize as yet its fuller implications. Thus at this time, if we may judge from *Guilt and Sorrow*, conceived on Salisbury Plain in August 1793, and finished before the end of 1794, he only accepted Godwin's necessitarianism (the crimes of the murderer being due to his circumstances), and hence his attack on criminal law and especially on capital punishment, his sympathy with the outcasts of society, who are what society has made them, his protest against wealth and property, and his hatred of war, and exposure of the calamities of war as they affect individuals.

During the next year (1794) the influence of the Revolution waned before his growing tendency to accept the fuller implications of Godwin's individualism. The fall of Robespierre at the end of July reawakened his faith in the immediate future; but when Frenchmen 'changed a war of self defence to one of conquest' he became for the time a whole-hearted Godwinian. [Godwin's Diaries record five meetings with Wordsworth between February and August 1795 (*v.* Moorman I, p. 262). H. D.] The question arises, when was that time, and how long did his subjection to Godwinism last?

Some critics have given the date 1798 to Wordsworth's recognition of the French as 'oppressors'. In this they are misled by the statement found in the second paragraph of the pamphlet on the *Convention of Cintra* (1809) to the effect that 'only after the subjugation of Switzerland and not till then' had 'the body of the people who had sympathized with the Revolution begun to regard the war against France as both just and necessary'. The subjugation of Switzerland was, indeed, the event which arrested the popular imagination, but it was significant of a change in French policy which had been noted by Wordsworth, and had brought about his second moral crisis, some years before. To accept 1798 as the date of Wordsworth's renunciation of France would be to falsify the whole chronology of *Prelude* X [XI], and that view is, indeed, falsified by all we know of Wordsworth's life and poetry in the Alfoxden days. He was doubtless deeply stirred by the subjugation of Switzerland, but politics were clearly not his prime interest at that time, and his moral crisis was over.

The date most usually accepted (Knight, Worsfold, Moore Smith) is 1796, when Napoleon undertook his first campaign in Italy; and Garrod has placed it slightly earlier, i.e. after the Directory (25 October 1795). But even this is too late to fit in with my interpretation of his changing states of mind as recorded in *The Prelude*, and it seems to me more likely that Wordsworth is referring to the close of 1794 and early months of 1795. The change in the policy of the French was in reality dictated by necessity rather than by the definite renunciation of an ideal. After the fall of Robespierre the Thermidorians, with a treasury drained dry, had to choose between disbanding their starving army (with the imminent danger that it would refuse to be disbanded and that its generals would come to Paris and effect another Revolution) and sending it beyond the frontiers to feed upon other nations. They chose what was obviously to them the lesser of two evils; but to Wordsworth, to whom the Revolution was the ideal of universal freedom and brotherhood, this was the renunciation of their faith. In the reports of the progress of the French armies which appeared in the English papers of this period Wordsworth found plenty of evidence of French aggression. In September and October 1794 France had successes in Spain and Italy, and still more in Holland, where they demanded 10 millions of Antwerp and took hostages to ensure its receipt; in Germany they were fighting for possession of all country west of the Rhine, and this they had obtained by 16 January following. The conquests of France, it is reported in *The Times* of 18 February, 'though they increase the glory of the Republic, are considered in Paris only as means of spreading ruin in foreign countries'. 'For eight months', said Hauffman in the National Convention of 24 February, 'our armies have subsisted on the produce of the conquered countries.' 'Let the public wealth of Holland', said Crétier two days later, 'be carried into France. It may be injustice, but any other policy is folly.'

There was plenty in all this to convince Wordsworth that the French 'had become oppressors in their turn'. In the last months of 1794 he was at Penrith at the bedside of his friend Raisley Calvert. In January Calvert died, leaving him the legacy which freed him from all immediate financial anxiety. [But see Moorman I, pp. 269–70 for evidence that for various reasons the Wordsworths were not freed from financial anxiety by the Calvert legacy. S. G.] Forthwith he hurried to London to be able to watch the progress of events at closer quarters, and here he stayed till he went to Bristol early in September, and then with Dorothy proceeded to Racedown, Dorsetshire. His change from faith in the practical issue of the Revolution to abstract Godwinism, I incline to date some time in the spring of that year, 1795, when he gives up his faith in the 'general will' and becomes for the time a pure individualist. But in my view his complete subservience to Godwin satisfied him for a much shorter period than is usually supposed, and indeed was passed by the time that, in September, he went to Racedown. At that time 'he had yielded up moral questions in despair'—a state from which he was rescued partly by Dorothy and partly by Coleridge 'about that time first known to me' (X. 905. N.B.—W. W. and S. T. C. met in September 1795). The period of moral despair is often confused with that of complete Godwinism. But Godwin, with his sublime optimism, was very far from giving up any question in despair. Despair came to Wordsworth from that scepticism and disillusionment which was the inevitable result of his discovery that Godwinism did not satisfy his nature. His cure from this state was slow and gradual, and cannot be said to have been completed till the summer of 1797. During that period, while he had given up Godwinism, or at least found it unsatisfying to his whole nature, he could yet find no faith with which to replace it. Hence I take the view supported by Hale White and Legouis, but denied by Garrod, that *The Borderers*, written in 1795–6, though unquestionably Godwinian in plot, is written rather as an exposure than an exposition of Godwinism. This is clear also from the essay which W. wrote as preface to *The Borderers* (printed, with a commentary by the present Editor, in *The Nineteenth Century and After*, November 1926). The essay was obviously written early (according to the I.F. note, while he was actually writing the play); for it is prefixed to a much corrected and obviously early draft. 'The general moral', says W. in that essay, 'is obvious—to show the dangerous use which may be made of reason when a man has committed a great crime', i.e. that reason when it sins against the emotions is a dangerous guide. Garrod asserts that both Oswald and Marmaduke fail because they do not trust their intellects enough, i.e. are not good Godwinians. But W.'s meaning surely is that they failed because they declined to listen to the call of the emotions which, on Godwinian principles, they rejected as unreasonable. Certainly Coleridge would not have admired *The Borderers* so immoderately if he had regarded it as Godwinian; for though he went through a period of modified Godwinism himself, and addressed a *Sonnet* to Godwin in the *Morning Post* of 10 January 1795, he was exposing the fallacies of Godwin before the end of the year.

819–29. *How glorious . . . independent intellect*: Cf. the words put into the mouth of the Godwinian Oswald, addressing his dupe Marmaduke after Herbert has been left to starve on the moor:

> You have obeyed the only law that sense
> Submits to recognize; the immediate law
> From the clear light of circumstances, flashed
> Upon an independent Intellect.   (*Borderers*, 1493–6.)

Legouis points out that ll. 821–9 are an exact poetical version of a saying of Godwin: 'The true dignity of human reason is, as much as we are able to go beyond them (i.e. general rules), to have our faculties in act upon every occasion that occurs, and to conduct ourselves accordingly.' *Enquiry concerning Political Justice* (2nd ed., i. 347). Cf. also *ib.* i. 398 'He who regards all things past present and to come as links of an indissoluble chain, will, as often as he recollects this comprehensive view, be superior to the tumult of passion; and will reflect upon the moral concerns of mankind with the same clearness of perception, the same unalterable firmness of judgement, and the same tranquillity as we are accustomed to do upon the truths of geometry.' The fact that Wordsworth soon found himself obliged to turn from the moral concerns of mankind and give them up in despair in favour of geometry shows that he was no longer a whole-hearted Godwinian.

837–8 [XI. 253–4]. *And spread abroad the wings of Liberty etc.*: A reminiscence of Spenser's *Muiopotmos, or, The tale of the Butterflie*, 209–11:

> What more felicitie can fall to creature,
> Then to enjoy delight with libertie,
> And to be lord of all the workes of Nature!

In *The Beggars* (composed 1802) Wordsworth draws upon this same stanza of *Muiopotmos* for the phrase 'a weed of glorious feature'.

849–55 [XI. 259–65]. *Enough, no doubt . . . part*: Cf. 645–56 and *note*.

862 [XI. 272]. *my mind*: Altered (1850) doubtless to avoid the jingle of sound; though 'mine', with 'minds' in the previous line, is hardly an improvement.

868–9.   *Having two natures in me, joy the one*
                                The other melancholy:

It is interesting to notice that in the A text Wordsworth refers to an element in his character which was doubtless in part responsible for the hold which Godwin had upon him—his addiction to melancholy. 'Now it is a question', writes Mark Rutherford ('Godwin and Wordsworth': in *More Pages from a Journal*, p. 209), 'whether Wordsworth's temporary subjugation by *Political Justice* was due to pure intellectual conviction. I think not. Coleridge noticed that Wordsworth suffered much from hypochondria. He complains that during the Scotch tour in 1803 "Wordsworth's hypochondriacal feelings keep him silent and self-centred". He again says to Richard Sharp, in 1804, that Wordsworth "has occasional fits of hypochondriacal uncomfortableness, from which, more or less, he has never been wholly free from his very child-hood", and that he "has a hypochondriacal graft in his nature". Wordsworth himself speaks of times when

            fears and fancies thick upon me came;
    Dim sadness—and blind thoughts, I knew not nor could name.

. . . During 1793, 1794, and part of 1795 this tendency to hypochondria must have been greatly encouraged. His hopes in the Revolution had begun to fail, but the declaration of war against France made him wretched. He wandered about from place to place, unable to conjecture what his future would be. "I have been doing nothing," he tells Mathews, "and still con-tinue to do nothing. What is to become of me I know not." . . . Hypo-chondriacal misery is apt to take an intellectual shape. The most hopeless metaphysics or theology which we happen to encounter fastens on us, and we mistake for an unbiased conviction the form which the disease assumes. The *Political Justice* found in Wordsworth the aptest soil for germination; it rooted and grew rapidly. [It] was falsified in him by Racedown, by better health, by the society of his beloved sister, and finally by the friendship with Cole-ridge. . . . Certain beliefs, at any rate with men of Wordsworth's stamp, are sickness, and with the restoration of vitality and the influx of joy they disappear.'

904–5. *then it was That Thou, most precious Friend*: omitted, doubtless, from later texts because the influence of Coleridge succeeded and did not precede that of Dorothy.

908 [XI. 335]. *the belovèd Woman*: *v. note* to VI. 216–45.

917 [XI. 344]. *Than as a clouded, not a waning moon*: The 'and' in E, in place of 'not', is an error. When [345] was added, [343] was omitted, and 'Than' [344] changed to 'Both'; when [343] was restored in 1850, the 'not' of [344] should also have been restored.

932 [XI. 359]. *rivet up*: There is no manuscript authority for 'seal up all', the reading of 1850.

932–3 [XI. 359–60]. *a Pope Is summon'd in to crown an Emperor*: on 2 December 1804, a ceremony to which Pope Pius VII had been summoned. But when the Pope was about to crown him, Napoleon took the crown from the altar, and put it on his own head himself.

949–50 [XI. 378–9]. *Syracuse, The City of Timoleon*: Coleridge was in Sicily from early in August to the beginning of November 1804.

Some time after the murder of Dion in 353 B.C. (cf. IX. 415 ff., *note*) Dionysius the younger again obtained possession of Syracuse, but in 343 B.C. was driven out by Timoleon, who came from Corinth at the request of the Greek cities in Sicily, to repel the Carthaginians from the island. Timoleon took Syracuse and 'at the sute of the citizens, made counsel hals, and places of justice to be built there: and did by this means stablish a free state and popular government, and did suppress all tyrannical power'. He then defeated a large force of the Carthaginians and drove them from the island, establishing democracies in the different cities. He died in 337 B.C. 'Thus did Timoleon roote out all tyrants out of *Sicilie* and made an end of all warres there. And whereas he found the whole Ile, wild, savage, and hated of the naturall countrymen and inhabitants of the same for the extreme calamities and miseries they suffered, he brought it to be so civill, and so much desired of all straungers, that they came far and neare to dwell there, where the naturall inhabitants of the country selfe before, were glad to fly and forsake it. For *Agrigentum* and *Gela*, two great cities, did witnesse this . . . whom *Timoleon* did not only assure of peace and safety to live there, but willingly did helpe them besides, with all other things necessarie, to his uttermost meane and ability, for which they loved and honoured him as their father and founder. And this his good love and favour was common also to all other people of *Sicilie* whatsoever.' Plutarch: *Life of Timoleon*, trans. by North.

968–9 [XI. 394–5]. *One great Society alone on earth,*
The noble Living and the noble Dead:

Cf. *Convention of Cintra* (1809), (Grosart, i. 170). 'There is a spiritual community binding together the living and the dead; the good, the brave and the wise, of all ages. We would not be rejected from that community: and therefore do we hope.'

985. *This heavy time of change*: *Lycidas*, 37: 'But O the heavy change now thou art gone.' The phrase was clearly put into Wordsworth's mind by his use of 'Thou art gone' in l. 980, *supra*.

997. *carrying a heart more ripe*: i.e. more ripe than Wordsworth's was when he visited the Alps in 1790.

1002–3 [XI. 419–20]. *O Flowery Vale Of Enna!*: Cf. *Paradise Lost*, iv. 268–71:

> that faire field
> Of Enna, where Proserpin, gathering flours
> Herself a fairer floure, by gloomie Dis
> Was gatherd.

1012 [XI. 434]. *Empedocles*: the philosopher of Agrigentum (*fl. c.* 444 B.C.), who according to tradition threw himself into the burning crater of Etna that he might be deemed a god. Cf. Matthew Arnold: *Empedocles on Etna*.

1013 [XI. 435]. *Archimedes*: of Syracuse, born 287 B.C., the most famous of ancient mathematicians. He constructed engines of war for Hiero, when defending Syracuse against Marcellus, and is said to have been killed by the Roman soldiers in 212 B.C., when intent on a mathematical problem.

1022 [XI. 444]. *Divine Comates*: Theocritus, *Idyll*, vii. 78 (*note* in 1850). 'And he shall sing how, once upon a time, the great chest prisoned the living goat-herd by his lord's infatuate and evil will, and how the blunt-faced bees, as they came up from the meadow to the fragrant cedar chest, fed him with food of tender flowers, because the muse still dropped sweet nectar on his lips. O blessed Comates, surely these things befell thee, and thou wast enclosed within the chest, and feeding on the honeycomb through the springtime didst serve out thy bondage.' *Idyll*, vii. 78–83, trans. by Lang.

BOOK XI

24–5. *when I was dead To deeper hope etc.*: The time referred to is clearly the spring of 1796 at Racedown, when Wordsworth, dissatisfied with Godwinism, yet having found no theory of life to take its place, had 'given up moral questions in despair'. These lines, fuller in A than in 1850, explain how it was that though he was 'dead to deeper hope' he could yet at times be cheerful, as both his own letters and Dorothy's written in the early Racedown days prove him to have been. They are thus a complete answer to Harper's scepticism as to his mental depression at this time (*v.* Harper, i. 289–90).

59–60.
> *The man to come parted as by a gulph,*
> *From him who had been:*

Cf. Godwin, *Political Justice*, 1st ed., ii. 494. 'Nothing can be more unreasonable than to argue from men as we now find them, to men as they may hereafter be made.' The whole passage down to l. 137 sums up the influence upon Wordsworth of his Godwinian hopes that the world would start afresh on the basis of pure Reason. 'A bigot to a new idolatry', he does not seem to realize that the 'mysteries of passion' (84), so strongly rooted in his own nature, are the true bond of brotherhood to the human race. Hence he gives up first history and then poetry; and even Nature becomes less deeply valuable to him (99–120).

64. *Patriot, Lover*: significantly changed later to 'warrior, patriot'. When Wordsworth first wrote the lines he would not allow the warrior, as distinct from the patriot, to be one of 'the great family'.

121–37. An interesting passage on the dangers of the analytic or scientific reason, though Wordsworth at the same time recognizes its value as a stage in mental development. Its result is presumption (152), superficiality (159), and a lack of penetrative imagination. Cf. *The Tables Turned*, 26–8.

[160–4. Printed from MS. B. The reading in MS. A has been completely erased. S. G.]

171–99 [XII. 127–51]. The attitude to Nature described in these lines is that which he first experienced on his visit to Tintern in 1793. On his return to England Man had absorbed his whole interest, but after the war with France had brought about his first moral crisis (i.e. in August 1793) he made a sudden return to Nature—

> more like a man
> Flying from something that he dreads than one
> Who sought the thing he loved.
> . . . the sounding cataract
> Haunted me like a passion: the tall rock
> The mountain, and the deep and gloomy wood,
> Their colours and their forms, were then to me
> An appetite, a feeling and a love
> That had no need of a remoter charm
> By thought supplied, nor any interest
> Unborrowed from the eye.

It is a new thing, and typical of his psychological state at this time, that he should come to Nature fleeing from something that he dreads, i.e. in reaction from his moral sufferings. He now finds distraction in purely sensuous pleasure, from which moral feeling and all his deeper 'inner faculties' are excluded. This attitude to Nature seems to have been dominant with him until, gradually, his cure was effected.

191. *from rock to rock*: Cf. *To the Daisy*:

> In youth from rock to rock I went,
> From hill to hill in discontent
> Of pleasure high and turbulent.

199 [XII. 151]. *I knew a Maid*: Mary Hutchinson. [Cf. MS. reading of line 200, 'her years ran parallel with mine'. *v.* P.; she was born in August 1770, four months after W. W. H. D.]

204 [XII. 155]. *barren intermeddling subtleties*: Cf. *The Tables Turned*, 26–8:

> Our meddling intellect
> Misshapes the beauteous forms of things:—
> We murder to dissect.

235. *As my soul bade me*: Notice Wordsworth's earlier insistence on natural emotion prompted by sensation only—'I felt, and nothing else' (238) rather than, as later, on external sanction—'as piety ordained' [185], supported by

reflection—'I felt, observed, and pondered' [188]. The change in the text (1850) really obscures his meaning.

[258. It is important that the reader should return to the parallel text *Prelude* and, from the information given about the MSS., work out the chronology of composition of the late books. Here it may just be noted that in Book XI, ll. 258–316 and 345–89, the childhood episodes, are taken from the work of 1799–1800, but ll. 316–45, where W. W. speaks of the loss of visionary power, were only composed when the poem was being completed in 1804–5. It cannot be stressed enough that *The Prelude* is more than an account of W.W.'s childhood and youth. It is also a sensitive record of W. W.'s growth *during the years of the poem's composition.* S. G.]

262–3 [XII. 212–13].   *Or aught of heavier and more deadly weight*
                                     In trivial occupations etc.:

   Cf. *Sonnet* 'I am not one who much or oft delight', and the lines from MS. quoted P. p. 606.

279–316. Mr. Gordon Wordsworth has identified the scene of this episode as the Cowdrake Quarry on the Edenhall side of the Penrith Beacon. Here in 1766 Thomas Parker, a butcher from Langwathby, was murdered by one Thomas Nicholson. Nicholson was executed at Carlisle on 31 August 1767, and his body afterwards hung in chains on a spot close to the scene of his crime. On the turf below the gibbet were cut the letters T. P. M. (Thomas Parker murdered). The initials were thus those of the murdered man and not, as Wordsworth states, of the criminal. The story must have been known to the child; hence his terror. His visit to the spot must have taken place either when on a visit to his grandparents, or in 1776–7, when, with Mary Hutchinson, he was attending Dame Birkett's infant school at Penrith.

283. *honest James*: not to be confounded with that James, one of his grandfather's servants, whose insolence was so galling to the Wordsworth children (*v.* Dorothy's letter to Jane Pollard, quoted in Harper, i. 76–7).

323 [XII. 266]. *The spirit of pleasure and youth's golden gleam*: This line is repeated from VI. 245 (q.v. *note*), where he recounts this same visit to the Border Beacon, near Penrith. Hence the 'two dear Ones, to my soul so dear', words which he omits from 1850. A later reading, 'with the maid To whom were breathed my first fond vows', is important, as it suggests that Mary Hutchinson was in fact the poet's first love, forgotten for the time in his passion for Annette.

326–43 [XII. 269–86]. A statement of the central point of Wordsworth's creed, that poetry 'takes its origin from emotion recollected in tranquillity', drawing its inspiration and its material from the great moments of the past, especially from the scenes of childhood and early youth, when feeling is strongest. Hence, perhaps, the falling off in the inspiration of his later poetic life, which he might be said to prophesy in ll. 338–9. Lines 333–4 owe something to Coleridge, *Ode to Dejection,* 47–8:

> O Lady! we receive but what we give,
> And in our life alone does Nature live.

For the idea expressed in the whole passage cf. *The Waggoner*, iv. 197–217, but especially the reference (210–12) to

> a shy spirit in my heart,
> That comes and goes—will sometimes leap
> From hiding-places ten years deep.

345 [XII. 287]. *One Christmas-time*: December 1783, at which time there would be three boys at school, William and his brothers Richard and John. Christopher did not go to Hawkshead till two years later. Wordsworth seems to have been in some doubt as to the number of horses sent, but two is probably correct. The scene of the look-out crag has been a matter of much discussion; and three out of four of Knight's conjectures are based on the false assumption that the horses were coming from Penrith, whereas they were coming from Cockermouth. Hence their route would run either over the Wrynose Pass, or, *via* Grasmere and Keswick—in neither case through Ambleside, as Knight imagines. Knight's fourth suggestion—by Randy Pike—is just possible, but far more likely is Mr. Gordon Wordsworth's—a short half-mile north of Borwick Lodge, on the ridge that overlooks the road to Skelwith and the now little-used track to Oxenfell.

345–89 [XII. 287–335]. Garrod (pp. 207–9) suggests that this passage has an added pathos as written in 1805, after Wordsworth had received news of the death of his brother John. But it is found in an early MS. which proves it to have been written in 1798–9.

[367 [XII. 308]. *two brothers*: *v.* D. W.'s letter (*M.Y.* 165). H. D.]

382 [323]. *Advanced in such indisputable shapes*: an echo of Hamlet: 'Thou camst in such a questionable shape', i.e. a shape that can be questioned. But it is the mist, and not its shape, that cannot be disputed with.

BOOK XII

31–2 [XIII. 27–8]. *But lifts The Being into magnanimity*: Notice the significant change in the text, not introduced before 1832.

66–8.   *I sought*
> *For good in the familiar face of life*
> *And built thereon my hopes of good to come*:

a contrast, deliberately stated, with his faith when as a Godwinian he

> had hope to see,
> I mean that future times would surely see
> The man to come parted as by a gulph,
> From him who had been. (XI. 57–60).

The 'individual man', in whom he is now interested, is 'no composition of the thought, Abstraction, image, shadow' (i.e. the ideal man of Godwin's *Political Justice*). The lines that follow (97–219) describe the frame of mind in which, as a revulsion from Godwinism, Wordsworth set himself to compose the more homely of the *Lyrical Ballads*. The attribution of 'genuine knowledge' to the rustic in l. 99 (altered later to the less debatable 'genuine virtue') was a definite defiance of Godwin. 'Godwin', says Legouis (trs. p. 307) 'had taught him to believe that virtue was dependent on the intelligence, which can itself be exercised only on knowledge already acquired. He had said that "in order to choose the greatest possible good" one "must be deeply acquainted with the nature of man, its general features and varieties" (*Pol. Just.*, 1st ed., pp. 232–3). He had asserted that "virtue cannot exist in an eminent degree, unaccompanied by an extensive survey of causes and their consequences' (*ib.*, p. 232). He had sneered at Tertullian for saying "that the most ignorant peasant under the Christian dispensation possessed more real knowledge than the wisest of ancient philosophers", and had shown the absurdity of pretending that "an honest ploughman could be as virtuous as Cato" (*ib.*, p. 254).'

149–50. *one bare steep Beyond the limits which my feet had trod*: i.e. the road to the village of Isel over the Hay or Watch Hill, which can be seen from the garden and the back of the house at Cockermouth where Wordsworth passed the first years of his life.

223–77. This passage was first printed as the conclusion of the Appendix to *Poems* 1835 (*Of legislation for the Poor, the Working Classes, and the Clergy*).

231–98. The whole of this passage should be compared with the lines written in 1798 and afterwards printed as the *Prospectus* to *The Excursion*; and also with the *Preface* to the *Lyrical Ballads*, 1802, especially with that part in which Wordsworth defends his choice of subject. 'Low and rustic life was generally chosen, because, in that condition, the essential passions of the heart find a better soil in which they can attain their maturity, are less under restraint, and speak a plainer and more emphatic language; because in that condition of life our elementary feelings coexist in a state of greater simplicity, and, consequently, may be more accurately contemplated, and more forcibly communicated; because the manners of rural life germinate from these elementary feelings, and, from the necessary character of rural occupations, are more easily comprehended, and are more durable; and, lastly, because in that condition the passions of men are incorporated with the beautiful and permanent forms of nature.' Cf. also the passage which follows, on the language of men of humble and rustic life, with ll. 253–64.

313–14. *a Traveller at that time Upon the Plain of Sarum*: On leaving the Isle of Wight, where Wordsworth spent a month in July–August 1793 (cf. X. 290–306), he went with William Calvert for three days walking over Salisbury Plain. Here it was that he conceived *Guilt and Sorrow* and wrote some of it (*v.* 359). Cf. I. F. note to *Guilt and Sorrow*. [De Selincourt's note does not make it clear that W. W. was left alone on Salisbury Plain after an accident had shattered the travelling carriage. See D. W.'s account of the accident, *E.Y.*, 109. W. W. was alone, without employment or prospects, with his feelings in tumult over the war and his enforced absence from France. He then walked a very long way over hard country. Late in life he played down his experiences (see a letter published in *Modern Lang. Rev.*, liii, 1958) but *The Prelude* gives a more credible account of what his feelings were during his trek. S. G.]

[357-65. In 1793-4 W. W. composed a poem called 'Salisbury Plain' or alternatively 'A Night on Salisbury Plain'. This poem was most likely read to Coleridge in autumn 1795. On settling at Racedown in 1795 W. W. at once revised the poem very extensively and renamed it 'Adventures on Salisbury Plain'. In 1796 he attempted to publish it, but plans were not realized, and only the story told by the woman, 'The Female Vagrant', appeared, in *Lyrical Ballads*, 1798. Nothing more was done to the poem until it was again revised for publication as 'Guilt and Sorrow' in the 1842 *Poems, Chiefly of Early and Late Years*. For a text of 'Salisbury Plain' ed. by Stephen Gill see *Studies*. In *Biographia Literaria* (1817) Coleridge wrote of the poem: 'I was in my twenty-fourth year, when I had the happiness of knowing Mr. Wordsworth personally, and while memory lasts, I shall hardly forget the sudden effect produced on my mind, by his recitation of a manuscript poem, which still remains unpublished, but of which the stanza, and tone of style, were the same as those of the *Female Vagrant*, as originally printed in the first volume of the *Lyrical Ballads*. There was here no mark of strained thought, or forced diction, no crowd or turbulence of imagery; and as the poet hath himself well described in his lines "on re-visiting the Wye", manly reflection, and human associations had given both variety, and an additional interest to natural objects, which in the passion and appetite of the first love they had seemed to him neither to need or permit. . . . It was not however the freedom from false taste, whether as to common defects, or to those more properly his own, which made so unusual an impression on my feelings immediately, and subsequently on my judgement. It was the union of deep feeling with profound thought; the fine balance of truth in observing, with the imaginative faculty in modifying the objects observed: and above all, the original gift of spreading the tone, the atmosphere, and with it the depth and height of the ideal world around forms, incidents and situations, of which, for the common view, custom had bedimmed all the lustre, had dried up the sparkle and the dew drops.' S. G.]

369-79. This passage in its original form expresses a vital element in Wordsworth's thought, and puts into intellectual terms a part of his own deepest experience. The growth of his mind was bound up with a process of continual action and interaction between his own inner life and the world without:

> my mind hath look'd
> Upon the speaking face of earth and heaven
> As her prime Teacher, intercourse with man

> Establish'd by the sovereign Intellect,
> Who through that bodily image hath diffus'd
> A soul divine which we participate,
> A deathless spirit. (V. 11–17.)

Here he differed from Coleridge, who held that

> we receive but what we give
> And in our life alone doth Nature live.

To Wordsworth, as to Coleridge, the poetic mind was creative, but unlike Coleridge, he held that it was stimulated and worked upon by the creative power of Nature, since Nature was possessed by that same divine being, which ran through all things, of whose presence he was conscious in his 'own interior life'. Hence the poet is a *sensitive* being, a *creative soul* (XI. 257). The first version of this passage simply asserts that the source of our inner life, 'That whence our dignity originates', is an active power which maintains a continual interaction between the mind and the objects of its vision, and is itself 'The excellence, pure spirit, and best power' of both. The later version substitutes for this 'power' a system of 'fixed laws', and makes the 'spirit' into a 'function', thus covering up the true significance of the passage in its relation with his earlier Pantheism.

BOOK XIII

2. *with a youthful Friend*: Robert Jones (*v.* VI. 339 and *note*). This excursion was in the summer of 1791.

71. *underpresence*: Note the significance of Wordsworth's use of nouns compounded with the prefix 'under'. Here, 'underpresence' *corr. to* 'underconsciousness' (neither of them in *The Oxford Dictionary*), 'Under-Powers' (I. 163; *Oxf. Dict.* gives no other ex.), 'under-soul' (III. 540; *Oxf. Dict.*, no ex. before 1868), 'under-countenance' (VI. 236; not in *Oxf. Dict.*), 'under-thirst' (VI. 489 [558]; not in *Oxf. Dict.*). He needed these words to express his profound consciousness of that mysterious life which lies deep down below our ordinary, everyday experience, and whence we draw our power—that one interior life:

> In which all beings live with God, themselves
> Are God, existing in the mighty whole.

The relation of this conception to the subconscious or subliminal self of the modern psychologist is obvious.

98–9. *they build up greatest things From least suggestions*: These words recall the first of Wordsworth's printed attempts to define the imagination, 'the faculty which produces impressive effects out of simple elements' (*note* to 'The Thorn', *Lyr. Ball.*, 1800).

101–2.   *They need not extraordinary calls*
                 To rouze them:

Cf. *Preface*, 1802: 'the human mind is capable of being excited without the application of gross and violent stimulants; and he must have a very faint perception of its beauty and dignity who does not know . . . that one being is elevated above another in proportion as he possesses this capability.'

113 [XIV. 120]. *whether discursive or intuitive*: Cf. Milton, *P.L.* v. 486–8:

> Fansie and understanding, whence the soul
> Reason receives, and reason is her being
> Discursive or intuitive.

138 [XIV. 160]. *a universe of death*: a Miltonic phrase. Cf. *P.L.* ii. 622–4:

> A Universe of death, which God by curse
> Created evil, for evil only good
> Where all life dies, death lives.

148. *All truth and beauty, from pervading love*: In later versions than A Wordsworth omits the statement that love is the source of all truth and beauty.

154–8 [XIV. 181–7]. *there is higher love etc.*: The 1850 change in the text here, with the introduction of a definitely Christian interpretation of the character of that 'higher love', is noteworthy, as is the change in the next line of 'intellectual' into 'spiritual'. Wordsworth would not, in 1804–5, have denied that the love was spiritual, but he prefers to emphasize his belief that it is essentially a part of the natural equipment of man as man, and does not depend, as in the later text, upon a definitely Christian faith and attitude to religion. The religion of the original version of *The Prelude* is the religion of the *Lines composed a few miles above Tintern Abbey*, and not the religion of the *Ecclesiastical Sonnets*. Cf. Aubrey de Vere, *Recollections of Wordsworth* (Grosart, iii. 491): 'It has been observed that the Religion of Wordsworth's poetry, at least of his earlier poetry, is not as distinctly "Revealed Religion" as might have been expected from this poet's well-known adherence to what he has called emphatically "The Lord and mighty paramount of Truths". He once remarked to me himself on this circumstance, and explained it by stating that when in youth his imagination was shaping for itself the channel in which it was to flow, his religious convictions were less definite and less strong than they had become on more mature thought, and that when his poetic mind and manner had once been formed, he feared that he might, in attempting to modify them, have become constrained.'

176 [XIV. 204]. *The feeling of life endless, the great thought*: Notice the very significant change of this line, to 'Faith in life endless, the sustaining thought'. It denotes a definite renunciation of that trust in the natural human feelings as the guide to truth which was characteristic of the earlier Wordsworth.

205 [XIV. 233]. *Elsewhere*: Cf. *note* to VI. 216–17.

218–19 [XIV. 245–6]. *that beauty, which, as Milton sings, Hath terror in it*: Cf. *Paradise Lost*, ix. 489–91:

Shee fair, divinely fair, fit Love for Gods,
Not terrible, though terrour be in Love
And beautie.

240–1 [XIV. 255–301]. *Coleridge! with this my argument, of thee*
                      Shall I be silent?:

It is curious that whilst this passage pays a beautiful tribute to Wordsworth's
love for his friend, so little acknowledgement is made of his incalculable
intellectual debt to him. Yet it was through Coleridge that he came first to
understand himself and his poetic aims, and he readily admits elsewhere how
much he owed to Coleridge's inspired conversation. Thus he writes to Sir
George Beaumont (1 August 1805) of *The Recluse*: 'Should Coleridge return,
so that I might have some conversation with him on the subject, I should go
on swimmingly.' And years later he said of Coleridge: 'He was most wonderful
in the power he possessed of throwing out in profusion grand central truths
from which might be evolved the most comprehensive systems.' In later texts
Wordsworth did something to correct this deficiency, but even so it is hardly
a complete expression of his debt.

343 [XIV. 355]. *The name of Calvert*: Raisley Calvert, brother of William Calvert
with whom Wordsworth stayed in the Isle of Wight in the summer of 1793.
The Calverts were sons of the steward of the Duke of Norfolk, who owned a
large estate at Greystoke, four miles from Penrith (Harper, i. 248). Raisley was
consumptive and Wordsworth proposed in October 1794 to accompany him
to Lisbon on a voyage of health, and when this plan fell through, attended
him through his last illness. He died in January 1795 and left Wordsworth
£900.

386. *Quantock's grassy Hills*: Wordsworth was at Alfoxden from July 1797 to
September 1798; Coleridge was living three miles off at Nether Stowey; the
Quantock hills rise behind both places. Both *The Ancient Mariner* and *Christabel*
were written in the late autumn of 1797 (*The Ancient Mariner* in November);
the summer therefore which Wordsworth here recalls was that of 1798. *The
Thorn* and *The Idiot Boy* were both written in 1798 (*The Thorn* on 19 March).

409. *a private grief*: the loss of his brother John. Cf. *Elegiac Verses, In Memory of
my Brother, John Wordsworth, Commander of the E. I. Company's Ship, The Earl of
Abergavenny, in which he perished by calamitous shipwreck, February 6th, 1805*. *Elegiac
Stanzas, suggested by a picture of Peele Castle etc.* were inspired by this same loss,
and in drawing his portrait of the *Happy Warrior* Wordsworth had in mind,
he tells us (I.F. note to the poem), many elements in his brother's character.
[De Selincourt suggested that W. W. moved towards orthodoxy as a result of
his brother's death. But the orthodoxy of W. W.'s later work has been much
overstressed. Moreover, W. W.'s thought evolved in subtle ways through
many processes. It did not suddenly change from one state to another. See

the 'Ode to Duty' (1804) for evidence that, before John's death in 1805, W. W. was already beginning to investigate new elements in man's relationship to other men and to God. S. G.]

437. *By reason and by truth*: Notice the significant alteration of the early text to 'By reason, blest by faith'.

SYNOPSIS OF THE POEM

Even those who know *The Prelude* well often find it difficult to remember the location of certain passages or the context of a particular episode. The following synopsis, with the relevant line numbers, is intended to be only a rudimentary finding-index, to help those who have *already read the poem*. It does not attempt to analyse 'themes'. S. G.

BOOK FIRST: INTRODUCTION—CHILDHOOD AND SCHOOL-TIME

Proem (1)—Choice of subject (157)—Childhood (271)—Birds nesting (305)—Stolen boat episode (372)—Skating (452)—Card-playing (541)—Concluding consideration of relationship of nature and child (571)

BOOK SECOND: SCHOOL-TIME (*continued*)

Boating (55)—Visits to St. Mary's Abbey (99)—Visits to inn and the 'Minstrel of our troop' episode (145)—'Bless'd the infant Babe' passage (237)—Continuing account of nature's education, emphasizing the development (281)—Concluding statement of the importance of this education in the current times of dismay (435)—Address to Coleridge (466)

BOOK THIRD: RESIDENCE AT CAMBRIDGE

Enters St. John's (44)—W.W. a 'chosen son' of nature (81)—Account of his attitude to University life (121)—'Imagination slept' (259)—Strengths and weaknesses of this life (328)—Vacation (669)

BOOK FOURTH: SUMMER VACATION

Return to Lakes (1)—Feelings in home surroundings (68)—A new 'human-heartedness' about W.W.'s love (222)—Dedication to poetry in a magnificent early morning (330)—Discharged Soldier episode (400)

BOOK FIFTH: BOOKS

Transience of monuments of intellect (1)—Dream of Arab on his dromedary (49)—Opposition to current education theory (223)—'There was a Boy' (389)—Memory of the dead man dragged from the lake (450)—Debts to imaginative stories (516)

BOOK SIXTH: CAMBRIDGE AND THE ALPS

Continuing life at College(19)—Growth of poet's spirit (55)—Importance of mathematics (135)—Vacation wanderings (208)—Address to Coleridge (246)—Visit to Continent (332)—Through France to Switzerland (360)—Crossing Alps (494)—'Imagination! lifting up itself' passage (525)—Simplon Pass (549)—Return (688)

SYNOPSIS OF THE POEM

BOOK SEVENTH: RESIDENCE IN LONDON

Recapitulation, 'Five years are vanish'd' (1)—London (63)—Panorama of city and account of experiences (81)—'Maid of Buttermere' (311)—Bartholomew Fair (650)

BOOK EIGHTH: RETROSPECT—LOVE OF NATURE LEADING TO LOVE OF MANKIND

Helvellyn Fair (10)—Transfigured Shepherd passage (81)—Discussion of love of humble life (144)—Shepherd and his son episode (222)—'Greenland Bears' passage (390)—More detailed account of the process by which love of nature leads to love of man (428)—Account of imaginative workings in the great city (797)

BOOK NINTH: RESIDENCE IN FRANCE

France (40)—involvement in Revolutionary fervour (96)—Friendship with Beaupuy (294)—Vaudracour and Julia story (556)

BOOK TENTH: RESIDENCE IN FRANCE AND FRENCH REVOLUTION

Paris (38)—Denunciation of Robespierre (83)—Return to England (188)—Moral shock when Britain leagues against France (227)—Isle of Wight stay (290)—Reign of Terror (307)—Overthrow of Robespierre (466)—New repression in England (645, 757)—French become oppressors (791)—W.W.'s torment of mind (859)—'Yielded up moral questions in despair' passage (888)—Importance of Coleridge, Dorothy, and nature (904)—Address to Coleridge in Sicily (941)

BOOK ELEVENTH: IMAGINATION, HOW IMPAIRED AND RESTORED

Continuing account of state of W.W.'s creative mind (42)—Importance of Nature, 'Oh, Soul of Nature, excellent and fair' (138)—Tribute to Mary Hutchinson (200)—'There are in our existence spots of time' (258)—Two examples, the gibbet scene (279) and the waiting for the horses (345)

BOOK TWELFTH: SAME SUBJECT (*continued*)

New recognition of strength and love of man (53)—Emphasis upon the importance of humble life (220)—New conviction of nature's power to consecrate even the humblest (277)—Account of experiences on Salisbury Plain (312)—Vision of a new world of interrelation with nature (365)

BOOK THIRTEENTH: CONCLUSION

The climbing of Snowdon (1)—Discussion of the meaning of the experience (66)—Tributes to Dorothy (204), Coleridge (239)—Brief biographical summary to 1798 (325)—Tribute to Calvert (342)—Further tribute to Coleridge and concluding statement of the mission still before both men (379)

INDEX

Bold-face figures refer to the text of *The Prelude*

INDEX

INDEX

INDEX

Ullswater, xxvi, 252
Ulverston, 254, 302

Vallon, Annette, 287, 295–6, 313 (and *v.* Julia; Wordsworth, William: *Vaudracour and Julia*)
Vaudracour, **166–76**, 296, 297 (and *v.* Wordsworth, William: *Vaudracour and Julia*)
Vauxhall, **108**, 280
Vere, Aubrey de: *Recollections of W.W.*, 318
Virgil, 257, 270; *Georgics*, 286
Voltaire, 290

Wales, **229**, **238**, 275, 289
Wallace, William, 7, 250
Walpole, Horace, 281; *Letters*, 280
Watts, Alaric, xiv
Wedgwood, Thomas, 266
Westminster Abbey, **108**
Westmorland, **17**
White Lion Inn, **24**, 254
White Moss Common, 280
Whittington, Dick, **108**
Wight, Isle of, **185**, 301, 315
Wilberforce, William, 300
Williams, Helen: *Letters written in France . . .*, 296
Windermere, **21**, **24**, **53**, 254, 261, 262
Wordsworth, Christopher, 272, 314
Wordsworth, Dora, 243
Wordsworth, Dorothy, xi, **91**, **234–5**, 243, 272, 275, 288, 307, 309, 311, 316; *Journals*, 276, 280, 283; *Letters*, xvii, 252, 269, 270, 271, 287, 313, 314
Wordsworth, Gordon, 251, 252, 254, 263, 272, 286, 313, 314
Wordsworth, John, 280, 288, 314, 319
Wordsworth, Jonathan, viii, 244
Wordsworth, Richard, 251, 289, 292, 314
WORDSWORTH, WILLIAM, b. 1770; childhood at Cockermouth, **8–9**, 251; death of mother (1778), **74**, 266; goes to Hawkshead School (Whitsuntide 1779), **9**, 251; death of father (1783), **215–17**, 314; goes to St. John's College, Cambridge (1787), **34–5**, 256; first long vaca-

tion, **53** ff., 261–3; return to Cambridge, **85**; second long vacation, **90–2**, 274; third long vacation, tour on Continent with Robert Jones, **94** ff., 275 ff.; returns to Cambridge, November, at Forncett in December and January 1791, to Cambridge to take his degree, in London in February, **106** ff., 280–83; in Wales, May, **229–30**; in France, November: in Paris, **152**, at Orleans and Blois, **154**, 289–90; friendship with Beaupuy, **159–63**, 292–3; relations with Annette Vallon, 295–7; in Paris on 29 October 1792, **178**, 297–9; recalled to England, January 1793, 300; sojourn in Isle of Wight, **185**, 301; crosses Salisbury Plain, **226–7**, 315–16; possible October 1793 visit to France, 292; at Rampside and Penrith, 1794, 303–4; in London January–September 1795, 307–8; at Bristol and then with D.W. at Racedown, 307; meets Coleridge at Bristol, September 1795, 274, 309; goes to Alfoxden, July 1797, 319; writing *Lyrical Ballads*, **240**, 319; settles at Dove Cottage, Grasmere, December 1799, 247; writes *The Prelude*, vii–viii, ix–x
works by:
  Address to Scholars, &c., 303;
  Appendix 'on . . . Poetic Diction', 270–1;
  Beggars, 308;
  Borderers, The, 307, 308;
  Butterfly, To a, 251, 273;
  Complaint . . . Indian Woman, The, 269;
  Convention of Cintra, 306, 310;
  Cumberland Beggar, The, 248
  Daisy, To the, 312;
  Descriptive Sketches, xiv, xv, 275, 276, 290;
  Dion, 293;
  Discharged Soldier, The, **63–6**, 248;
  Elegiac Stanzas on Peele Castle, 303, 319;

329